D0962295

SPY SCHOOLS

SPY

SCHOOLS

· ·

HOW THE CIA, FBI, AND FOREIGN
INTELLIGENCE SECRETLY EXPLOIT
AMERICA'S UNIVERSITIES

· ·

DANIEL GOLDEN

HENRY HOLT AND COMPANY   NEW YORK

Henry Holt and Company
Publishers since 1866
175 Fifth Avenue
New York, New York 10010
www.henryholt.com

Henry Holt® and 🝔® are registered trademarks of
Macmillan Publishing Group, LLC.

Library of Congress Cataloging-in-Publication Data

Names: Golden, Daniel, 1957– author.
Title: Spy schools : how the CIA, FBI, and foreign intelligence secretly exploit
  America's universities / Daniel Golden.
Description: New York, New York : Henry Holt and Company, [2017] |
  Includes bibliographical references and index.
Identifiers: LCCN 2016056352| ISBN 9781627796354 (hardcover) |
  ISBN 9781627796361 (ebook)
Subjects: LCSH: Intelligence service—United States—Officials and employees—Recruiting. |
  Spies—Recruiting—United States. | Universities and colleges—United States. |
  Espionage—United States.
Classification: LCC JK468.I6 G625 2017 | DDC 327.12730071/1—dc23
LC record available at https://lccn.loc.gov/2016056352

Our books may be purchased in bulk for promotional, educational, or business use. Please
contact your local bookseller or the Macmillan Corporate and Premium Sales Department at
(800) 221-7945, extension 5442, or by e-mail at MacmillanSpecialMarkets@macmillan.com.

First Edition 2017

Designed by Kelly S. Too

Printed in the United States of America

1 2 3 4 5 6 7 8 9 10

To Steven

CONTENTS

THE FBI GOES TO COLLEGE

On an April morning in 2009, Dajin Peng shaved and dressed for a normal day of teaching. Then the University of South Florida professor of international studies sat down at the desktop computer in his bedroom and began surfing the Internet for the best way to kill himself.

Peng was reeling from an abrupt tumble down the academic ladder. With little warning or explanation, South Florida had placed him on leave as director of its Confucius Institute, a China-funded language and cultural program. He was trying to find a painless poison, and one he could buy without attracting attention, when he heard his father calling to him from another room. Somebody was knocking on the front door.

Visitors seldom climbed the outside staircase to Peng's second-floor apartment in the drab, rust-colored roadside complex. He opened the door to a tall woman with an athletic build and shoulder-length brown hair, who was forty years old but looked younger. Although sunny, the weather was cool for spring in Florida, and she wore a coat over an off-white blouse.

Giving him a reassuring smile and a business card, she introduced herself as Dianne Mercurio, a special agent for the Federal Bureau of Investigation. Although she grew up in South Carolina, where she had been a high school track star, her voice bore little trace of a southern accent.

Peng briefly feared that the FBI intended to arrest him, but her friendly demeanor indicated some other purpose.

As they shook hands, she said, "Nick Abaid sends his regards."

With a jolt, Peng recognized the name from his days as a graduate student at Princeton's Woodrow Wilson School of Public and International Affairs. Abaid, an FBI special agent, had cultivated Chinese students at Princeton who might become useful informants. He had identified Peng, who had gone to a university run by China's spy service and had ex-classmates in the highest reaches of its government, as a potential prize. Abaid had taken him to lunch several times, usually just before or after Peng's trips home to China. Explaining that he was worried about theft of American technology, Abaid had asked Peng if he had noticed anything suspicious about other Chinese students. Peng said he hadn't.

Mercurio's reference to Abaid convinced him that she did indeed work for the FBI. It also put him on his guard. His last conversation with Abaid had been in 1994, when Peng joined the University of South Florida's faculty. Abaid had asked him to stay in touch with the FBI's Tampa bureau, an offer Peng politely declined, hoping he had seen the last of U.S. intelligence. For the next fifteen years, Peng and the FBI had gone their separate ways. Now the bureau was hounding him again.

When Mercurio asked if he had time to talk, Peng suggested a walk outside. He wanted to avoid disturbing his father, a frail widower, who lived with him. As they strolled up and down a corner of the parking lot, Mercurio told him she was aware of his predicament at the university.

Glad to have a sympathetic audience, especially an attractive woman, Peng recounted his tale of woe in fluent but heavily accented English. Funded by an affiliate of China's education ministry, Confucius Institutes had sprung up in the past five years on campuses worldwide. As founder and director of South Florida's branch, he deserved credit for its expanding array of courses, community outreach, and new cultural center. He had even arranged for the director of all Confucius Institutes to schedule a trip to USF, and he had expected her to lionize him and proclaim his institute a model for the world.

Instead, weeks before her visit, he was ousted. Peng's boss at USF handed him a curt notice that he was not allowed to return to the institute or have any contact with its staff, "pending investigation into allegations of inappropriate management of the Confucius Institute." He could still teach his regular courses in international political economy and business, but that was scant consolation. The dean provided no details of the accusations against him, nor did she name his accusers. He would have expected such injustice in the China of his youth, but not in America.

As if worried that Peng might connect her visit with his downfall, Mercurio volunteered that she had no influence over the university, and nothing to do with his difficulties. He accepted her statement at face value. Later, he would wonder how she knew about his troubles, and would suspect the FBI of instigating them to gain leverage over him.

Mercurio's next comment disturbed him. She wanted to know more about the Confucius Institutes, she said, because they harbored Chinese spies. Since the Chinese government funded them, and Chinese universities supplied most of their staff, they made ideal listening posts and recruiting stations, she explained. Left unsaid, but as unmistakable as a tabloid headline, was the accusation that Peng himself was a Chinese agent.

"You're wrong," Peng told Mercurio. She asserted her opinion as fact, but where was her evidence? "China would never use the Confucius Institutes for spying," he said. "They are too important. The government wouldn't want to risk the U.S. shutting them down."

She didn't argue with him. For Mercurio, who had recently taken over the China beat on the counterintelligence squad, an informant of Peng's prominence and connections could make her career. Later, as their relationship ripened, she would ask him to spy on the Confucius Institutes and their Chinese government sponsors, as well as Tampa's Chinese community and his Chinese colleagues at South Florida. Her CIA counterparts would have plans for him as well. In return, she would be prepared to protect his professorship and, if necessary, keep him out of prison. The FBI had pressured mobsters, drug dealers, and loan sharks to cooperate; why not a Princeton-educated professor?

But first she needed to assess his enthusiasm for espionage. Peng was a U.S. citizen now, she reminded him. He understood her meaning. He'd been a Chinese national when he spurned Abaid's request to stay in touch. Now he owed his patriotic allegiance to his adopted country, not his homeland. She asked him directly whether he would serve his country. Despite inner misgivings, he had little choice. He agreed.

They had walked for almost an hour.

As she said good-bye, she arranged a lunch date with him, and told him that she would set up an email account where he could contact her. She cautioned him not to mention her visit to anyone at South Florida.

Afterward, a neighbor dropped by his apartment. She and her husband, both Chinese, were among his closest friends; he had used his university position to help them obtain visas to study in the United States. They shared his fury over his ouster from the institute, and fretted about his bleak mood.

She had seen Peng with Mercurio, and her curiosity was aroused. Peng's female friends were usually Chinese.

"Who was your visitor?" she asked.

"An FBI agent," he blurted out. Distracted from suicide, his mind raced ahead, groping to understand why the bureau had reentered his life and what it meant for his future.

THE WORLD THAT we encounter in our adolescence tends to entrench itself permanently in our minds. In the time and place where I grew up, FBI director J. Edgar Hoover was a bigger villain than the thugs on the bureau's "Ten Most Wanted" list. In the 1960s and early 1970s in Amherst, Massachusetts, where my parents and most of my friends' fathers taught at the University of Massachusetts, Amherst College, or Hampshire College, the FBI's snooping on the civil rights and anti–Vietnam War movements had sullied its reputation.

The CIA, which sabotaged Marxist regimes popular with many intellectuals, ranked even lower in academic esteem. Protests and sit-ins greeted campus recruiters. As late as 1986, demonstrators against CIA recruiting occupied a building on the UMass campus. Fifteen people, including Amy Carter (daughter of former president Jimmy Carter) and ex-Yippie Abbie Hoffman, were arrested and charged with trespassing and disorderly conduct. During their jury trial in Northampton, Massachusetts, just across the Connecticut River, they admitted breaking the law but argued that protests were needed to raise awareness of CIA crimes in Latin America and elsewhere. Emblazoned on their T-shirts was the slogan "Put the CIA on Trial." Left-wing icons such as Daniel Ellsberg, leaker of the Pentagon Papers, and former U.S. attorney general Ramsey

Clark testified about the agency's complicity in assassinations and misinformation campaigns. The defendants were acquitted.

I was slow to recognize that this conflict in my youth between academia and U.S. intelligence was a historical aberration, or at least the nadir of a cycle, preceded and followed by eras of closer cooperation. After the terrorist attacks of September 11, 2001, though, the thaw was too evident to ignore. In 2002, I reported in the *Wall Street Journal* on a rapprochement between the CIA and the Rochester Institute of Technology. A decade earlier, a scandal about the CIA's influence on research and curriculum had spurred the resignation of the school's president, who had concealed his own work for the agency. Now the CIA was back, recruiting top students and proposing topics for senior theses.

Later, at Bloomberg News, I wrote about the growing threat of foreign espionage to U.S. universities. Then, in May 2014, University of South Florida associate professor Dajin Peng, a native of China, contacted me to complain that the FBI had forced him into an unappetizing choice: lose his job and face prison for alleged fraud, or spy on China. Although his tale struck me as bizarre, I checked it out, and found that it was largely true.

I realized that globalization—the influx of students and professors from China and other countries; the outflow of American undergraduates to overseas universities; and the proliferation of China-funded Confucius Institutes and far-flung branches of U.S. colleges—had raised the academic stakes for foreign and domestic intelligence services alike. Often in hidden ways, they were penetrating higher education more deeply than ever. Academia, resistant in my youth, was acquiescing, despite the tension between its open, global values and the nationalistic, covert culture of espionage.

The premise for this book crystallized when I was having lunch in a quiet corner of a suburban restaurant with a former U.S. government official. With some trepidation, I laid out my concerns about the invasion of academia by intelligence services—including his own. He thought it over for a moment, and then nodded.

"Both sides are exploiting universities," he said.

Academia's close relationship with the CIA in its early years, and the subsequent breach between them in the 1960s and 1970s, are well documented. But no one has chronicled the resurgence of clandestine U.S. intelligence activity at American universities. Several memoirs by former CIA officers, in which they mentioned trolling for recruits at universities or academic conferences or having been referred by their professors for agency employment, whetted my curiosity. Regarding foreign services, their cyber-espionage, especially against U.S. corporate and government targets, has overshadowed their use of student and faculty compatriots to acquire information, contacts, and sensitive research at American universities.

I set out to explore how and why intelligence services were targeting American higher education, and what the implications were for national security and academic freedom. When I had looked into Professor Peng's allegations, an open records request to the University of South Florida for its correspondence with FBI agent Dianne Mercurio had proven fruitful. Recognizing that the bureau, which famously investigated Hillary Clinton's emails, could itself be electronically indiscreet, I extended the same tactic nationwide, asking a dozen public universities for their communications with the CIA and FBI. The CIA didn't seem to mind, but the FBI did. Evincing a Hoover-esque hostility toward my inquiries, it took the counterintuitive legal position that its emails to universities still belonged to it, not to the recipients.

After the New Jersey Institute of Technology notified me in April 2015 that its communications with the bureau were "voluminous," eight FBI personnel reviewed the material for two days. At the FBI's bidding, the institute withheld 3,949 pages due to various exemptions. It did release another 500 pages, but most were heavily blacked out. (The FBI later identified 1,500 additional pages, adding up to about 6,000 in all.) With the help of attorneys at the Reporters Committee for Freedom of the Press, I appealed to a New Jersey state court. The case ended up in federal court, and NJIT, in consultation with the U.S. Department of Justice, handed over most of the documents. The notation "Per CIA," next to redactions in several emails, indicated a review by that agency as well.

Gregory M. Milonovich, the FBI's academic liaison, disparaged my project in a May 2015 email to the University of California, Davis's, chief of staff, which the university provided in response to my public records request. "Dan Golden . . . is trying to . . . build a book regarding the relationship between academia and the intelligence community," Milonovich wrote. "I'm not overly concerned that he is going to turn up anything worth writing about." He copied four FBI colleagues, asking them to confer on how to help UC Davis in dealing with me.

My approach met resistance in other quarters as well. Some liberals were unhappy that I was investigating foreign spies; some conservatives, that I was investigating American ones. Nevertheless, many people in the academic and national security realms were extraordinarily candid and helpful, and to them I am grateful.

I have divided this book into two parts, examining foreign and American espionage on campus in turn. Among the episodes revealed in Part 1: A Chinese graduate student poaches Pentagon-funded invisibility research from a Duke University lab—and then is staked by the Chinese government to launch a competing venture in Shenzhen that makes him a billionaire. A Puerto Rican admirer of the Castro regime, who both spied for Cuba herself and recruited a graduate school classmate who would become one of the most damaging moles ever inside the U.S. government, now teaches high school in Sweden, beyond the reach of American authorities. To attract full-paying Chinese students, an Ohio college affiliates with a Beijing university run by China's intelligence service—and sends its professors there to teach future spies about American culture.

In Part 2: The CIA stages academic conferences so that it can lure scientists in Iran's nuclear weapons program to defect. CIA officers who enroll undercover in Harvard mid-career and executive education programs cultivate unsuspecting foreign officials. And Dajin Peng, the beleaguered South Florida professor, matches wits with FBI agent Dianne Mercurio.

IN RECENT YEARS, U.S. universities have become a favored arena for the secret jousting of spy versus spy. While often portrayed as enclaves of scholarly learning and athletic prowess, or playpens for teenagers cavorting on the cusp of adulthood, they have taken on a disquieting real-world dimension as a front line for espionage. "Intelligence," which in academia used to refer to brainpower, increasingly means "information and knowledge about an adversary."

In labs, classrooms, and auditoriums, espionage services from countries such as China, Russia, and Cuba seek insights into U.S. policy, recruits for clandestine operations and access to sensitive military and civilian research. The FBI and CIA reciprocate, developing sources among international students and faculty. With close connections to government, business, and technology, plus the technical expertise needed to compete in a knowledge-based economy, professors, graduate students, and even undergraduates find themselves coveted as informants by all sides.

"Most if not all spy services view universities as a prime recruiting ground," says Chris Simmons, a former counterintelligence officer at the U.S. Defense Intelligence Agency, the Pentagon's intelligence arm. "People are most pliable in their late teens and early twenties, when they're young and inexperienced. It's easy for someone trained in the art of manipulation to steer them in a direction they're already inclined, or help convince them it's what they intended all along." It's also cheaper and less conspicuous for an intelligence service to enlist a student or professor who can be placed later in a federal agency than to lure someone already in a sensitive government position.

Open campuses make it simple for foreigners and Americans alike to gather intelligence. Most classrooms, student centers, and even laboratories (except for the growing number that conduct classified government research) offer easier entry than a gated residential community in Florida. Spies with no academic affiliation can slip unnoticed into lectures, seminars, and cafeterias and befriend the computer scientist or Pentagon adviser sitting beside them.

Hidden and sometimes deceptive, the spy services exploit—and taint—the traditional academic ideals of transparency and independent scholarship. Nevertheless, as universities pursue revenue and global prominence by opening branches abroad, allowing China to fund and staff institutes on their campuses, and ramping up enrollment of full-paying international students, they have ignored or even condoned espionage. Columbia Business School, for instance, didn't rescind the master's degree of Cynthia Murphy, a suburban New Jersey mother of two, when she turned out to be a Russian spy named Lydia Guryeva, tasked by Moscow to "strengthen . . . ties w. classmates on daily basis incl. professors who can help in job search and who will have (or already have) access to secret info."

Two trends have converged to create the surge in academic spying. The first is the growing intimacy between U.S. intelligence and academia, driven partly by patriotic fervor and terrorism fears in the wake of the September 11, 2001, attacks. Deterred by student protests and faculty hostility during the Vietnam era, the CIA, FBI, and other security agencies have returned in force, forging a tenuous alliance of spies and scholars.

"September 11 led to a quiet reengagement of a lot of the academy with the national security community," says Austin Long, who teaches security policy at Columbia University.

Second, and perhaps even more important, is the globalization of higher education. Globalization has built friendships and understanding between hostile countries, and improved the quality of teaching and research. It has also fostered foreign spying at American universities and their branches overseas, as well as a corresponding spike in U.S. efforts to recruit international students and professors. Academic migration to and from the United States has soared, with both directions offering opportunities for espionage. More U.S. students and faculty are heading overseas. The number of Americans studying abroad has doubled since 2001 to 304,467 in 2014–15. The sun never sets on American universities. There are more than 160 American-style universities in eighty countries, from Italy to Kurdistan. Most are branch campuses of U.S. institutions, or foreign-run schools seeking U.S. accreditation. More than half have opened since 2000.

Often located in politically sensitive regions such as the Middle East and China, these branches provide targets for foreign intelligence agencies and likely listening posts for our own. Foreign intelligence services, especially China's, seek to recruit young Americans abroad and place them in key U.S. government positions. If they are fluent in the right languages, U.S. intelligence may also tap them.

The CIA and FBI "think nothing of finding a linguistically appropriate young American, whom they know has a wanderlust and has decided to spend two or three semesters overseas, and asking them to gather intelligence," a former federal official told me. The FBI even urged the University of South Florida to open a China branch, where Peng could be assigned as a cover for his spying.

At the same time, foreign students and professors have been pouring into the United States, though the election of Donald Trump as president on an anti-immigrant platform could stanch the flow, especially from Iran and other Muslim countries. There were almost one million (974,926) international students at U.S. universities in 2014–15, more than six times the 1974–75 total (154,580) and more than double that in 1994–95 (452,635). The number of foreign-born scientists and engineers working at U.S. colleges and universities rose by 44 percent, from 360,000 in 2003 to 517,000 in 2013. While most international students, researchers, and professors come to the United States for legitimate reasons, universities are an "ideal place" for foreign intelligence "to find recruits, propose and nurture ideas, learn and even steal research data, or place trainees," the FBI reported in 2011.

The FBI and CIA set their sights on international students, professors, and visiting scholars in the United States, assessing them as potential threats or "assets"—espionage lingo for spies managed by CIA officers. In a 2012 poll of staff at U.S. universities who work with international students, 31 percent, or almost one-third, reported that the FBI had visited students within the past year. (The poll didn't ask about the CIA.) It's likely that the FBI approached more students without the staff's knowledge.

"When it comes to counter-intelligence," Milonovich, the FBI liaison to academia, wrote to a group of university presidents in May 2014, "the FBI is interested in 3 primary areas: 1) students, both foreign and domestic, 2) faculty, both foreign and domestic and 3) research and development."

With so many foreigners on campus, U.S. intelligence prioritizes them based on such factors as country of origin, field of study, access to sensitive research, family background, and whether their home government is paying their tuition. If an academic has access to a country that's both hostile and hard to penetrate, U.S. intelligence can be very persistent. Take the case of an Iranian-born scientist who travels frequently to his native land. "He was first contacted by the FBI with the excuse that they wanted to know his opinion about what was happening in Iran," says a friend of his. "He met with the FBI agent. Then, after a few email exchanges, he was told by the FBI agent that the CIA was interested in recruiting him. He turned them down.

"Sometime later the same FBI agent asked the scientist to reconsider his decision, but he rejected the CIA offer again. Several months later he was invited to a security conference, which was known to be populated by CIA agents." The conference was "about Iran and how young Iranians, particularly young scientists, become foot soldiers for the Iranian hard-liners, and help them with all sorts of things, including Iran's nuclear program." The scientist "turned down the invitation. Several months later, he was asked to meet with the representative of a British company, and was told that 'the British Consulate in San Francisco' had suggested the meeting. But it turned out that the company did not exist, so that was probably another attempt for recruitment. The meeting did not take place."

Although the CIA is noted for its feats and failures abroad, its National Resources Division operates clandestinely in the United States, primarily recruiting foreign nationals. Henry Crumpton, who headed the division from 2003 to 2005, said that it relied on a network of "campus cooperators" numbering in the "low hundreds" to identify prospects.

"We have cooperative contacts at the universities," Crumpton told me. "I would meet with them sometimes. These are American citizens, for the most part, or persons legally here, cooperating because they think it's the right thing to do."

CIA officers must acknowledge their intelligence affiliation when recruiting U.S. citizens and permanent residents, but not foreigners. Working from "lists of foreign students studying at US universities," one former CIA officer used "a plethora of commercial aliases" to make appointments with them, according to his memoir, written under the pseudonym Ishmael Jones. "I'd meet them to see if they had access to any secrets of interest to the US and if they did, advance the relationship and then recruit them. . . . Typically I sought out graduate students from rogue states whose educations were being paid for by their governments and were studying something useful to the rogue state—such as nuclear science."

Some CIA officers on clandestine missions pretend to be professors. While they aren't supposed to represent themselves falsely as employees of a specific U.S. university, the policy leaves room for hazier cover. "I'm an associate professor of Middle Eastern Studies at the University of Texas at Austin" is forbidden, but "I'm a professor doing research for a book on Middle Eastern politics" is allowed. Such distinctions may blur in the field. "I don't know of any restriction on posing as a pointy-headed college professor, and I have done so," Jones told me.

Based on his campaign promises and first months in office, President Trump's policies are likely to spur more domestic and foreign spying in academia. Less shackled by civil liberties and privacy restraints, the CIA and NSA may be expected to step up recruiting and surveillance of foreign students and professors, though Trump's anti-Muslim rhetoric is likely to undermine efforts to win over Middle Eastern students and send them home as American agents. His threatened trade war with China may embolden its government to siphon off more technologies developed at American universities, while his appeasement of Russia could encourage Vladimir Putin to infiltrate the Ivy League with more spies. China, Russia, and Iran may also seek campus informants on the arms buildup vowed in Trump's December 2016 tweet that "the United States must greatly strengthen and expand its nuclear capability." Even our allies, bewildered by the president's unreliability and belligerent posturing, may furtively gather academic insights into his policies and intentions.

After lower courts had blocked Trump's plan to restrict entry to the U.S. from Iran and five other predominantly Muslim countries, the Supreme Court in June 2017 reinstated part of the travel ban. But it exempted foreigners with "a bona fide relationship with a person or entity" in the U.S. Those still free to come here, the court said, include students admitted to U.S. universities and lecturers invited to address American audiences. It would hardly be surprising if their nations' intelligence agencies, with other avenues of espionage stymied by the ban, would press some of these students and speakers into service.

WHILE MANY PROFESSORS work hard, their official duties aren't especially protracted. They teach ten to fifteen hours a week, hold office hours twice a week, and have summers off. That leaves plenty of unstructured time for writing, research, preparing lectures, grading papers, serving on university committees, consulting, traveling internationally to academic conferences—and moonlighting for U.S. intelligence.

Their assistance comes in many forms and levels of engagement. When they return from places of interest, they may be debriefed by the CIA, or volunteer a nugget. "Occasionally, I will report something of my own volition if I've had a particularly interesting conversation with a high government official," says Harvard political scientist Joseph Nye, a former National Intelligence Council chairman. "I might say, 'I saw the foreign minister. Their official position is this. Over drinks, he said the opposite.'"

Although CIA policy prohibits using journalists, clergy, and Peace Corps volunteers except under extraordinary circumstances, students and professors are fair game. Two globe-trotting professors were among the agency's "most energetic and incompetent" recent agents, according to Ishmael Jones. They invited a young scientist from a "country with a nascent nuclear program" to the United States and ushered him on a private tour of the Massachusetts Institute of Technology's cutting-edge laboratories, inadvertently disrupting another CIA officer's efforts to recruit him.

On a separate occasion, the faculty duo used CIA funds to create "a scientific conference specifically designed" to entice a nuclear scientist from a hostile nation, and arranged a scholarship for him to an American university. Rather than help the CIA, though, he "used his university connections and scholarship to gather additional scientific information for his country's nuclear program."

A professor at one top-tier East Coast university enjoys wearing his eight-hundred-dollar Victorinox Swiss Army watch to dinner parties. It's the ultimate conversation piece: a bribe from a Russian spy.

As a student, he had considered a CIA career, but the agency wasn't hiring. He'd gone into academia instead, making his name as a foreign policy expert, and still occasionally wondering if he had a talent for espionage.

Then, in 2010, he got an unexpected chance. He was moderating a campus discussion on arms control. Afterward, a Russian diplomat approached him and one of the panelists, gave them his card, and invited them to lunch.

Because they held security clearances, the professor and his colleague were obliged to run this overture past the FBI. A contact at FBI counterintelligence soon called the professor and said that the diplomat was believed to be a foreign intelligence officer.

"I guess I won't meet him for lunch," the professor said.

"That's one option," the FBI agent said. "We'd prefer you to meet him." The bureau wanted to use the professor as a double agent to learn about "Russian collection priorities, tradecraft, and things like that," he told me. "Just knowing what the other side is really interested in is very valuable."

Over the next two years, the Russian and the FBI each treated the professor to ten lunches. He would dine with the Russian spy at Mexican restaurants, French bistros, and steakhouses: never the same place twice, because his host was worried about countersurveillance. The Russian always paid cash: hundred-dollar bills, straight from an operational fund. Afterward the professor would call the FBI agents, who would take him to lunch a few days later and debrief him.

The spy was in his late thirties, muscular and swarthy, with a high forehead and deep-set eyes reminiscent of Russian president and former KGB officer Vladimir Putin. He offered to help the professor find a Russian publisher for his scholarly articles and books, saying he had connections in Moscow publishing circles because his father had worked for the Soviet news service—a frequent cover, his listener knew, for KGB agents. The spy also plied the professor with gifts of increasing value, first a fine bottle of Posolskaya vodka—which was especially appropriate coming from a spy under diplomatic cover because *posolskaya* means "ambassador" in Russian—and then the Swiss watch.

"Do you want the watch?" the professor asked the FBI agents. "Don't you want to check for bugs?"

No need, they told him; it was unlikely to be bugged. He could keep it.

Initially, the spy elicited the professor's views on the sort of topics often discussed in the faculty lounge or a current events seminar, such as U.S. policy in Afghanistan. Gradually, his questions over lunch became more pointed. How well did the professor know a certain U.S. general, and what did they talk about? Avoiding specifics, the professor did his best to act cagey, but intrigued.

"You want to play smart and dumb," the professor later explained to me. "You want to seem a little more oblivious than you are. It's a courtship. You can't seem too eager to betray your country."

At last, the Russian proposed a trade: cash for information. The amount of the payment would depend on the quality of the information. To prevent exposure, he said, the professor should buy a laptop that he would never connect to the Internet, write on it, and supply the file to the Russian on a flash drive. The spy would then insert the drive into a secure computer in the nearest Russian diplomatic facility, and send a cable to Moscow.

The FBI instructed the professor to play along without providing any classified secrets. He wrote an authoritative-sounding discussion of the Afghanistan war on his own laptop and gave the flash drive to the Russian.

At their next lunch, the spy handed over two thousand dollars in hundred-dollar bills. He also made clear to his recruit that publicly available information, no matter how well analyzed, would not suffice.

"We appreciate it, but we didn't think it was that sensitive," he told the professor. "We can pay you more if you give us more."

Familiar with the revolving door in the United States between academe and government, he encouraged the professor to seek a job in the State Department or Pentagon—where, both men understood without saying, Russia would pay dearly for an inside source.

The professor turned the money over to the FBI. Soon afterward, the Russian rotated back to Moscow. He assured the professor that his replacement would be in touch, but no message came. Possibly the professor's banal analysis had persuaded Russian intelligence that he knew nothing of value. Or they guessed that the FBI was running him. Either way, his foray into espionage was over. While he had discovered "nothing earth-shattering," the professor concluded, he had benefited national security, and scratched his intelligence itch.

SPY SCHOOLS

PART 1

FOREIGN ESPIONAGE AT AMERICAN UNIVERSITIES

1
. . . .

CLOAK OF INVISIBILITY

Brandishing a light saber, and sporting a dark cloak and hood that concealed his eyes but not his grin, Jedi Master Obi-Wan Kenobi pranced about the stage of Window of the World Caesar's Palace in Shenzhen, China, on the evening of January 30, 2016. So did Jedi warriors, imperial stormtroopers, and other Star Wars characters. Pulsating spotlights and jets of smoke alternately illuminated and clouded the spectacle as a cheering audience of seven hundred waved yellow, green, and purple sabers.

Titled "Battle of Future—A New Dawn," the Star Wars parody highlighted an extravaganza that also featured live music, sensual dances, people's faces (poked through a screen) atop puppet bodies, and a tribute to China's military. It marked the sixth anniversary of Kuang-Chi Institute of Advanced Technology and Kuang-Chi Science Ltd., which aim to conceive and commercialize breakthroughs in the fast-growing field of metamaterials. Ruopeng Liu, the Obi-Wan Kenobi, is the founder and head of these ventures; the other Jedis, their executives; the performers and audience, their workers. Several members of the audience won prizes epitomizing the fearless, innovative spirit that Liu preaches: trips to the North Pole, the South Pole, and Near Space.

Still in his costume but now sans saber, Liu clutched an enormous bouquet of flowers in his left hand and a microphone in his right, and glorified his accomplishments in song. "No matter how thrilling it is outside, I behave with perfect composure," he crooned in Chinese. "You can't say how hard the trip is, it's fortunate we kept a cool head." Then he segued into the chorus from the Beatles' "Hey Jude."

Chubby-cheeked and endearingly boyish at the age of thirty-two, Liu had a lot to celebrate. His majority stake in Kuang-Chi Science, which is traded on the Hong Kong stock exchange, made him a billionaire with a business empire extending to the United States, Norway, Canada, and New Zealand. Chinese media dubbed him the "Elon Musk of China," equating him as a visionary with the iconic founder of electric car maker Tesla. By the end of 2015, his fledgling institute had sought an astounding total of 3,289 patents, and received 1,783. China's government showered him with honors and responsibilities for technology policy, and President Xi Jinping, as well as many prominent ministers and party officials, toured Liu's enterprises in Shenzhen.

Yet Liu's wealth and fame are a mask, like his costume at the anniversary gala, or the invisibility cloak that he helped design as a Duke graduate student in electrical engineering, under renowned professor David R. Smith. They hide an unsettling reality that has never been made public: he owes much of his success to what one might call a higher education form of economic espionage. Liu exploited an unwary professor, lax collaboration guidelines, and Duke's open, global culture by funneling Pentagon-funded research to China. He arranged for Chinese researchers to visit Smith's lab and reproduce its equipment, and passed them data and ideas developed by unwitting colleagues at Duke. He secretly started a Chinese website based on research at Duke, and deceived Smith into committing to work part-time in China. His activities compromised the United States' edge in an emerging technology that could someday conceal a fighter jet, tank, or drone, affecting the outcome of a war or covert operation. Once Liu returned to China, a grateful government invested millions in his start-up ventures.

Looking back, some of Liu's former colleagues in the Duke lab feel that he violated their trust. "When you toil away in academia, only about ten people know it's your idea," one member of the lab, Jonah Gollub, told me. "Ideas were flowing from here to China. In retrospect, people feel they weren't given the full picture."

The Liu case illustrates how vulnerable academic research is to foreign raiders, and how little universities do to protect it. Eager to attract international students and open branches abroad, universities are reluctant to offend China and other countries by cracking down on research theft. Yet, by looking the other way, they're betraying the government agencies, and ultimately the American taxpayers, funding the research. We pay taxes for our military to defend us, only to have universities compromise that security by pursuing global prominence without acknowledging or addressing the collateral damage.

Although Liu has never been charged with any crime, the FBI looked into his activities and briefed university presidents and law enforcement officials about them. At an October 2012 closed-door session of the National Security Higher Education Advisory Board at FBI headquarters, according to an agenda obtained through a public records request, Smith recounted how, "without his knowledge, a Chinese national targeted his lab and . . . created a mirror institute in China. The episode cost Duke significantly in licensing, patents and royalties and kept Smith from being the first to publish ground-breaking research." An FBI video interview with Smith about the episode, shown to an invitation-only audience in September 2015, was titled simply "The Theft of a Great Idea."

Liu "was definitely filled with intent," and his actions "could have tremendous economic impact in the future," Smith wrote me in July 2015. "I think if people understood how something like this happens, and how those with potentially ill intent can take advantage of the natural chaos that occurs in US academic environments, they might become more aware and avoid things like this in the future."

ACADEMIC RESEARCH OFFERS a valuable, vulnerable, and low-risk target for foreign espionage. Despite pursuing groundbreaking technologies for the Pentagon and the intelligence community, university laboratories are less protected than their corporate counterparts, reflecting a culture oriented toward collaboration and publication. Typically, university researchers aren't required to sign nondisclosure agreements, which run counter to the ethic of openness.

"There's a lot less control than in a company like Boeing," says John Villasenor, a professor of electrical engineering at the University of California, Los Angeles. "Universities are ripe pickings for anybody who's interested in accessing intellectual property."

Ignorance about intellectual property safeguards, or even hostility toward them, is rife among science students and faculty. There is "zero instruction" on the topic outside law school, Villasenor told me. Significant proportions of UCLA engineering graduate students whom he surveyed couldn't define a patent (21 percent), copyright (32 percent), trademark (51 percent), or trade secret (68 percent). Never contemplating the possibility of espionage, American professors sometimes comply with requests from acquaintances or strangers overseas for research advice, manuscript reviews, or unpublished data. A civil engineering professor at Penn State once phoned Graham Spanier, then the university's president, to say that a foreigner had emailed him asking how to build an underground concrete structure that could withstand a megaton explosion.

"I was about to hit send, when it dawned on me, I'd better ask," the professor said. "I don't know this person." Spanier notified the FBI, which traced the request back through seven intermediary layers before losing the trail. The elaborately disguised source was never unmasked.

The casual university attitude belies the growing threat. Academic solicitation, or "the use of students, professors, scientists or researchers as collectors," tripled from 8 percent of all foreign efforts to obtain sensitive or classified information in fiscal 2010 to 24 percent in 2014, according to the Defense Security Service, a Defense Department agency that protects American technology.

American college graduates with a flair for engineering or computer science typically join high-technology companies, or start their own, rather than continue their educations. As a result, international students dominate graduate programs in those fields at U.S. universities, forming the backbone of their workforce for cutting-edge research. In 2012–13, foreign students earned 56.9 percent of doctorates conferred by U.S. universities in engineering and 52.5 percent of those in computer and information sciences. They comprise more than 70 percent of graduate students nationwide in Smith's specialty, electrical engineering.

"Foreign intelligence services, foreign corporations and foreign governments often target these students in an attempt to have them provide the results of the research they are working on or other proprietary and intellectual property that belongs to the United States government or to United States corporations that are funding the research," David W. Szady, former FBI assistant director for counterintelligence, wrote in a July 2014 newsletter. "Foreign militaries can develop state-of-the-art weapons systems by stealing research from colleges and universities that is sponsored by the United States Department of Defense."

AMERICAN TAXPAYERS FUND a significant amount of academic research and development. The U.S. government spent $27.4 billion on it in 2014, up from $16.9 billion in 2000 and $9.1 billion in 1990. That includes $2.4 billion in 2014 from the Pentagon and intelligence agencies (not counting the CIA, which doesn't report expenditures), up from $1.7 billion in 2000 and $1.2 billion in 1990.

Some of this research is off-limits to foreign students. If it's classified, only people with security clearances can work on it, usually in secure, off-campus facilities. If it's export-controlled, the next level down on the secrecy scale, the university must obtain a license from the government for a foreign national to participate. Such licenses are typically denied for students from countries such as China and Iran.

The bulk of federally funded university research, though, is fundamental, and open to all students. Since it can also be published without restriction, one might wonder, why bother stealing it? The answer: to save time, and avoid mistakes. Access can provide insights beyond the results published in an academic journal. "It's great to know the solutions, but the process is arguably just as important," says historian Vince Houghton, curator of the International Spy Museum in Washington, D.C. "You can see the paths not taken, the failures and dead ends." With a mole in a U.S. university laboratory, researchers overseas can publish and patent an idea first, ahead of the true pioneers, and enjoy the consequent acclaim, funding, and surge in interest from top students and faculty.

A foreign government may be eager to scoop up a fundamental breakthrough before its applications become so important that it's labeled secret—and foreign students lose access to it. J. A. Koerner, the former head of counterintelligence in the FBI's Tampa office, has a term for such promising science: pre-classified. "Once it becomes integrated into a military system, it will be classified and harder to get at," he says.

The very openness of U.S. universities denies them recourse against foreigners who siphon American ideas abroad. Economic espionage laws require the owner of stolen trade secrets to have taken reasonable precautions to protect them, like Coca-Cola's famed vigilance in defense of its formula. Lacking nondisclosure and collaboration agreements to safeguard intellectual property, universities can't meet that standard.

Reflecting his prominence at Duke, Professor David Smith has two offices in different buildings that face each other across a well-manicured lawn. He runs both his own research group out of the Fitzpatrick Center for Interdisciplinary Engineering, Medicine and Applied Sciences, which has a stone façade and modern amenities like "smart bridges," as well as the department of electrical and computer engineering out of older, red-brick Hudson Hall.

When we talked in April 2016 in the Hudson Hall office, where a remodeling had left the walls and shelves bare, Smith displayed none of the self-importance that one might expect from a department chair and award-winning scientist often touted as a Nobel Prize candidate. Casually dressed, he came across as soft-spoken and unpretentious.

The case of Ruopeng Liu, his former student turned Chinese billionaire, had taught him how easily the relationship of trust that scientific collaborations depend on can be abused, he told me. "No one has any training in intellectual property," he said. "It's something we're all grappling with—where to draw the line."

SMITH WAS BORN in 1964 in Okinawa, Japan, where his father served in the U.S. military. When he was a baby, his parents divorced, and he had no more contact with his father. His mother worked odd jobs, and they lived all over California: Riverside, San Diego, Carlsbad, San Francisco, Palm Springs, and finally Escondido, where he spent his last three years of high school.

He earned his bachelor's degree in 1988 and his doctorate in 1994, both from the University of California, San Diego. His hobby in graduate school was blackjack. He learned to count cards, a strategy that improves the player's chances by predicting the value of cards remaining in the deck. "I ended up organizing a group that played blackjack in Las Vegas for a while." Scammed by dealers using marked decks at a casino on an Indian reservation near San Diego, he sued to recover his losses. After five years of litigation, during which Smith "learned quite a bit about Indian gaming law," a California appeals court ruled against him.

Smith was a latecomer to academic stardom. At UCSD, he "was a fairly typical graduate student with no expectations on that level at all," said David Schurig, who overlapped with him there and later was a researcher in Smith's lab at Duke. "It's quite an impressive rise."

As a postdoctoral student at UCSD, Smith became involved with a biotech company his adviser was starting, and hardly published any research. He decided to leave academia for industry, but thought that a few publications first would help his career. As it happened, his articles helped launch the field of metamaterials—artificial materials with properties not found in nature—and "I was lucky enough to turn things around."

Around 1998, he began collaborating with Sir John Pendry, an English physicist and professor at Imperial College London, who theorized that metamaterials could warp the path of light as it moves through space. At a scientific meeting in San Antonio in 2005, Pendry suggested what he regarded as an "amusing" application. "I said, 'By the way, we can make something invisible,'" he later recalled. "I just gave a sketch and one slide with a formula on it and I sat down and I expect everybody to laugh. Straight faces."

Smith, who had joined Duke's faculty in 2004, missed the conference, but two members of his lab attended Pendry's speech. "Pretty soon the phone lines were hot, and David said, 'We've got to build this stuff,'" Pendry recalled.

"I and my group thought it would be a fun challenge and we realized right away we could do the experiment and the design," Smith told me. "I never expected that interest in this topic would be so huge."

Invisibility has always fascinated humankind. After killing Medusa, Perseus donned an invisibility helmet to elude the Gorgons. Long before Harry Potter and Frodo Baggins, King Arthur and Tom Thumb wore invisibility cloaks, while Gyges, a shepherd featured in Plato's *Republic*, sported an invisibility ring to murder a king and seduce the queen.

Journalists crave invisibility for professional benefit; we long to be unnoticed observers, flies on the wall, albeit flies with notebooks, pens, cameras, and tape recorders. Similarly, the obvious advantages of invisibility in war and espionage have long intrigued strategists. The British Army employed a stage magician and a filmmaker as invisibility consultants in World War II. For a 2002 *Wall Street Journal* article about the CIA's resurgence at the Rochester Institute of Technology, I sat in on a meeting where the agency's chief scientist, John Phillips, suggested projects for college seniors. High on his list was bending light rays to keep a spy in the shadows.

"Make me invisible," the six-foot-three, 250-pound Phillips exhorted.

In June 2006, Pendry, Schurig, and Smith coauthored an article in the prestigious journal *Science* explaining how to make an invisibility cloak. The following October, in a report published online by *Science,* those scientists, together with other members of Smith's lab, unveiled the first successful cloak. Composed of thousands of copper circuits, it "can make light curve around an object, and then emerge just as if it had passed in a straight line," Smith later wrote. "Think of it like water flowing past a rock in a stream."

There was one major caveat. The cloak only concealed objects from microwaves, not the human eye. Since visible light waves are 10,000 times shorter than microwaves, the metamaterials would need to be correspondingly tinier. Such a difference in scale creates a practical difficulty that remains to be solved: the metals used in those smaller metamaterials mostly absorb light, rather than diverting it. Still, the discovery had a range of potential applications, from improving cell phone reception by bending waves around a building or other obstacle, to reducing interference by antennas in military signaling.

The two *Science* publications spurred a media blitz. The diffident professor of electrical engineering found himself famous, with his research admired—and, in some quarters, coveted—worldwide.

"I would never have imagined that someone would believe our group to be so important," he told me. "I could barely find students to join our group, and finding funding is a nonstop struggle that is never certain. It just would never have seemed a possibility that anyone would seek to obtain intellectual property from us."

In August 2006, as Smith was adjusting to sudden celebrity, he welcomed a graduate student from China into his lab. He had high expectations for Ruopeng Liu. While Chinese candidates, who made up more than 80 percent of the department's applicant pool, were "very difficult to evaluate," Liu stood out as an "outstanding prospective student," Smith recalled.

The professor and his new pupil had contrasting personalities. While Smith was diffident, thoughtful, and precise, Liu was gregarious, eager, self-confident, and prone to hyperbole. As the youngest member of the group, "he came across as a lovable, bumbling, enthusiastic kid," Smith said.

Liu was "a very high-energy guy, almost in a cartoonish sort of way," another professor recalled. "Pretty outgoing, very friendly, bopping around. Awkward at times, but endearing. When he introduces himself, he'll bounce into a room. Easy to be around. He was remarkably open to different and new ideas. He was willing to take a crazy idea and see how far it could go."

Where Smith was a late bloomer, Liu was something of a prodigy. Born in Shaanxi Province, in northwest China, he moved south at the age of nine to Shenzhen. A fast-growing manufacturing and financial center across a river and a bay from Hong Kong, Shenzhen is home to telecommunications giant ZTE Corporation, where Liu's parents worked. As a sophomore at Zhejiang University, he encountered the hot new subject of metamaterials. A year later, Tie Jun Cui, one of the leading Chinese scientists in the field, became a visiting professor at Zhejiang, and Liu's mentor. Liu began taking a train each weekend to work in Cui's lab at Southeast University in Nanjing. "He conducted his research in my group" for two years, Cui told me. Liu also assembled a group of Zhejiang students to explore mathematical modeling.

"He's very energetic and ambitious, and he knows how to organize people," said Da Huang, a friend of Liu's at Zhejiang who later joined Smith's lab. "When he's focused, he thinks fast." In his leisure time at Duke, Liu enjoyed grilling meat for potluck dinners and watching a Chinese television drama about Mongol emperor Genghis Khan.

Liu came to Duke with "a thousand ideas" and wasn't shy about sharing them, recalled Jonah Gollub, another member of Smith's lab. Within a week, Liu organized an hour-long seminar to discuss his research in China. "He came in with this grand unified theory of metamaterials," Gollub said. "It's not how science is usually done, but there was the sense he was brilliant. He doesn't sleep, he's one hundred percent focused on science, one hundred percent enthusiasm for what he was working on."

"Ruopeng was a very unusual graduate student," another lab member recalled. "He hit the ground running. He was having debates with David Smith and postdocs on day one. That's something you normally see at the end of the first or second year."

When he arrived, Liu was one of only five students in Smith's group. It would swell to half a dozen graduate students and three or four postdoctoral fellows by 2010. They worked primarily on fundamental research, though occasionally a project was export-controlled. They exchanged ideas at weekly meetings. The lab relied on federal funding, especially from the U.S. military's research branches.

As the boss, Smith was supportive but not intrusive. He expected researchers to be independent and solve problems on their own. "At the time, I found David's approach to be very frustrating, very hands-off," Gollub said. "You didn't necessarily feel that you were strongly guided in any direction. If you were struggling, you couldn't necessarily count on him to notice."

Liu stepped into the void. Acting more like a professor than a mere graduate student, he familiarized himself with all of the projects in Smith's lab, and many in other Duke engineering groups, dispensing ideas and encouragement and initiating collaborations. "He was really more of an organizer and manager than a scientist," Smith said. "His strongest skills were not in science, but he seemed to have an extraordinary ability to get others to do things."

Rarely, though, did Liu knuckle down himself to the rigorous tasks of analyzing and testing his creative notions. "He was a talker," Schurig said. "He spent all of his time talking to people. He was a good communicator. You never saw him spending long hours focused on his computer. I'm always a little suspicious of people like that. They're gleaning their ideas from others."

SOON AFTER JOINING Smith's group, Liu suggested collaborating with his former team, run by Cui at Southeast University in Nanjing. Liu told Smith that Cui had a large, talented roster of scientists whose projects would mesh with the Duke lab's research.

Smith liked the idea. His international association with Pendry had proven fruitful, and Cui was a respected scientist. At San Diego, Smith told me, his adviser "had been extremely paranoid and xenophobic. That really harmed us as a group, and when I began to be more independent, my feeling was to be as open and collaborative as possible."

Like most collaborations that bubble up from student or faculty interactions, the one between Smith's group and Cui's was unwritten. No formal agreement was drawn up that might have set limits on sharing intellectual property. "The majority of collaborations are just informal, people getting together at meetings and brainstorming," Smith said. It's "another nebulous area in the system that is in need of clarity."

Liu became the liaison between the Duke and China teams. "He had this kind of advantage of being able to shift between universes, our group and the Chinese group," Gollub said.

Then Liu broached another proposal: Smith should enhance the collaboration by inviting Cui's team to Duke. When Smith objected that he didn't have the budget, Liu told him to relax: China would pay. So the researchers visited Smith's lab, where they photographed the equipment: mainly, two big plates of aluminum separated by one centimeter, on mechanical stages. Then they measured the length of the plates, the thickness of the metal, and other dimensions.

Taking pictures of other teams' laboratories is controversial in academia. To maintain a competitive advantage, some research groups at U.S. universities ban the practice. Though dismayed, Smith reasoned that his collaborators were entitled to study the equipment. According to the FBI, the lab was later reproduced in China.

As a member of Smith's group, and coauthor of the October 2006 *Science* article, Bryan Justice designed the apparatus. He could tell from later publications by Cui's group, he told me, that they had "painstakingly duplicated" it and "had everything down to the nuts and bolts . . . a little more closely than you should be able to by reading our papers."

Justice said he "spent probably a semester and a half developing, troubleshooting, and debugging that system before it was ready for prime time." Cui's group could "duplicate it in a couple of weeks because we've already done the heavy lifting." However, according to Smith, they failed to reproduce the cloak itself, which limited their ability to collect data with the apparatus.

In emails to me, Cui didn't deny that his team photographed and replicated the equipment, but he downplayed the benefit, and said he was surprised that anyone would regard it as a violation of academic ethics. Smith's group had already published a description and picture of the apparatus, which was simple in concept and design and easy to build, Cui wrote. "By the way, I have seen at least five similar equipment in China, UK, Singapore, and Hong Kong."

The collaborations between his group and Smith's, he added, were "properly scientific."

A talk by Cui at Duke also raised suspicion about his—and Liu's—intentions. At the time, Liu was working with a postdoctoral fellow in Smith's group who had devised a new application of transformation optics, or using metamaterials to bend light. The postdoc, who asked not to be identified in this book, told me that he supplied files and data from his simulations to Liu, who was "supposed to find an implementable design and to fabricate a structure that would comply with the material parameters I calculated."

Instead, the fellow was stunned to hear Cui deliver the simulation results, as if the Chinese team had discovered them. "For me, it was obvious that Ruopeng reported my results to T. J. Cui and most likely sent him the files," he continued. "I was really upset and I think one day after the talk I reported the case to David Smith."

Again, Smith shrugged off the concerns. "With me believing that we were in a collaboration, I felt that we just needed to tune things a bit," he told me. He told the postdoc that "he was not obliged to share details of his project if he felt uncomfortable with the situation." The postdoc ended the collaboration with Liu and virtually stopped speaking to him. In retrospect, Smith said, "he made a very good choice to be cautious with his results around the lab!"

Surfing the Internet, the postdoctoral student noticed that Liu was coauthoring scientific articles with Cui's team. The fellow notified Smith, who didn't know about the publications. "Being new to all of this, I assumed the best, and thought they just didn't understand that you shouldn't do that," Smith said. He talked with Liu, who said it was a misunderstanding, and wouldn't happen again. But it would.

After the Chinese team's visit to Duke, Liu began inviting his colleagues in Smith's group to reciprocate. Still angry that Cui had appropriated his data, the postdoctoral student declined. But Smith and several other members of his lab agreed to go to China. The offers were hard to resist, because the trips were free: China's government footed the bill.

Early in 2008, Jonah Gollub accompanied Liu to China and gave talks on his research at five universities. "I was confused about why he was bringing me over there," Gollub told me. "We saw many, many different groups. It was kind of weird. Even at the time, I was saying, 'Why are we doing this?'" Gollub added that "it was clear they had money for this sort of thing."

In November 2008, Smith, Liu, Schurig, and other Duke researchers participated in an international metamaterials workshop that Cui organized at the Jinling Riverside Conference Hotel in Nanjing. Along with Cui, Smith and Pendry were listed as cochairs. "I'm not positive that I agreed," Smith told me. "In retrospect, I think they were trying to sell us as active collaborators in China."

"A whole bunch of us visited China," recalled Schurig, who is now a professor at the University of Utah. "At the time, we were pretty excited about it. We'd never been to China. They were great hosts. It was a really fun trip. A lot of research was presented by the Chinese and the visitors. China paid for everything."

Smith almost backed out of the conference, he told me. He was hoping to save one day for sightseeing, but Liu was demanding that he cancel his touring. Since Cui and China were picking up the Duke group's expenses, Liu told him, he should devote all of his time to giving technical advice and talks to Cui's group. The two of them argued in Chicago's O'Hare International Airport as their flight to China was about to depart. "He began trying to add constraints and things to all of the invited speakers," Smith recalled. "I told him that my understanding was that this was a conference and that we were invited speakers, and we weren't there to work for Professor Cui. Ruopeng got upset and said that it was important for the program that we provide some technical input to Cui's program."

Smith finally threatened to turn around and go back to North Carolina. Liu "clearly was under pressure from China to make our trip worthwhile," Smith said.

It's likely that Chinese officials anticipated Smith's full cooperation because Liu had persuaded him to join a program called Project 111. Cui was associated with Project 111, and set up the metamaterials workshop under its aegis.

Liu had explained to Smith that Project 111 would strengthen the collaboration with Cui and fund research. But he didn't divulge its true purpose, or the commitment that Smith was making. China's Ministry of Education and its State Administration of Foreign Experts Affairs established Project 111 in 2006 to spur "scientific renewal" of Chinese universities by recruiting renowned scientists as "overseas academic masters." In return for travel fees, allowance, housing, and medical services, each master was expected to work at least one month at "innovation centers" established on Chinese campuses.

Liu sought to enlist other Western metamaterials experts besides Smith in Project 111. One of them, a China-born professor at the University of California, became suspicious. He translated the contract into English and warned Smith that it required working in China. Smith went back to Liu, who assured him that everything was fine, and not to worry about it.

"I was incredibly naïve about all this," Smith said.

IN A NUMBER of high-profile cases, the U.S. government has wrongly accused Chinese-American scientists of economic espionage. Most notably, Professor Xi Xiaoxing, chairman of Temple University's physics department, was cleared in 2015 of sending a secret design to China of a superconductor device known as a pocket heater, when it turned out that the blueprints were for entirely different equipment. A study by Thomas Nolan, a California defense attorney specializing in economic espionage cases, shows that people with Chinese surnames were sentenced on average to 32 months in prison for stealing trade secrets, as against 15 months for everyone else.

False accusations and unfair sentencing are inexcusable. Nevertheless, they stem from a disturbing reality: foreign theft of American science and technology is running rampant, and China is the leading culprit. The 2013 report of the Commission on the Theft of American Intellectual Property, cochaired by former U.S. ambassador to China Jon M. Huntsman Jr., concluded that China accounts for between 50 percent and 80 percent of the more than $300 billion in intellectual property that the

United States loses annually. Almost two-thirds of all economic espionage cases alleging a foreign destination for stolen trade secrets involve China. Of China-related cases between 1997 and 2016, twenty-four led to convictions or guilty pleas, three were reduced to lesser charges, eight were dropped or dismissed, and thirteen were pending.

Project 111 is one of a vast array of Chinese "brain gain" programs that, intentionally or not, encourage theft of intellectual property from U.S. universities. These initiatives to attract overseas scientists, especially those born in China, offer such generous salaries, laboratory facilities, and other incentives that a borderline candidate may be tempted to improve his chances by bringing back somebody else's data or ideas.

Chinese recruitment programs "pose a serious threat to US businesses and universities through economic espionage and theft of IP," according to a September 2015 FBI report. Koerner, the FBI's former head of counterintelligence in Tampa, sums up the implicit message to Chinese researchers in the United States: "Don't come home empty-handed."

In March 2013, Huajun Zhao, a research assistant at Medical College of Wisconsin, was arrested and charged with stealing three vials of a cancer-fighting compound from his professor, Marshall Anderson, who had patented it. Zhao, who claimed that he invented the compound and wanted to bring it to China for further study, had applied for funding from Chinese agencies that support research and overseas recruitment. One application was an "exact translation" of an old grant proposal by Anderson, according to the 2015 FBI report, which was distributed only to law enforcement and corporate security members of its Domestic Security Alliance Council. Zhao later pleaded guilty to a reduced charge of illegally downloading research data and was sentenced to the four-and-a-half months he'd already served plus two years' probation.

Since its inception in 1949, the People's Republic of China has recognized the importance of foreign-trained scientists in accelerating technological progress. Established that same year, the Chinese Academy of Sciences "soon welcomed over 200 returning scientists who contributed to CAS the high-level expertise they had acquired abroad," according to its website. Driven out of the United States as a suspected communist on flimsy evidence, California Institute of Technology rocket scientist Qian Xuesen returned to China in 1955 and built its space and missile programs.

After the Cultural Revolution, when Chinese leader Deng Xiaoping decided to send throngs of students to the United States, he hoped that 90 percent would return and foster China's technological prowess. Instead he spurred a brain drain that peaked after the 1989 Tiananmen Square massacre. Students who had opposed the crackdown feared prosecution in China, and the U.S. government allowed them to stay.

In response, China's national, provincial, and municipal governments embarked on aggressive efforts to lure back the most successful expatriates. Of the slew of initiatives, the best known are the Hundred Talents Program and the Thousand Talents Program. Hundred Talents seeks up-and-coming scholars under age forty. Thousand Talents, established in 2008 by the Communist Party's powerful Organization Department, woos prominent professors of Chinese ethnicity under age fifty-five. Aside from salaries, laboratories, and research funds, the perks include housing, medical care, jobs for spouses, and top schools for children. The government also rewards Chinese universities for landing foreign experts.

"In fact, the Chinese government has been the most assertive government in the world in introducing policies targeted at triggering a reverse brain drain," David Zweig, a professor at Hong Kong University of Science and Technology, and Huiyao Wang, director general of the Center for China and Globalization in Beijing, wrote in 2012.

Such initiatives have attracted numerous foreign scientists. In the 296 national research programs approved by China's Ministry of Science and Technology from 2006 to 2011, 47 percent of the chief scientists earned their doctorates abroad, and 32 percent came to China via the Thousand Talents Program. Of Chinese students who received science and engineering doctorates at American universities in 1996, 98 percent remained in the United States in 2001. Among the corresponding cohort a decade later, 15 percent left the United States, likely due to China's enticements.

Hong Ding was one of the Thousand Talent Program's biggest prizes. The tenured full professor of physics at Boston College accepted what Ding called a "very attractive" package, including a $147,000 relocation allowance, to lead two projects for the Chinese Academy of Sciences.

Boston College faculty "were shocked," Ding told *China Daily*. "People thought staying in the US was good for my career. But I wanted to contribute to basic research going on in China." China made Ding "unbelievable offers of salary and equipment," a Boston College physics professor told me. "He was an up and coming star."

Still, China has snared relatively few scientists of Ding's status from U.S. universities. Most are reluctant to uproot families and leave tenured sinecures in the creative disorder of American academia to work in an authoritarian society. As a result, Thousand Talents and similar programs have modified their rules to allow recruits to keep their jobs abroad and come to China two or three months a year, much like Smith's contract with Project 111. Yitang Zhang, a University of California, Santa Barbara, math professor who has won a MacArthur "genius" award, rejected a full-time offer from the Chinese Academy of Sciences in 2013. Instead, Zhang, a former Chinese dissident, teaches graduate students at CAS in Beijing for two months in the summer. The Chinese have a phrase for such summer returnees: "migratory birds."

Even a part-time commitment was too much for Xiaochun He, a nuclear physicist at Georgia State University and Brookhaven National Laboratory. For both family and career reasons, he rejected a Thousand Talents offer to spend three months a year at a Chinese university with a higher salary and bigger laboratory.

"My friends in China, they have a whole floor of lab space," he told me. "My biggest concern is the research environment, and whether it's dominated by government policy instead of my free will. I'm a scientist. I do what I'm interested in."

Disdained by elite scientists, the talent programs appeal primarily to those on the fringes of American academia: untenured or adjunct professors, postdoctoral students with uncertain prospects. They realize what China wants—rapid progress in fields where it lags behind the West—and may be tempted to enhance their credentials by plundering American research.

"The structure, particularly of the Hundred Talents, encouraged people to bring back technology that was not available in China if they wanted to get a position," Zweig told me. "People do plan to go out look-ing for something they know is missing. They know that's their compara-tive advantage."

LATE IN 2008, Liu and a Duke graduate student in statistics, Chunlin Ji, developed a new invisibility cloak. Ji wrote the computer code for the design, and Liu translated the algorithms into the layout of wires needed to make the cloak. It could hide a bump on a flat surface from a broad spectrum of wave frequencies, bringing tantalizingly closer to fulfillment the dream of making objects invisible to the human eye.

Smith was pleased. Still, after the paper was submitted to *Science*, he asked Liu, the lead author, for a clearer explanation of the break-through. "I really had wanted him to be able to present—for his own education—all of the details in his own words," Smith said. Liu stalled him, and Smith wondered why. "This is the point where I started becom-ing very suspicious, because Ruopeng would never produce the tech-nique by which he achieved the design of the cloak. I probably asked him fifty times, and he kept saying he'd get to it. It was okay for a while, as we were finishing up the paper and it clearly worked. . . . But he kept stonewalling."

Exasperated, Smith finally asked Nathan Kundtz, another member of the team, to figure out the method. Two weeks later, "I had the tool, and presented it to the group," Kundtz recalled. "I was not thinking, I'll show Ruopeng. I was blissfully ignorant that anyone would care."

One listener did care. As Kundtz spoke, Liu "sank in his chair, looked incredibly angry, and was silent," Smith said. Liu was not only chagrined that a colleague could replicate his technique and frustrated that he couldn't keep it for himself, but also brooding about a shift in the group's pecking order. Kundtz, a graduate student in physics who had joined the lab in January 2008, was eclipsing him as the star student.

When Kundtz came to the lab, he told me, Liu was "the most charis-matic" member, and published the most. "He had his own de facto sub-group, and he would run the meetings like a professor." Initially the two were "very friendly," Kundtz said. But tensions developed. Kundtz was just as ambitious, stubborn, and aggressive as Liu, and a more pains-taking researcher.

Liu began sulking, and his research contributions diminished. "Certainly Ruopeng was unhappy that David was taking a liking to Nathan and spending more time with him," Gollub said.

Smith, in fact, was increasingly disenchanted with Liu's grandiose approach to science. Liu had developed what he called a theory of metamaterials and was determined to publish it, but Smith wouldn't let him, because the analysis was flawed. "As time progressed, his theory fell apart," and Liu couldn't correct it, Smith said. Finally, Smith fixed it himself in a published article.

"Ruopeng would often find interesting things," Smith said. "The theory wasn't right. He'd present it, and look so confident, that a lot of people thought he was brilliant. It was hard to tell in half an hour that it was all nonsense."

Soon after Kundtz unveiled Liu and Ji's invisibility cloak technique, several postdoctoral students arranged a confidential lunch with Smith. They complained that Kundtz was stealing ideas and urged Smith to expel him from the group.

One of them, Aloyse Degiron, told me that their demand had nothing to do with Kundtz reconstructing the cloak technique. He said Kundtz's abrasiveness had antagonized his colleagues: "It was very difficult to work with Nathan. He has this very strong personality. Clearly he had a very high opinion of himself. If someone said something stupid, he wouldn't hesitate to say it was stupid."

However, Gollub said that the postdocs felt "a certain sympathy" for Liu. "People felt some of these projects that were originally pushed along by Ruopeng were getting unfairly shifted to Nathan."

Smith believes that Liu incited the mutiny: "He was so mad about Nathan spilling the beans on his theory." When Smith went around the table, asking each postdoc what ideas Kundtz had stolen, "one after the other of the postdocs said they didn't know firsthand but heard it from someone else," he recalled. He told them that they should blame him instead, because he had assigned Kundtz to get a handle on the projects.

"A bunch of smart people were allowing themselves to be manipulated, and I was pretty irritated," Smith said.

• • •

THE JANUARY 16, 2009, publication of "Broadband Ground-Plane Cloak" in *Science,* with Liu and Ji as lead authors and Smith and Cui among the coauthors, should have been a triumph for Smith's group. It drew wide attention, including a joke in Jay Leno's *Tonight Show* monologue: "Scientists are developing a cloak that bends light to make you invisible—like being an actress over forty in Hollywood." Bada boom.

Smith heralded the advance in a Duke publication. "The difference between the original device and the latest model is like night and day," he announced. "The new device can cloak a much wider spectrum of waves—nearly limitless—and will scale far more easily to infrared and visible light."

For Liu, the article generated both prestige and profit. As another incentive for technological achievement, China's government rewards Chinese scientists for bylines in premier journals. It paid Liu more than ten thousand dollars, according to Smith.

But the celebration was short-lived—and all because of a footnote. It cited funders for the research: not only Smith's patrons, such as the Air Force Office of Scientific Research and defense contractor Raytheon, but also Cui's, which included the National Basic Science Foundation of China, the National Basic Research Program of China, and Project 111. In late January, Smith's project manager at the Air Force sent him "a very harsh email" telling him that the Pentagon wanted to know why he was taking money from China. Presumably the Pentagon had invested in Smith's research because it hoped to mask a fighter jet or other weapons from enemy radar. It didn't want China, a potential adversary, to have the same capacity.

Alarmed, Smith pulled out of the collaboration with Cui's group and Project 111. "It all just fell apart after our sponsors became so concerned," he said. Smith told Liu not to work with Cui's group any longer, and to distinguish clearly in his dissertation between his own research and that of collaborators at Duke and in China.

As LIU PLUGGED away at his doctoral dissertation on "Designing and Building Microwave Metamaterials" in 2009, he began preparing for his career after Duke. He was torn between two paths: academia and business.

He had a knack for entrepreneurship. One night in the lab, he talked with a colleague about technology opportunities in Africa, such as manufacturing cheap cell phones. But he could also see himself as a professor, guiding his own group's research. "Ruopeng wanted to do something innovative and real, and also to be a business success," Da Huang, his friend from Zhejiang University and Smith's group, told me.

Armed with recommendations from Pendry and Smith, Liu applied to top U.S. universities. "I believe that Ruopeng did make a positive scientific contribution and one or two of his ideas I would describe as creative," Pendry told me. "I wrote positive references for him." He added that their "limited interactions were entirely scientific . . . although I certainly heard the rumours connecting espionage."

The Massachusetts Institute of Technology, which had an opening for an assistant professor, invited Liu to give a presentation. Smith agreed to help him by glancing over it beforehand. On April Fool's Day 2009, over lunch at a restaurant on the Duke campus, Liu ran through the slides for his job talk on his laptop. One of them caught Smith's eye. It depicted an elaborate website, complete with contact phone numbers and email addresses, the details of Liu's experiments, and an article from a Duke science publication.

Smith pointed out that Liu needed Duke's permission to reprint the article. Liu answered that the site wasn't real; he had only created it for the MIT interview.

After returning to his office, Smith did some checking and discovered that Liu's website was hosted on a server in China. "I was on to him," Smith told me.

Liu had been shirking his Duke responsibilities, both in Smith's lab and in a course on electromagnetism, where he was supposed to be a teaching assistant but rarely showed up. "You're doing no work for the group, no one can find you, and yet you put all this effort into a website?" Smith asked him the day after the lunch.

Sobbing, Liu insisted that he had cobbled the site together quickly. "I came here at twenty-two years old," he said. "I'm naïve."

'We both know that's not true," Smith replied. "You know what you're doing." It was the venture, Smith concluded, for which Liu had hoped to save the cloaking technique.

Similarly, Liu's commercial ambitions in China seemed to explain why he sometimes sought to delay publication of Duke research. "Ruopeng would show the material to Cui in advance of publication, and then slow down the publication," Kundtz told me. "It was a timing game."

Despite those slowdowns, Liu was startlingly prolific. Scouring the Internet a few days after their lunch, Smith took a close look at Liu's publications, which the postdoctoral fellow had warned him about in 2008. He found at least forty-three scientific articles that Liu had coauthored at Duke. A typical graduate student has between zero and five publications; a remarkable student, perhaps a dozen. He had amassed his astonishing total largely by inspiring other students with his visionary babble, and then feeding off their ideas and data. He hadn't told Smith about at least a dozen papers that he wrote with Cui's group, although several listed Smith as a coauthor, exploiting his name and reputation. One of Liu's published collaborations with the Chinese addressed a topic on which Smith had assigned him to work with a Duke student. That was a "clear violation" of academic ethics, Smith told me.

Smith summoned Liu to his office. The professor sat behind his desk, with the offending publications stacked on his lap, hidden from Liu's view. Then he trotted out one paper, as if it alone concerned him, and reminded Liu that they had agreed to sever ties with Cui's group. Liu at first protested that he had told Smith about the article, but then admitted he had forgotten, just that once.

Smith pulled out another publication, and another. Liu grew very quiet. He eventually blamed his Chinese collaborators and "made a big show of telling everyone that they shouldn't do that again," Smith said.

Liu similarly misled Smith about a different sort of collaboration. After the 2008 Nanjing conference, Liu suggested publishing its proceedings, which is customary in academia. He asked Smith to compose an introduction. Smith said he was too busy to write or edit fresh material, which wasn't needed anyway. Liu agreed and said he would write the abstracts for each presentation by Smith's group. "There was no mention of this being a book, and I was so busy that I just ignored all of the subsequent correspondence," Smith said. "Later, Ruopeng began to call it a book, and I'd stop him and I'd say, 'This is just a collection of conference papers, right?' and then he'd nod and agree." One day, a box of books showed up at Smith's door, and he saw himself listed as the volume's co-editor, and coauthor of six chapters, which Liu had written. "It was filled with broken English and not very high quality," Smith said. Liu had again exploited Smith's fame to fulfill his ambitions and boost his reputation.

Smith's tolerance was exhausted. On April 21, 2009, he took away Liu's key to the lab and told him to finish his dissertation at home. Later that year, Smith also nixed Liu's prospects for a postdoctoral fellowship at Princeton by telling an old friend there about Liu's rogue collaborations with Cui's group.

Understandably, Liu feared an even more severe blow: that Duke would deny him a doctoral degree. Duke's graduate school standards of conduct prohibit academic dishonesty, such as "representing someone else's work as your own." According to a person familiar with the procedure, "There usually has to be a panel assembled to evaluate the evidence if formal charges are brought. That takes weeks and weeks to get done. It would have delayed his graduation certainly."

Instead, Liu defended his dissertation on November 30, 2009, without incident. The discussion was purely technical: Smith didn't even tell the other professors on the committee about Liu's pipeline to China. "It would have been very difficult at the time to show that he had done anything unambiguously wrong," Smith told me. The website in China, for example, could be "excused by a Chinese student not really understanding the rules well enough," or even praised as entrepreneurial zeal. Smith discussed his suspicions with some Duke administrators and professors, but received no guidance, he said.

Duke may have wanted to avoid a brouhaha for another reason: it was forging ahead with plans for a branch campus in China. A week after Liu's dissertation defense, Duke trustees approved continuing negotiations with Chinese officials to build a campus in the city of Kunshan, which would supply the land and facilities for free. "Duke, like the other universities that aspire to be world class, recognize that they need to have a presence in China" if they are "going to get the best students, the best resources, the best faculty," said Dan Blue, chairman of Duke's board. It would have been an awkward time to punish a Chinese researcher already renowned in his homeland for his prestigious *Science* article.

Liu received his doctorate on December 30, 2009. Like Princeton, MIT had turned him down, but China was beckoning. His mentor,

Cui, had ties to a brain-gain program, and Liu could bring Duke's metamaterials research and some of its most promising China-born scientists back with him. He likely could have named his price. He told a friend over dinner that, through one of its ventures to lure overseas talent, the government offered him as much as $100 million to start a metamaterials center. "They would pay for the equipment, they would hire as many engineers as he needed," the friend said. "There were companies in China that would be in the pipeline to productize the technologies that he would invent. Before he left America, he knew of this institute that he was going to be leading."

Liu returned to China in January 2010 with his wife, Weizi Huang. She had been working on her own dissertation at Duke—on statistical models for identifying genetic risks for ovarian cancer—and planned to earn a doctorate in computational biology in another year. One day she told her adviser, Edwin Iversen, that she had to go back to China with her husband. She settled for a master's degree.

"She wasn't happy to leave," Iversen told me. "She wanted to complete her PhD." Her consolation prize was to be a founding member of Kuang-Chi Science.

AT MY REQUEST, and armed with a series of questions that I had prepared, a Shenzhen-based freelance journalist interviewed Liu in June 2016. They met in the billionaire's office on the second floor of Kuang-Chi's Shenzhen headquarters. The office, which overlooks a nearby pond, is spare and functional: white walls, whiteboard, file cabinet, desk with a globe and a photo of himself, sofa, conference table with oranges in a plastic bowl, coffee table with some of his awards and a model helicopter.

Cornering Liu wasn't easy. He'd canceled a prior appointment after a two-hour wait, and then left for Singapore and Beijing. Back in Shenzhen, he was an hour late for the rescheduled interview, but finally materialized, smiling and affable, wearing a light gray blazer and a white shirt.

During the ninety-minute conversation, he acknowledged that Smith had accused him of "stealing stuff" and taken away his key to the lab, that he had been "a little worried" that the university would withhold his doctorate, and that "the FBI went to Duke to investigate all the stuff after I left." Still, he said he did nothing wrong, and "nothing was stolen," because all of the research was basic and open, and sharing of ideas is integral to academic collaboration.

"I'm not working in any kind of classified lab," he said. "I worked in fundamental research and published papers and they can be seen by everyone in the world. Everyone right now can download the paper and see what I have done; it is all transparent."

He maintained that he started Kuang-Chi with fifty thousand dollars borrowed from his mother; China's government did not send him to snatch American technology and did not pay him to return. The Duke research "is not all that valuable. . . . We cannot solve any problems in reality and it is all in academic environment and everything is transparent. Anyone can look at anything we have done and it is published, so if China and Shenzhen funded as a reward this kind of fundamental research, I think it would spend all of its money."

Asked about criticism from his former Duke colleagues of his scientific prowess, Liu clapped his hands together twice, and then laughed. "We'll make things work," he said. "Comments cannot change the world. Build the machine. Make it fly."

He suggested that Smith had turned against him for fear of losing research support after the Pentagon backlash. "Probably what people can do is prevent future funding," he said. "That's why I can understand that Dave had concerns with that, and he should have concerns with that; otherwise it would influence the funds for the whole team."

He recalled the argument with Smith in the Chicago airport: "Some people wanted to have a tour, and then no one would be able to chair the seminar, so I said no. . . . We just needed someone to chair the global academic session." He blamed Chunlin Ji, his coauthor from the statistics department, for starting the China-based website that featured Duke's research, and T. J. Cui's team for publishing articles, without Smith's knowledge, that listed Liu and sometimes Smith as coauthors. "They wanted to put the other party, the team at Duke, because they do think that they have worked together a lot with Dave."

Liu was less forthcoming on other episodes that alarmed members of Smith's lab. He had a habit of responding, "That's interesting," and then equivocating. For example:

Did visitors from Cui's lab take pictures of the equipment so they could reproduce it in China? "That's interesting. So how could people go to the lab? Duke has to invite people, then people can get the visa, and they come to the lab, it is an academic exchange."

Did he mislead Smith about Project 111? "If he says I set him up for Project 111 without telling him, then how could he spend time in China? I have no right to kidnap him. Right?"

Did he dodge Smith's request to explain how the invisibility cloak worked because he was saving the method for his business in China? "What's the proof? So if we do not put all the algorithms and the stuff out, how can we publish a paper?"

Was Liu upset that Kundtz figured out the technique, and did he stir up the protest against him? "That's interesting. Actually, when Nathan came, I was about to graduate. He wanted to work together with me on some projects but at the time I was about to graduate. . . . I was not concerned about who actually replaced me as a star student because I was leaving as a star student." In fact, Kundtz joined Smith's group twenty-three months before Liu graduated.

Did he write the chapters for the metamaterials book, and list Smith as coauthor, after assuring the professor that it would only be a collection of conference proceedings? "That's interesting. At that time I was still his student and wrote up the conference proceedings and put my adviser's name. . . . It was basically from the conference, but also with some new type of stuff."

A TRIP TO Kuang-Chi's battleship-gray, twelve-story headquarters isn't complete without stopping at the exhibit hall on the first floor, displaying the company's latest technology. A guide touts the Metawifi, which uses metamaterials to eliminate interference and serve crowded areas such as shopping malls and concert arenas where traditional Wi-Fi is overloaded. Visitors can try the Photonic Systems, which, by scanning a fingerprint and then shining a beam on a receptor, offer more secure building access than key cards do. "There is no equipment that can decrypt it," the guide says.

The next section depicts Kuang-Chi's space gadgetry, including the Traveler—a tourism pod attached to a balloon—and a blimp called the Cloud. Connected to fiber-optic cables, it's "much cheaper than a satellite," stays aloft 24/7, and tracks ships and cars, the guide says.

A screen presentation introduces Kuang-Chi. One slide shows the founders, including Liu, his wife, Chunlin Ji, and two other Duke alumni. Another boasts that Kuang-Chi has filed 86 percent of all current patent applications for metamaterials worldwide. A third describes the company's mission with the kind of grandiose rhetoric that has been Liu's trademark since his Duke days: "empowering machines with souls and bringing happiness and human connection."

Since his return to China, Liu and his enterprises have made quite a splash, with official help. Kuang-Chi was the third recipient of funding under Shenzhen's Peacock Program, initiated in 2010 to lure overseas professionals. Overall, municipal records show, Shenzhen and Guangdong Province have awarded $13.7 million to Kuang-Chi.

"We do receive great support from the Shenzhen government," Liu said in a March 2016 interview on Phoenix Television, a Hong Kong–based broadcaster.

"Since 2010, Guangdong and Shenzhen have launched a lot of schemes to attract talents. We happened to catch these opportunities."

In 2012, Liu was chosen as a metamaterials expert for a national government committee overseeing scientific research and investment, the youngest person ever to hold such a position. That December, Liu escorted Xi Jinping around Kuang-Chi's exhibit hall, showing off the Metawifi high-density coverage, the photonic security system, and other technology. The Communist Party leader was impressed.

"After watching your research results and listening to Mr. Liu Ruopeng's introduction just now, I am very glad to see such a young entrepreneurial team full of passion and enthusiasm," Xi told Kuang-Chi executives, according to its news release. "The old generation of scientists, such as Qian Xuesen, overcame tremendous obstacles in USA, returned to China with the same patriotic obsession. . . . At the reform and opening-up era, you returned to China to realize Chinese dream."

Liu accompanied President Xi to New Zealand in November 2014 and met Glenn Martin, inventor of the "jetpack" flying machine. Its potential applications range from transport of emergency medical and rescue workers to military supply and surveillance. Soon afterward, Kuang-Chi Science bought a controlling share in Martin Aircraft. Visitors to Kuang-Chi's exhibition hall are strapped into a jetpack simulator for practice flying. Kuang-Chi has taken stakes in other firms, too, such as Solar Ship, a Canadian maker of solar-powered airships to haul freight to remote locations; and Zwipe, a Norwegian start-up with U.S. offices in Illinois and Denver, which embeds fingerprints in credit cards to authenticate transactions.

KUANG-CHI HAS STOCKPILED intellectual property, applying for one patent after another. Most of its patents are in China, and it's hard to tell how many of them are based on Duke research, or how important they may become. "I heard he patented a ton of stuff that was probably developed at Duke," Schurig told me. There could have been "lots of ideas floating around the lab that nobody was going to pursue. It could represent a significant value."

Asked if Kuang-Chi had patented ideas nurtured at Duke, Liu scoffed. "We have three thousand patents," he said. "I'm a talent that can generate three thousand patents from three years at Duke? Then call me Superman." Later, he added, "We actually are going in a very different direction of the field, to build something greater and has no relationship to work we did in fundamental research because that is far away from the industry."

Kuang-Chi does hold twenty-six U.S. patents, primarily for advances in metamaterials, with Liu named as co-inventor on all of them. Kuang-Chi and Liu also have more than thirty pending applications for U.S. patents. On several filings, patent examiners questioned Liu's purported inventions on the grounds that they were anticipated by Smith's prior research.

For example, Liu and two other Kuang-Chi scientists—including cofounder Lin Luan, who also received her doctorate at Duke—applied in September 2012 to patent a metamaterial structure for a small antenna. In April 2015, a U.S. patent examiner disallowed nineteen of their twenty claims. The examiner found that two of these supposed improvements had been anticipated by Smith, and others would have been "obvious to one of ordinary skill" who was familiar with Smith's work. Although the rejection was labeled "final," the inventors revised their claims, and a patent was issued in December 2015.

Kuang-Chi's website highlighted Liu's time at Duke, crediting him with a pivotal contribution to the field of metamaterials. "With his diligence and wisdom, Doctor Liu received his PhD degree in less than four years," it stated. "Dr. Liu is not only a visionary as well as a doer, he is also a charismatic team leader. During his graduate study, he developed the frontier technology with other Kuang-Chi founders. . . . In the beginning of 2010, holding the keys to the 'invisible cloak,' they returned to China."

Smith pointed out that his team conceived and executed its first invisibility cloak before Liu joined it. Liu "has not demonstrated any capabilities" to justify the website's praise, he told me.

Smith has forsaken invisibility research, at least temporarily. "The prospect of true invisibility and cloaking remain highly speculative," he emailed me. "The path to a full cloak is fraught with enormous challenges and not very practical at this point. We've become more interested in research that might transition sooner."

Liu hasn't given up. The Kuang-Chi Metamaterial Center, fifteen miles from the exhibit hall, produces ultrathin copper sheets that are treated with a film, then etched with patterns and rinsed in chemicals and water. "The structure is so tiny, so sensitive to certain waves with a particular waveband, it is able to fulfill the function of invisibility, so it cannot be detected by radar," an engineer said, adding that it has military applications. In a control room, three workers used microscopes to measure patterns of metamaterials.

FROM AFAR, SMITH and members of his lab have followed Liu's rise with both amazement and skepticism. Like some analysts and investors tracking Kuang-Chi's stock, they wonder whether all the patents and plugs will translate into real scientific or commercial success. Could their discoveries at Duke end up benefiting China instead of the United States? Or is Liu fooling the Chinese government the way he once fooled them?

"He's good at inspiring people with grand ideas and grand ambitions, but I don't think he can execute anything," Gollub told me. "It takes more than contracts and intellectual property transfers to get things off the ground."

"Clearly, he's a genius in terms of sensing what's hype and how to sell it," Aloyse Degiron added. "Scientifically, I'm not sure."

Smith minimized the loss. While Kuang-Chi's accumulation of patents confirmed his suspicions about Liu, "Ruopeng was not really capable enough to figure out the real value of the research we were doing, so that the patents he has filed are really not clearly detrimental, even if they might infringe," he said. "Most of them are not of great value."

Because he had pressed Liu to notify Duke about potential inventions, he said, "we were able to preserve the IP." Otherwise, "certainly Ruopeng would have been patenting everything in China and we would have lost out on what has become a very important technology."

Liu's onetime rival, Nathan Kundtz, who also earned his Duke doctorate in 2009, runs a company that may be closer than Kuang-Chi to profiting from metamaterials innovations. Based in Redmond, Washington, Kymeta Corporation makes tiny flat antennas that replace satellite dishes and improve broadband service. Smith is a strategic adviser to Kymeta, which raised $62 million in January 2016 from a group of investors led by Bill Gates. In a sense, Kundtz and Liu are still competing, because the Kuang-Chi Metamaterial Center is experimenting with small portable antennas.

The September 2015 FBI report on "Chinese Talent Programs" examined the Liu case and the role of Project 111. Without naming Smith, the report faulted him for letting himself be gulled.

While Smith and Cui were supposed to share ideas, "the US researcher eventually realized most of the ideas were coming from his lab," it said. "By convincing the US researcher to collaborate with Cui, Liu was able to freely share information and invite visitors to the lab. Although this was not restricted research, the metamaterials research could have both military and civilian applications. The US researcher risked his research by allowing visitors to come into his lab without personally looking at their background and being too trusting of his scientific relationship with Liu."

Smith disputed this conclusion. "At all points in this process, I took the steps that I thought were correct, and so did others at Duke," he told me. "I don't feel that I or Duke have risked anything, since we took it as seriously as we could have."

While Smith still takes Chinese students on government scholarships, he said that he would never accept direct funding from China or participate in China-funded collaborations, and that he sizes up candidates for his group more carefully. "I now look for signs of that sort of behavior—the overeagerness, the seeming agenda."

Asked whether he has returned to the United States since leaving Duke, Liu dodged the question. "Uh, my team has visited the U.S. many times," he said. Pressed again, he said he hasn't. "We don't have business in the U.S.," he explained, apparently forgetting the Zwipe offices. Given the FBI's concerns about him, it seems likely that Liu would have difficulty obtaining a visa.

He has contacted Smith only once. In 2011, Liu wrote to his former professor, asking him to collaborate. Smith had no desire to give him another chance. "I told him, 'when you were here, you didn't do things right. As you go forward, pay more attention to ethics.'"

THE CHINESE ARE COMING

The phone rang at 3 a.m. in the White House bedroom of President Jimmy Carter and his wife, Rosalynn. Carter, who had given instructions not to wake him except for a crisis, thought, Oh my, there's a tragedy somewhere in the United States.

On the phone was Carter's national science adviser, geologist Frank Press. "Frank, what's happened, another Mount Etna, or something like that exploded?" Carter asked.

"No, I'm in China with Deng Xiaoping," Press said.

"What has happened with Deng Xiaoping? What's wrong?"

"Deng Xiaoping insisted I call you now to see if you would permit five thousand Chinese students to come to American universities."

Furious over losing sleep, the president shouted, "Tell him to send a hundred thousand," and slammed down the phone.

Once he calmed down that morning in July 1978, Carter welcomed Deng's overture. The United States had opposed the 1949 communist revolution in China, and afterward recognized the exiled Nationalist regime on the island of Taiwan as China's true government. Academic contacts waned. Then, with visits to China by the U.S. table tennis team in 1971 and President Richard Nixon in 1972, the two powers began edging toward reconciliation.

Carter's administration, eager to normalize diplomatic relations through educational exchanges and other cooperative programs, expected China to send only a handful of students to American colleges. But Deng, who was emerging as a leader after Mao's death two years before, was determined to modernize China. He had reopened universities that had been shuttered as part of the Cultural Revolution's assault on scholars and intellectuals, and reinstituted competitive entrance exams.

At the same time, he recognized that U.S. universities far surpassed China's, especially in science and technology. Dispatching thousands of students across the Pacific would narrow the gap—especially if they returned home with the latest American innovations.

The zeal of a famously insular communist country to expose so many of its young people to American capitalism and democracy startled even Americans who were fully awake. "I had no idea about the size of the exchange the Chinese were interested in, but my State Department advisors thought we should press for a large number, perhaps five hundred per side," recalled National Science Foundation director Richard Atkinson, a member of Press's delegation, who handled the negotiations in Beijing.

During those talks, a Chinese vice premier, Fang Yi, asked Atkinson how many students from other nations were enrolled at U.S. colleges. Atkinson cited figures from six or seven countries, including 25,000 Iranians and 9,000 Taiwanese.

"How many can China have?" Fang asked.

Perhaps a thousand, Atkinson said, naming the highest total that the U.S. side dared hope for.

"Why can't we have as many as other countries?" Fang demanded.

The Americans, Atkinson later wrote, were "stunned, but secretly delighted."

THE OPENING OF China's student pipeline to the United States would prove to be a pivotal moment in the globalization of American higher education—and in the rise of academic espionage. While other countries already used students and visiting scholars to filch academic research and penetrate U.S. government or business, China would take the strategy of targeting academia to a new level—and prompt the United States to respond in kind. In the last quarter of the twentieth century, "Chinese intelligence flooded the United States with students, scientists, businessmen, and émigrés from all walks of life to harvest America's political, economic, and scientific secrets," wrote Michael Sulick, the former director of the CIA's clandestine service.

Of the almost one million international students at U.S. universities in 2014–15, 31 percent (304,040) came from China, up nearly eightfold in two decades. Of the more than half a million foreign-born scientists and engineers working at U.S. universities in 2013, about 15 percent, or 78,000, were natives of China, more than of any other country, and up two-thirds from 47,000 in 2003. The vast majority pose no threat and, like other newcomers, infuse American universities with energy and fresh perspectives. Some, like Ruopeng Liu, may have other agendas that aren't immediately apparent.

Accustomed to hosting visiting scholars, Professor Daniel J. Scheeres didn't hesitate to grant a request by Yu Xiaohong to study with him at the University of Michigan. She expressed a "pretty general interest" in Scheeres's work on topics such as movement of celestial bodies in space, he told me.

She cited an affiliation with the Chinese Academy of Sciences, a civilian organization. Yet the Beijing address Yu listed in the Michigan online directory was the same as the Academy of Equipment Command & Technology, where instructors train Chinese military cadets and officers. Scheeres wasn't aware of that connection, nor that Yu cowrote a 2004 article on improving the precision of antisatellite weapons.

Once Yu arrived, her questions made Scheeres uncomfortable, and he stopped accepting visiting scholars from China. "It was pretty clear to me that the stuff she was interested in probably had some military satellite-orbit applications," he said. "Once I saw that, I didn't really tell her anything new."

Positions in academic laboratories provide a plausible excuse for students from countries under U.S. export restrictions, such as China or Iran, to acquire advanced American technology, which they then smuggle home. "No one is going to pay attention to your name or ethnicity if you're coming from an American university," says Vince Houghton, curator of the International Spy Museum in Washington, D.C. "If you're tied to the Ivies or a technical university like MIT, you're beyond suspicion."

WENTONG CAI COUNTED on being "beyond suspicion." Born in Inner Mongolia, he enrolled in 2009 as a graduate student in veterinary microbiology at Iowa State University. In 2012 and 2013, using his university email address, he negotiated to buy one or more angular rate sensors from Applied Technology Associates in Albuquerque, New Mexico, pretending that he needed them for his research. Actually, these sensors are designed for line-of-sight stabilization and motion control systems in military and civilian planes and ground vehicles. They had no use in Cai's research on how *E. coli* bacteria cause urinary tract disease.

Wentong was acting on behalf of his cousin, Bo Cai, a businessman in China who wanted the sensors for an unnamed buyer. The U.S. government banned exporting them to China because of their military applications. So Bo drafted Wentong.

"His status as a student at Iowa State would make it easier for us to commit this crime," Bo Cai later explained. "We knew the manufacturer would not send ARS-14s to me or my customer in China but we figured the manufacturer would send ARS-14s to Iowa State and we could smuggle them to China from there."

"Me and my cousin Bo grew up like brothers," Wentong later wrote. "Just because of the help and support I received, whenever my family and friends asked help from me, I don't generally deny, considering as returning favor."

As he dickered over the sensors, Wentong let slip in an October 2013 email to Applied Technology that "we finally obtained support from a Chinese company that we constantly collaborate with. I am thinking if I should involve them in this order." Aware of the U.S. embargo on sending military equipment to China, Applied Technology alerted the Department of Homeland Security. Posing as the firm's international distributor, a DHS undercover agent contacted Wentong, who confided that the sensors were destined for China. Both cousins traveled to New Mexico in December 2013 to meet the distributor and check out the merchandise. Wentong, a devotee of the television drama *Breaking Bad*, also hoped to visit the Albuquerque locations where it was filmed. Ironically, the protagonist of *Breaking Bad*, like Wentong, was a scientist-turned-criminal.

The agent showed them three sensors, and Bo arranged to buy them. As he prepared to board a flight back to China, with one sensor hidden in his luggage, he was arrested. Wentong was then arrested in his Iowa State lab in January 2014, five months after marrying one of his lab mates and being honored by the university for "outstanding research accomplishments," and two weeks before he was to defend his dissertation. In lieu of a doctorate, he was awarded eighteen months in prison and then deported.

"I feel so unfortunate to get caught up in this situation," Wentong told the court. "But I am still positive about my future. . . . It encouraged me so much that a paper coauthored by me was published even in the midst of my incarceration."

Unlike Cai, other foreigners earn degrees and find jobs in the United States first, and then steal technology. A study conducted for this book yielded an eye-popping statistic: at least thirty people born or raised in China and charged since 2000 in U.S. courts with economic espionage, theft of trade secrets, and similar offenses attended American colleges or graduate schools, including Harvard, Stanford, Columbia, and Cornell. College enables a foreign agent to "develop a history" in the United States, Houghton told me: "You build your bona fides, lose your accent, get a job."

AT THE TIME of China's opening, Iranians made up the largest contingent of foreign students in the United States. The CIA took a strong interest in Iran, which was not only a major oil producer, but was ruled by Shah Mohammad Reza Pahlavi, whom the agency had entrenched in power in a 1953 coup. The agency scoured academia for Iranian informants who could return home and keep an eye on the shah and his enemies.

Ahmad Jabbari, an Iranian graduate student in economics at Washington University in St. Louis, secretly tape-recorded a series of conversations in 1974 with a CIA agent, to whom a friend of his U.S. host family had introduced him. Inviting Jabbari to his hotel room, the agent offered him an immediate $750 and a monthly stipend to return to Iran and get a job in the government for at least two years. The CIA would then help him become a permanent U.S. resident or naturalized citizen.

"If you had knowledge of dissidents, that would be of interest," the agent told him. "Anything you might gather would be interesting."

Alternatively, the agent said, Jabbari could spy on other foreign students in the United States, because the CIA wanted to know how they felt about their governments. Jabbari, though, was a campus activist opposed to the shah. He declined both options.

"I wasn't the only one," Jabbari, now a publisher of scholarly articles on Iran and central Asia, said in a 2015 interview. The CIA "was all over the campuses."

After the 1979 Islamic revolution toppled the shah, Iranian students no longer flocked to the United States. But their numbers have rebounded dramatically in recent years, from 1,885 in 1999–2000 to 11,338 in 2014–15. Because Iran doesn't maintain formal diplomatic relations with the United States, it can't send spies here under foreign-service cover, as other nations do. Instead, a former U.S. official told me, "the way the Iranians collect intel is through their student network."

IN THE 1970s, only a few dozen students a year trickled into the United States from its Cold War rival, the Soviet Union. Their occupations might have warned President Carter to be leery of welcoming a larger contingent from the other communist superpower, China. Of 400 Soviet exchange students who attended U.S. universities from 1965 to 1975, the FBI identified more than 100 as intelligence officers. The Soviets had also tried to recruit more than 100 American students at universities in the USSR.

Soviet intelligence had long been notorious for recruiting communist sympathizers at English universities. By cultivating "young radical high-fliers from leading universities before they entered the corridors of power," the KGB had enlisted its greatest agents, the students and fellows from the University of Cambridge in England known as the "Cambridge Five": Kim Philby, Donald Duart Maclean, Guy Burgess, Anthony Blunt, and John Cairncross. "By the early years of the Second World War all of the Five were to succeed in penetrating either the Foreign Office or the intelligence community," former KGB archivist Vasili Mitrokhin observed.

"The volume of high-grade intelligence which they supplied was to become so large that Moscow sometimes had difficulty coping with it."

Fresh from his Harvard graduation at the age of eighteen in 1944, physicist Theodore Hall worked on the Manhattan Project in Los Alamos, New Mexico, which developed the atomic bomb. The "youngest major spy of the twentieth century," he passed atomic secrets to the Soviets because, he later said, "it was important that there should be no monopoly, which could turn one nation into a menace."

The KGB helped choose Soviet students for academic exchanges with the United States "and trained many of them as talent-spotters." It steered them to universities that were accessible to the USSR's diplomatic residences in San Francisco, such as Stanford and the University of California, Berkeley; in Washington, D.C. (Georgetown, George Washington); and in New York City (Columbia, Cornell, Harvard, Princeton, MIT).

Semyon Markovich Semyonov became the first Soviet agent to enroll at MIT in 1938. "The scientific contacts which he made . . . helped to lay the basis for the remarkable wartime expansion of S&T collection in the United States," Mitrokhin wrote.

KGB officer Oleg Kalugin entered Columbia University's journalism school in 1958. After graduation, posing as a Radio Moscow correspondent at the United Nations, he attended events at Columbia and reported back to Moscow on them. His report on a speech about U.S.-Soviet relations by Zbigniew Brzezinski, then a Columbia professor and later national security adviser to President Carter, earned kudos from the Communist Party's Central Committee.

After that, "I went all across the country, from Harvard to Columbia and the West Coast, listening to what people said and reporting it if I thought it was interesting," Kalugin told me. He rose to become a KGB general and head of its foreign counterintelligence branch.

U.S. intelligence monitored the Soviet students. "We had a program to Americanize them," recalled former FBI supervisory special agent David Major. "The idea was to show them the good things of America. I was the supervisor in Baltimore. We'd take them out on a boat, or have crab cakes and beer." The agents hid their occupation, typically posing as businessmen.

The Soviet Union didn't rely solely on student spies. Scientists sent on goodwill visits and exchange programs by the Soviet Academy of Sciences, the State Committee for Science and Technology, and similar government-affiliated organizations sought sensitive information on engineering and applied technology—aircraft control, weapons systems, and the like—at more than sixty U.S. universities in the early 1980s, up from twenty in the late 1970s. Three times as many Soviet-bloc scientists visited MIT as any other university, with Harvard second. The guests also "were involved in spotting and assessing U.S. scientists for potential recruitment as agents."

In 1976, one of the FBI's biggest campus coups foiled Soviet espionage. The KGB had placed Boris Yuzhin in a graduate program in journalism at the University of California's flagship Berkeley campus and assigned him to befriend scientists and opinion makers. Instead America's prosperity and political freedom entranced Yuzhin, and the FBI recruited him.

When the KGB sent him back to California in 1978 as a correspondent for a government news agency, Yuzhin became a valuable FBI informant, using a miniature camera hidden in a cigarette lighter to photograph documents in the Soviet consulate in San Francisco. He "largely taught a new generation at the FBI how the KGB was organized, what it did worldwide, and what it was doing in the U.S.," former CIA and FBI counterintelligence officer Christopher Lynch wrote. After Robert Hanssen and Aldrich Ames—Soviet moles in the FBI and CIA, respectively— identified him in 1985 to the KGB as a double agent, Yuzhin was confined to a Siberian prison camp. Released in 1992, he returned to California, where he still lives.

In December 1978, the first fifty-two Chinese students left Beijing for New York—via Paris, there being no direct flights. By 1979–80, there were 1,000 Chinese students in the United States; by 1984–85, 10,100. They consisted mainly of graduate students who had learned some English in or after college. Few entering freshmen had the requisite language skills, because Chinese high schools at the time offered little English instruction. Although China gave students only about fifty dollars apiece, U.S. universities provided generous scholarships, and some American companies that hoped to enter the Chinese market chipped in.

Intelligence gathering was part of the students' mission. U.S.-bound students underwent two weeks of training beforehand at a foreign language institute in Shanghai, one student who enrolled in an Ivy League graduate program in 1982 recalled. They learned the niceties of American etiquette, such as not asking a woman's age. In addition, in one-on-one meetings, an official from the Chinese foreign affairs ministry instructed them to pass along any important information they came across in the United States to the Chinese government. If they belonged to the Communist Party, they were instructed to omit their membership from their visa applications, which were submitted together to U.S. officials. One trainee was actually an intelligence officer, with academic credentials trumped up to fool his American university.

In the United States, the Chinese embassy kept tabs on them. So did FBI special agent I. C. Smith, whose beat was Chinese counterintelligence. "Deng Xiaoping knew that allowing students to travel to the United States there would be some who wouldn't return, but he was willing to take that chance," Smith told me. "Essentially he overwhelmed us with sheer numbers, all of whom were expected to siphon any and all information that was available. There appeared to be little specific targeting of information, just a vacuum cleaner approach."

I. C. SMITH HAD BEEN fascinated by China since his boyhood in rural Louisiana. He idolized General Claire Chennault, who had grown up in the same region and headed the U.S. Army Air Forces in China—known as the "Flying Tigers"—during World War II. Smith enlisted in the Navy, serving in the Pacific and visiting Hong Kong. "How can one ride the Star Ferry, experience the hustle and bustle of that dynamic city, and not become enamored of that part of the world?"

After college and a stint in the Monroe, Louisiana, police department, Smith joined the FBI. He handled criminal matters in St. Louis and political corruption in Washington, D.C., before arranging a transfer to the Chinese squad in 1980. While, to his regret, he didn't learn China's language, he familiarized himself with its culture and politics. He took courses at the CIA, the Defense Intelligence Agency, the U.S. State Department, and the Smithsonian Institution, and reached out to old China hands in government. They recommended readings, shared experiences, and offered advice. "They were invaluable in getting first-hand insights into China, which was difficult due [to] the strain of relations."

Elevated to squad supervisor in 1982, Smith led the investigation of Larry Wu-Tai Chin, the most enduring mole in U.S. history. As a translator and analyst for the CIA's Foreign Broadcast Information Service, Chin spied on the United States for China from 1952 to 1985. He used his access to top-secret documents to betray dozens of the agency's Chinese informants, resulting in their imprisonment or execution, and to alert his handlers in advance to U.S. policy, such as Nixon's plan to visit China and establish diplomatic ties.

Over the years, China paid him more than $1 million, which he laundered by buying Baltimore tenements and gambling at Las Vegas casinos. Reflecting Chin's dexterity, he was honored by the CIA in 1980 and China's Ministry of State Security in 1982, which is roughly equivalent to being feted by both Planned Parenthood and Operation Rescue. After a tip from a source—whom Smith code-named "Planesman," borrowing a term from his Navy days for the controller of a submerged submarine's buoyancy—that China had penetrated U.S. intelligence, the FBI fingered Chin. He was convicted of espionage in 1986, and two weeks later asphyxiated himself to death in his prison cell.

"The Chin case was a harbinger of espionage to come," Sulick wrote. "By the dawn of the twenty-first century, Chinese intelligence collection against the United States would eclipse Russian espionage efforts."

In 1984, Smith was promoted to FBI headquarters for one purpose: to develop a response to the deluge of Chinese students. Unlike the KGB, the Chinese disdained traditional tradecraft such as setting up dead drops, writing in invisible ink, or using disguises. The students gathered reams of material. Most was open and unclassified, but it satisfied Chinese authorities.

"Virtually all of those early students engaged in information gathering, mainly to support the demands of their parent institute," Smith told me. "They were simply expected to siphon any and all available information and send it back to China. And they did!"

The bureau began noticing signs of an increase in campus spying, such as a spike in the use of copying paper. As the FBI's senior resident agent from 1982 to 1984 in Madison, Wisconsin, Harry "Skip" Brandon watched the surge of Chinese graduate students at the University of Wisconsin.

"Sometimes their Xeroxing bills were very high, almost humorously so," he told me in January 2016. "We wondered how they shipped all this stuff back." Unlike Smith, Brandon believed that the Chinese students sought specific documents. Rather than "collecting blindly," they followed instructions, presumably from the Chinese consulate in Chicago, he said.

WITHIN THE FBI, Smith advocated for recruiting Chinese students. "I took the position then and now that having those students on our soil, while presenting a very real counterintelligence problem, also presented a considerable intelligence and counterintelligence opportunity. . . . That turned out to be the case."

Many students agreed to help because they resented how they and their families had been mistreated during the Cultural Revolution. "The Cultural Revolution was still very much a sore point and it wasn't something that even the most fervent People's Republic of China supporters could support." One evening, a Chinese-American acquaintance arranged for Smith to meet an older Chinese student, in his midfifties. "I sat with the two and listened for a lengthy time as he related, with tears, his mistreatment during the Cultural Revolution, and how he just couldn't return, how he thought it could happen again." He became a useful FBI source.

The Cultural Revolution victimized many of China's elite political families. Their children, who grew up in the shadow of their parents' humiliation, came to study in the United States, and often became the FBI's biggest prizes.

"It was those golden youth who, among all the students that traveled to the United States, saw the hypocrisy of communism," Smith said. "For after all, some had suffered during the Cultural Revolution, simply because of who they were . . . and not what they stood for. Further, it was the golden youth that had shopped in special stores in the PRC, lived in larger homes, had access to chauffeured vehicles, etc.," and recognized that these luxuries belied the austere lifestyle that Chinese leaders professed to follow. "For us, that presented an opportunity."

Like Boris Yuzhin, Chinese students accustomed to communist propaganda about the United States were impressed by its well-stocked capitalist stores. One student, whom Smith took shopping, couldn't make up his mind which toothpaste and clothes to buy.

"He knew that they had been lied to, for the PRC under Mao had painted a picture of the U.S. as a wasteland. He had never seen such a vast array of choices and we ended up making choices for him. He had herded sheep during the Cultural Revolution, simply because his father was a ranking cadre of a major city, and his girlfriend had killed herself by drinking rat poison. He had little desire to help with the Four Modernizations."

The pitch was discreet. "We would not ask those students who may have foreign intelligence information to betray the PRC, but to enter into discussions that would allow for the betterment of relations," Smith said. "If there was a chance that one of those students would become a source, I advocated *not* formalizing the arrangement," especially since the FBI had to run any formal recruitment of a foreign student past the State Department. "As long as the information flowed, who cared how they justified the relationship?"

It wasn't hard for the agents to establish contact with the newcomers, either directly or through an intermediary such as a classmate or Chinese-American community member. An agent, typically pretending to work for some cover company or group, might arrange to run into a student by accident—a "bump," as it's known in espionage parlance—in a relaxed setting such as a ballgame.

"Some agents even brought in their families, something I didn't necessarily endorse, but I did recognize that was important to the Chinese culture. I was willing . . . to entertain just about anything that would further the effort. It could be risky, but I was willing to take that chance."

Initially, the FBI preferred using Chinese-American agents to recruit Chinese students, but Smith soon found that the strategy could backfire. "It was well down the whole effort before a Chinese-American agent had a true success." Unfamiliar with the assimilation of second-generation Chinese-Americans, a newcomer would wonder whether the recruiter secretly represented Taiwan or even the People's Republic: "How could a Chinese-American agent truly be loyal to the U.S. when they're Chinese?"

In fact, the FBI agent's biggest challenge sometimes was fending off competitors from friendly espionage services, from Taiwan's National Security Bureau to the CIA. In the 1970s, worried that the United States would normalize relations with China, Taiwan was developing nuclear weapons. After those fears came true, the National Security Bureau used Taiwanese students and researchers at top universities to recruit students from Communist China, said one former student whose friends were targeted.

"Taiwan, feeling betrayed by President Carter's normalization, was also interested in contact with those from the PRC," Smith told me. While foreign intelligence services weren't supposed to operate unilaterally in the United States, "we all know that at times they ignored that edict."

Like Communist China, Taiwan also coveted American technological know-how. As a CIA officer in Taiwan from 1976 to 1979, Robert Simmons monitored its efforts to develop nuclear weapons. He noticed that many older students whom Taiwan sent to MIT were actually military officers tasked with learning how to build a bomb. "They were sheep-dipped as students," said Simmons, who later served three terms in Congress.

THE INFLUX OF Chinese students intensified the turf wars between the FBI and CIA. "An immense tension existed between FBI agents and Agency officers because there was an overlap of mission—both were trying to recruit foreigners in the US," one former CIA officer wrote. "Agency officers were supposed to check with the FBI before doing any operation involving the more important targets such as Soviets, Iranians, and Chinese."

Both the FBI and CIA coveted one Chinese graduate student at an Ivy League university. He hated the Chinese government because it had sent his father to a labor camp for ten years during the Cultural Revolution. Hearing from campus sources about a likely prospect, an FBI agent knocked on his door in 1983, showed credentials, and invited him for a beer at a nearby restaurant. They ended up drinking quite a few, and the student readily agreed to cooperate.

As time went on, he alerted the FBI about students and visiting scholars who were working for Chinese intelligence or had access to sensitive scientific research. He kept the bureau abreast of activities of student groups controlled by the Chinese government. He even cleared up confusions over common Chinese names—for example, whether a certain Wang or Chen was related to a similarly named Politburo member.

Then the CIA's local station chief asked for the FBI's permission to talk to the student. The FBI agreed that a CIA agent could approach him, posing as a representative of a U.S. think tank with China operations that wanted to hire him as a researcher. But his FBI handler set one condition: the CIA could not ask the informant to return to China. It would be too dangerous, and the FBI would lose control over him, because the CIA was in charge of spying overseas.

The agent promised—but asked anyway. The informant, who had no desire to go back to China, saw through the CIA man's cover—and was furious with both the agency and the bureau. The FBI agent confronted his CIA counterpart, who apologized.

The informant "was very upset," the FBI agent recalled. "It hurt our relationship for a while."

The FBI's courting of Chinese students also caused strains with university administrators. Some deans or registrars—or their staffs—quietly supplied nuggets about a student's family background, financial status, aspirations, or adjustment issues. Others bristled.

As supervisor of a counterintelligence squad at the FBI's Baltimore office in 1984, David Major sent agents to Johns Hopkins University to recruit Chinese students. According to Major, some of the students complained to a dean there about the FBI's approaches. The dean assured them that they were guests of the United States and Johns Hopkins, and under no obligation to cooperate with the bureau. He instructed them to report any further contact from the FBI to him.

Major stormed into the dean's office. He told him that counterintelligence was the FBI's responsibility, which he would carry out with or without the dean's support. "I said, 'We're not stopping, and you won't interfere with my job.'"

WITH THE 1991 dissolution of the Soviet Union, America's premier intelligence target since World War II, politicians and editorialists advocated increased investment in social services and other domestic priorities. "Peace dividend" became a catchphrase, and Congress slashed funding for the military and spy agencies.

As counterintelligence suffered, the number of foreign students rose from 386,850 in 1990 to 514,723 a decade later. That divergence worried

I. C. Smith, the China expert who served from 1990 to 1995 as the FBI's section chief for analysis, budget, and training, and represented the bureau on the National Foreign Intelligence Board. He called for restricting both the number of students from China and the Middle East allowed into the United States, and the fields they could pursue.

"My proposals were made in part due to the FBI being overwhelmed with sheer numbers and in the aftermath of the demise of the Soviet Union and the Cold War, the rush, including some ill-advised individuals within the FBI who had no understanding of counterintelligence, to cut back on counterintelligence resources to work such things as street gangs in Washington, D.C."

Smith's plan, though, conflicted with the interests of universities and business. Both sought a global talent pool and a presence in China and the Middle East. Full-tuition-paying foreign students were a growing revenue stream for universities. A cap also ran counter to traditional U.S. policy that exposing as many foreign students as possible to American democracy would in the long run reap allies and influence worldwide.

"Any proposal to restrict numbers wasn't going to happen," Smith continued. "Businesses looked at China as a future source of profits and of course, they had greater influence on Capitol Hill than did the intelligence community in that regard. It's always the profits!"

The participation of foreign students in terrorism attacks against the United States seemed to justify Smith's concern. Eyad Ismoil, a Jordanian, entered the United States on a student visa in 1989. Four years later, he parked a van packed with explosives in the garage of the World Trade Center in New York City, where it blew up and killed six people. Also on a student visa was Hani Hanjour, who flew a plane into the Pentagon on September 11, 2001.

Instead of curbing foreign enrollment after 9/11, the U.S. poured dollars and manpower into counterterrorism and counterintelligence. The number of foreign students and professors on campus continued to soar. So did espionage. By 2013, the FBI's counterintelligence division considered developing a national "Academic Security Awareness Program" to alert students, professors, and administrators to the growing threat.

"Counterintelligence threats to academia (people and research) have increased and evolved," according to the proposal by Dean W. Chappell III of the division's strategic partnership program. Yet "some institutions do not have an 'open door' policy for the FBI." The program should be "accessible to the widest possible audience on an ongoing basis to achieve national impact."

Its message to students: "You may find yourself studying a language overseas or working on sensitive research. These activities can make you appealing to a foreign government."

To professors: "You may find yourself teaching a language overseas, recruiting foreign students, or conducting research on sensitive technologies. These activities can make you appealing to a foreign government."

To administrators: "You may find your institution has the interest of foreign governments due to locations you have outside the US or the research your school does in sensitive and economically valuable technologies."

I asked FBI spokeswoman Susan McKee whether the bureau adopted Chappell's proposal. The Academic Security Awareness Program has moved from the FBI's counterintelligence division to its Office of Private Sector, which handles outreach initiatives, and is "in flux at this time," she said.

IN THE INTERNET age, China, Russia, and other countries complement human intelligence gathering at U.S. universities with cyber-spying.

At first, they primarily exploited academic computer networks as platforms for hacking into American businesses. Because the networks—like campus buildings—were unusually accessible, and because emails from ".edu" addresses were unlikely to draw a second look from university information security staff, they were a perfect launching pad for economic espionage.

Increasingly, though, universities have become not just stepping-stones but targets, with scientific research and faculty emails both vulnerable. In 2015, Pennsylvania State University and the University of Virginia announced that Chinese hackers had compromised their networks. The Virginia attackers sought emails of employees who worked on China-related matters. Penn State conducts weapons research for the Navy and ranks third in national security funding among U.S. universities behind Johns Hopkins and Georgia Tech, but its cyber-defenses proved inadequate. The breach of its engineering school's computers went undetected for more than two years, until the FBI alerted the university. Investigators identified two groups of hackers. One was connected to China, while the origin of the other couldn't be located.

Penn State responded by establishing an Office of Information Security. "We had been infiltrated by advanced persistent threat actors operating at a level higher than we were used to," Provost Nicholas Jones told me. "We needed to step up our game." Universities are "not only desirable but soft targets. The way we operate, we tend to be very open. We're places where great work is being done, great discoveries are taking place. A lot of information is of potential interest."

Corporations typically have stronger cybersecurity than universities do, says Laura Galante, intelligence threat director for security firm FireEye Inc., which investigated both the Penn State and Virginia break-ins. Universities focus on other information technology priorities, such as making sure that new students' emails work. While the average intrusion at a business or government office isn't discovered for 220 days, the lag time at universities is "far higher," she says.

A September 2015 handshake agreement between President Barack Obama and Chinese president Xi Jinping not to "conduct or knowingly support cyber-enabled theft of intellectual property, including trade secrets or other confidential business information for commercial advantage," could actually increase the risk for universities. The pact rules out cyberattacks on American businesses but leaves some wiggle room regarding academic research that has potential economic applications but has not yet been licensed to a manufacturer. "You have a much stronger case, sitting in China, who will deny it happened as they always have, to say, 'No, we were interested for national security purposes, or to understand the future of a certain issue,'" Galante says.

Like Russia, China phishes for political secrets, often on the eve of military or strategic meetings with other countries, with the goal of gaining an advantage in discussions. Several days before Harvard's John F. Kennedy School of Government hosted military officers in charge of China's nuclear arsenal at a conference, a nuclear expert at a Washington, D.C., think tank emailed Kennedy School professor Matthew Bunn. Attaching a PowerPoint file, she wrote that she was sending Bunn in advance her presentation on "Cooperative Threat Reduction"—Bunn's specialty—and would welcome his comments.

Bunn clicked on the attachment, triggering a warning from his Macintosh computer. It turned out that his friend hadn't sent the email—and that other conference guests had received similar messages from the same address, each one tailored to the attendee's field of expertise. Unlike his Mac, their personal computers didn't balk at the malware. The FBI later traced the attack to China.

SPY WITHOUT A COUNTRY

Beside a busy highway leading out of Stockholm stands Thorildsplans Gymnasium, a three-story yellow brick building divided into five adjoining blocks. Modest in size by U.S. standards, with an enrollment of 1,300, it's one of the biggest public high schools in Sweden's capital. Founded in the 1940s, Thorildsplans is mainly a technical school, specializing in fields such as Web design, electrical engineering, architecture, and computer networking, and attracts an economically and ethnically diverse student body. Co-principal Robert Waardahl told me in April 2016 that the school was gearing up for an influx of refugees from Syria and other war-torn countries. "We are the school for everyone," he said. "That is our motto." While Thorildsplans competes in basketball and other sports, he added, its teams generally lose. "In our school, it's good to be a nerd."

Like thousands of other high schools and colleges worldwide, Thorildsplans uses an information technology curriculum developed by Cisco Systems Inc. in San Jose, California. It periodically sends students and staff on field trips to Cisco's headquarters and nearby attractions such as Stanford University and San Francisco's Golden Gate Park. Many teachers at Thorildsplans leap at this perk, but not Marta Rita Velázquez. The popular teacher of Spanish and English shows no interest in visiting the United States even though she's an American, born and raised in Puerto

Rico, with degrees from Princeton University, Georgetown University Law Center, and Johns Hopkins University.

"She's been asked to come to California with the class," Waardahl said. "She has rejected it. We never asked why."

Velázquez can't go home again. In April 2013, an indictment was unsealed against her in federal district court in Washington, D.C., accusing the former lawyer for the U.S. Agency for International Development of spying for Cuba for fifteen years. Most significantly, as a graduate student at Johns Hopkins's School of Advanced International Studies (SAIS), Velázquez allegedly recruited classmate Ana Belén Montes for Cuban intelligence. They overlapped at SAIS with a professor who worked for the State Department and was also a Cuban spy. Though they don't appear to have formed a classic espionage "cell," the presence of three Cuban agents inside one of the top feeder programs to U.S. diplomatic and intelligence services shows just how deeply the Castro regime penetrated American academia.

Montes would rise to become the premier analyst on Cuba at the Pentagon's military intelligence arm, the U.S. Defense Intelligence Agency, and the most effective Cuban mole ever to burrow into the federal bureaucracy, feeding classified briefings to the Castro regime while softening U.S. policy toward it. Michelle Van Cleave, who headed U.S. counterintelligence under President George W. Bush, described Montes in 2012 congressional testimony as "one of the most damaging spies in U.S. history."

SAIS professor Piero Gleijeses, an expert on U.S.-Cuba relations, knew and liked both Montes and Velázquez. Montes was one of his best students, and Velázquez one of his favorite research assistants. "These are two people who took very serious risks for their beliefs," he told me.

Montes was eventually exposed and imprisoned, but Velázquez fled to Sweden, beyond the grasp of U.S. authorities. With the help of a Stockholm-based journalist, I traced her to Thorildsplans. Few of her colleagues and students there are aware of her history, or the charges pending against her. Waardahl said he had heard a "rumor," but didn't look into it because it had no bearing on her employment. "She is very friendly, very competent," he said. "She's good at what she does, and a good colleague."

"This sounds like something out of a spy novel," Morgan Malm, another English teacher at Thorildsplans, said as he hurried to class. "She's a friend and colleague and I fail to see how this could have any basis in fact."

No FOREIGN GOVERNMENT has divided American public opinion more in the past half century than Cuba's. Is it a totalitarian regime, with a discredited communist ideology, that persecutes dissidents while destroying its own economy, as Cuban exiles and other critics contend? Or is it a progressive beacon that overthrew a dictator, reformed education and medical care, and aided other populist insurgencies against U.S.-backed tyrants in Latin America and Africa, as supporters, including many on American campuses, have maintained?

Either way, most experts on espionage agree that Cuba boasts one of the world's best intelligence services, which is fixated on its main enemy, the United States. Trained by the KGB in the days when Cuba was a satellite of the Soviet Union, Cuban intelligence emulates its Russian mentors in focusing on U.S. universities. Like Russian intelligence, which views the constant shuffling of policy makers between the federal government, think tanks, and academia as a vulnerability of the U.S. system, Cuba courts professors with high-level connections and students who may be steered into jobs at key federal agencies.

"The Cuban intelligence services are known to actively target the US academic world for the purposes of recruiting agents, in order to both obtain useful information and conduct influence activities," the FBI warned in a September 2014 advisory. "A large part of the work and effort of CuIS [Cuban Intelligence Services] departments targeting the United States is devoted to influencing American and Cuban-American academics, to recruiting them if possible, and to converting them into Cuban intelligence agents. Likewise, students from these universities are the subjects of assessment and recruitment because many of them, after completing their studies, are going to hold important posts in private enterprise or the US government."

Globalization has deepened U.S. academic ties with China and Russia, but not Cuba. With each country frowning on travel to the other, only 94 Cubans attended American colleges in 2014–15, down from 190 in

2004–05. Unable to rely on homegrown students to collect information in the United States, Cuban intelligence has tapped into the pool of American students and faculty who sympathize with the Castro regime. Cash-strapped Cuba rarely pays agents, preferring ideologically driven volunteers over mercenaries for whom the United States might outbid it.

Once the students become agents, they stop wearing Che Guevara T-shirts and start applying for U.S. government jobs. "When you recruit a younger guy, nineteen or twenty years old, you suggest, in the future, you cannot talk about socialism," said Enrique Garcia Díaz, who ran Cuban undercover operations in seven South American countries from 1978 to 1988 before defecting to the United States. " 'Change your mentality. You are not on the left, not on the right.' Then you suggest, good, join the FBI, CIA, or another U.S. government agency. In five years you will have this guy inside the government, like Ana Montes."

Cuba's intelligence service, according to former officers who have defected, is especially active at universities near its diplomatic missions in New York and Washington, which have the usual complement of spies, and in South Florida, the epicenter of the exile community. Such schools include Harvard, Yale, Columbia, New York University, Hunter College, American University, Georgetown, Johns Hopkins, the University of Miami, and Florida International University. Cuban intelligence tracks all of the publicly available information on these universities, from their undergraduate and graduate programs to the views and publications of administrators and faculty members.

When it identifies a sympathetic professor, it enlists a Cuban academic in the same field to strike up a friendship, which ripens through meetings and meals at conferences, "and even invitations to visit Cuba," the FBI reported. A department of Cuban intelligence arranges academic travel to Cuba and monitors the visitors' rooms in government-run hotels, hoping for compromising videos or recordings.

"I learned blackmail at the Russian academy," said García, whom Cuba sent to study at KGB schools near Moscow in 1980 and 1985. When I asked how he would reel in a married professor who was caught with a woman in his hotel room while attending a conference in Havana, he gave a knowing look and said he would prefer a subtle approach. "Just showing knowledge. 'How was your night with the lady? We can help you, protect you, nobody will never know.' "

When Harvard professor Jorge Domínguez visited Havana to research a book on Cuban foreign policy in 1985–86, Cuban intelligence seized its chance to pump him. After he interviewed Cuban officials, Domínguez recalled in June 2016, they asked to interview him in return. He agreed. As they pressed him for names and personal information of influential Cuban-Americans in Florida, he realized that, despite titles from other government branches, they belonged to the intelligence service. He told them that they had the wrong guy; all he knew about the Florida scene was what he read in the newspapers.

Cuban-American professors at U.S. universities are trapped in the middle of a spy war. Intelligence services in both countries zero in on them. Much as it pressured a Chinese-American professor, Dajin Peng, to spy on his homeland, the FBI asked one Cuban-American professor to persuade a friend of his in the Cuban government to defect to the United States. He consulted an administrator at his university, who told him, "You go to Cuba as an academic, not as an intelligence agent." The professor declined the FBI's request.

ALMOST EVERY LAWYER in Puerto Rico knew Miguel Velázquez Rivera, whom they called "Don Miguel" as a token of respect. Not only was he a prominent judge noted for his influential opinions, and later a University of Puerto Rico School of Law professor so admired that a moot court competition is named after him, but he also ran a popular—and lucrative—side business preparing students for the Puerto Rican bar exam. Striding around the auditorium that he leased from the school, he would pepper his pupils with questions and regale them with tales of a fictional family whose disputes and misfortunes illuminated the fine points of the law.

"His cast of characters are legendary in local law," says attorney Charles Hey-Maestre, who credits the course with helping him pass the exam. "They were always having problems. He'd say, 'Juan Péres López and his wife are getting a divorce. Their child is going to college. What does the law say about paying support?' Giving a hypothetical example made it more fun." The study guides that he sold to accompany the course featured the same characters, along with actual cases and statutes.

Don Miguel's life embodied the American dream of upward mobility. Of mixed race, with dark skin and blue eyes, he rose from a poor childhood in the town of Moca to own a large San Juan home shielded from urban bustle by a bevy of trees, bushes, and flowers. His slender, long-haired wife, Dominga Hernandez, painted at an easel in the back of the house; her colorful art was once exhibited in the Puerto Rican Bar Association building. They sent their eight children, two daughters and six sons, to a Catholic high school in San Juan and then to fine universities in the continental United States, including Princeton, Stanford, and Carleton College. The eldest, Teresa, now a pediatrician in Virginia, was encouraged as a child "to read, learn, work hard, be patient and stay healthy and happy," according to the website of her medical practice.

Despite his success and affluence, Don Miguel wasn't satisfied with the status quo. He made no secret of his support for the independence of Puerto Rico, which was invaded by the United States in 1898. He was in a distinct minority; only about 5 percent of Puerto Rican voters have backed independence in referenda over the years. Many more of them sympathize with nationalist aspirations but fear that Puerto Rico couldn't sustain itself economically as a separate country.

His pro-independence stance may have hampered his career advancement, but Don Miguel thought there was another reason why he never achieved his ambition of serving on the Supreme Court of Puerto Rico. The island's white, old-boy network, he believed, passed him over because of his color.

"He was convinced that, were it not for his race, he would have been named to the Supreme Court," said Professor José Julian Alvarez, who was his student and law school colleague. "He always resented that. It was something that really pissed him off."

Don Miguel was especially close to his younger daughter, Marta, who was born in July 1957. "He was the motivator, he encouraged her to excel," said another law school professor, Roberto Aponte Toro, who also served as dean from 2007 to 2011. "She was very involved with him. He was an excellent father. She was an excellent student and an excellent daughter." Marta revered Don Miguel and inherited his devotion to independence and racial equality. Both causes likely spurred her interest in another Caribbean island: Cuba.

Puerto Rico and Cuba have many historical and cultural affinities. They were the last two Spanish colonies in the Western Hemisphere, and their economies both depended on sugarcane. José Martí, the nineteenth-century Cuban patriot and revolutionary, envisioned both islands in an independent confederation. A poem that many Puerto Rican children read in school describes them as "two wings of the same bird," an image that Cuban folksinger Pablo Milanés borrowed in his "Son de Cuba a Puerto Rico."

The Castro regime, which took power when Marta was a toddler, would have appealed to a young, mixed-race Puerto Rican *independentista*. Fidel Castro touted progress in race relations that appeared to contrast with continuing discrimination in the United States. Politically, he defied the behemoth to the north, insisting on Cuba's right to shape its destiny. He sought the same right for Puerto Rico. Cuba financed its independence movement, advocated for its self-determination before the United Nations decolonization committee, and established a house in Havana—Casa Puerto Rico—for visiting members of the independence movement.

Aside from the merits of the issue, pushing Puerto Rican independence served two purposes for Castro. It irritated the U.S. government, and it attracted Puerto Ricans, who are U.S. citizens by birth, to spy for Cuba on their homeland. "Cuba was working very hard that topic of the independence of Puerto Rico against the U.S. and it was an objective to recruit Puerto Ricans in any part of the world," former Cuban intelligence officer Orlando Brito Pestana told me.

Said García: "Cuba used Puerto Rico like a special support group to infiltrate agents inside the U.S., because they are Americans and have U.S. documents."

TERESA VELÁZQUEZ ENROLLED at Princeton in 1972, and her sister, Marta, followed three years later. They joined a small contingent of students of Puerto Rican heritage that also included Sonia Sotomayor, now a U.S. Supreme Court justice. Sotomayor was Teresa's friend and classmate, and a mentor to younger Hispanic students, so it's likely that she knew Marta as well.

While Teresa was a pre-med biology major, Marta majored in politics—both in and out of the classroom. Rarely did she miss a student rally on behalf of women, minorities, and other targets of discrimination. She protested against the university's investments in apartheid South Africa, chanting, "Princeton, divest, like all the rest / 'Cause if you don't, we will not rest / We're gonna fight and fight and keep on fighting some more / Princeton divest . . ." and petitioning the administration to "commit itself immediately to the complete divestiture of its securities in these institutions." She organized a Latino Festival proclaiming "Independence and Socialism as the Only Political Alternative for Puerto Rico," and a Third World Cultural Festival featuring Puerto Rican poetry, African dance, a Chinese folk song, a Chicano singing group, and a Native American exhibition.

"We are all part of oppressed nationalities throughout the world," Velázquez told the *Daily Princetonian*. "Here at the university, which is very conservative and white-male-oriented, if we can put together a performance as successful as this one was, it's almost unbelievable."

Velázquez occasionally took a break from politics. She enjoyed dancing, movies, and weekends in Manhattan, making the rounds of restaurants and clubs. Still, she was a young woman of deep convictions, even on mundane matters, as her college friends recall. "What I remember about Marty is just her intensity," said Nilsa Santiago, a professor at John Jay College of Criminal Justice. "When she spoke, it's like the words vibrated through her whole body. Her head, her neck, her torso would move in time with the earnestness of her words.

"She was very idealistic, very earnest about whatever she was talking to you about. She really, really believed it, and she wanted you to believe it. If she said something that she thought you would know but you weren't familiar with, a quizzical look of disbelief would register on her face."

One afternoon, as they were walking into the student center, Velázquez said to Santiago, "Let's have yogurt."

"I've never had yogurt," Santiago replied.

"What? This is unbelievable," Velázquez said. She marched Santiago into the cafeteria and selected a Dannon blueberry yogurt. "She remedied my ignorance and I now had a new favorite snack," Santiago recalled.

For her senior thesis, Velázquez chose a topic close to her—and her father's—heart. Describing herself as "the descendant of an African woman who lived in a sugar plantation on the sister island Puerto Rico," she explored "Race Relations in Cuba: Past and New Developments."

Starting with a long quotation from Cuban poet Nicolás Guillén, a communist and Castro supporter, she recounted Cuba's history of slavery and racial discrimination, finding that it was crueler, and aroused fiercer resistance among black Africans on the island, than was generally thought. The United States, she wrote, "continued this oppression by allying itself with the Cuban oligarchy," and with former Cuban dictator Fulgencio Batista, who, while mixed-race himself, was "the defender of a powerful racist class."

She had nothing but praise for the revolutionary who overthrew Batista: Castro. "The government has instituted an informal but well understood policy of de-emphasizing any racial differences," she wrote. "They have gone about this, however, in a unique form. Instead of trying to assimilate the black population into the European culture of the dominant society, the government has pointed at the common African heritage of all the Cuban people. . . . The new Cuba is not only latin, but latino-african in its political and social identity.

"This has perhaps proved to be the wisest course ever taken by a Cuban leader. . . . When compared to the situation of absolute rejection and powerlessness felt by blacks and mulattoes before the 1959 revolution, the new state is indeed a blessing."

President Carter had lifted restrictions on travel to Cuba, and Velázquez, joining a trip sponsored by Princeton's Latin American Studies program, conducted "a brief period of field research" there for her thesis. The highlight of her visit, according to a college friend, was an unscheduled exposure to the Yoruba culture that West African slaves brought to Cuba. She attended and recorded a concert of Afro-Cuban jazz.

"She had gotten to go to this unauthorized, underground Yoruba gathering in Cuba," the friend recalled. "Black people in Cuba kept this culture alive. She was able to see it for herself." Back at Princeton, she played the tape for her friend: "She seemed to think it was relevant, or exciting," he said.

It's not clear how she gained access to the jam session. Perhaps Cuban authorities gave permission because the African-influenced music pertained to her thesis topic. If so, her request may have drawn the attention of Cuban intelligence. Or they may have noticed her anyway. Exceptionally bright, dedicated to Puerto Rican independence, and sympathetic to the Castro regime, with an Ivy League education as a gateway to an influential position in U.S. government or academia, she was an ideal candidate for recruitment.

LOCATED IN WASHINGTON, D.C., near Dupont Circle, Johns Hopkins University's School of Advanced International Studies has spawned an impressive roster of U.S. diplomats and cabinet members, including former secretary of the treasury Timothy Geithner, former secretary of state Madeleine Albright, and former U.S. ambassador to Iraq April Glaspie. Its pipeline to power invites attention from foreign intelligence services, including Cuba's.

"SAIS was always one of the most important universities, because of its access to the U.S. government," said Pestana, the former Cuban intelligence officer. Officials at the Cuban Interest Section, Cuba's diplomatic outpost in Washington, "always had that as a priority."

Cuba succeeded in penetrating the school, which offers master's degrees in fields such as international affairs, international economics, and global policy. In the early 1980s, at least three people at SAIS were in contact with Cuban intelligence. All would spy for Cuba while working for the U.S. government, according to court documents. One was a professor, Kendall Myers. Two were students: Marta Rita Velázquez and Ana Belén Montes.

Velázquez and Montes had so much in common that they seemed destined to be friends, even if one wasn't recruiting the other for espionage. Montes was born in 1957, four months before Velázquez, on a military base in West Germany where her father, a U.S. Army psychiatrist, was stationed. Like Don Miguel Velázquez, who favored Puerto Rican independence, Alberto Montes took an interest in the island's political future, though his views are in dispute. He "strongly supported" independence and "voiced that opinion freely in letters and articles," according to former Defense Intelligence Agency investigator Scott Carmichael.

Shortly before his death in 2000, Alberto wrote a paper advocating independence for Puerto Rico, in connection with a United Nations hearing, Ana's mother, Emilia Montes, told me in a phone conversation. Another relative, though, believes that Alberto "had very moderate views and thought it was best for PR to remain a commonwealth."

The family eventually settled in Towson, Maryland, a Baltimore suburb, where Montes attended high school. Both Velázquez and Montes
studied Latin American politics at prestigious universities—in Montes's
case, the University of Virginia—and graduated in 1979. Both enrolled
at SAIS three years later. In the interim, Velázquez earned a law degree
at Georgetown University, where she edited a journal on immigration
law. While attending SAIS, both had jobs in the federal government.
Montes worked full-time at the U.S. Department of Justice, handling
public records requests, and Velázquez was a legal intern at the State
Department's Agency for International Development.

Montes brought Velázquez to her parents' home in Maryland on
several occasions, said a relative who requested anonymity. "They seemed
to be best friends." Velázquez was "sweet, warm, and friendly. We all
liked her."

"They were good friends," Emilia Montes said. "Marta seemed to be
a nice girl, very social and smart and clever."

Both classmates opposed the Reagan administration's policy in Latin
America, and especially Nicaragua, where a proxy war was raging
between Cuba and the United States. They favored the Cuba-backed Sandinista government, which had overthrown dictator Anastasio Somoza
in 1979, and were appalled by U.S. efforts to topple the Sandinistas by
funneling arms and money to a rebel group known as the Contras.

SAIS was a magnet for debate over U.S. policy. Wayne Smith, a career
diplomat who favored rapprochement with the Castro regime, quit as
head of the U.S. Interests Section in Havana in 1982 in disagreement
with the administration's hard-line stance. In the spring of 1984, Montes's and Velázquez's second year, Smith taught a course at SAIS on Cuban
history since the 1959 revolution.

Montes "gained her first real insight into what she described as the
cruel and inhumane nature of U.S. Government policy supporting the
Contra rebels in Nicaragua during her graduate studies at Johns Hopkins," the Pentagon's Office of Inspector General reported in 2005. "Most
of the other students and professors at Johns Hopkins shared her views
about the unjustness of U.S. policies."

Montes clashed with one of her professors, Riordan Roett, who taught
an introductory course on Latin American politics. "She disliked me and
my staff completely, and thought we were fascists," Roett told me. "Every

time I said something that was pro-America, prodemocracy, pro-NATO, she would protest."

Montes and Velázquez gravitated toward a more like-minded professor, Piero Gleijeses, who taught "U.S. Relations with Latin America" in 1982–83, and "The United States and Central America" in fall 1983. The Italian-born Gleijeses, who told me that he was "the most left-wing" professor at SAIS, rejected an overture from the CIA in 1983. A woman visited his office and "made a little pitch. . . . She said, at the time I was writing a fair amount about Central America, perhaps I had information. This would help the United States develop policy. I said I was not interested. There was absolutely no insistence, absolutely no pressure."

For a book Gleijeses was working on about the 1944 Guatemalan revolution and the United States, Velázquez pored over Guatemalan newspapers on microfilm. "We never discussed politics," Gleijeses told me. "We discussed the work we were doing together. I told her what I was looking for. We would meet once a week or after she had done a number of hours of work. She would give me the printout and we would discuss what she had found," he said. "She was excellent. I remember Marta as a very pleasant person and excellent research assistant. I have a soft spot for her."

Kendall Myers taught British politics and European history at SAIS, where he'd earned his doctorate in 1972. Beginning in 1977, he was also an instructor at the State Department's Foreign Service Institute, where he prepared government employees for overseas duty. At Cuba's urging, he applied for an analyst position at the CIA in 1981, but was turned down.

Six foot six with a walrus mustache, an accomplished yachtsman and WASP blue-blood whose ancestors included telephone inventor Alexander Graham Bell, Myers was infatuated with the Castro regime. Invited by a Cuban intelligence officer in New York, Myers visited Cuba in December 1978. "Everything one hears about Fidel suggests that he is a brilliant and charismatic leader," he wrote in his diary. "He has helped the Cubans to save their own souls. He is certainly one of the great political leaders of our time." He and his wife, Gwendolyn, joined up six months later.

The couple passed information to their handlers by switching shopping carts in crowded Washington supermarkets, and also hooked up with Cuban intelligence in Trinidad and Tobago, Mexico, Brazil, Ecuador, Argentina, Italy, France, and the Czech Republic. His biggest thrill was a four-hour audience in Havana in 1995 with Fidel Castro himself.

Myers received a top-secret security clearance in 1985 and rose to become a senior analyst at the State Department's Bureau of Intelligence and Research from 2001 to 2007, giving him access to sensitive intelligence. He also coordinated State Department conferences and research projects.

"I would see him once every couple of months" at CIA headquarters, when Myers dropped by to discuss upcoming conferences, recalls Fulton Armstrong, former national intelligence officer for Latin America. "I'd try to snag him for a cup of coffee to lobby him for more conferences on Cuba and Latin America. Not once would he show me a glimmer of interest in anything to do with Cuba." Perhaps Myers was concealing his fidelity to Fidel.

Chris Simmons, a former specialist on Cuban intelligence at the Defense Intelligence Agency, says that the U.S. secrets Myers supplied to Cuba were less valuable than his assessments of which SAIS students were ripe for recruitment.

Whether Myers recommended Velázquez or Montes to Cuban intelligence isn't certain. "In my opinion, Myers suggested Rita Velázquez, and Rita suggested Montes," said García, the former Cuban intelligence officer.

According to her indictment, Velázquez began spying for Cuban intelligence in 1983. That September, she traveled to Mexico City, intending to meet with Cuban agents. The planned rendezvous was aborted because Mexico had just arrested two Cuban officials. She also began cultivating Montes by appealing to their mutual disdain for U.S. policy in Nicaragua. In the summer of 1984, she took Montes to dinner and explained that she had friends who were "looking for someone to translate Spanish language news articles into English" and could fulfill Montes's "expressed wish to assist the people of Nicaragua."

Around that time, they finished their studies at SAIS and Velázquez became a lawyer for the U.S. Department of Transportation, with a security clearance. That July, she wrote to Montes, "It has been a great satisfaction to me to have had you as a friend and comrade during this time we've spent as students. I hope our relationship continues outside the academic sphere."

It did. In December 1984, and again in early 1985, they rode by train to New York to see a Cuban intelligence officer. Montes "unhesitatingly agreed to work through the Cubans to 'help' Nicaragua," according to the inspector general's report. At the instruction of Velázquez, who also supplied the typewriter, Montes wrote an autobiography, describing her Justice Department job. Then, in the spring of 1985, they traveled on false passports via Prague and Madrid to Cuba, where they were given intelligence training in how to receive encrypted radio messages and how to pass lie detector tests that might be required for employment at U.S. intelligence agencies. (Montes later explained that the technique required tensing the sphincter muscles.) Montes applied to the Office of Naval Intelligence, the Arms Control and Disarmament Agency, and the Defense Intelligence Agency. Velázquez gave her a character reference, and DIA hired her as a researcher—a gateway to scoping out U.S. military plans and intelligence activities involving Cuba.

Possibly for security reasons, once Montes established herself at the DIA, she and Velázquez stopped hanging around together—and made sure everyone knew it. "I vaguely remember Marta telling me, they used to be friends, but weren't anymore. Ana Montes had broken relations," Gleijeses said. "I would imagine they intentionally broke relations."

"They had a falling-out," Emilia Montes said. "They stopped speaking to each other. I don't know why."

The rupture "was odd," said the relative who asked not to be identified. "I had never heard of Ana arguing with a friend before. I'm sure now it was a lie."

Although Montes had completed her SAIS coursework in 1984, Johns Hopkins withheld her master's degree in Latin American studies until 1989 because of unpaid tuition. According to Simmons, who helped expose Montes as a spy and debriefed her after her arrest, she "got into a philosophical argument" with the university, insisting that her education should be free. On graduation day, Emilia Montes said, Ana marched with her classmates and received what looked like a diploma sheath but was empty inside. She explained to her mother that she was behind on her bill.

Montes hit up her father, but he refused to pay, Simmons said. Finally, Cuban intelligence stepped in. Making an exception to its usual practice of expecting agents to spy gratis, it covered her bill.

"She met with her case officer and said she owed her tuition and couldn't pay it," Simmons said. "The case officer was horrified. Operationally, it puts Cuba at risk. You don't want a spy with a credit history issue. It's a security issue. The Cubans paid it not because they wanted to, but because they had to."

In 1994, with the personal approval of Fidel and Raúl Castro, Gleijeses was granted unusual access to Cuba's historical archives. His coup spurred a visit from his former student, Ana Belén Montes, by then the DIA's top analyst on Cuba, who began asking him for his impressions about Cuba and its military. Gleijeses told her that he wouldn't share information with her because he opposed U.S. policy on Cuba.

Ostensibly, Montes was seeking his help on behalf of the U.S. government. But Gleijeses later wondered if she was on a mission from her Cuban handlers. Some Cuban officials thought he was a CIA spy and that giving him free rein in the archives was a mistake. Under a pretext, Montes was testing his scholarly independence.

"Once I realized she was a Cuban agent, I thought that perhaps she had been sent by Cuban intelligence to see how I was behaving," Gleijeses told me. "They wanted to see how I might respond. I clearly passed with flying colors."

Montes's dual role in their encounter—ostensibly as a U.S. official, actually as a Cuban agent—illustrates her double life in her heyday. "By day, she was a buttoned-down GS-14 in a Defense Intelligence Agency cubicle," a 2013 *Washington Post* profile observed, referring to her federal pay grade. "By night, she was on the clock for Fidel Castro, listening to coded messages over shortwave radio, passing encrypted files to handlers in crowded restaurants and slipping undetected into Cuba wearing a wig and clutching a phony passport."

Montes enjoyed a meteoric rise to the highest circles of federal policy making on Cuba. She briefed the Joint Chiefs of Staff and the National Security Council, and badgered the U.S. Drug Enforcement Administration about its investigations of Cuban drug trafficking. She successfully opposed a U.S. military response to Cuba's 1996 shooting down of two civilian planes, operated by the Miami-based group Brothers to the Rescue, that were releasing leaflets over Cuban territory.

She struck colleagues as aloof and arrogant, but also smart and well prepared, skilled at testing arguments against empirical evidence. "She kept to herself, and showed patience as she developed an argument and hit you between the eyes with it," Fulton Armstrong recalls. She could puncture another analyst's long-winded presentation with a brusque "So what you're saying is you don't know?"

"Everybody would try to crystal ball what Fidel and [his brother] Raúl are thinking about," Armstrong said. "She would say, 'Look, we don't know. Our views represent our biases more than our facts, and it's useless to speculate.'" Possibly she eschewed such speculation for fear of accidentally revealing that she did know what Cuban intelligence officials were thinking about, if not the Castro brothers themselves.

Montes is often credited with shaping a controversial Defense Department assessment that dismissed Cuba as a "negligible" threat with "minimal conventional fighting ability." Congressional critics and Cuban-American politicians attacked the assessment for ignoring Cuba's support for guerrilla insurgencies and terrorist groups. However, Armstrong says that Montes's first draft aimed at placating Republicans by hyping the Cuban threat. He and another intelligence official then rewrote it, eliminating the alarmist tone.

Armstrong has searched his memory in vain for clues to Montes's treachery, "including whether she advocated analytical lines that would serve the Cuban government's interests," he said. "But I reached the personal conclusion that she didn't want to call attention to herself by advocating. If she'd written an exculpatory paper, people would have said, 'She's soft on Castro.'"

The U.S. director of central intelligence named her an exceptional intelligence analyst and rewarded her with a year's sabbatical, on full pay, to study the Cuban military. Her report, which was likely guided by her Cuban handlers, exaggerated the Cuban high command's interest in a relationship with the U.S. military, according to former CIA analyst Brian Latell.

"I was very impressed with Montes," said Jorge Domínguez, the Harvard professor of Latin American politics, who met her at a session on

Cuban military capabilities. "She was knowledgeable, smart, articulate, and precise. She focused on the facts, without spinning. There was this aura of competence."

Pinned to the wall of Montes's DIA cubicle was a handwritten quotation: "The king hath note of all that they intend / By interception which they dream not of." It was a private woman's private joke; although Shakespeare was referring to Henry V, the couplet applied equally well to Montes's "interception" for her king, Fidel. As she ate lunch alone at her desk, she memorized page after page of classified documents on Cuba, which she would type at night in her apartment into her Toshiba laptop. She would transfer the floppy disks to her handlers over dinners at Chinese restaurants in the Washington area, during her Caribbean vacations, and on trips—official or clandestine—to Cuba itself.

She supplied Cuban intelligence with names and biographical sketches of more than four hundred Cuba watchers in the U.S. government, Simmons said. "Montes compromised all Cuban-focused collection programs, calling into question the reliability of all U.S. intelligence collected against Cuba," Van Cleave, the former national counterintelligence executive, told Congress in 2012. "It is also likely that the information she passed contributed to the death and injury of American and pro-American forces in Latin America."

"What makes Ana Montes so extraordinary, though, is that she not only had access to the United States' innermost secrets but also actually *created* many of the secrets—the highly classified assessments representing what we thought we knew about Cuba," Carmichael wrote. "Fidel Castro himself might as well have dictated our policy and positions concerning Cuba."

WITH THE BREAKUP of the Soviet Union, prospects seemed ripe in the early 1990s for détente between its former satellite, Cuba, and the United States. Many Cuban-American professors longed to connect with the island of their birth. They joined organizations such as the Institute of Cuban Studies and the Cuban Committee for Democracy (CCD), which held conferences both in Cuba and the United States advocating for reconciliation.

The Cuban intelligence service was curious about these groups, wondering if they were sincere or CIA/FBI fronts, and whether it could recruit any of their members. A comment at one Havana conference by Fordham University sociologist and CCD member Orlando Rodriguez, that many Cuban-Americans have dual loyalties to the United States and Cuba, marked him as a possibility. Bearing a gift of fine Cuban cigars, a man whom Rodriguez guessed to be an intelligence officer congratulated him on the remark, calling it "very cathartic for us."

Back in the States, a diplomat from the Cuban mission to the United Nations, also presumably a spy, dropped by Rodriguez's office to ask about his views on Cuba and about Fordham. Rodriguez sent him a university catalog and other materials. "As a member of the CCD, which wanted dialogue, I couldn't say to the diplomat, 'I don't want anything to do with you,'" he told me. After Rodriguez's son, an assistant vice president at Cantor Fitzgerald, was killed in the September 11, 2001, attack on the World Trade Center, a staffer from the Cuban mission visited Rodriguez at Fordham again, expressing condolences and discussing events in Cuba.

Likely sensing that Rodriguez wouldn't help, Cuban intelligence never progressed beyond chatting him up. But, unbeknownst to Rodriguez, one of his friends and fellow academics, Carlos Alvarez, a member of both the CCD and the Institute of Cuban Studies, was a Cuban agent.

Born in Cuba, Alvarez participated in an underground anti-Castro student movement and then fled to Venezuela. He studied for the priesthood but left the seminary for the United States, where he earned his doctorate at the University of Florida. In 1974 he joined the faculty of Florida International University (FIU), which has about seventeen thousand Cuban-American students, the most of any U.S. university. A psychologist specializing in conflict resolution, he sought to apply his expertise to improving relations between his homeland and the United States.

In classic fashion, Cuban intelligence used a fellow academic to recruit him. In New York for an Institute of Cuban Studies meeting, Alvarez began chatting at a party with a Cuban diplomat, who was actually an intelligence officer. When Alvarez said he wanted to visit Cuba to promote dialogue, the diplomat referred him to a Cuban psychologist who could arrange an invitation to the University of Havana, and would also appreciate his insights for a paper she was preparing on the Cuban-American community in South Florida. Alvarez had lunch with her the next day. Her husband was assigned to Cuba's mission at the United

Nations in New York, and soon Alvarez was in contact with handlers there. (In an ironic twist, the psychologist who recruited Alvarez would be convicted in Cuba in 2013, along with her husband, of spying against the regime. She was sentenced to fifteen years in prison, half as long as her husband.)

Alvarez received instructions from Cuba through "personal meetings, messages written on water-soluble paper, coded pager messages, and encoded electronic communications via shortwave radio," according to court documents. Unlike Ana Montes, Alvarez lacked access to classified documents and high-level federal officials. He supplied Cuban intelligence with various tidbits, including the phone number of an FBI analyst who was one of his students, and an assessment of FIU president Modesto Maidique, a close friend. Although prosecutors said in court documents that Alvarez prepared a report to Cuban intelligence containing "sensitive information" about Maidique's personal finances and private business ventures, Maidique told me that Alvarez "didn't have a fucking idea of my finances."

He said what Alvarez told Cuban intelligence about him was harmless, and they remain friends. "The totality of information that he provided them was that I was a very proud guy and egocentric, which is not inaccurate," said Maidique, who described himself as the first Cuban-American university president in U.S. history. "Carlos is one of the finest men I have met in my whole life." Alvarez is so kindhearted and innocent, Rodriguez told me, that when a prostitute solicited him on the streets of Havana, he tried to counsel her.

With what he later called a "heavy dosage of idealism and naïveté," Alvarez figured that he could manipulate Cuban intelligence. If he cooperated even minimally, it would let him travel to Cuba and run programs and workshops, fostering unofficial communication between Cubans and Cuban-Americans and liberalizing the Castro regime. "By [the] mid-eighties, I had already identified the intelligence service as a potential change agent in the island," he wrote. "In exchange for providing them with my analysis and other innocuous information regarding the Cuban-American community in South Florida, I expected to get access to decision-makers in the island, whom I would convince of the importance of establishing the channel for unofficial dialogues. I believed that I could control the situation."

He didn't reckon with the FBI. After four years of surveillance, two agents confronted him outside a Miami grocery in 2005. Telling him that it was the most important day of his life, they persuaded him to accompany them to a hotel room for what became a three-day interrogation. They assured him that he wouldn't be prosecuted if he cooperated fully.

Alvarez confessed, but the agents expected more. "Since you helped the . . . Cuban government, we want you to help the United States now," agent Rosa Schureck told Alvarez. "Okay? Do you understand?"

Unlike South Florida professor Dajin Peng, who would later finesse FBI agent Dianne Mercurio's request to spy on China, Alvarez flatly refused. "I want something else," he answered. "I want peace in my life." He pleaded guilty to conspiring to act as an unregistered Cuban agent, and was sentenced to five years in prison.

While Alvarez hardly damaged U.S. national security, his exposure did tarnish the credibility of academia. It prompted Florida to ban using public funds for educational travel to Cuba, and widened the breach between the state's Cuban exiles and Florida International.

"The case affected us all at FIU," Sebastián Arcos, associate director of its Cuban Research Institute, told me. "There was a lot of suspicion in the Cuban-American community that universities were full of pinkos who can't be trusted. The community said, 'Ha, told you so.'"

It also reverberated at prestigious Harvard University. Using tactics common to both higher education and espionage, Alvarez had cultivated Professor Herbert Kelman, founding director of Harvard's Program on International Conflict Analysis and Resolution, at conferences in the United States and Spain. "It was clear he had read my work, was familiar with the principles and concepts, and was eager to apply it to Cuba," Kelman recalled.

The flattery worked. In 1997, Alvarez became an affiliate of Kelman's program and Kelman lectured at Florida International. In 1998, both men and Donna Hicks, deputy director of the Harvard program, lobbied Cuban authorities in Havana for permission to bring together young Cubans and Cuban-Americans. Alvarez then ran several workshops, including one at Harvard in 2003.

Kelman defends Alvarez. "I'm absolutely convinced he didn't find the Cuban political system attractive in any way," Kelman told me. "He had an attachment to the country. He was bothered that young Cuban-Americans grew up hating and shunning the country."

Jorge Domínguez reacted differently. The scholar of Latin American politics was director from 1995 to 2006 of Harvard's Weatherhead Center for International Affairs, where Kelman's program was housed. As president of the Institute of Cuban Studies from 1990 to 1994, he was cordial with Alvarez. Domínguez enthusiastically supported Kelman and Alvarez's plan to foster dialogue between Cubans and Cuban-Americans.

"When he was arrested, I didn't want to believe it," Domínguez told me. "This was my friend. I thought I knew him. I thought, maybe the Bush administration or the FBI was being overzealous." As it became evident that Alvarez did work for Cuban intelligence, "I went from leaning over backwards to give him the benefit of the doubt, to feeling personally betrayed. He wasn't just spying on people like me. He was spying on me."

Harvard's workshop initiative, Domínguez adds, "could have been of interest to Cuban intelligence. The most extreme scenario would be that Carlos sold it to the Cuban government as a means to penetrate the Cuban-American community. For all I know, some of the Cubans who participated in the workshops could have been intelligence agents, and that's why they were chosen. In retrospect, it looks awful."

After a complaint by the state's surgeon general, Alvarez relinquished his license to practice psychology in Florida in 2008. The American Psychological Association, to which he belonged, reviewed his case but took no disciplinary action.

Like Maidique, Rodriguez remains close to Alvarez, and he isn't bothered that his friend informed on him. "After he was released, we got together in Miami," Rodriguez told me. "I said, 'I don't care what you said about me. It doesn't matter. I accept it in the context of your naïveté, playing games with the Cubans, making believe you were pliable when you weren't.'"

According to Rodriguez, Alvarez believes that Cuban intelligence betrayed him to the FBI. His criticism of the Castro regime's refusal to liberalize society, and his value as a public example of how Cuban intelligence had infiltrated the Cuban-American community, made him expendable. Now retired, he reads theology, and maintains his interest in reconciliation, though not between Cubans and Cuban-Americans. "He doesn't want anything to do with Cuba anymore," Rodriguez said. "I think he feels he was a jerk."

AFTER VIOLETA CHAMORRO defeated Daniel Ortega, the Cuban-backed Sandinista president of Nicaragua, in his bid for reelection in 1990, the U.S. Defense Intelligence Agency dispatched Ana Montes there. She briefed Chamorro about the Cuba-trained Nicaraguan army that the new president had inherited. Perhaps, after the sting of his ally's defeat, Fidel Castro took some consolation in knowing that his agent had the ear of the winner.

Another U.S. government employee in Nicaragua whom Chamorro got to know was also a Cuban spy. With the Sandinistas defeated, the U.S. Agency for International Development returned to Nicaragua. Its regional legal adviser was none other than Marta Rita Velázquez. She had left the transportation department for USAID in 1989 and, like Montes, positioned herself to inform Cuba about U.S. activities and personnel in Latin America. USAID, which strives to end extreme poverty and promote democracy, worked with Chamorro on trade and education issues. She referred to Velázquez affectionately as "my little puertoriqueña."

Velázquez worked long hours in USAID's Nicaragua office, reviewing its grants and contracts, which were closely scrutinized by congressional Republicans. They accused the office, which had a development budget of more than $700 million, of funding entities associated with Sandinista leaders, and forced it to void one such contract. "We had struggles with the USAID mission in Nicaragua," recalled Daniel Fisk, a former staff member of the House and Senate foreign relations committees. "It was an outpost of the Sandinistas."

Daily life in Managua, the Nicaraguan capital, was chaotic. "Housing was substandard because the Sandinistas had devastated the country," one former USAID employee told me. "Marta's house had no running water for a year." The currency was so unstable that workers spent their pay over the weekend, knowing it would be worthless on Monday. "The first two years, we worked on stabilizing the economy."

Velázquez liked socializing with other expatriates. She brought fried bananas, mashed in the Puerto Rican style, to dinner parties, and rarely missed dances that the U.S. Marine Corps held every Friday. "She was very outgoing, had that Puerto Rican spark," a coworker said. "A great sense of humor. One time, we were going to an event at the embassy, and she said, 'I almost made a huge gaffe. I was going to wear a red and black dress. I remembered just in time those are the Sandinista colors.'"

The U.S. embassy discouraged employees from fraternizing with Nicaraguans. Instead, Velázquez began dating Anders Kviele, a Swedish diplomat. Their political views were likely compatible, because Sweden was sympathetic to the Castro regime. In 1975, Swedish prime minister Olof Palme, a harsh critic of the Vietnam War, had become the first Western European head of state to visit Cuba since the revolution, and praised Castro's "forces of freedom."

Velázquez and Kviele were married in March 1996 at the Second Union Church in Puerto Rico. About two hundred guests attended the reception at the Caribe Hilton, an oceanfront San Juan hotel, including her father's colleague Roberto Aponte Toro. "The wedding wasn't lavish, but it was very nice," Aponte Toro told me. "There was the family from Sweden, and the rest of the people were from San Juan."

Velázquez had given a guest lecture to one of Aponte Toro's classes in Puerto Rico, and he had encouraged her to join her father on the law school faculty. But she declined, possibly because she was flourishing at USAID. After leaving Nicaragua in 1994, she became the agency's chief legal officer for the Middle East and Asia, supervising two lawyers in Washington and seven more abroad. She gave legal advice in cases related to the Middle East peace process and nuclear proliferation in Asia. From 1998 to 2000, she was on leave in Sweden with her husband, but still pinch-hit for the permanent legal adviser at USAID's mission in Moscow. In 2000, she returned to Latin America, this time to Guatemala, as director of the regional office of trade and economic analysis, heading a team of nine people on trade and economic development issues.

Her indictment specifies several alleged contacts during her USAID career with Cuban intelligence. In 1996, it furnished her with encryption software. In 1994 and 1997, she disclosed identities of U.S. spies. After Marta gave birth to a son, Ingmar, in January 1997, Cuban intelligence passed along the joyous news to Montes.

Ingmar inherited his father's Nordic looks. When Velázquez wheeled him around in the baby carriage, a former USAID colleague told me, "people thought she was the nanny. She thought it was very funny."

In August 1999, Velázquez had a daughter, Ingrid. By giving her children impeccably Swedish names, she may have hoped to insulate them from attention or controversy in the event of her exposure as a spy.

THE SOVIET UNION's collapse didn't end Russian spying at U.S. universities. Since ex–KGB officer Vladimir Putin became president for the first time in 2000, the country that taught Cuba to pinpoint academia has stepped up its own espionage in the United States, especially on campus, and is believed to share information with its former satellite.

"The Russian intelligence presence in the United States is now at or above its Cold War levels," Van Cleave said in her 2012 testimony. "While Moscow's intelligence liaison relationships with Cuba may have waxed and waned, it is prudent to assume they haven't gone away."

Since 2000, about five thousand Russian students a year have attended U.S. colleges. That doesn't include so-called illegals, spies without diplomatic protection whom Russia sows across the United States, including at universities. Like the KGB duo who pose as suburban travel agents in the popular FX drama series *The Americans,* illegals assume false names and nationalities. They enjoy two advantages over traditional agents based under diplomatic cover at Russia's embassy and consulates, who also troll campuses for gullible students and professors. First, since they're underground, illegals generally face less FBI surveillance. Second, if they aren't identified, they can stay in the United States even if it severs diplomatic relations with Russia and kicks out embassy personnel.

Russian intelligence's reliance on illegals, who may take years or decades to pay off, or even go native and shed their loyalty to the motherland, illustrates its fabled patience. "It has always been a characteristic of Russian intelligence operations that they 'farm long-term' and are not under any obligation to produce instant results," intelligence historian Nigel West told me. "They take the view that a small investment now, spread widely, may pay dividends later. The Chinese MSS [Ministry of State Security] has adopted the same strategy, sometimes known as a 'scattergun' approach. In contrast, Western agencies tend to concentrate, like a sniper, on targets with proven access, and are under pressure to provide instant results."

After a decade-long investigation, the FBI arrested ten Russian illegals in 2010. Largely overlooked in the media furor over Anna Chapman, the so-called sexy spy, was that Russia had placed seven of the other nine in universities, including Harvard, Columbia, The New School, and the University of Washington. One agent, Mikhail Semenko, who received a graduate degree from Seton Hall University, spoke Mandarin and had studied at Harbin Institute of Technology in China, possibly a sign of coordination between Russian and Chinese intelligence.

Cynthia Murphy, who worked at an accounting and tax services firm in Manhattan, earned a bachelor's degree from NYU's Stern School of Business in 2000, and a master's degree at Columbia Business School in 2010. Her real name was Lydia Guryeva, and her assignments from Russian intelligence were quite different from her Columbia homework. Moscow's marching orders were to "strengthen . . . ties w. classmates on daily basis incl. professors who can help in job search and who will have (or already have) access to secret info" and to report "on their detailed personal data and character traits w. preliminary conclusions about their potential (vulnerability) to be recruited by Service."

She was ordered to dig up information on classmates applying for jobs at the CIA, or already hired there. Via radiograms or electronic messages concealed by special software, she funneled names of potential Columbia recruits to Moscow Center, which checked them against databases of agents for other countries' intelligence services to determine if they were "clean." She gathered "v. usefull [sic]" information on prospects for the global gold market that her handlers sent to the ministers of finance and economic development. She also cultivated financier Alan Patricof, a fundraiser for Hillary Clinton's 2008 presidential campaign. Patricof said he talked to Guryeva in person and on the phone, but only about personal finances, not politics or world affairs.

She and her husband, who was also a spy, asked Moscow in 2009 for permission to buy a house, a colonial with a hydrangea-lined walkway, in Montclair, New Jersey. The director of Russian foreign intelligence personally denied the request. Moscow Center would own their home in their names instead.

"You were sent to USA for long-term service trip," the center told them. "Your education, bank accounts, car, house etc.—all these serve one goal. . . . to search and develop ties in policymaking circles in US."

Another illegal, Mikhail Anatolyevich Vasenkov, taught a course on Latin America at Baruch College in 2008–09 under the name Juan Lazaro.

He criticized U.S. foreign policy so vehemently that he was dismissed at the end of the semester.

The illegals apparently made few American converts. Putin's defiance of the United States hasn't captured the imagination of American academics the way that Fidel Castro's did, and his brand of state capitalism lacks the appeal that communism held long ago for the Cambridge Five. "No one's spying for the Russians because they have an ideological message," says Mark Galeotti, a Russia expert and professor of global affairs at New York University.

The illegals pleaded guilty to conspiring to act as unlawful agents of the Russian Federation within the United States, and were traded back to Moscow. Reached by phone in Russia, where Guryeva works for Vnesheconombank, a state corporation that supports economic development, she pretended it was a wrong number and hung up.

Three years after the FBI busted the illegals' ring, it recorded two Russian spies under diplomatic cover, Igor Sporyshev and Victor Pobodnyy, discussing efforts to recruit several young women with ties to New York University. Both men specialized in economic espionage and were supposed to gather information on U.S. alternative energy initiatives, as well as on sanctions against Russia.

While Sporyshev elicited "a positive response without any feelings of rejection" from one woman, he told Pobodnyy in April 2013, another reacted less favorably. "I have lots of ideas about such girls but these ideas are not actionable because they don't allow you to get close enough. And in order to be close you either need to fuck them or use other levers to influence them to execute my requests. So when you tell me about girls, in my experience, it's very rare that something workable will come of it."

Ana Montes expected to spend 2001 at Langley on a prestigious National Intelligence Council fellowship that would have brought more classified documents within her grasp. But her assignment was postponed, on a pretext.

Cuba's uncanny ability to anticipate U.S. military and intelligence maneuvers in Latin America, as well as suspicions of Montes's loyalty by DIA counterintelligence analysts, had spurred a DIA-FBI mole hunt. Information from a senior official in the Cuban Intelligence Services also implicated Montes. Ten days after the September 11, 2001, attacks, amid concerns that she might transmit U.S. plans for the invasion of Afghanistan to her Cuban handlers, she was arrested.

U.S. authorities initially considered seeking the death penalty for Montes's treason, but the Department of Justice "raised the evidence threshold so high it could never be met," Simmons told me. Likely facing life in prison, Montes pleaded guilty in federal court in Washington, D.C., and agreed to cooperate with the FBI, in return for a twenty-five-year term. At her sentencing, she read an unrepentant statement in her black-and-white prison garb. "Your honor, I engaged in the activity that brought me before you because I obeyed my conscience rather than the law," she said. "I believe our government's policy toward Cuba is cruel and unfair, profoundly unneighborly, and I felt morally obligated to help the island defend itself from our efforts to impose our values and our political system on it. . . . I did what I thought right to counter a grave injustice. My greatest desire is to see amicable relations emerge between the United States and Cuba. I hope my case in some way will encourage our government to abandon its hostility towards Cuba and to work with Havana in a spirit of tolerance, mutual respect, and understanding."

Gleijeses praised his former student's statement as "dignified, very impressive." Emilia Montes was—and remains—heartbroken. "I no longer believe in causes," she told me. "She wasted the best years of her life."

The FBI is still curious about Montes. Around 2013, two agents interviewed Gleijeses for an hour at SAIS. He told them how Montes had pretended to seek his inside knowledge on the Cuba military, while actually testing whether the Castros could trust him. They didn't explain why they were interested in Montes, who by then had served half her sentence. "They said they were reviewing something about her case," Gleijeses said.

Montes's arrest alarmed Kendall Myers, the aristocratic, Castro-worshipping SAIS instructor and State Department analyst. He and Gwendolyn began taking more precautions, and only met their Cuban handlers outside the United States. Then, in April 2009, on Kendall Myers's seventy-second birthday, an FBI agent purporting to be a Cuban intelligence officer accosted the professor in front of the SAIS building, giving him a Cuban cigar and regards from their superiors in Havana. The encounter spurred a series of meetings in hotel lounges, ostensibly to solicit the professor's political insights, at which Myers and his wife were gulled into confessing their espionage.

"I have great admiration for Ana Montes," Myers told the agent. "She's a hero. . . . But she took too many chances." He added that he and Montes supplied some of the same information to Cuban intelligence. "There was duplication. . . . Because I read the stuff that she gave."

After the Myerses were arrested in June 2009, Castro said that they "deserve every honor in this world." Instead, in July 2010, Kendall Myers was sentenced to life imprisonment; Gwendolyn received eighty-one months, almost seven years. "Our overriding objective was to help the Cuban people defend their revolution," Myers said in court.

With Montes and Myers in prison, only one member of the SAIS troika who had spied for Cuba was still at large: Velázquez.

STRICKEN WITH ALZHEIMER'S, Don Miguel died in December 2006. He was buried in his native Moca. Mourners at his funeral looked in vain for his beloved daughter. If her siblings and mother knew that Velázquez would be arrested if she set foot on American soil, they didn't betray it.

"The family said they could not find her," recalled Aponte Toro, who spoke at the funeral. "It was an extraordinary situation. Nobody knew why. I thought there was some break between the family. It was not that."

According to another law school colleague, Don Miguel had been aware of his daughter's predicament. "I was told that, when he wanted to see her, he had to leave the United States, because she could not come in," Professor Luis Muñiz Argüelles told me.

With his death, Marta lost not only a father, but a mentor who had shaped her views and understood the sacrifices she had made. "He would have been proud of Marta, though he probably wouldn't have said so openly," Hey-Maestre said.

Velázquez's greatest espionage triumph, recruiting Montes, proved to be her downfall. During Montes's debriefing, she identified Velázquez as a Cuban agent. But the United States didn't catch Velázquez. Aware from press reports that her onetime friend and classmate was talking, she resigned from USAID and fled from Guatemala to Stockholm. Sweden bans extradition for a "political offense," a category that, under

Swedish legal precedent, includes espionage. With her husband's help, Velázquez became a Swedish citizen in February 2003, while keeping U.S. citizenship.

"The FBI dropped the ball," Simmons said. "They had Montes first, and she gave Velázquez. The FBI talked to Montes for three or four weeks. Then we interrogated her for three months. The FBI knew Velázquez was a talent spotter for three months while she was working for the State Department. They could have gotten her anytime. Then she fled to Stockholm."

A 2004 indictment for conspiracy to commit espionage was sealed to avoid alerting Velázquez, but she stayed out of the reach of the U.S. government anyway. She "is undoubtedly aware" that Montes "has cooperated with the United States and would have exposed" that Velázquez helped recruit her, the Justice Department said in a 2011 court filing.

Traveling on a Swedish passport with the privileges accorded to a diplomat's wife, she accompanied Kviele on his assignments in Europe, which included postings to Vienna, where he attended an International Atomic Energy Agency conference in 2004, and Lisbon. Like Sweden's, the extradition treaties that Austria and Portugal have with the United States exclude political offenses.

Unwilling to return to the United States to stand trial, burdened with a secret past that could burst into public scandal at any moment, Velázquez had every reason to lie low, but she was too ardent and restless to be a stay-at-home mother. Instead, still driven to improve society, she embarked on a second career—as an educator. She taught English at a vocational education institute for adults in Vienna in 2005–06. Then, in Portugal, she tutored students at an international school in Spanish, and taught business English to engineers at BP/Global Alliance and to board members of the commission that supervises the stock market. Surprisingly, she even worked for the government of the United States' close ally, the United Kingdom, teaching English in 2009 for its international cultural arm, the British Council. Seeking new friends to replace old ones in the United States whom she could no longer visit, she joined International Women in Portugal, a social group.

Its patience exhausted, the U.S. Justice Department offered to negotiate a deal, with the warning that otherwise it would make her indictment public. Apparently Velázquez refused, because the government fulfilled its threat, stunning her former classmates and USAID colleagues. "I can't tell you how often a group of us from the mission has gotten together" and talked about Marta's spying for Cuba, one told me. "None of us had a clue." Friends in the United States were unable to contact her; Princeton's alumni directory lists her address as "lost" as of May 1, 2013, six days after her indictment was unsealed.

Her brother Jorge Velázquez, a lawyer in Puerto Rico who runs Don Miguel's old firm preparing students for the bar exam, represents her. Like his sister, he has degrees from three eminent U.S. universities: Stanford (bachelor's), Northwestern (master's in American history), and Cornell (law). He told me that he would not discuss her case, and had instructed all family members not to do so, either, "because anything they say could attract questioning from the FBI."

After reading her senior thesis and talking with her father's friends, her Princeton classmates and teachers, and her colleagues at USAID and Thorildsplans, I began to feel a certain affinity for Marta Rita Velázquez. We were the same age and attended Ivy League universities at the same time; I had protested against Harvard's South Africa investments, though less zealously than she had against Princeton's.

Pointing out that we had "a fair bit in common," I emailed her to request an interview. There was no reply.

STYMIED FOR MORE than half a century, hopes for better U.S.-Cuban relations may finally be coming true. President Barack Obama eased restrictions on trade, tourism, and financial transactions and in 2016 became the first sitting president to visit Cuba since the Castros took power in 1959. The American embassy in Havana reopened in 2015, and plans were afoot for a Cuban consulate in Tampa. Fidel Castro—hero of Montes, Myers, and Velázquez, and long a U.S. nemesis—died in November 2016.

It was reported in June 2016 that the Obama administration was considering trading Montes herself to Cuba for fugitive former Black Panther Party member Assata Shakur. Cuba gave Shakur asylum after she escaped in 1979 from a New Jersey prison where she was serving a life sentence for the 1973 murder of a state trooper. California congressman Devin Nunes, who chairs the House Intelligence Committee, denounced the idea of releasing Montes as "preposterous . . . it is difficult to overstate the damage caused by Ms. Montes's treachery."

Like U.S. corporations, American higher education is poised to capitalize on the rapprochement. Academic exchanges with Cuban universities are springing up. A 2013 study by a consultant to Florida International University, where Cuban agent Carlos Alvarez taught from 1974 until his 2006 arrest, urged it to explore establishing a campus in Cuba. In 2015, the New Jersey–based Educational Testing Service administered the Test of English as a Foreign Language in Cuba for the first time. U.S. colleges rely on the TOEFL to evaluate international applicants. Because of Cuba's poverty, most of its students would need scholarships, but for many U.S. universities, the cachet of a Cuban connection might justify the extra expense.

A thaw in hostilities, though, would be unlikely to reduce academic espionage—or the harm it can cause. On the contrary, if the effect of globalization elsewhere is any guide, more educational traffic between Cuba and the United States would spur a corresponding increase in spying. Cuba would probably rely on homegrown students and professors, along with American disciples like Montes, Myers, and Velázquez, to collect information in the United States.

Moreover, the documents stolen or whispers overheard by these agents might circulate beyond Cuba. Even if Cuba itself becomes friendlier to the United States, it trades intelligence with countries that aren't. "The sale and barter of U.S. secrets is one of the major revenue sources sustaining the Cuban regime," Simmons told me. Some of Montes's dispatches to Cuba ended up in Beijing and Moscow, he said.

Montes "compromised programs of broader scope—highly sensitive intelligence of limited value to Cuba, but potentially very high value to other adversaries," Van Cleave said in her testimony. "There is a continuing market for such stolen U.S. secrets. . . . The damage to the United States from the loss of sensitive national security information to Cuban espionage is not bounded by the national security threat presented by Cuba alone, but also by its value to potentially more dangerous adversaries."

THE CENTRAL SQUARE of Spånga, a suburb of Stockholm, reflects the diversity of modern Sweden, where 17 percent of the population is foreign-born. A Thai restaurant has leaflets in Arabic explaining Sweden's health care system. A woman wearing a hijab sells strawberries at the entrance to the commuter rail station.

The Kvieles live in Spånga's posher section, about four hundred yards from the square, in a two-story yellow house with a tile roof, a basement, and two balconies facing south. They bought it in 2013 for about $500,000, moving there from a more glamorous Stockholm address just a few months after the indictment against Velázquez was unsealed. Like Velázquez's childhood home in Puerto Rico, the six-room Spånga house is surrounded by greenery, including a garden with pine and birch trees, and an apple tree with a birdhouse. There's a 2010 Volvo in the driveway, and a brick porch with a twenty-inch religious statuette, perhaps reflecting Velázquez's Catholic heritage and schooling.

One day in June 2016, a Stockholm-based journalist who was helping me with this chapter approached the statue for a closer look. From inside the house, a rap on a window warned him to retreat. In response to a follow-up phone call, a woman's voice—presumably either Velázquez or her daughter—asked, "Who is this?" in Swedish. When the journalist identified himself, she hung up.

No longer posted abroad, Kviele has worked in recent years as a regular desk officer in the Swedish foreign ministry. Velázquez, who speaks fluent Swedish as well as Portuguese, English, and Spanish, blends into the scene, just one more transplanted foreigner with a complicated history in a cosmopolitan capital. "If you look closely at the Latin American population in Stockholm, many of them were involved in leftist politics," says a Thorildsplans colleague.

For a fugitive from U.S. justice, Velázquez appears to lead a settled and productive life. Since she and Kviele returned to Sweden from Lisbon around 2010, she has continued to teach English and/or Spanish: at the now-defunct International School for Justice and Peace, at an adult-education program called Folkuniversitetet, and then at Thorildsplans.

In 2014, she joined the Thorildsplans staff, teaching beginning Spanish and advanced English to college prep students aged sixteen to nineteen. Although she lacks the requisite teaching certificate, schools in Sweden with shortages of credentialed teachers may hire unqualified candidates. Offsetting her lack of teacher training, her degrees from three elite U.S. universities likely impressed school administrators. She also has an English-teaching certificate from the University of Cambridge, according to her curriculum vitae on file with the school district. She works on a year-to-year contract, earning about four thousand dollars a month, while pursuing a teaching degree to meet the qualifications set by the Swedish National Agency for Education. She expects to complete her degree in 2017, and then will move into a permanent slot, Waardahl said. "Marta gets very good reviews from her students."

Velázquez remains intense and idealistic, a crusader for social justice—a trait she passed on to her son, Ingmar, who graduated from another Stockholm high school in 2015, and has signed petitions for releasing prisoners of conscience in Eritrea, and against deporting two Ethiopian children from Sweden. One of her students in English at Thorildsplans in 2015–16 said Velázquez went out of her way to emphasize the importance of human rights. Somewhat surprisingly, she assigned her pupils to write an essay about an organization that has assailed the Castro regime for repressing dissidents and independent media: Amnesty International. Perhaps, unlike Montes, Velázquez regrets spying for Cuba.

FOREIGN EXCHANGE

Magnolia and crabapple trees were blossoming pink and white on a blustery Saturday afternoon in April 2016 on the hillside campus of Marietta College in southern Ohio, where red-brick, Georgian-style buildings overlook the Ohio and Muskingum rivers. Beside the McDonough Rock—actually a hunk of concrete found near a bridge and hauled up the hill—about thirty people gathered to dedicate a sapling and a plaque in memory of Andrea Parhamovich, a Marietta alumna and prodemocracy activist killed in Iraq in 2007. It was fitting to honor Parhamovich there, a Marietta administrator told the crowd, because the rock is a "symbol of free speech."

Many in the group then headed inside the nearby McDonough Center for Leadership and Business for a student presentation on relations between the United States, China, and Russia. Here, though, there was no mention of democracy or free speech. The six American students discussing their research sounded like mouthpieces for the Chinese government. Their historical overview omitted the Tiananmen Square massacre, and their discussion of covert action ignored Chinese economic espionage and cyberspying. Instead, citing mutual interests in promoting international trade and fighting global health epidemics, they predicted an era of unprecedented cooperation.

"The U.S., Russia, and China have a greater opportunity to work together than ever before," one sophomore declared.

The same tone prevailed during the question-and-answer session. When a member of the audience asked whether Japan's rearming might cause tensions between the United States and China, the sophomore dismissed the possibility. "China's relationship with us is a lot stronger than our relationship with Japan," he said. Another questioner wondered how to change the perception of most Americans that China and Russia are "bad guys." A female undergraduate rejected the premise. Her generation sees Syrian refugees and illegal Mexican immigrants as villains, she explained, not Russia or China.

I was tempted to attribute the students' apparent brainwashing to their teacher, Yingjie Luo, who was listening intently in the front row. His participation in the conference was the reason that I had chosen this particular weekend to visit Marietta. Luo wore glasses, and a natty blue suit without a tie; his dark hair was tinged with silver. After a Marietta dean introduced him as a "renowned scholar" on China-Russia relations, Luo himself thanked the students and the audience.

"Today is very important for me," he said. "I never think I can teach a course in the U.S."

LUO DIDN'T EXPLAIN why teaching in this country had seemed so far-fetched. He was probably alluding to his lack of English fluency, but perhaps also to the unique status of the university in China that sent him to Marietta. Luo was a visiting scholar from the University of International Relations (UIR) in Beijing, which U.S. diplomats have described as the Chinese Ministry of State Security's "elite institute for preparing its new recruits." UIR is affiliated with and partly funded by the security ministry, China's intelligence organization, which plucks promising candidates from the university to replenish its ranks. The special attention that the FBI has long lavished on UIR graduates in the United States triggered South Florida professor Dajin Peng's travails.

Luo owed his presence at Marietta to one of the strangest partnerships in higher education, between a Chinese spy school and a small, isolated liberal arts college in the American heartland. At the very least, like the Confucius Institutes in the United States, UIR's Marietta connection represents an exercise in soft power, instilling Chinese propaganda in unwary undergraduates like the presenters at the McDonough Center. At most, it may be a security breach, a successful ploy by Chinese intelligence to gain an inconspicuous foothold in the United States by taking advantage of the guileless hospitality of the American Midwest. A more far-fetched theory is that it's a CIA tactic to penetrate China's spy school. Whatever the explanation, the relationship turns some Marietta professors into functionaries of China's security ministry, which pays them to come to Beijing and teach American culture to UIR summer students, likely including future intelligence officers.

"I'm thinking, 'I'm so naïve,'" a former Marietta provost told me. "I personally never questioned the UIR relationship."

Few people have. Created and overseen by a magnetic, mysterious Marietta professor with ties to Mao Zedong and Chinese president Xi Jinping as well as the U.S. State Department, the partnership benefits both schools. UIR has helped Marietta, which has a modest endowment and depends primarily on tuition revenue, to attract a flood of full-paying Chinese students. The windfall has been sizable enough to squelch any doubts within the Marietta administration about the wisdom of collaborating with a spy school.

In return, as UIR's only strategic partner in the United States, Marietta gives it both legitimacy outside China and a low-profile outlet where its students and faculty can experience America firsthand. Jonathan Adelman, a University of Denver professor who specializes in Chinese and Russian national security policy, has lectured and taught extensively in China, including at UIR. When I asked him how the Marietta connection benefited UIR, he said he wasn't familiar with it, but added, "If I had to make a guess, I'd guess somebody got up and said, 'We need to find an all-American place, so we can learn the habits of America.'"

The partnership has many facets. Chinese high school seniors take Marietta's English-proficiency exam on UIR's campus. Once they enroll at Marietta, they can fulfill its general education requirements by taking UIR summer courses. Marietta hosts twenty to twenty-five UIR students and two faculty members for two weeks each summer, and as many as ten exchange and transfer students and one or two professors, such as Professor Luo, during the academic year. The exchange students typically pay board but no tuition; the visiting professors stay for free in Marietta's International Scholars House, a blue cottage on campus.

Delegations of top administrators from each institution visit the other's campus almost every year, and the two colleges have sponsored joint conferences in Beijing. Half a dozen Marietta professors teach in UIR's summer program. UIR paid for publication of a 2013 book (on Chinese advertising) coauthored by one of its professors and a Marietta faculty member. Marietta's choir performed at UIR in 2006.

Only one aspect of a standard exchange program is missing. Marietta doesn't send American students to UIR; its Asian studies majors generally spend their required semester abroad at other Chinese universities. When Marietta sophomore Michael Fahy considered enrolling at UIR in 2013, his adviser, political science chairman Mark Schaefer, discouraged him. Fahy wanted to work for the State Department someday, and Schaefer told him that attending UIR, or even socializing with its students, could hurt his chances for a security clearance.

"He was pretty clear about what the school was," Fahy told me.

"I have a recollection of saying that UIR, to some government agencies, would be a red flag he'd have to deal with," Schaefer said.

Fahy heeded Schaefer's advice and attended the Beijing Foreign Studies University, which is run by the Ministry of Foreign Affairs. When he asked his classmates and professors there about UIR, they would say, "You know what that school is about."

Marietta's administration instructed faculty members, if I contacted them for interviews, to refer me to communications director Tom Perry. (Thankfully, many of them disregarded that edict.) Perry said in a statement, "Marietta College and UIR have enjoyed a positive relationship for two decades, and we continue to be partner institutions. Our faculty have and continue to teach courses at UIR. We are also proud of the cultural diversity that is created on campus by the hundreds of international students who attend Marietta College each year."

Perry did arrange for me to interview then-president Joseph Bruno in February 2016. I asked Bruno whether he was aware that UIR is connected to the security ministry. "I heard they used to be," he said. "I didn't know they still were. It was mentioned once by one of the faculty visitors on campus. I think she mentioned that some of them have a rank in the Army. I was curious about it. . . . I do largely think it's irrelevant. We're in it for the educational benefits, and that's all I've ever seen out of the interactions with the university."

LOCATED NEAR THE Summer Palace in a scenic area of northwest Beijing replete with greenery and weeping willows, and shielded by security gates and guard posts and a row of pine trees, the University of International Relations forms what one alumna calls a "Golden Triangle" with Peking and Tsinghua universities, China's Harvard and Yale. Especially by Chinese standards, UIR is small. It has about three thousand undergraduates and graduate students, and specializes in teaching international politics and economics, foreign languages, and public relations. All students must take advanced English language courses, a 2009 graduate told me. UIR has five research institutes, including a center for international strategy and security studies.

UIR operates day-to-day like a typical college, with the usual array of extracurricular clubs and sports, including tennis and golf. On its website it describes itself as "one of the 'key national universities' under the administration of the Ministry of Education," and doesn't mention the security ministry. On a subcampus, its Center for International Education teaches Chinese language and culture courses, lasting anywhere from two weeks to one year, to hundreds of international students, who stay in a separate dormitory.

Still, while the education ministry confers the university's degree-granting authority and makes sure it runs smoothly, the security ministry sets its direction, supplies funding, and takes its pick of graduates. In U.S. terms, the Chinese spymasters are the board of trustees.

UIR "probably fits on the Ministry of State Security organizational chart," said Peter Mattis, a fellow at The Jamestown Foundation in Washington, D.C., who studies and writes extensively on Chinese espionage. "I'd be completely confident that there is a relationship, and a continuing relationship that's not just arm's-length."

Jeremy Wang, a Marietta professor of information systems and one of its first Chinese graduates, teaches at UIR every summer. He also makes arrangements at Marietta for visiting scholars from UIR like Yingjie Luo. Based on his conversations with UIR faculty, he told me, "the top students will have an opportunity to work for the security department. There's a very strict process of selection. They have to be very good, with that kind of mentality."

UIR professors argue about the university's future, Wang said. Some want it to shed the spy school stigma by severing ties with the security ministry and moving under the education ministry's umbrella. Others are reluctant to lose a deep-pocketed patron. "Some faculty members say it's better to stay with the security ministry, because it's more funding," he said. "If you go with the Ministry of Education, you compete against many other schools."

I asked Wang if, as a teenager in China, he considered applying to UIR. He laughed. "Never," he said. "At that time, we know UIR is a [Chinese] CIA school, we don't like it. I'm not into politics, I'm into business. At that time, if you want to enter UIR, it's an honor for a family. Personally, I just don't like politics."

FOUNDED IN 1949, the same year as the People's Republic of China, the then–Institute of International Relations was placed under the security ministry in 1965. The security agency needed people trained in international relations because Chinese leader Mao Zedong, who suspected the professional diplomats in his civil service of Western leanings and disloyalty to communism, gave his secret police unusual power over foreign affairs.

"Mao hated the upper-class foreign-service types," Adelman told me. As early as 1940, when Mao realized he would be likely to assume power if the Japanese were defeated in World War II, he asked the head of his personal security to run foreign policy. "Ever since then, the party elite has turned to the security people to provide them with vital information." UIR, Adelman added, "is not that up front about its relationship with the security ministry. If you can't hide your own university in plain sight, what good are you?"

Ironically, as a feeder school for the security ministry, UIR became one of China's most cosmopolitan and outward-looking universities. It couldn't afford to reject the West or take refuge in political slogans, because future intelligence officers needed to understand what the rest of the world was actually like. When China under Deng Xiaoping began emerging from the Cultural Revolution, it was one of the few Chinese universities with professors who had studied in the United States, and its library was stocked Western publications and videos. "We had a greater latitude in learning about foreign cultures," a former student recalled. "We watched CNN every night, and that wasn't accessible by students elsewhere." Now that Western-trained teachers are commonplace in China, UIR has lost some of its competitive edge, and its prestige has declined. Greater awareness of its link to the security ministry may also have hurt its academic reputation.

"Some of the teachers had previously studied in the U.S.," recalled I. C. Smith, retired supervisor of the FBI's China squad. "They not only had the language skills but could talk with some authority about the U.S. as a country, its history, and its people," at a time when there was a "dearth of information available to those inside China." Students "weren't being taught traditional tradecraft, but instead, cultural, political, economic awareness of the countries they were going to be targeting for analytical assessments."

Unlike their peers at other Chinese universities, UIR professors hold military ranks. Also as a privilege of its Ministry of State Security (MSS) affiliation, UIR enjoys priority in selecting students. If high school seniors identify UIR as one of their college choices, and excel on the national entrance exam, it can scoop them up first, shutting out other universities that they listed. "It gives the ministry a first cut and allows them to get a look at these students," Mattis said.

UIR heavily recruits from border provinces, where the security ministry maintains a strong presence. "Training for most MSS intelligence officers begins at the Beijing University of International Relations," global consulting firm Stratfor reported in 2010. "The MSS taps university-bound students prior to their university entrance exams, choosing qualified students with a lack of foreign contacts or travel to make sure they haven't already been compromised." Loyalty is one of four virtues highlighted on UIR's Internet home page, along with diligence, practicality, and innovation.

U.S. officials have long been aware of UIR. When China began sending students to the United States in 1979, "the intelligence community went through a period of trying to sort out what institutes were important," I. C. Smith, then supervisor of the FBI's Chinese squad, told me. "The International Relations Institute was identified as being important. We were quite familiar with it." The FBI nicknamed it "School of Spies" and tracked its graduates in the United States.

China was also keeping tabs on its alumni, perhaps worried that U.S. intelligence would turn them against their homeland. In 1984, Fei-Ling Wang earned a master's degree in international economics at the institute. Twenty years later, as a Georgia Institute of Technology professor of international affairs visiting China on a research trip, he was charged with espionage and detained for two weeks, including four days in solitary confinement.

Wang declined to discuss his case, but commented generally on the institute in a May 2015 email. "IIR is affiliated to the PRC Ministry of State Security and many of its graduates are later presumably employed by the Ministry. However, many IIR graduates have left and pursued other lines of work," he wrote, using the school's former acronym. ". . . I would not be surprised that IIR graduates living in the U.S. might have gotten special attention from U.S. government."

How MANY UIR alumni work for Chinese intelligence is unclear. The majority—like Liu Huan, China's most famous singer-songwriter, who performed at the opening ceremony of the 2008 Olympics in Beijing— pursue other careers. Three UIR students told Adelman in the late 1980s that the security ministry hired one-fourth of its graduates. "The other 75 percent were told, 'We'll keep in touch with you.'" Some alumni may ostensibly have other jobs, but the security ministry pays their salaries, according to one graduate.

Mattis disputed Stratfor's finding that UIR trains "most" Chinese intelligence officers. He said "most" is an exaggeration, because the ministry employs more than thirty thousand people. "Is one small college in Beijing going to be able to train everyone for that?"

One indication of UIR's true master is its extensive overlap with the China Institutes of Contemporary International Relations, a prominent think tank that conducts research for the Chinese government. According to Mattis, CICIR is a bureau of the security ministry. "It was previously the number eight bureau, and now I believe it's number eleven," Mattis said. The ministry "pays most of" CICIR's bills, David Shambaugh, a professor of international affairs at George Washington University and director of its China Policy Program, wrote in 2002.

Traditionally, applicants to UIR's graduate school were tracked to become either professors at the university or researchers at CICIR. A 2011 CIA report found that nearly half of the think tank's senior leaders had taught or studied at the University of International Relations. The two institutions appear "to have a close relationship," it concluded. Tao Jian, the university's president (and an alumnus), used to be a vice president of the think tank. Many researchers at the think tank also teach at the university, Mattis told me. He believes they act as talent spotters, referring promising students to the security ministry. UIR and CICIR also offer a joint doctoral program.

MANY UIR GRADUATES leave China. Of 636 bachelor's degree recipients in 2014, 120 went abroad for further study. A LinkedIn site for UIR alumni identified 314 of them in the United States in 2016, including 72 in the New York City area. They not only attend premier graduate and professional schools, including Harvard Law School, but also work for major banks, high-tech companies, and investment and accounting firms, as well as nonprofits and municipal governments. It's unlikely that they're intelligence officers, since in that case it would be foolhardy for them to parade their spy school degrees on LinkedIn.

The FBI was more worried about UIR graduates who tried to conceal their alma mater. "In most cases we ran into in the bureau, people masked their affiliation with the school," a former agent told me. "They don't list it on their resume. That's a sure sign they're operational."

Perhaps eager to distance themselves from Chinese intelligence, alumni from each of the past four decades told me that UIR's connection to the security ministry was weakest in their era. For example, a 1989 graduate said that the security ministry hired less than 5 percent of his class. Today, he said, the percentage of graduates going into intelligence work is higher. "The affiliation is stronger, closer, and more students are specially recruited," he said. The ministry "found that the past way is too loose."

Most of the UIR alumni in the United States whom I interviewed told me that they had little or no contact with Chinese intelligence, either in college or afterward. One exception was a former UIR student who completed his education in the United States. When he returned to China, working in a sensitive position for a Western organization, he began running into his former UIR professors in unlikely locations, such as cafés far from campus, and they would chat over tea. He sensed that the meetings were not accidental.

"I think they wanted to recruit me," he told me. "I feel very uncomfortable about that. If you refuse, they can turn against you." He quit his job and left China.

FEW AMERICAN BUSINESSES and nonprofit groups appear familiar with UIR, or to regard an affiliation with the school as cause for concern, much less a deal-breaker. Courtesy of a well-known American human rights organization, one UIR graduate gained a front-row seat at an event of likely importance to Chinese intelligence.

After earning a master's degree at UIR in 2008, Xie Tingting became a researcher for the Charhar Institute in Beijing, which was established in 2009 and calls itself a "non-governmental think tank." Like Confucius Institutes, Charhar is an instrument of Chinese soft power. It "focuses specifically on improving China's overseas image," David Shambaugh has written.

Charhar is also a partner of the Carter Center in Atlanta. Founded by Jimmy Carter, who as president had welcomed the first influx of students from the People's Republic, the Atlanta nonprofit monitors elections around the world to help ensure that the process is democratic and the results are accurate. Although deploying a representative from an authoritarian regime to safeguard a democratic election might seem counterproductive, the Carter Center draws observers from a variety of nations and has worked on village elections in China.

Yawei Liu, director of the Carter Center's China program and an adjunct political science professor at Emory University in Atlanta, is a senior fellow at Charhar. At his urging, the Carter Center sent Xie Tingting to East Africa for eight to ten days to observe the January 2011 referendum on self-determination for southern Sudan. Liu told me that his recommendation was "based on her research interest" at the China Foreign Affairs University, where she was pursuing her doctorate. "We need someone from China to participate in the observation. We want people to see how elections are conducted in developing countries. You have to debunk the fallacy that, if you're not developed, you're not able to hold elections. The Chinese always say they're not developed enough."

Liu wasn't worried about Xie's connection to UIR. "That was just undergraduate," he said. When I pointed out that actually Xie had been a graduate student there, he said, "No difference. I don't think it's under MSS any longer. I just don't know the exact relationship. My impression is, right now, when they graduate, they go anywhere they want to go. It's just like any of the American students from Harvard or Georgetown or anywhere to be recruited by CIA or FBI."

The Sudan referendum posed a diplomatic conundrum for China. Sudan was one of its biggest oil suppliers in Africa, and China had invested heavily in oil production facilities there. It had also sold arms to the Sudanese government in Khartoum to help it suppress the rebels in the south. But now South Sudan, where most of the oil is located, was about to become a separate country, and China would need to conciliate it. Almost 99 percent of voters favored independence, and South Sudan seceded six months later.

"There would be Chinese interest in following the 2011 referendum," another observer told me. "They certainly had/have significant commercial interests and also quite significant political interests as well. . . . My impression is that with China expanding so much in Africa they have wanted to increase their own knowledge on the continent and boost their own ranks of Africa specialists."

David Carroll, director of the Carter Center's democracy program, said he must have met Xie Tingting, but didn't remember her. While "you're not going to learn anything of a sensitive nature as a short-term observer," he told me, "we would not normally take somebody who works for an intelligence service in their country."

After returning from Sudan, Xie became a visiting scholar at Emory University in Atlanta from August 2011 to May 2012, studying international relations on a Fulbright fellowship. According to Liu, she's now a professor at a university in Quanzhou, China. She didn't respond to my email to her LinkedIn account.

If China's security ministry was looking for a low-profile college where future intelligence officers could absorb American culture undisturbed, it couldn't have found one more suitable or receptive than Marietta. Former president Larry Wilson calls it "centrally isolated" and "two hours from anywhere, Columbus, Pittsburgh, Cleveland." Established in 1835, it has 1,200 students and seven "core values," including "global perspective and diversity." Its baseball team has won six small-college national championships.

Marietta, Ohio (population: 14,053), oozes small-town hospitality. Former mayor Michael "Moon" Mullen, a Marietta alumnus and bluegrass musician, hosts UIR students every summer. Once, at the downtown pizzeria Mullen owns, he and a UIR coed crooned a folk ballad together. Another time, he invited the Chinese students to his home for a cookout.

"It was a night in the life of an American family, what we do for fun, we get together with friends, sit around the campfire, play our guitars," Mullen says. "I give them authenticity. This is Middle America, simpler, slower, the life that I love. The more they feel welcome and at home here, the more they'll come back. It's good for the economy, good for cultural exchange."

Mullen is fully aware that international students have a "huge impact" on the college's bottom line. With only a $71.3 million endowment in 2015, less than a tenth of Ohio competitor Denison University's $797.1 million (Denison has about twice as many students), Marietta relies on tuition. International students usually pay the sticker price, or close to it, while domestic students receive more financial aid.

With a well-regarded petroleum engineering program, Marietta attracts a sizable Middle Eastern contingent, including 58 Kuwaitis in 2015. But they're outnumbered by Chinese enrollment, which peaked at 144 in both 2011 and 2012, when it comprised about 10 percent of the student body. That's a high proportion, especially for an obscure liberal arts college; Chinese families tend to aspire to brand-name schools, like the Ivy Leagues and large public universities. Nor is Marietta a bargain: for years, it has required Chinese students to pay fifty thousand dollars up front, even before setting foot on campus.

"They're the lifeline of the college," Luding Tong, a professor of Chinese language and director of Marietta's Asian studies program, told me. "They're the ATM machine."

LIVING UP TO its team name, the "Pioneers," Marietta was one of the first liberal arts colleges to take advantage of China's opening to the West after the Cultural Revolution. Marietta first gained a toehold in 1985, when the late professor of economics Wen-Yu Cheng arranged a faculty exchange with the Sichuan Institute of Finance and Economics (now Southwestern University of Finance and Economics) in his native city of Chengdu. As that relationship fizzled in the wake of China's massacre of student protesters in Beijing's Tiananmen Square in 1989, a princeling arrived at Marietta who would establish a more durable and lucrative bond with China's spy university.

Marietta received a U.S. Department of Education grant for a tenure-track position teaching both Chinese language and political science. From a handful of candidates, it chose Xiaoxiong Yi, a doctoral student at American University in Washington, D.C.

Yi proved to be a dynamic teacher, and was awarded tenure in 1995. Michael Taylor, a management professor whose office was across the hall from Yi's classroom, occasionally sat in on his classes. "He was as good as I've seen," Taylor told me. "He really knows his subject, really listens to his students. He could get them involved. They were asking questions all the time. I wanted to see how he got that much engagement from U.S. students who are taking the course because they need a course in international stuff to graduate. He had a tremendous following of American students. They understood that he cared about what they had to say."

Gradually, word spread at Marietta about Yi's lofty background. His father, Yi Lirong, an early member of the Chinese Communist Party and comrade of Mao Zedong, became labor minister when Mao took power in 1949, the same year that UIR was founded. Xiaoxiong Yi grew up in a compound for senior leaders and their families in Beijing, where children "were groomed to become China's ruling elite." Like so many of his brethren, Yi Lirong fell from favor during the Cultural Revolution and was imprisoned for a decade. Tainted by his father's downfall, Xiaoxiong Yi also served time, and spent years as a fugitive in the countryside.

When Yi Lirong was rehabilitated, his family moved to a housing complex where current Chinese president Xi Jinping, son of another prominent official who had been purged and pardoned, lived across the hall. Xiaoxiong Yi and Xi Jinping became friends and talked almost every day for five years. While Xi Jinping embarked on a political career, Xiaoxiong Yi "descended into the pursuit of romantic relationships, drink, movies and Western literature," and then left China to pursue graduate studies in the United States. In 1987, Xi Jinping visited Xiaoxiong Yi in Washington, D.C.

At Marietta, Yi shared a coffeepot with a colleague, and the two men often chatted over java about opportunities for the college in China. Eventually, Yi approached the administration and offered to travel back and forth to China and bring in a few children from families that he knew there.

There was one caveat. At the time, U.S. colleges could only recruit in China if they had a tie-in with a local university. Yi had one in mind—the University of International Relations.

"My understanding is that there was a faculty member at UIR who had a pretty good personal relationship with Xiaoxiong," Jeremy Wang told me. "It evolved into an institutional relationship. We started to use UIR as a recruiting agent."

Given Yi's background, he must have known about UIR's affiliation with the security ministry. It's likely that Yi, who declined to be interviewed for this book, recognized and acted upon a mutual interest: Marietta's desire for diversity and revenue, and UIR's for credibility and firsthand experience of American culture.

Peter Mattis, the Jamestown Foundation expert on Chinese espionage, speculated that the security officials overseeing UIR trusted Yi because they were familiar with his father. "In the MSS, if you want to get promoted, you have to be the son or daughter of someone," he says. "They believe that breeds loyalty and people who understand the system." Yi "may go back and say to MSS, 'There's this kind of opportunity, why don't we put something together?'"

Yi also cultivated U.S. Department of State contacts, which helped in obtaining visas for Chinese students. "My impression is that Xiaoxiong does have connections with the State Department," a Marietta colleague told me. "They value him very much as an informed person. I know he has friends there who often take his advice."

UIR began supplying prospective students with information about Marietta and steering them there. According to Tong, Marietta paid UIR at least $1,000 for each enrollee. One UIR administrator who had a high-ranking relative in Inner Mongolia helped Marietta connect with students there.

The first group of a dozen Chinese students came to Marietta in 1995. UIR and Yi recruited all of them except Jeremy Wang, who transferred to Marietta for his senior year from Southwestern University of

Finance and Economics. In the early years, Yi often tapped China's premier families. He He Li, who attended Marietta in 1997–98, was the son of Li Zhaoxing, then China's ambassador to the United States and later its foreign minister. Li Zhaoxing delivered Marietta's commencement address in 1998 and received an honorary degree.

Initially, the arrangement with UIR bothered some Marietta professors. "A lot of faculty questioned this," Tong told me. "Why we want to do it with a spy school? There was no answer. Then, all those years go by, we need the income from the Chinese students, it became a reality."

Michael Taylor, the management professor, recalled the early discussions. "I was told, whatever State Security spy training was being done, wasn't being done there," he said. UIR "was still basically owned and operated by State Security, because institutions in China don't just give up and say, 'We'll turn this over to the education ministry.' In China, the education ministry was the weakest link. They had the least money to spare. Nobody wanted to hand over their school, with the buildings and professors, whatever clout you had, to the education ministry."

In the college leadership's view, the benefits—financial and otherwise—outweighed the risks. As I interviewed them, I was continually taken aback by how easily most Marietta administrators, past and present, rationalized the college's connection to China's spy university. "I didn't have misgivings," Larry Wilson, Marietta's president from 1995 to 2000, told me. "We certainly talked about it, what were the implications of it. Our feeling was, students coming to the U.S. would learn about our country in very positive ways. Then, when they went home, they would bring positive aspects about America back to China.

"Did we have any students who were working for the Chinese government? If we did, we didn't know it. Of course, they wouldn't want us to know it."

UIR's budding relationship with Marietta raised eyebrows at the American embassy in Beijing. In November 2002, the embassy sent a four-page cable, marked "secret" and "priority" and titled "China's MSS Training School Begins to Seek 'Real World' Contacts," to the secretary of state in Washington, D.C. It copied the American consulates in Shanghai, Shenyang, Guangzhou, and Hong Kong; the Taipei office of the American Institute in Taiwan, which represents the U.S. government; the U.S. embassies in Tokyo and Seoul; and the commander in chief and joint intelligence center of the U.S. Pacific Command, based in Honolulu. In response to my 2015 public records request, the State Department supplied a summary of the document, though it withheld the body, which it said was classified.

"Beijing's University of International Relations, the Ministry of State Security's elite institute for preparing its new recruits, is seeking 'exchange agreements' with a number of overseas institutions of higher learning," the cable stated. "The decision to pursue this route, which is being pushed within the UIR by students and within the ministry by 'progressive' young technocrats, is still being hotly debated. Nonetheless, UIR's president has already concluded an agreement in the United States with Marietta College in Ohio, which so far has for the first time allowed UIR professors 'real world' opportunities to teach for short stints at Marietta."

As MORE CHINESE high school seniors applied to Marietta, the college streamlined the process. It opened a Beijing office, where Yi could meet students and parents and help with visas and other concerns. Eventually he gave up teaching and stayed in China almost year-round, in part for family reasons. His father died in 1997 at the age of ninety-nine, but his mother was still living there. "He was getting worn to a frazzle" doing two jobs and commuting to China, Taylor told me.

From his perch in Beijing, Yi controlled Marietta's China operations. Unlike his counterparts at branch campuses of other U.S. universities, he reported to the president, rather than to the vice president for enrollment management or director of admission, according to former staff members. At times he relaxed Marietta's usual academic standards. The result, according to his critics at the college, was letting in some Chinese students who weren't ready or who lacked English fluency.

For example, in other foreign countries, Marietta applicants had to pass the standard English-proficiency exam, the College Board's Test of English as a Foreign Language. Although Professor Janie Rees-Miller, Marietta's director of English as a second language, recommended requiring the TOEFL in China as well, Yi overruled her. Instead, Rees-Miller designed Marietta's own English test. It's not as accurate as the TOEFL, but "it's better than nothing for damn sure," she told me. While the TOEFL costs $153 and lasts four hours, Marietta's exam is free and takes half the time. The college's admissions director would fly to China to proctor the exam, which was given in a UIR conference room, and interview prospects; he could accept or reject them on the spot. Marietta awarded small stipends to its better Chinese applicants, who relished not only the financial savings but also the prestige of a merit scholarship.

Although their tuition was important to the college, former admission dean Jason Turley didn't feel pressure to accept Chinese applicants, he told me. "Every trip I made, there were students who didn't get in," he said. "Their speaking was not adequate, and they were denied. . . . From the president to the CFO, there was never an implication, 'Make sure you bring in more.' It was, 'If you're going to accept them, they'd better be good.'"

Yi raised Marietta's profile in China. "Xiaoxiong liked taking the president and the provost over and squiring them around, wining and dining and introducing them to bigwigs," one former administrator recalled. "He's very big on politicking and relationship building."

Of the dozen Chinese students whom I interviewed at Marietta in April 2016, Yi had personally recruited almost all of them, including several through UIR. The uncle of Zi Hui Yu, a junior majoring in advertising and public relations, knows a UIR professor who recommended talking to Yi. The mother of freshman Yi Si Wang teaches computer science at UIR and knows Yi. The aunt of Zhen Ze Mi, a petroleum engineering major, is Yi's friend. The high school volleyball coach of sophomore Jie Yu Song gave her the phone number of Yi's assistant.

"All of us come here for" Yi, Da Chuan Nie, a senior and finance major from Shenzhen, told me as we chatted on the Marietta mall, a stone walkway bisecting the campus, with islands of greenery and a tall flagpole with an American flag.

Yi had recruited Da's older brother to Marietta. Da's own first choice had been the University of Missouri, but his TOEFL score was below its bar, he told me. He took Marietta's English exam at UIR with a roomful of other students—"All of us passed"—but still yearned for Missouri. "This town is too small. Very boring. I have no entertainment. I just play games in my room."

Yolanda Feng, a junior English major with a fondness for romantic Victorian novels like *Jane Eyre* and *Wuthering Heights,* was an exchange student from UIR. Yi was in touch with her in Beijing, and then picked her up at the airport in the United States. "I like the peaceful life here," she told me. "I have to spend a lot of time reading, but it's very rewarding. It's a good opportunity to practice English for English majors or those who want to pursue further study in the U.S."

As at other colleges, Chinese students at Marietta mostly socialize with each other. Several told me that they had tried rooming with American students for a semester, but cultural differences and their limited English fluency made it awkward. There's also a financial gap: the Chinese students are generally richer than the Americans, and more likely to own expensive cars, which stirs some resentment. Robert Pastoor, Marietta's former vice president for student life, told me that Americans could request international roommates on the housing form, but the measure "was probably not very effective." Some Chinese students pair up with local "mentor families," who have them over to their houses for dinner or birthday parties, or take them to church.

One taboo topic between Chinese and American students is UIR's reputation for espionage. Americans "who took Mandarin and were involved in Asian studies kind of knew that it was the spy school," Matthew Heinzman, a 2012 graduate in Asian studies and international business, told me. "We didn't really talk much about it with the UIR students. It's kind of a touchy subject."

Indeed, I raised the issue with several Chinese students, and didn't get far. "I'm not very interested in politics," Feng told me.

"UIR students are just normal students," Michelle Yu said. "When they graduate, some work for the . . ." She paused to choose the right word. "Government. Others choose by themselves."

UIR students have also transferred to Marietta. One told me that, as a high school senior, he marked UIR as a college option without knowing much about it. It has first dibs in admissions, and picked him, so he had to go. He spent two years there, studying political science. He gradually realized that he preferred engineering and natural sciences, but UIR's offerings in those fields were meager. After visiting Marietta for the two-week summer program, he decided to go there full-time.

Some of his UIR classmates, he acknowledged, wanted to work for the security ministry. "Most of the students there are the same as anybody else."

After graduating, the bulk of Marietta's Chinese students work for corporations, either in the United States or China. One exception was Wei Tan, a 2004 graduate who joined the Clinton Foundation's China office and served as former president Bill Clinton's interpreter on a 2005 visit to Hunan Province. "It was a lot of talking to do," Tan told Marietta's magazine.

Under Yi's guidance, the UIR-Marietta alliance expanded beyond recruiting. In 2001, UIR began sending a faculty member or two to Marietta each semester. The professors have taught a wide range of subjects, from ballroom dancing to martial arts to Chinese law.

Since 2007, at UIR's request, twenty-three of its students and two professors have visited Marietta each summer, learning about interest groups, public opinion polls, and other real-world influences on U.S. foreign policy. They divide into teams to explore how the United States and China could cooperate on an international issue, such as food safety. In their spare time, they shop at outlet stores and Wal-Mart and sample Americana, from minor-league baseball to the former mayor's pizzeria, Over the Moon.

"It's the coolest thing I do on the side," says Mark Schaefer, the program's academic director. "I want to leave them with a good impression of the U.S. and a more accurate sense of how the U.S. works. Most of them probably go on to work in business. It would be very interesting if someone goes to work as a spy or for the Chinese government. At least they'd have a better understanding of the U.S."

In 2013, UIR opened its own summer program in Beijing, where its undergraduates can choose among forty courses taught primarily in English by foreigners, including about half a dozen Marietta professors. Classes meet for 16, 24, or 32 hours over one to three weeks, with 30 to 60 students in each class. UIR pays teachers about $125 per hour, plus round-trip airfare and free accommodations in spacious, well-equipped apartments.

"The rumor is that the security ministry sponsored the summer program," Jeremy Wang told me. "I go there, I heard some faculty members saying that the security ministry funded the summer school."

The courses fall into two categories: enrichment, or academic. Enrichment courses untangle baseball, country music, and other peculiarities that any student of American culture—especially one who expects to be an intelligence officer in the United States or handle an agent there—should be familiar with. Deborah McNutt, an English as a second language instructor at Marietta, teaches a summer UIR course on "American Culture and Practical American English," such as idioms and slang.

"The goal and learning objectives of this course is to help foreign born people better understand what makes up an American," according to her syllabus, posted on UIR's website. "By understanding the reasons Americans behave as they do, a person from another country will be able to do business with more understanding." The textbook: *What Foreigners Need to Know About America from A to Z.*

For a "brief biography of instructor," McNutt wrote that she is a lifelong Marietta resident. "Although my home is small, for the last two summers I have opened up my home to visiting UIR students and professors as a 'model' of what an American home looks like from the inside."

Professor Jacqueline Khorassani, chair of economics and business at Marietta, offers an academic summer course in her field at UIR. She doesn't care if the security ministry is paying her, "as long as they don't interfere and I have academic freedom to teach what I want to teach," she told me. "I teach economics, no matter where."

Though no one has censored Khorassani's lectures, foreign professors at UIR may not have complete freedom. One of them noticed a "minder" monitoring his class. After showing a video that criticized the Chinese and U.S. governments, the teacher wasn't invited back the next summer.

Xing Li had his heart set on studying foreign languages and international relations in UIR's graduate program. When it spurned him, he went abroad to Aalborg University, a small public school in northern Denmark. Founded in 1974, Aalborg is known for its innovative approach to learning: students work in groups to identify and solve real-life problems.

Xing earned his master's and doctorate there, and joined Aalborg's faculty. UIR noticed his progress. In 2009, at its invitation, he attended its sixtieth anniversary celebration. In 2010, the university that had once rejected him named him an honorary professor. He also was inducted into a talent program for overseas scholars, which paid him for teaching in China.

The courtship bore fruit: a 2011 partnership with Aalborg that gives UIR a foothold in Western Europe, much as Marietta has done in the United States. The biggest difference is that, while UIR sends undergraduates to Marietta, the UIR-Aalborg initiative involves a master's degree program in China and international relations. Twelve graduate students from each university spend the first year in Denmark, and the second in China, earning degrees from both universities. There's also a joint research center located at UIR, and an academic journal that publishes two issues a year, one in English and one in Chinese. Xing Li is editor in chief.

No one at Aalborg questioned the collaboration at first. Denmark is seeking closer ties with China, one of its biggest export markets for everything from pork sausages to insulin. Then, in 2014, a faculty member searching the Internet stumbled on UIR's affiliation with the security ministry. His complaint spurred a debate that raged through Xing's department of culture and global studies, and then the faculty of social sciences, and up to the rector, or president.

The rector consulted the Danish intelligence services, which didn't consider the program a security risk. "I heard they said they were more concerned with Chinese industrial espionage," Ane Bislev, academic coordinator for the joint master's degree, told me. "We know there is cooperation" between UIR and the security ministry. "We don't know the extent. We talk to students about it, and tell them."

While the Ministry of State Security selects some UIR graduates for further intelligence training, most pursue other fields, Xing told me. "As long as the joint program is purely academic and professional, it allows no room for any politicization," he added in an email.

THROUGH A FRIEND of Xing Li, UIR also gained entrée to a public university in the United States. Timothy Shaw, a Canadian who has taught international politics and development at universities in fourteen countries on five continents, spent 2000–2001 as a visiting professor at Aalborg, where he got to know Xing.

In the fall of 2012, Shaw became director of the Global Governance and Human Security doctoral program at the University of Massachusetts Boston. He told me that UMass Boston's future lies in cultivating emerging countries such as China, Brazil, and the United Arab Emirates.

In 2013, he agreed to host two visiting scholars from UIR, Rihan Huang and Wang Hui. It was an easy decision, he said, because it cost UMass Boston nothing. China paid their way. An assistant professor at UIR, where he also earned his bachelor's, master's, and doctorate, Rihan had received government funding to study cybersecurity, with a focus on China and the United States. Wang, an older associate professor, had a Ministry of Education grant to research American perceptions of China's rise.

They chose UMass Boston, Shaw said, because they had heard of him through Xing Li, and because "they know Boston is a very good city, very academic. They also know that if they apply to Harvard, they wouldn't get a reply."

Their duties were up to Shaw, and he didn't give them any. Neither Rihan nor Wang took or taught courses at UMass Boston; indeed, they didn't have offices at the university, and hardly showed up there. Instead, they rode the subway most mornings from the suburban Chinese neighborhood where they lived to other academic institutions in the area: Boston University, Northeastern University, MIT, and especially Harvard's Kennedy School of Government. There they sat in on seminars, conferences, and other events that they had found on the Internet. Later, they might remark to Shaw, "Did you know what was happening at MIT last week?"

Going to conferences is, of course, a favorite academic pastime. It's also a popular way for espionage services to make contacts and gather unclassified but valuable information. "One of the things that the Chinese intelligence system is very good at is understanding how to collect information that doesn't come from documents and you won't read in the media, that you'll only get by showing up at these events, and being in place, and just listening," Mattis told me.

Shaw was pleased that they weren't bothering him. "I was worried they would need a lot of hand-holding," he told me. "They needed no hand-holding. It never occurred to me that they might be spooks, sniffing around. They didn't have the demeanor. I just assumed they were enjoying their six months here in a very different environment. I was just glad they weren't in my hair."

Wang Hui had lunch with another UMass Boston professor to discuss his research topic of U.S. perceptions of China. Wang complained that Hillary Clinton, then secretary of state, only attacked China's human rights record. The professor contradicted him, pointing out that Clinton had chided Israel and other countries. Wang "reflected the Chinese government to a T," the professor told me. "He couldn't have been more establishment."

As Shaw welcomed the visiting scholars, he also persuaded UMass Boston to develop a formal relationship with UIR. Schuyler Korban, vice provost for international affairs, traveled to Beijing in October 2013 and met with UIR president Tao Jian. They exchanged gifts: a Plexiglas pen holder with "UMass Boston" engraved on it for Jian, a cardboard box with packets of green tea for Korban.

Korban, a molecular biologist, said he had "no inkling" of UIR's position in Chinese intelligence. "All I knew was that it had a strong academic reputation," he told me. "We're academics, we look at academic programs. Beyond that, of course, you look at things a little more carefully if you know where the resources are coming from. . . . If I had that knowledge ahead of time, I would have looked at it a little differently."

That December, Shaw went to UIR for a conference, bringing a memo of understanding signed by top UMass administrators. At a ceremony in the Exchange Academic Center on UIR's campus, President Jian, Vice Chancellor Rubai Wang, and international exchange director Hao Min added their signatures. Shaw and Xing Li were on hand as well.

Under the five-year agreement, the universities agreed to promote student and faculty exchanges, "transnational research," and other joint activities. The only follow-up so far is that Shaw taught in UIR's summer program in 2016.

After returning to UIR, Rihan Huang coauthored a 2015 article with UIR graduate and Charhar Institute researcher Xie Tingting, the former Carter Center observer in South Sudan and Emory University visiting scholar, about how China could exploit the European refugee crisis. "Of course, China should seize the opportunity to become an advocate of the international migration governance mechanism and rule maker of the global governance," they wrote.

The article appeared in the *Journal of China and International Relations*—the joint UIR-Aalborg publication edited by Aalborg professor Xing Li.

MARIETTA'S BEIJING OFFICE is tucked in an upscale residential complex a mile from the American embassy, behind a BMW headquarters and a Donna Bella International Beauty Clinic. A security guard monitors the compound entrance. On an impromptu Wednesday afternoon visit in May 2016, children squealed on a shaded playground with a jungle gym and plastic tic-tac-toe boards, and a young woman walked her shih tzu past a basketball court.

No sign identified the college's office on the fifth floor of a twenty-two-story tower with large square windows, and no one responded to initial knocking. On a second try, twenty minutes later, a middle-aged Chinese woman opened the door. Inside, the office looked like any cluttered apartment, with an overstuffed kitchen and a dining room table, except for displays of books about Marietta's history and photos of Professor Xiaoxiong Yi with faculty and students. A framed English-language newspaper clipping hung near the table, with Yi's picture and a headline about improved relations with China.

The woman declined to give her name or be interviewed, saying that her job was to speak only with parents and students—none of whom were there. She said that Yi rarely comes to the office. Asked about Marietta's success in recruiting Chinese students, she downplayed it. "Marietta is just Marietta," she said.

The slow day was no aberration; Marietta isn't attracting as many Chinese as it used to. The number of Chinese students plunged 39 percent, from 144 in fall 2012 to 88 in fall 2015, contributing disproportionately to an overall 17 percent decline in Marietta's enrollment from 1,432 to 1,193 over the same period. The resulting financial crisis precipitated faculty cuts and the resignation of President Joseph Bruno.

Along with greater competition from other U.S. colleges, one factor in this slump may have been a confidential 2009 cable from the U.S. Embassy in Beijing to the State Department in Washington, which WikiLeaks made public in 2011.

Titled "Portrait of Vice President Xi Jinping: 'Ambitious Survivor' of the Cultural Revolution," the 3,735-word cable described "multiple conversations" from 2007 to 2009 between a political officer at the embassy and "a longtime Embassy contact and former close friend" of Xi. The contact described Xi's parents, childhood, Cultural Revolution exile in the countryside, and early career, as well as his personality and political views.

The source clearly knew Xi well, and had ambivalent feelings about him. He portrayed the future president as confident, calculating, focused, and so ambitious that he joined the Communist Party "while his father still languished in a Party prison for alleged political crimes." Peers had underestimated Xi's intelligence, and women found him "boring." Should Xi take power, the informant accurately predicted, he would "aggressively" tackle China's corruption, "perhaps at the expense of the new moneyed class."

The cable didn't name the contact, but it brimmed with clues. Born in 1953, he was the son of "an early revolutionary and contemporary of Mao" who became "the PRC's first Minister of Labor." He attended Beijing Normal University and graduate school in Washington, D.C. Now an American citizen, he "teaches political science at a U.S. university."

These details matched one man: Professor Xiaoxiong Yi. The Marietta recruiter's frank assessment of Xi for the U.S. government spread among Chinese students and prospective applicants, and their parents. "I was told about it by a colleague who had been to China and heard about it from some families," Rees-Miller recalled. After the cable was published, a posting on Chinese social media included Yi's name on a list of suspected U.S. spies, also causing a stir at Marietta. "A lot of students saw it at the time," a former Marietta employee told me.

Especially after Xi became general secretary of China's Communist Party in November 2012, some Chinese families may have avoided Marietta, fearing that Yi's candor might have displeased their country's new leader, or even that Yi was working for U.S. intelligence. "I would be uneasy to send my kid," Professor Tong said. "They think, 'Marietta is the American spy school.'"

The cable didn't deter China's spy school and Marietta from strengthening their bond. In October 2011, they extended their partnership for five more years. In 2015, presidents Bruno and Tao Jian met at UIR, along with Yi and other Marietta officials.

The number of UIR exchange students at Marietta increased from one or two per semester to four in spring 2016 and six that fall. Marietta held an event for Chinese alumni on UIR's campus in April 2016. UIR officials "were generous in offering their campus as a venue," Bruno told me.

Khorassani, Marietta's economics chair, has proposed a dual degree program to boost Chinese enrollment. UIR economics majors would spend two years there and two at Marietta, and receive degrees from both. The Marietta diploma would help them get into U.S. graduate schools, by showing that they could read and write English at a college level, she told me. "I thought it would be something Chinese students are interested in," she said, adding that it hasn't been adopted yet.

"The two institutions are looking at some dual degree options but as of now they are in the very early stages," spokesman Perry told me.

Following his students' presentation at the McDonough Center about relations between the United States, China, and Russia, I chatted in the hallway with Yingjie Liu, the visiting scholar from UIR. After initial pleasantries—Yingjie said he liked Marietta because its fresh air gave him relief from Beijing's smog—I asked him why the students never mentioned human rights or cyber-spying.

"The topics are already set in several areas," he said.

"By whom?"

"The students."

Mystified, I changed the topic to UIR's relationship with Chinese intelligence. While the university receives funding from the security ministry, its support from the education ministry has increased in recent years, he said.

"It's just a very normal college," he told me. "Like Marietta."

SHANGHAIED

During the summer after his freshman year in college, Glenn Duffie Shriver fell in love with China. And, though he didn't speak its language yet, China seemed to fall in love with him.

Shriver was one of the youngest of eighteen Grand Valley State University students from western Michigan's conservative cornfields, plunged for six eye-opening weeks in 2001 into a vast and alien country. "There were a number of us who were just fascinated with China," another student recalled. "A lot of us, Glenn included, were on a 'high' or sensory overload, especially the first week or so. It was like you couldn't get enough of it. Everywhere you turned, you were blown away."

Based at East China Normal University, amid the throngs and skyscrapers of Shanghai, they studied Chinese philosophy, hung out with Chinese students eager to practice English, and dined on snake and jellyfish. They made excursions to the Great Wall and to Beijing, where a traditional Chinese healer examined them and deduced from the warmth of their livers that several students—including Shriver—were drinking too much. They could have told him that.

On another side trip, they stopped at a rural one-room elementary school in southwest China where the children had never seen foreigners. The Americans taught them to dance the Hokey Pokey, and Grand Valley student Michael McCann pulled out a video camera.

"Some of these kids had never seen their own reflection except in a pool of water," he recalled. "I don't think they had mirrors in the village. I flipped the viewfinder over and let them see themselves. They realized it was them. They were waving at the camera and then hid from it." Before leaving, the American students donated two hundred dollars to the school, the equivalent of three years' funding.

Eight thousand miles and an ocean away from home, Shriver felt—and sometimes acted like—a rock star. He trash-talked Chinese opponents in pickup basketball games on East China Normal's courts. He reveled in attention from Chinese women, and boasted about his conquests. He dominated class discussions, even when he had no idea what he was talking about. Older, more knowledgeable students laughed at him, and told him to shut up, but he didn't.

Attending an ethnic minority cultural pageant, the handsome Shriver was selected from the audience to wear onstage the traditional garb of the Yi people, who live in the mountains of southwest China. "He looked like a dignified young prince," said Grand Valley professor Peimin Ni, who led the Grand Valley group.

Shriver was always ready for adventure. One evening in Beijing, he, McCann, and two other students decided to roam the capital's back alleys, with no particular destination. "We didn't want to see tourist things," McCann recalled. "We wanted to see what Beijing was really like. We started wandering around the streets, found a restaurant, found a bar, met up with two Russian guys. Found some karaoke bars. Had a great, great night. Glenn was tearing it up on karaoke. He loved to drink, to sing, to have fun."

One day, he went too far. The Grand Valley group was touring the Stone Forest, a national park featuring enormous formations of limestone that tower over the hills of Yunnan Province like medieval battlements. Other students heeded signs prohibiting climbing in the Stone Forest, which is sacred to the local tribespeople. Not Shriver. He clambered all over the rocks, risking his limbs and the university's reputation, until Professor Ni warned him to stop.

Two Chinese girls hung around with Shriver and his friend Michael Weits. When the program ended, they rode with the group to the airport, and "shed some tears over our leaving," Weits recalled. By then Shriver had resolved to learn the language and return to China to study and work. Later, when he fulfilled that vow, he would again stray from the path of safety: this time, into the embrace of Chinese intelligence.

"When I saw the news, I had to chuckle," one of his Grand Valley study-abroad companions told me in 2015. "I'm like, 'I could see it happening.' If it was anyone in our group, it would be him. He seemed quite confident. He didn't necessarily care what other people thought. He walked to his own drum. There were some times on the trip when I felt like, 'Seriously, let's cut with the antics.'"

IN SPYING, AS in sports, the home team enjoys the advantage. Knowing the native language, culture, and geography, the buildings and the byways, makes it easier to blend in. There's no risk of being caught by the authorities: instead, their cooperation can facilitate covert operations.

That's why U.S. universities become more vulnerable to espionage when they're transplanted overseas via study-abroad programs, branch campuses, research centers, and the like. Even if the administrators and faculty are mostly Americans, the support staff—janitors, cafeteria workers, librarians, mail carriers—tends to be local. Restricting foreign students' access to sensitive research, hard enough in the United States, becomes that much more difficult in their own countries. And if U.S. intelligence wants to use an overseas campus for spying, as the FBI's Dianne Mercurio proposed to the University of South Florida, it risks exposure and embarrassment.

American universities haven't let such worries interfere with international expansion. Touting its "dynamic global network," New York University has opened degree-granting campuses in Shanghai and Abu Dhabi, along with study-abroad centers from Buenos Aires to Prague, Accra to Tel Aviv. By requiring its Shanghai students to spend at least one semester at another NYU campus, including Manhattan, and encouraging Abu Dhabi students to do so, NYU may unlock a gateway to the United States and other countries for spies.

Not to be outdone, Cornell, Northwestern, Texas A&M, Georgetown, Carnegie Mellon, and Virginia Commonwealth universities all have branches in Qatar. Carnegie Mellon also offers degrees with local institutions in Rwanda, Singapore, Bologna, Nanjing, and South Korea. The University of Chicago's Booth School of Business boasts campuses in the

United Kingdom and Hong Kong. Duke University's campus in Kun-shan, China, offered its first classes in August 2014; two months later, Yale opened a center in Beijing as a "convening space and intellectual hub for all of Yale's activities in China."

The number of U.S. students who travel abroad for academic credit more than tripled from 1993–94 to 2013–14. In 2006, Goucher College in Maryland became the first liberal arts school in the United States to require study abroad for undergraduates. China is the fifth most popular destination, and first outside Western Europe. President Obama's five-year goal, announced in 2009, of sending 100,000 U.S. students to China was met in 2014, counting noncredit and high school students. In 2015, the State Department opened a study-abroad office to promote participation by minority and low-income students. More than 350 U.S. colleges and universities have joined an Institute of International Education initiative to boost the number of Americans studying abroad to 600,000 by 2020.

Although study abroad undoubtedly has educational value, it can also benefit U.S. universities' bottom line. Many private U.S. universities require a student who attends an institution overseas for a semester or a year to pay their regular tuition; they then reimburse the other school. If their tuition is higher than the foreign university's tab, as is usually the case, they pocket the difference. Moreover, at some U.S. schools, American students forfeit their university-funded scholarships while they're abroad. Finally, U.S. universities can enroll and house more students, betting that a percentage of their enrollment will be sojourning overseas.

Branch campuses may also be lucrative. Not only are they often staffed by low-salaried adjuncts rather than expensive tenured professors, but—like football and baseball stadiums in the United States—they may enjoy tax breaks and other perks from grateful hosts. In both Abu Dhabi and Qatar, the royal families are bankrolling the branch campuses.

Most academic expatriates are too engrossed in their new surroundings to wonder if a particularly affable or generous foreigner might be a spy. "If I'm in a university in Florence, the last thing on my mind is that the Russians are targeting me," says a retired CIA officer. "The better thing to do is drink wine and go to school and enjoy being twenty-two." Students "don't ask why Sergei wants to buy me drinks or invites me to take a trip with him."

Occasionally, though, the approaches are too blatant to ignore. A graduate student at Columbia University, who also taught at a U.S. military academy, was leading a group of cadets to China in 2015 when intelligence agents there tried to recruit him. "They peeled him off the group," a person familiar with the incident told me. They explained that if he was ever dissatisfied, he should let them know.

At one university in northeast China, the administrator in charge of foreign faculty arranged in 2006–07 for a young American who taught English there to earn extra money by tutoring an older Chinese man. The lessons consisted of conversation in English while the middle-aged pupil escorted the American to tourist sites and fancy restaurants with "real and fake plants . . . poisonous snakes in cages, and octopuses in tanks—to order," the teacher wrote in emails home. The "50-year-old 'sugar daddy,'" he realized, was "trying to buy me through trips and dinners."

Once, a friend of the student joined them for a multicourse banquet. Describing himself as a security official, he denounced the Falun Gong, echoing the Chinese Communist Party's attacks on the religious group as a dangerous cult that undermines social stability. Then he asked the American to help Chinese authorities combat the threat. When he returned home, would he gather information about the Falun Gong exile community in the United States? As a reward, the official promised a gem—literally. "He would give my mom some jade," the American told me.

The teacher was "freaked out" but didn't want to be rude. "I didn't really give them a straight answer," he said. "I smiled and nodded and tried to disassociate myself." He quit his job and fled to another Chinese university, hundreds of miles away, but his ex-pupil pursued him, showing up one day with another man in the lobby of the teacher's dormitory. "He had invested a significant amount of money and time into cultivating me," the American said. "I had to go awkwardly confront them and awkwardly refuse to do anything."

Michigan State University president Lou Anna K. Simon contacted the CIA in late 2009 with an urgent question. The school's campus in Dubai needed a bailout and an unlikely savior had stepped forward: a Dubai-based company that offered to provide money and students.

Simon was tempted. She also worried that the company, which had investors from Iran and wanted to recruit students from there, might be a front for the Iranian government, she said. If so, an agreement could violate federal trade sanctions and invite enemy spies. The CIA couldn't confirm that the company wasn't an arm of Iran's government. Simon rejected the offer and shut down undergraduate programs in Dubai, at a loss of $3.7 million.

CONSCIOUSLY OR NOT, intelligence services often engage in what's known as "mirror-imaging": that is, assuming that their counterparts around the world think and behave the way they do. Thus countries that send students and researchers to spy on the United States expect it to do the same to them. While mirror-imaging can be a mistake, because every nation is different, such suspicions often snag efforts by American universities to establish campuses or conduct research overseas. And once those branches or laboratories open in China, Russia, or the Middle East, the host country's intelligence service is likely to regard them as potential outlets for U.S. espionage, and try to infiltrate them.

China has long perceived the CIA's hand in U.S. academic expansion there. The staffing of the first American campus in China stoked these fears. In 1986, Johns Hopkins's School of Advanced International Studies—the same school where Marta Rita Velázquez had recruited Ana Belén Montes to spy for Cuba not long before—established the campus as a joint project with Nanjing University.

For American co-director, Johns Hopkins chose Leon Slawecki, cultural affairs officer at the U.S. embassy in Beijing and, earlier, at the U.S. consulate in Hong Kong. In November 1984, with plans for the center already under way, a Chinese-language Hong Kong newspaper, the *Oriental Daily,* reported that Slawecki worked for the CIA. Slawecki told me that the allegation was false, and that the newspaper leaped to the wrong conclusion, perhaps because he had been one of the first U.S. officials in Hong Kong to cultivate communist contacts, or because a Beijing-based CIA officer had posed in the boondocks as a cultural officer.

Soon after the article's publication, Slawecki showed it to the Chinese co-director, Wang Zhigang, and assured him that he was never a spy. "I trusted him," Wang said. "We had very good working relations, and we have been friends all these years."

Nonetheless, an atmosphere of mutual wariness prevailed at the new center. Some Americans believed that the Chinese were watching them. "When service desks were moved without warning to the end of each dormitory corridor, Americans concluded it was to surveil them better," Slawecki later wrote. "The Chinese explained it was to serve them better."

"Every Chinese person our folks came in contact with in China, we assumed was a spy, whether they were students or a cabdriver or a person cleaning the buildings," recalled Lloyd Armstrong, dean of arts and sciences at Johns Hopkins from 1987 to 1993. "I'm positive they thought all of us were spies."

The Chinese tapped the center's phone lines and read its mail. They also continued to suspect that Slawecki worked for the CIA. When he stepped down after two years, they tried to figure out who would assume that role. They settled on Professor Larry Engelmann. An expert on the Vietnam War, Engelmann had recently visited Vietnam, which was feuding with China, and had brought boxes of documents marked "classified" with him to Nanjing. They had been declassified, but the Chinese authorities didn't realize it.

Meihong Xu, a Chinese military intelligence officer, enrolled at the center with orders to investigate Engelmann. She took his courses, became friendly with him, and took advantage of occasional times when he naïvely left her alone in his office or apartment to read his papers, letters, and diary. She soon realized that he wasn't a spy. Meihong, who was married, also fell in love with him. Aghast, the People's Liberation Army spirited her out of the center, interrogated her, stripped her of her rank as a first lieutenant, and discharged her. At the insistence of the Chinese, and over the American faculty's protests, Engelmann was also tossed out of Hopkins-Nanjing. "The Chinese wanted him out for having a relationship with a married PLA officer," said Richard Gaulton, who succeeded Slawecki as the American co-director. Engelmann and Meihong married in 1990 and moved to California, but a divorce in 1999 spoiled the Hollywood ending.

As the U.S. academic presence in China expanded, so did Chinese scrutiny. Before Eric Shepherd became Dajin Peng's rival at South Florida, he was the program officer for US/China Links, an initiative funded by the Pentagon and U.S. intelligence to teach Chinese to young Americans and plug them into Chinese business, academia, and government. It aimed to develop a cadre of Americans who understood Chinese decision making.

The program drew attention from China's security services, which likely viewed it as a U.S. plot to infiltrate key institutions. Shepherd, who lived in China, was followed, and his emails and phone calls were monitored. "I had Chinese friends distance themselves from me," he told me. He was careful about what he said and wrote, and after six months the surveillance diminished.

If visiting American professors have any links to the Pentagon or CIA, Chinese intelligence pumps them for information. "From the moment I land in China, the minders are after me," said Indiana University political scientist Sumit Ganguly, an expert on India and Pakistan who has been to China four or five times. They usually pose as advanced graduate students or affiliates of an institute; once, when he taught at prestigious Fudan University in Shanghai, "there was actually a minder in the classroom.

"They badger you. Sometimes it's done more subtly, sometimes it's very heavy-handed. 'Do you think there's going to be an imminent settlement of the China-India border dispute? Do you think the U.S. will sell ballistic missiles to India?' They think I know things." Ganguly has held security clearances, and the Chinese "might surmise I have access to classified information."

"I can't stand it," he added. "I don't know how my colleagues who are China experts stand it. I find it very uncomfortable. I am not a spy. I am a professor who happens to consult for American intelligence and defense agencies." Ganguly has reported the hounding and the minders' names to U.S. intelligence.

GLENN SHRIVER INHERITED his energy, swagger, and iconoclastic streak from his father. Six foot two and two hundred pounds, with blue eyes and brown hair, Jon Michael Shriver was strikingly handsome, and had a certain charisma. He grew up in a prosperous family, and, like so many teenagers in the 1960s, rebelled against parental and government authority. He married in 1972 but was arrested a year later and sentenced in Richmond City Circuit Court to ten years in prison for dealing heroin. He took college English courses in prison and became lifelong friends with his teacher. While he was behind bars, his first son—Jon Michael Shriver Jr.—was born, and his wife divorced him.

Paroled in 1980, he was married again in April 1981, in Richmond, Virginia, to Michigan native Karen Sue Dawson. Seven months later, they had a son, whom they named after his maternal grandfather, Glenn Duffie Dawson, a U.S. Navy veteran. The couple split up in September 1983, and Karen returned to Michigan with the toddler.

"Being married to Jon would be difficult, from a woman's point of view," says Linda Kimble, a family friend and retired high school English teacher in North Carolina. "I think the world of him. He's good-looking, he's interesting to talk with, enjoys life. But he demands a lot out of life, and he's constantly on the go."

The 1988 divorce judgment gave Karen custody of Glenn, and required Jon Michael to pay fifty-six dollars a week in child support, which he often didn't. Although the Michigan court sought to garnish his wages from his employers, Century Data Systems of Raleigh, North Carolina, and W. Harold Pettus Metal of Drakes Branch, Virginia, Jon Michael owed $2,297 by August 1993. The court issued a warrant for his arrest. In 1998 it held him in contempt for nonpayment, but dismissed his debt at the request of Karen Shriver, who was by then remarried. Jon Michael eventually went into the antiques business, restoring and selling old furniture.

Glenn visited his father and half brother during summers and Christmas vacations. He attended junior high and the first two years of high school in the city of Wyoming, Michigan, the largest suburb of Grand Rapids, where he and his mother lived in a modest bungalow. As a high school junior, he traveled to Barcelona on a study-abroad program and learned Spanish.

"I knew early on that this country was going to need people who knew a multitude of languages" and were "able to work in a multicultural work force," Shriver said later. "And that's what I set out to achieve, and I did."

Gregarious and intellectually curious, the teenage Shriver conversed easily and on equal terms with adults. "He wanted to learn as much as he could," Kimble recalled. "He was very approachable. You walk into a crowd of four or five people, and he'd be the one to make you feel very welcome. . . . I know he had big plans for himself. He wanted to make a difference."

His mother married Luis Chavez, a Guatemalan immigrant, in 1997. The family moved the next year to a one-story tan ranch house in another Grand Rapids suburb, Jenison. She and Chavez, who worked for a trucking company, divorced in 2003.

As a senior at Jenison High School, Glenn impressed Stephanie Wagener, a classmate in world history. "He knew all the answers, and I was really jealous," she told me. "Everybody liked him. He was funny, and smart. . . . He just thought he knew everything. But he did. I thought he was going places. I guess he went the wrong places."

He enrolled at Grand Valley State, where his mother has worked in student accounts for more than thirty years. Established in 1960, Grand Valley had 18,579 students in 2000; its enrollment has since risen to more than 25,000. Amway cofounder Richard DeVos, father-in-law of U.S. Secretary of Education Betsy DeVos, has fueled Grand Valley's expansion, having donated $36 million to the university in the past 30 years.

Professor Ni had established Grand Valley's summer program in China in 1995 but struggled to attract students. He recruited them at study-abroad fairs, in history classes, and by word of mouth. "It's even hard for students here to think about going to China," he told me. "Too remote, too hard to imagine." Already an experienced traveler, Glenn could imagine it, and signed up. Professor Geling Shang, the group's co-leader, warned students at orientation to avoid drugs, prostitutes, and politics. The threat of espionage wasn't on anyone's mind.

While in Shanghai, Shriver and several other Grand Valley students visited an elementary school where an American was teaching English. The teacher told them that they could follow his example and earn enough to "live like a king" in Shanghai, McCann recalled. "A lot of us felt like that would be really amazing." Several, including Shriver, seized the chance to teach at the school for a short time, he added.

"Glenn was like, 'Yeah, I'm going to come back and do this,' " said another member of the group, Jill Gunnerson.

Grand Valley allows students with at least a 2.5 grade point average to spend their junior years abroad, and Shriver returned to East China Normal University in 2002–03. There he improved his Mandarin and acted in a Chinese-language beer advertisement that aired on video bill-boards on campus.

"He was driving a convertible, holding a beer," Professor Shang said. "Every time we take the elevator, he showed up with a beer. I always pointed to him with our students: he's a GVSU guy, now he's on a commercial."

Back at Grand Valley for his senior year, Shriver took modern Chinese history with Professor Patrick Shan. Shriver "offered very penetrating remarks" and his essays were well organized and insightful, Shan said. After class, he and Shan would stroll back to the professor's office, speaking Chinese so that Shriver could polish his language skills.

"He was such a talented student, he could have been a scholar," Shan recalled. "He is very confident. Sometimes you could use the word *over-confident*. He talked a lot in class. I still have a vivid memory of his participation."

After Shriver earned his degree in international relations in 2004, he told Shan that he was interested in graduate school. Shan recommended him, but Shriver was rejected. He headed back to Shanghai.

INTELLIGENCE COMMITTEE CHAIRMAN David Boren left a meeting about stockpiling minerals and made his way to the Senate chamber. How much more important it would be, he mused, to create a strategic reserve of human talent that understood foreign languages and cultures. So many intelligence failures over the years stemmed from American ignorance of the world. He scrawled the title of an amendment on a torn brown envelope and sent it to the floor, squelching the Senate parliamentarian's protests that it wasn't in proper form. The Oklahoma senator then pushed it into law in 1991, without any hearings, by holding the entire intelligence budget hostage.

Thus he created what are today named after him: the Boren Awards. Funded by congressional appropriation through the defense and intelligence budgets, and overseen by a board that includes the director of the CIA, the program provides as much as $20,000 to undergraduates and $30,000 to graduate students to live abroad and learn less commonly taught languages spoken in regions critical to U.S. security. Afterward, recipients must work in national security for at least a year, with priority given to the Pentagon, State Department, Department of Homeland Security, and the intelligence community.

"The most important thing you can have is a group of highly intelligent people who are extremely well educated, who understand the cultures, who speak the languages, who can go into those countries and be advocates for the United States, run our programs, collect intelligence, do all the things we need to do for national security," Boren said. In other words, today's students abroad would be tomorrow's spooks.

That notion caused an uproar among academic specialists on Africa, Latin America, and the Middle East who feared for their own credibility and their students' safety. Many governments on whose goodwill they depended for their research detested the CIA and had no desire to incubate American spies. Their scholarly associations warned that "linking university-based research to U.S. national security agencies, even indirectly, will restrict our already narrow research opportunities; it will endanger the physical safety of scholars and our students studying abroad; and it will jeopardize the cooperation and safety of those we study and collaborate with in these regions."

Although the service requirement was originally looser, and the law prohibited recipients from gathering intelligence for the U.S. government during their Boren stint, many professors refused to recommend students for Boren Awards, and prominent universities debated whether to support the program. The University of California, Berkeley, deferred participation, while the University of Minnesota and University of Pennsylvania warned prospective applicants about the risks.

After Boren resigned from the Senate in 1994 to become president of the University of Oklahoma, his brainchild teetered on the brink of extinction. "I have no nerve endings left," Robert Slater told me over coffee in January 2016 at a Panera Bread in a Washington, D.C., suburb. From 1995 to 2010, Slater served as director of the National Security Education Program, which oversees Boren and other language-training programs bankrolled by the Pentagon and intelligence. "We were always one *Post* story away from being done: 'Boren fellow arrested in Russia on spy charges.'

"Everything was done that could possibly be done to protect academic integrity," he continued. "There's no way to mollify these people. Younger scholars who didn't share these views wouldn't risk their careers. . . . Why is it bad if a bright kid, who studies in Lebanon and learns Arabic, comes back and works for the CIA?"

The Boren program avoided scandal and gradually gained acceptance, aided by the study-abroad boom, and academia's warming to intelligence agencies after the 9/11 attacks. The awards have become increasingly prestigious and selective: in 2014, only 271 of 1,365 applicants, or 19.9 percent, were chosen.

Some critics remained. While American University in Washington, D.C., led the nation with twenty-three Boren recipients in 2014, its executive director of study-abroad programs, Sara Dumont, advocates warning host families abroad that they're sheltering future spies. "I feel like telling these families, watch out for these students," she said. "Later on, they may try to use you or your family." When "their clear career goal is to be a spy for the CIA, I worry about the ethics of what we do in study abroad."

Of Boren alumni in federal jobs, 7.5 percent work for the CIA or other intelligence agencies, well behind the State Department (34 percent) and Defense (22 percent), according to a 2014 survey. That likely understates the true percentage, as one would expect many spies either not to answer or to use their employment cover. David J. Comp, who advised Boren candidates at the University of Chicago from 2000 to 2011, told me that two-thirds of them wanted to parlay the awards into intelligence jobs.

"The program was a life-changing experience that . . . broadened my world perspective and set me on a course to accept intelligence agency rotational assignments overseas," one respondent to the 2014 survey wrote.

More Boren alumni would likely have joined the intelligence community if the agencies had moved more aggressively to hire them. Two CIA offices offered analyst positions to Steven A. Cook after his 1999 fellowship. But the security clearance and other red tape took so long that he opted for the Council on Foreign Relations, where he is a senior fellow for Middle East and Africa studies. "The CIA would have been a blast," Cook told me. "It would have made for a fun career. It also seemed, given my skills and background, a natural place to go."

Fears that the intelligence connection endangered Boren recipients were overblown, Cook said. "In Egypt and Turkey, where I went to do field research, if I said I have a Boren fellowship, nobody would have known what I was talking about."

As the Borens and the other National Security Education Programs become more recognized, though, some of those early forebodings are starting to be fulfilled. Michael Nugent, Slater's successor as NSEP director, was expected to address a group of university presidents in October 2013 about "a recent incident with students under his program being aggressively targeted by a hostile intel service," namely Iranian intelligence, and "the choices he had to make," according to the meeting's agenda.

Then, in 2014, two Boren fellows apparently alarmed Russian intelligence by visiting U.S. consulates there and by sending emails to .gov and .mil domains. Local intelligence assumed that they were seeking instructions for espionage. Actually, the students were starting to look for national security jobs, although, under the Boren rules, they were supposed to finish their fellowships and return home first. One, a former U.S. military officer, hoped to rejoin the armed forces; the other wanted to work in the federal government. Both were studying Russian language at a state university in northwest Russia.

Russian agents checked the Boren website and learned about the service requirement, which raised their suspicions. They interviewed the fellows in a dormitory room, asking about their careers, why they had gone to the consulate, whether they had security clearances, and much more.

They threatened to detain one of the Boren fellows, according to a person familiar with the incident. "You're scheduled to leave here tomorrow," the agents told him. "If you want that to happen, you'll talk to us now, you'll tell us the truth. We don't like people who mislead us."

After two hours of questioning, he was let go, and returned to his room "a little shaken." At the airport the next morning, his computer was seized.

Perhaps on the theory that the two were part of a spy ring, Russian intelligence interviewed a third Boren fellow in the same region. He was questioned twice in ten days by a total of three agents from the Federal Security Service, or FSB, successor to the Soviet Union's KGB.

"They thought I was some sort of spy," this Boren recipient told me. "They openly came out and asked me more than once, 'Are you working for the government? Are you working for the security service?'"

The agents asked him about his dissertation on the Russian navy but "seemed to lose interest in it once they realized it was purely historical." They examined the contacts on his cell phone. Then they grabbed a blank sheet, drew up a nondisclosure agreement, and ordered him to sign it. When he balked, saying it had no legal standing, "they threatened that they'd say I cooperated even if I didn't, and that would prevent me from getting a job down the road."

He signed. In August 2014, the Boren program quietly pulled out of Russia. Recipients were no longer permitted to study there; they now learned Russian in neighboring countries such as Kazakhstan.

WITH HIS APTITUDE for languages, Glenn Shriver could have earned a Boren and ended up working for U.S. intelligence. Instead, he went the other way.

Hard-pressed for money in Shanghai, he answered an ad in October 2004 on an English-language website that offered payment for political essays by people with a background in East Asian studies.

A young woman who called herself "Amanda" contacted him and gave him $120 to write about tensions between the United States and China over Taiwan and North Korea. She praised his work and assigned him more papers, and he soon regarded her as a close friend. Eventually she introduced him to her associates, "Mr. Wu" and "Mr. Tang," in a hotel penthouse suite. They handed him business cards with only their names and phone numbers listed.

Although they posed as employees of Shanghai's municipal government, Amanda, Wu, and Tang worked for China's foreign intelligence service. The attractive woman, the paid essays, the business cards that didn't list an employer, the hotel rendezvous: all were classic spycraft, used by intelligence agencies worldwide to entice students and researchers. "Businessmen don't meet in hotel rooms, spies do," says former FBI supervisory special agent David Major, founder and president of the CI Centre, a counterintelligence training company. "Beware of writing a paper and meeting in hotel rooms."

Good-looking, personable, and multilingual, Shriver likely impressed the Chinese agents as a human missile that they could guide into the highest reaches of the U.S. government. "Shriver was able to present fairly well, he was relatively articulate, he spoke more than passable Mandarin, and he clearly showed an affinity for 'things Chinese,'" Philip Boycan, a retired CIA counterintelligence officer who worked on Chinese matters for eleven years and investigated the Shriver case, told me. "Shriver was, on the surface, a nice-looking, seemingly all-American kid. . . . To the Chinese intelligence way of thinking, Shriver would be a good candidate to attempt to penetrate the U.S. government because he is not ethnic Chinese." Chinese intelligence "undoubtedly thought that Shriver would be less likely to fall under suspicion and scrutiny than a person who had been born on the mainland, or for that matter, even a native-born U.S. citizen who was ethnic Chinese."

Shriver also "had no regular employment or means of support and obviously needed a way to generate some income," Boycan added. He "presented a unique opportunity" to Chinese intelligence because of "his accessibility, financial vulnerability, and, in my view, his personality traits. . . . He was motivated by money and, in my opinion, susceptible to the ego-stroking that he undoubtedly received from the Chinese."

Expressing a desire to help promising young Americans with living expenses, Wu and Tang gave Shriver more cash. Over a series of meetings, which they asked him to keep confidential, they inquired about his career plans and encouraged him to work for a U.S. government agency, especially the State Department or CIA. If he did, they said, "we can be close friends."

Gradually, Shriver realized who they really were. Just to make sure, he asked them, "What exactly do you guys want?"

"If it's possible, we want you to get us some secrets or classified information," they told him.

Shriver didn't balk. Money was the primary lure; it's also possible that, subconsciously, he sought to please his antiestablishment father by outfoxing the U.S. government. In April 2005, he took the exam in Shanghai to become a State Department foreign-service officer. Although he failed, Wu and Tang gave him $10,000. A year later, he flunked again, but received $20,000. Such up-front payments are "unheard-of" for Chinese intelligence, Major says. "That shows how aggressive they're becoming." His test scores indicated that Shriver perhaps wasn't as clever as he considered himself, or as capable of matching wits with China's intelligence service. He didn't realize that it now owned him. If he had landed a job with the State Department or CIA, and then refused to spy for the Chinese, they could have blackmailed him.

Shriver took a job with a tattoo supply company in Los Angeles. In communicating with his Chinese handlers, he adopted a pseudonym, Du Fei, which was a common Chinese name as well as a pun on his middle name, Duffie. In June 2007, he applied online to the CIA's clandestine service. That September, he flew to Shanghai, where he told Chinese intelligence officers about his CIA application and requested $40,000, which they supplied in U.S. currency. He understood the unspoken deal: if he succeeded in penetrating the CIA and supplying classified information to the Chinese, they would continue to pay him.

"It was very unusual and lavish for a PRC intelligence service to spend the amount that they did on Shriver," Boycan said. "If Shriver had not asked, I personally doubt that the Chinese would have given him that much at one meeting. The fact that they did, however, suggests the potentially high value—and probability of success—that the Chinese ascribed to the Shriver operation."

Shriver strapped the $40,000 to his belly and smuggled it through customs on his return to the United States. He gave part of the money to his father and brother, describing it as profit from an English-language school he had opened.

Shriver didn't hear from the CIA for more than two years. In the meantime, he relocated to South Korea, where he taught English. In December 2009, the CIA got in touch with him, inviting him to Washington the next spring for what it described as final employment processing. It's likely that the CIA revived his application after so long, and hinted that it was planning to hire him, because it had been tipped off about his relationship with Chinese intelligence. The agency was baiting a trap.

Shriver fell for it. Amanda had asked him to meet her in Shanghai or Hong Kong, but he put her off, figuring that federal agents conducting his background investigation would be curious about a trip to China. "I am making some progress for us," he wrote to her. "But right now is a bad time for me to come visit. Maybe you can wait six months. In six months I will have good news"—in other words, CIA employment.

From June 7 to June 14, 2010, the CIA interviewed Shriver. Asked in polygraph tests if he had ever been approached by, been affiliated with, or accepted money from a foreign intelligence service, he lied each time. Next it was the FBI's turn. As he was driving away from CIA headquarters, the FBI called and told him to pull off at the next exit and go to a hotel. There its agents confronted him, and he confessed.

The bureau wasn't quite sure how to deal with him. Unlike moles caught inside the target government, Shriver never got that far. Despite accepting more than $70,000 from Chinese intelligence, he had no security clearance, never gained access to the U.S. intelligence community or any classified secrets, and claimed he never meant to betray his country. "My father says, if I give you a thousand dollars to buy drugs, but you don't buy drugs, you didn't commit a crime," he told one FBI agent. (Shriver, or his father, was mistaken; it could still be a criminal conspiracy.)

U.S. intelligence considered using Shriver to spy on his contacts in China. "Recruiting Shriver as a double agent was suggested by some, which I argued strenuously against," the CIA's Boycan said. To deter further attempts to penetrate the CIA, Boycan felt, Shriver should be imprisoned. "I also believed that the utility of operating Shriver against the Chinese would be marginal."

While the FBI and CIA deliberated, Shriver made up their minds for them. On June 22, 2010, he was about to fly from Detroit to South Korea when FBI agents boarded the plane and arrested him. He pleaded guilty in October 2010 to conspiring to commit espionage for a foreign government and was sentenced to four years in prison.

"I think I was motivated by greed," he told the judge at his sentencing in January 2011. "I mean, you know, large stacks of money in front of me. And them saying, 'Hey, don't worry, you don't have to do anything for it.'"

THE MORE THE FBI and CIA examined the Shriver case, the more alarmed they became. Shriver was bright and talented, but no more so than many young Americans in China. Perhaps Chinese intelligence was making overtures to them as well. Indeed, eight to ten other American students in China reported that a woman matching Amanda's description, but using a different name, had approached them, too. The male students found her alluring, and at least one female student thought the woman "was hitting on her," a person familiar with the Shriver investigation told me. The Ministry of State Security, this person said, had created a separate unit to recruit Western students in China.

"I suspect other people than Shriver responded to the ad," another insider said. "There was something about him they found attractive.

Someone just graduated from college, incredibly young, impressionable, and not otherwise employed. That's what makes this case so interesting. It's not like he was a U.S. government employee and traveled over there. It's the fact you have a blank slate with which you ultimately can infiltrate a government service."

U.S. investigators even suspected collusion at Grand Valley State. One of Shriver's companions in the summer program at East China Normal also applied to the CIA later, as well as the FBI. The bureau wondered if program organizers might be identifying susceptible students with an interest in U.S. government service and steering them to China for recruitment. After Shriver's arrest, both professors Ni and Shang were interviewed by the FBI and searched as they passed through customs with their study-abroad acolytes.

"There were a few years that, every time I go through U.S. customs, I get checked thoroughly," Ni told me. "They open everything, all my luggage, even my handbag, open my folders and flip through the pages and ask what is this, what is that." Once, leaving the United States via San Francisco, "I had all the students' information and material in my bag. They asked me why did I bring copies of students' passports. I told them it was just in case students lost their passports.

"I asked the FBI guy, he came later and talked to me again about the Shriver case, he said it's just a random check, it's unrelated. Personally, I don't think it's a random check."

Customs inspectors were "so rude," Shang said. "They opened everything, even the syllabus." Like Ni, Shang complained to FBI agents about his treatment. Shang told them that "both Ni and I were dissidents in China. So we are fighting for democracy, we are fighting for freedom. The way we teach our students is to let them experience the actual life, the actual China, to let them make their own judgment."

Neither professor was charged with any wrongdoing, and immigration authorities eventually stopped hassling them.

THE BUREAU DECIDED to alert universities nationwide that foreign intelligence agencies could be recruiting their students abroad. Agent Thomas Barlow, who had elicited Shriver's confession, gave more than twenty talks about the case, primarily on college campuses. The FBI also hired a production company, Rocket Media Group, to make a film about it. *Game of Pawns: The Glenn Duffie Shriver Story* is a twenty-eight-minute docudrama with actors playing Amanda, Wu, Tang, and Shriver, who is both protagonist and narrator. A *dizi,* or Chinese transverse flute, warbles in the background.

"There is an old Chinese proverb," it begins, in a manner unfortunately reminiscent of the old Charlie Chan movies. "Life is like a game of chess, changing with each move. And to win the game, you must often sacrifice your pawns."

It repeatedly returns to the chess metaphor. "Do you think the Chinese would have just let you say no?" an FBI agent is shown asking Shriver. "Don't you think they documented every meeting you had with them? If you didn't give them what they wanted willingly, they would have used those recordings to blackmail you. You were just a pawn, one of many."

As the credits roll at the end of the film, Shriver himself addresses viewers from prison. "Recruitment's going on, don't fool yourself," he says. "The recruitment is active, and the target is young people. Throw lots of money at them, see what happens . . . Espionage is a very big deal, a very big deal. You're dealing with people's lives, and that's why it's such a big deal."

Although FBI invitations to the January 2013 premiere of *Game of Pawns* billed it as a "compelling true story," the movie was partly propaganda. It fictionalized two important elements of Shriver's saga in an effort to persuade students that it could happen to them, too. First, it left the impression that Shriver was in college when China recruited him, rather than a recent graduate. Second, the cinematic Shriver took far longer than the actual one to catch on that Chinese intelligence was recruiting him. He was more naïve and less cocky than his real-life counterpart.

"We endeavored to make Shriver better and more sympathetic than he was," screenwriter Sean Paul Murphy told me.

The bureau invited members of its higher education advisory board to the premiere and urged colleges nationwide to show the movie to students traveling abroad. However, instead of awakening universities to the threat of espionage, the FBI's energetic promotion of *Game of Pawns* revived the academic mistrust of study-abroad intrusions by U.S. intelligence that had flared up two decades earlier over the Boren Awards. Many universities spurned the film, protesting that it was melodramatic or too long to fit into orientation, or that espionage simply wasn't a major concern.

At the University of South Florida, where the FBI had pressured Dajin Peng to spy on China, dean of undergraduate studies W. Robert Sullins asked education-abroad director Amanda Maurer in April 2014, "Are we doing anything with the *Game of Pawns* film?"

"We have not shown the video to outgoing students for our summer programs," Maurer answered. "I think that it is something that we could show to the semester students (we have more orientation time with them), but I want to take the time to view it with a couple of my staff members. I know that one faculty member feels very strongly that it is the wrong message to send students who are about to study abroad."

"I too think it might be the wrong message—overkill at best," Sullins responded.

When an FBI agent played the movie for University of Akron administrators, encouraging them to show it both at a school-wide event and at orientation for study abroad, Steven Cook was ready. Then assistant director for education abroad, and no relation to the Boren fellow of the same name, Cook had researched the Shriver case, previewed the film, and identified the inconsistencies. Shriver "knew what was going on," Cook told me. "He made his bed. The film made it look like he was duped." As a compromise, both Cook and the FBI agent talked about Shriver at orientation for students heading overseas; the film wasn't shown.

The University of Minnesota also begged off. The FBI "sure did push" the movie, said Stacey Tsantir, then the university's director of international health, safety, and compliance. "They had an edict from the central office to get that out and spread to universities and campuses and in front of students. We accepted the DVD from the guy at our FBI field office, looked at it, and sent him pages and pages of feedback on why it wouldn't work for our population."

Minnesota needed to inform students going overseas about issues like drinking, mental health, and cultural adjustment, not espionage, she said. "In the context of a university that sends thousands of students abroad a year, and where we have a couple of hours to give them pre-departure health and safety information, that is really not at the top of our list. Our statistics don't show our students approached by intelligence agencies. I totally believe it's happening, but there's a risk-benefit analysis that as an educator you have to go through." FBI agents "look at the world through an intelligence lens, which we value. We look at the world through a very different lens."

At American University, Dumont advocated full disclosure. If the FBI truly wanted to protect students, she told one agent, it should alert them that they might be approached abroad not just by foreigners but also by U.S. intelligence. "I said to the FBI, 'It's not a bad idea to warn about foreign security agencies,'" she recalled. "'I just want you to warn them about domestic security agencies.' The FBI said, 'That's not our problem.'"

DUMONT WAS SPEAKING from experience. From 2006 to 2010, American University sent undergraduates to study for a semester at the University of Havana. The George W. Bush administration had restricted educational exchanges with Cuba, and American was one of the few universities licensed for study abroad there.

One year, CIA officers in Washington approached the program coordinator before the group left for Havana. A graduate student at American, the coordinator spoke fluent Spanish and had numerous contacts in Cuba. The agents asked to have dinner with her; they said they just wanted to talk, but she understood that they were interested in recruiting her. Although they persisted, she managed to put them off.

"She was very rattled," Dumont told me. "At one point, they said, 'We can pick a restaurant near your apartment.' That disturbed her: how did they know where she lived?"

That's not the only time that the U.S. government has sought to use students to spy on its adversaries in Latin America, notably the Marxist regimes in Cuba and Venezuela. Fulbright scholar Alexander van Schaick was in Bolivia interviewing peasant leaders for a research project on land tenure when an official at the U.S. embassy there told him in November 2007 to provide the names, addresses, and activities of any Cuban or Venezuelan doctors or field workers he encountered. Funded by the State Department, the Fulbright program provides stipends for teaching and

Four Duke University researchers who worked on the ground-plane invisibility cloak, pictured in Professor David Smith's lab: (from left) Smith, Ruopeng Liu, Jack Mock, Chunlin Ji. (Photograph courtesy of Duke University)

The invisibility cloak developed by Ruopeng Liu and other Duke University researchers. (Photograph courtesy of Duke University)

Marta Rita Velázquez's senior picture in the Princeton yearbook. (Photograph courtesy of Seeley G. Mudd Manuscript Library)

Marta Rita Velázquez at Thorildsplans Gymnasium.

Marta Rita Velázquez's house in Stockholm. The religious statuette is behind a bucket on the porch. (Photograph by Niklas Larsson)

Cuban spy Ana Belén Montes with Marty Scheina, her supervisor and chief of the Defense Intelligence Agency's Latin America Division (Photograph courtesy of the DIA)

The gate of the University of International Relations in Beijing
(Photograph by Michael Standaert)

Xiaoxiong Yi, the Marietta College professor with ties to both the Chinese and U.S. governments who established Marietta's partnership with the University of International Relations (Photograph courtesy of Gray Television Group, Inc.)

Glenn Duffie Shriver, second from left, during Grand Valley State University's study-abroad program in China (Photograph courtesy of Peimin Ni)

Glenn Duffie Shriver in the traditional costume of the Yi people at a cultural pageant during the Grand Valley State University study-abroad program (Photograph courtesy of Peimin Ni)

Dajin Peng's mother, Lixin Peng, at a 1956 education conference in Beijing. She is in the fourth row, sixth from the left (part of her face is hidden by the man in front of her). Dignitaries in the front row include Zhou Enlai, then China's premier, and Zhu De, former commander in chief of the People's Liberation Army. (Photograph courtesy of Dajin Peng)

Dajin Peng as a three-year old
with his mother, Lixin Peng
(Photograph courtesy of Dajin Peng)

Dajin Peng with his parents and sons in 1994 soon after they moved to Tampa (Photograph courtesy of Dajin Peng)

Dajin Peng's parents in 1980, after their remarriage
(Photograph courtesy of Dajin Peng)

Dajin Peng in front of the
University of International
Relations in 1985, when he
was a graduate student there
(Photograph courtesy of Dajin Peng)

Both sides of the Warren Medal presented to Graham Spanier by the CIA (Photographs courtesy of Graham Spanier)

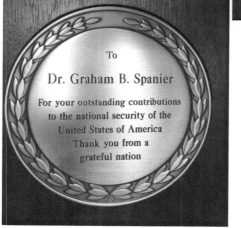

Former Penn State president Graham Spanier (center) with Director of National Intelligence James Clapper (second from left) and officials of the Applied Research Laboratory. (Photograph courtesy of Graham Spanier)

Former CIA officer Rob Simmons, who attended Harvard's Kennedy School of Government under cover, in a coffeehouse in Stonington, Connecticut, where he is first selectman. (Photograph by Patrick Raycraft, courtesy of the Hartford Courant Media Group)

The late CIA officer Kenneth Moskow's entry in the Harvard Kennedy School mid-career program's picture book, which falsely described him as a State Department employee (Photograph courtesy of Kennedy School of Government)

University of South Florida President Judy Genshaft (Photograph courtesy of the University of South Florida)

research; scholars are prohibited from engaging in political activities in their host countries.

"We know the Venezuelans and Cubans are here, and we want to keep tabs on them," the embassy official told the appalled van Schaick, who didn't comply.

CIA officers, perhaps under foreign-service cover, are likely to chat now and again with professors at American branches overseas, said Mark Galeotti, the professor of global affairs at NYU and former special adviser to the British foreign office. "You're a Western intelligence service," he told me. "Where else would you find someone embedded abroad who already has language skills?"

AT GRAND VALLEY'S summer-abroad orientation, professors Ni and Shang bring up the Shriver case. A student in this very program—"a very nice kid, just a little bit naïve, as most of you are," Ni likes to say—was once recruited by Chinese intelligence to spy on the United States. So be alert, Ni tells them. And remember that no gift is truly free.

They don't show *Game of Pawns*. Although it doesn't mention Grand Valley by name, the film's failure to clarify that Shriver had graduated before answering Amanda's ad annoyed both professors. Also, it does identify East China Normal University, where Shriver spent his junior year. Officials at East China, which still hosts the Grand Valley summer students, have lamented to Ni and Shang that the film damages their school's reputation.

Neither professor is in touch with Shriver. The last time Shang talked to the FBI, he asked about Glenn. The agent said that Shriver was doing okay, and promised to pass along Shang's greetings. "Why can't he have another chance to do some positive things? He's got ability, talent, personality," Shang told me. "He just made a stupid mistake. We were good friends. I care about him."

Shriver earned a master's degree in international business in prison, and was released in December 2013. Afterward, he visited Linda Kimble, the family friend and high school teacher, who had cancer. "He made it a point to come over and say hello," Kimble said. "That spoke volumes."

"Glenn and I are doing really well," his mother wrote in a September 2015 email that their lawyer shared with me. "If I could only have known the future I would not have been so stressed in the past."

When I asked Shriver, through his mother, for an interview, his answer reminded me of his susceptibility to the bribes from Chinese spymasters.

"How much does it pay?" he responded.

She says he meant it as a joke.

PART 2

COVERT U.S. OPERATIONS
IN HIGHER EDUCATION

6

· · · · · · · · ·

AN IMPERFECT SPY

I first heard of Dajin Peng in 2011, when I was looking into the China-funded Confucius Institutes sprouting up on U.S. campuses. I came across a *St. Petersburg Times* report that the University of South Florida had suspended him as director of its Confucius Institute for taking thousands of dollars under false pretenses and violating immigration rules, among other offenses.

Asked why Peng wasn't punished more harshly, university spokesman Michael Hoad had cited his job security as a tenured professor. A follow-up editorial urged the university to fire Peng. Tenure "should not be a shield for unethical behavior," it said.

The *Times* clearly didn't buy Professor Peng's own explanation for his troubles. The FBI "decided to force me into a spy for the U.S.A.," Peng told the newspaper. "This scheme goes all the way to President Obama."

Although it sounded ludicrous, I was curious. I emailed Peng, who declined to comment. I also called Hoad and asked if the FBI played any role in Peng's case.

USF had "no FBI contact that I'm aware of," Hoad told me. "Our reaction is that anybody who is a spy doesn't discuss it with a newspaper reporter." Peng, he suggested, was just "frustrated and upset."

Years later, after leaving the university, Hoad apologized for misleading me. He said it was unintentional; he had no idea that the FBI was involved, because the university lawyers who briefed him never mentioned it. "My guess is that they wouldn't tell me about it for the fairly simple reason that if they did, I would have to answer the question truthfully."

As a public institution, South Florida was susceptible to pressure from national security agencies, Hoad added. "A state university is going to be immensely deferential to the FBI."

I was talking to Hoad again because Peng had gotten in touch with me in May 2014, saying he wanted to tell his story and had "key evidences," including FBI emails, to support it. After reading the emails, I realized that Peng's experience might offer a rare glimpse of U.S. intelligence's increasingly brazen campaign to co-opt American universities.

I booked a flight to Florida.

MEETING PENG WASN'T easy. When I tried to firm up an appointment, he responded by email, "I am not allowed to use my office since I am in suspension. I do not think it is a good idea for us to meet at my apartment because I am afraid it might be taped [sic]. For the same reason it is not good for us to preset a restaurant."

On landing in Tampa, I called him from the airport. He suggested a rendezvous in a Walgreens parking lot, where he left his car, presumably as a precaution against being followed. We drove in my rental car to a Chinese restaurant run by a friend of his. There he led me through the dining area to a back room with bare walls, a flat-screen television, and one table, and closed the door. The waitress who served lunch knocked each time she entered.

After this display of tradecraft, Peng relaxed. He was wearing a white shirt with the sleeves rolled up to his elbows and his Samsung phone in a front pocket. He eyes were reddened and puffy, perhaps due to jet lag. He had just returned from Beijing by way of Dubai and Cape Town with his father.

Chatting companionably in accented English as he selected dishes for us both, he struck me as affable, even gregarious. His charm, I would later realize, was like octopus ink, a camouflage to avoid predators. His childhood in China had taught him the value of deception, and the penalty for speaking his mind. Even his mentor and closest friend at South

Florida, Professor Emeritus Harvey Nelsen, who helped hire him there, admits he doesn't know Peng well.

"He's honest, but he's also secretive," says Nelsen, himself a former China analyst for U.S. intelligence. "He doesn't lay all his cards on the table."

Divorced, with two sons at elite U.S. universities, Peng was living with his widowed father, Xianyu Zhi. Through no fault of his own, Xianyu had been absent during most of Peng's youth, and his very identity had been a mystery to his son.

Xianyu had served as an officer in the Nationalist army of Chiang Kai-shek. After the Chinese communists under Mao Zedong overthrew Chiang in 1948, he became a teacher in Wuhan and coauthored a geography textbook. The largest city in central China and the capital of Hubei Province, located at the confluence of the Yangtze and Hanjiang rivers, Wuhan was "a politically and economically prominent city" in the early and mid-twentieth century, though later in the century it would be "left behind by the country's economic wave."

When Mao invited candid appraisals of his policies in 1956, urging his people to "let a hundred flowers bloom and a hundred schools of thought contend," Xianyu unwisely took him at his word and criticized the government at a school meeting. He didn't realize that the party chairman's apparent tolerance was a ploy to flush out dissidents. Xianyu was arrested and sent to a labor camp, leaving his pregnant wife, Lixin Peng, at home. A high school teacher and administrator, Lixin was so respected for her success in preparing students for college that in 1956 the Chinese government invited her to a conference in Beijing, where she met Premier Zhou Enlai and Vice Chairman Zhu De, former commander in chief of the army.

Ten days after their only child, a son, was born in 1958, Lixin was forced to divorce Xianyu to save her job, which she needed to support the family. The baby was given his mother's family name and a first name, Dajin, that meant "Great Leap Forward"—a politically correct tribute to the disastrous industrialization program introduced by Mao that year.

The government humiliated Xianyu by making him pull a coal cart through his Wuhan neighborhood. As he trudged through the streets, he would sometimes seek out his son and give him candy, defying a ban on contact with his family. Or Lixin, holding Dajin by the hand, would secretly meet her ex-husband at a friend's house. She continued to see him even after authorities reprimanded her for it in her job evaluation. They wanted her to know that she was being watched and that her career and freedom were at stake.

Afraid that the boy would accidentally disclose the forbidden trysts, his mother told Dajin that Xianyu was just a friend, not his father. The confusion left him with a lifelong insecurity. It also taught him an early lesson about intelligence services—and the damage they can inflict on ordinary people.

"I was very puzzled," Peng told me. "My father was communicating, through his actions, he was my father. I believed my father, too. That's why, when I was very young, I suffered a lot. Friends would laugh at me, and I didn't know how to respond."

The puzzle wasn't solved until he was eight years old. One day, Xianyu brought sweets for him and his grandmother. After Xianyu left, Peng's grandmother said, "That's your father."

His mother and grandmother doted on the bright, gregarious child, pushing him to excel academically and restore the family's status. His mother was principal of the Boone School in Wuhan, which had been founded by American missionaries. After Dajin attended it for one semester, she noticed that teachers were going easy on him because he was her son, and she made him transfer to another school, where classmates mocked and bullied the fatherless boy. He tried to ignore them or at least deflect the worst of their verbal and physical blows by retreating into his own world. His favorite hobby was a solitary one: observing the stars and constellations in the night sky. Their grandeur made his own sorrow seem insignificant. Gifted with a spongelike memory, he learned their names by heart.

His mother did arrange for him to use Boone's library, where he read voraciously, and to sleep in a school bedroom. From the age of twelve to twenty he often stayed there, enthralled by the maps on its walls of China and the world.

After his high school graduation, Peng taught middle school while studying on his own, hoping to go to college. During the Cultural Revolution, Mao's bloody purge of suspected "revisionists," the government canceled university entrance exams and limited admission to Communist Party loyalists. It wasn't until China restored entrance exams in 1977 that Peng, who passed them easily, could enroll in Wuhan University. Even then, the university hesitated, placing his application in a special category because of his father's disgrace. In 1978, as Deng Xiaoping consolidated power and began liberalizing China, Peng's parents were allowed to remarry. They had remained devoted to each other despite separation and hardship, and their relationship taught Peng an important lesson: it was possible to outwit and outlast state-sanctioned pressures.

Peng studied English at Wuhan University. As a reward for his hard work, he was named study monitor, which entitled him to organize academic competitions for his class. He then taught for two years at a financial and economics college in Wuhan. During this period, he began dating Xianai Mi, who had also grown up in Wuhan and studied foreign languages at Wuhan University. They would marry in 1985.

His wife "adored him in the early stages and took care of him," says a former Wuhan classmate, Hongshan Li, now a history professor at Kent State University. Once, when Li was visiting their apartment, Mi fetched a basin of water and washed Peng's feet. "That is something that most wives don't do in front of people. The whole family worked together to help him become successful. I envied him that he had such a devoted wife."

In 1984, PENG enrolled as a graduate student at what was then known as the Institute of International Relations—the same spy school that would later affiliate with Marietta College in Ohio. The institute's alumni enjoyed preference for employment at the security ministry, and its professors and administrators had connections at the highest levels of China's government. Peng's own faculty adviser had been chief of a government section that analyzed the American economy. Chinese leaders, including Mao and Zhou Enlai, consulted him regularly. "Until now, in his eighties, my adviser is still providing advice to the Chinese government on the U.S. economy," Peng said.

At the time Peng became his protégé, the adviser had recently returned from a research stint at the World Trade Center in Dallas, Texas, where U.S. intelligence had approached him. "Knowing his importance, the FBI and CIA were trying to recruit him and made very generous offers," Peng told me. "My adviser rejected their offers because he just wanted to be a scholar, not spying for anyone, not to say for a foreign country. He has also advised me not to work for any intelligence [service]. That influenced me a lot and it was partly why I tried to avoid the FBI whenever possible."

Applicants to IIR's graduate school chose one of two career tracks: either to become teachers at the institute, or researchers at its sister organization, China Institutes of Contemporary International Relations. Established in 1965, CICIR was—and remains—a bureau of the security ministry. Its deputy director of American research in Peng's era was Geng Huichang, who has been China's minister of state security since 2007.

Peng opted for the CICIR route, but worked there for only a month after earning his master's degree. In 1986, he left China to continue his education in America. His wife, who would join him in the United States a year later, and his parents came to the Beijing airport to say good-bye. It was the first time he had ever seen his mother cry.

He was bound for the University of Akron in Ohio, which had awarded him a full scholarship. Soon after he arrived, the FBI interviewed him for the first time. Asked about the Institute of International Relations, Peng told his favorite joke about his alma mater: "Do you know why they always put guards in front of the gate? They don't want people to know that there are no secrets inside."

At Akron, Peng earned another master's, this time in economics. Then he pursued a doctorate at three universities, climbing the prestige ladder from the University of Cincinnati and the University of Texas at Dallas to one of the world's premier centers for international relations. In 1989, he was admitted to the Woodrow Wilson School of Public and International Affairs at Princeton University.

Relishing his Ivy League status, Peng dove into his dissertation topic: the rise of economic cooperation among Asian Pacific nations. "He was a fine student, and his mastery of Japanese as well as Chinese was very useful in the kind of research he was doing," said Lynn White, one of his Wilson School professors.

His family life flourished as well. His sons were born in 1991 and 1994. They grew up bilingual, speaking Chinese at home with Peng's parents, who had arrived from China in 1990. His mother cooked and babysat while his wife waitressed. Xianai Mi "sacrificed everything for this guy," says Kate Zhou, a college classmate of Peng, who was also studying at the Wilson School. "The day she delivered her second child, she was still working in the restaurant."

Peng also gained a luncheon companion: FBI special agent Nicholas Abaid. Peng dined several times with Abaid at the FBI's expense. He thought it would be impolitic to refuse, since he was attending Princeton on a scholarship and a student visa through the grace of the United States.

"We became good friends," Peng recalled. Abaid asked Peng about other Chinese students and their access to sensitive research. "He complained to me that Chinese students were able to get technology from the U.S. He was very alarmed about this."

Based in the FBI's Trenton office, Nick Abaid worked counterintelligence at Princeton from 1982 to 1999, he told me as we strolled across the largely deserted campus on a hot, humid June afternoon in 2015. Kindly and white-haired, limping slightly from a knee replacement, Abaid knew the university as well as any official tour guide, but from the unique perspective of someone whose main business there was recruiting Chinese students as spies.

Working from State Department lists of international students, he developed sources among the Princeton staff who tipped him off about the newcomers' family backgrounds, adjustment issues, needs, and aspirations. "Universities get a bad rap as anti-FBI, anti-CIA," Abaid said as we walked through the Wilson School, Peng's old stomping grounds. "If there are ways universities can help us protect the country, they'll do it."

When we dropped by the faculty dining room, where Abaid used to meet Princeton's head of security, he complained that the 1984 Buckley Amendment, which prohibits universities from divulging all but the most basic student records without consent, made his job harder. Then he brightened. "If you approached it properly, and kept it confidential, maybe you could squeeze a little more," he said. Universities "don't want to be embarrassed by nefarious activities among their students. So they're willing to cooperate as long as we don't get too nosy."

We strolled to Nassau Hall, Princeton's oldest building. George Washington's troops had used its hallway as a bowling alley, my guide told me. We mounted the original steps to our destination, the office of the dean of foreign students, where Abaid had often visited. He was taken aback to find that it was now the waiting room of the vice provost for institutional equity and diversity.

Abaid's low-key, avuncular manner went over well with Chinese students. He helped them to open bank accounts and showed them the Norman Rockwell side of America, inviting them to cookouts and minor-league baseball games. He told them that in the United States, unlike China, they had freedom of choice. They controlled their destinies, and could decide for themselves whether to cooperate with him or not. Often, they did. Of the two hundred Princeton foreign students, mostly Chinese, whom he interviewed during his career, about fifty helped short-term with a specific fact, and about ten became productive longtime informants. "Recruiting assets is what the game is all about," he said.

His most important recruit, though, wasn't Chinese or a student, but a foreign nuclear physicist who came to Princeton as a visiting scholar. The physicist, who held a military officer's rank, had rebuffed the CIA's overtures overseas, so the agency asked the FBI to approach him at Princeton.

Based on information supplied by Princeton about the scientist's research, personality, and family, the FBI set up an undercover operation. An agent posing as a magazine salesman began to socialize with the scientist, who was a heavy drinker. Since the agent had to keep up, he was usually drunk by the time Abaid debriefed him at the end of the evening.

The physicist finally said to the agent, "I think you're CIA." He denied it. Then the scientist surprised him by saying, "Well, I want to talk to the CIA."

"I'm not CIA, but I have a friend in the FBI," the agent said, maintaining his cover. "Would that be okay?"

The scientist set one condition for his cooperation: his son had to study at a U.S. university. The FBI and CIA agreed, and smoothed the way, but the youth turned out to be bright enough to be admitted on his own.

Abaid and other agents interviewed the scientist as many as sixteen hours a day for several weeks, working around his Princeton schedule and meeting in a different building every day to protect his identity. When they ran out of questions, other federal agencies, including the State Department and the Pentagon, provided more. The scientist identified many of the intelligence agents in his country's diplomatic corps and "gave a very good update" on its military technology.

"He was extremely helpful," Abaid said. "He wasn't a spy himself, but he knew the agents because they briefed him."

Eventually the FBI handed him over to the CIA, which sent him home to collect more intelligence. When the FBI agents asked what he would like as a going-away present, he suggested a watch for his wife. They showed him an array of watches in a catalog, but all of them were too small. "My wife has a wrist like an elephant," the physicist said. They settled on a necklace instead.

PENG WASN'T ONE of Abaid's triumphs. Wary of U.S. security organizations as well as China's, he parried the agent's questions. In 1994, a year before he completed his Princeton doctorate, Peng became an instructor at South Florida. When Abaid asked him to check in with the FBI in Tampa, Peng mustered his courage and refused.

Accompanied by his parents, wife, and children, Peng left the Ivy League for an up-and-coming state university dotted with palm trees. Founded in 1956, 210 years after Princeton, USF mushroomed into one of the largest public universities in the United States. It has 48,400 undergraduate and graduate students, including 3,300 international students, from more than 130 countries.

Its main campus in Tampa—it also has branches in St. Petersburg and Sarasota—resembles a corporate office park, with imposing research centers and dormitories separated by well-kept lawns. It prides itself on research and entrepreneurship, and regularly ranks among the top fifteen universities worldwide in the number of U.S. patents granted.

National security is Tampa's business. The city is home to the U.S. Central Command and U.S. Special Operations Command, both hosted by MacDill Air Force Base, and a $14 billion military industry specializing in everything from cybersecurity to veterans' health rehabilitation. Nine of the top ten U.S. defense contractors, from Raytheon to Honeywell, have plants in the Tampa Bay area.

As Peng began teaching at USF, revelations of ties between two faculty members and Middle East terrorism strained the university's relationship with its surrounding community. One was Ramadan Shallah, executive director of World and Islam Studies Enterprise, a campus think tank on Middle Eastern issues. In 1995, Shallah became leader of the Iran-backed Palestinian Islamic Jihad in Damascus, Syria.

The other was Sami Al-Arian, a tenured computer engineering professor who in 1990–91 founded World and Islam Studies Enterprise. His long-running case would draw national attention and foster a bond between the FBI and the University of South Florida.

After a 1994 public television documentary accused Al-Arian, a Kuwaiti-born Palestinian, of raising money for terrorism, the FBI began investigating him. With a lack of Arabic speakers to translate the tens of thousands of documents seized from Al-Arian's home as well as wiretapped conversations, the probe became "a seven-year root canal," says J. A. Koerner, who headed counterintelligence and counterterrorism in the FBI's Tampa field office at the time.

The allegations against Al-Arian forced the university to weigh competing values of national security and academic freedom. Withstanding pressure to fire him, USF president Betty Castor, a former Democratic state senator, placed him on paid leave pending the FBI investigation's outcome. In 1998, after a university-commissioned inquiry found no wrongdoing, she let him resume his academic duties.

Because much of the evidence against Al-Arian was classified, the FBI couldn't share it with Castor. "We told her as much as we could, but we couldn't give her all the jewels we had," Koerner told me in September 2015. "I felt bad for Betty" when her opponent's criticism that she was soft on terrorism cost her a U.S. Senate seat in 2004, he added.

The university's posture shifted after the September 11, 2001, attacks—and an appearance two weeks later by Al-Arian on Fox News' *The O'Reilly Factor.* Host Bill O'Reilly showed a videotape of Al-Arian shouting "Death to Israel and victory to Islam" in a 1998 speech and said, "If I was the CIA, I'd follow you wherever you went." USF, O'Reilly speculated, "may be a hotbed of support for Arab militants." Al-Arian responded that he had meant "death to occupation, death to apartheid, death to oppression" and wasn't threatening anyone's life.

So many complaints and threats poured into the university that it evacuated the computer science building the next afternoon. In December

2001, university trustees ordered Judy Genshaft, who had replaced Castor as president, to dismiss Al-Arian "as quickly as university processes will allow."

Genshaft didn't balk. A former administrator at Ohio State University and the State University of New York, she was a newcomer to Florida, but the state's predominantly Republican political establishment and the businessmen on the university's board regarded her as reliable. Although she doesn't belong to a political party, Genshaft "was known as a Republican when she got here," said a former USF administrator. "She got the job because she let people know she's a Republican." She's a director of a family-owned Ohio meatpacking business that was founded by her father and is run by her brother, Neil Genshaft. He has donated thousands of dollars to Republican candidates, including George W. Bush, Mitt Romney, and congressmen James Renacci and Kirk Schuring.

Legal grounds for firing Al-Arian, though, were wanting. On a Saturday morning in November 2002, the university agreed in principle to pay him almost $1 million to resign, despite the likely public uproar over enriching an alleged terrorist. The next Monday, the university called off the deal.

Robert McKee, then Al-Arian's lawyer, told me that he suspects that the FBI had a hand in the about-face. His theory is that the bureau learned about the impending settlement from a wiretapped conversation and alerted the university that Al-Arian would soon be indicted, giving USF grounds to fire him. Indeed, FBI agents would later tell Peng that university officials were grateful to the bureau for sparing them the embarrassment and expense of buying out Al-Arian.

However, Al-Arian said in a 2007 radio interview that Richard Beard, the chairman of USF's board of trustees, had nixed the settlement "because of the anticipated political fallout." Beard then confirmed that he had objected: "I saw it as a payoff." Also, retired FBI agent Kerry Myers, who oversaw the criminal side of the investigation, told me that he never spoke to USF about the indictment in advance. "I'd be shocked if anyone had gone to USF and done that without my knowledge."

Al-Arian and seven others were arrested and indicted in February 2003 on charges of racketeering and conspiracy to commit murder. In December 2005, a jury acquitted him on eight of seventeen counts and deadlocked on nine others. The next February, he pleaded guilty on one count of conspiracy to aid Palestinian Islamic Jihad and was sentenced to fifty-seven months in prison. After further legal battles, he was deported to Turkey in 2015.

The ordeal scarred Genshaft. "It was a very devastating and painful time for the university and particularly for the president," says a former USF administrator. "She's very sensitive. She doesn't want to go there again."

USF sought to mend the rift with key constituents. In 2009, it hired a retired three-star general in the U.S. Marine Corps, Martin R. Steele, who promotes military partnerships and oversees a research initiative on veterans' health. In 2011, USF signed a memorandum of understanding with the U.S. Central Command to collaborate on "activities of mutual value," such as workshops, conferences, guest speakers, and professional exchanges. That same year, it became one of twenty universities designated by the Office of the Director of National Intelligence as Intelligence Community Centers for Academic Excellence. It has received almost $2 million to train students for certificates in national and competitive intelligence, and has placed interns at the Defense Intelligence Agency, the White House, the Secret Service, and the State Department. In 2014, the state of Florida created a cybersecurity center at USF, which helps faculty attract grants for unclassified research projects. The center also worked with South Florida professors to create an online master's degree program in cybersecurity.

USF has made "a healthy transition from a university that was anti-military, anti-intelligence to one that wants a partnership," says Walter Andrusyszyn, a former State Department official who runs USF's intelligence certificate program. Because of the Al-Arian tempest, "some folks there started seeing things in a different light."

PENG FLOURISHED AT USF. He offered courses in international political economy, Japanese business, U.S.-China relations, and other topics, earning tenure and a promotion to associate professor in 2001 and winning an award for outstanding teaching. He enjoyed impressing students with feats of memorization, rattling off the population and capital of any nation they named. On a website for grading their professors, anonymous students praised Peng as knowledgeable, helpful, and an easy grader, though some grumbled that he was disorganized or digressive. Sample comments:

"He is one of my favorite professors at USF! He knows his stuff and cares A LOT for his students. I took wealth/power with him and the class was a breeze. He gives you essay questions and terms in advance for the exams. Gives a lot of extra credit too. Soo nice and yes he has a thick accent, but he knows that and makes fun of himself at times. Take him!!!"

"Peng is great. He's not very organized and NEVER checks his email, but he's friendly & genuinely wants you to do well. It's not a tough class. He curves heavily."

"Dr. Peng is one of the most knowledgeable, dynamic professors I've ever had. Yes he strays off topic, but mostly it makes the class less boring."

"Peng has trouble keeping on topic & is unorganized. Overall, I learned more from the book than his lectures. However, I did like the way he related the class material to current events."

He became a citizen in 2000, proudly swearing his allegiance to the United States. (Six years later, his father followed his example.) Peng split his time between his new and old homelands. Taking advantage of the flexible academic schedule, he began supplementing his USF salary by teaching mid-career business students in China—starting at Nankai University in 2005, then gradually adding more universities, including three in his hometown of Wuhan. Money wasn't the only motivation for his trans-Pacific teaching load. With his Princeton doctorate, he impressed the fair-weather friends who had snubbed his family when his father was sent to the labor camp. With every trip, he felt as if he reaped prestige and respect for the family name.

Peng's international commuting is typical of his generation of China-born scholars, said his college friend Zhou, now a professor at the University of Hawai'i. "They like the United States but they also want to benefit from the rise of China," she said.

His China excursions distracted him from family turmoil. In 2004, his mother died of cancer, and Peng and his wife split up. Under the 2005 divorce terms, their two sons stayed primarily with Mi and visited Peng twice a week.

For now, the kind of opportunity that only comes once in a career beckoned. USF's dean of international affairs, Maria Crummett, asked Peng in May 2007 to use his contacts in China to establish Florida's first

Confucius Institute at USF. He had to find a partner university in China and then gain approval from Hanban, a Chinese education ministry affiliate that operates Confucius Institutes worldwide.

Peng rapidly secured both a partnership with Nankai University and Hanban's blessing. Hanban agreed to supply $100,000 in start-up funds, which increased to $200,000 in the second year, plus staff salaries and educational materials. Nankai provided the institute's co-director and staff.

"I believe you have magical powers," Crummett emailed Peng in August 2007. "Great work in moving forward with all your ability to convince that USF is the right institution and that we are committed."

As director, Peng choreographed the opening ceremonies in March 2008, which featured a lantern-festooned dinner, a magic act, a boat tour of Tampa bay, and a trip to the Salvador Dalí Museum in St. Petersburg. The Chinese consulate general from Houston and dignitaries from Nankai University and the Chinese embassy in Washington, D.C., were on hand. Renowned Chinese artist Fan Zeng donated a portrait of Confucius.

"Thank you for planning and orchestrating such a marvelous opening event," USF provost Ralph Wilcox emailed Peng and Crummett. "You made my job easy; extended a warm welcome to our guests from out of town; ensured that USF 'shone' in the Tampa Bay Community; and generally represented the university so very, very well."

Outside USF, Confucius Institutes were drawing less favorable attention. The program started in 2004 and grew rapidly, fueled by at least $1 billion in Chinese spending. By the end of 2015, Hanban had seeded 500 Confucius Institutes worldwide, including 109 in the United States. It was also operating 1,000 Confucius Classrooms for elementary and secondary school students. More than one-third, 347, were in the United States. In 2013 alone, China spent $278 million on Confucius Institutes, an amount roughly matched by host universities.

Instruments of "soft power," as former Chinese president Hu Jintao described them in a 2007 speech, the institutes typically provide instruction in Chinese language, history, and traditional arts such as calligraphy, though some specialize in one area, such as research, business, or tourism. They toe the Chinese government line, avoiding topics such as China's treatment of Tibet, or the 1989 suppression of student protests in Tiananmen Square.

"By peddling a product we want, namely Chinese language study, the Confucius Institutes bring the Chinese government into the American academy in powerful ways," Jonathan Lipman, a professor of Chinese history at Mount Holyoke College in South Hadley, Massachusetts, told me in 2011. "The general pattern is very clear. They can say, 'We'll give you this money, you'll have a Chinese program, and nobody will talk about Tibet.'"

For instance, Hanban attached a caveat to its $4 million offer to Stanford to host a Confucius Institute and endow a professorship: the professor couldn't discuss controversial issues like Tibet. Stanford yielded, using the funds for a chair in classical Chinese poetry.

In 2014, the American Association of University Professors urged universities to cease involvement with Confucius Institutes unless they could gain control from Hanban over all academic matters. "Confucius Institutes function as an arm of the Chinese state and are allowed to ignore academic freedom," the faculty union said. Subsequently, both the University of Chicago and Pennsylvania State University cut ties with their Confucius Institutes.

Western intelligence agencies have a different concern about Confucius Institutes: espionage. "There's no getting around the fact that they are outposts of Chinese state outreach and absolutely obvious places to assign people as agents," said Mark Galeotti, the New York University professor of global affairs. "The Confucius Institute is ideal because it's outward-looking. The whole purpose is to have more people come through its doors. It's where I would be looking to recruit people if I were a Chinese spymaster."

The Canadian Security Intelligence Service suspected the institutes of serving as "a cover-up for a gigantic system of siphoning and draining away of other people's scientific research." The FBI considered starting an investigation of all Confucius Institutes in the United States before deciding it didn't have enough grounds, according to a former federal official. The bureau looked for connections between the institutes' locations and China's business interests, the person said.

"We think it's an influence operation at the very least," the former official said. "At worst, it could be far more nefarious."

While Hongshan Li, Peng's college friend who teaches at Kent State, was attending his son's graduation from Harvard University, he received a call on his cell phone. It was an FBI agent, asking about his efforts to help Kent State set up a Confucius Institute. "I told them clearly, 'I was invited by the university to do this job.' I said, 'I won't talk to you,'" Li recalls. "'You want information, talk to them.'"

The FBI contacted one of Li's faculty colleagues as well. Kent State partnered with Shanghai Normal University to apply for an institute, but it didn't pan out. "To me, that's a relief. If it's established, I will be involved, it takes too much of my time," Li said.

It seems far-fetched that the Chinese education ministry would tailor the Confucius Institutes for espionage, since exposure would imperil a program in which it has invested so much. More likely is that China's powerful security services, either bypassing or overriding education officials, directly recruit institute staff or teachers—much as the FBI would try to enlist Peng.

"Chinese intelligence does see Confucius Institutes as a way to gather information," Zao Cheng Xu, director of the Confucius Institute at Indiana University–Purdue University Indianapolis (IUPUI), told me. "That's not the intention of Hanban or headquarters. Different agencies have a different agenda." The spy services "can approach a teacher, a student, anybody."

I had called Professor Xu, a neurologist at Indiana University School of Medicine, after reading a comment he had made on a Listserv for directors of Confucius Institutes in North America. With the subject heading "more trouble for Confucius Institutes," another director had circulated my February 2015 Bloomberg News article about Peng, and Xu was responding to it. "I am sure many of us have been contacted by FBI," he wrote. "We are in the middle of politics and secret service between the two countries."

Xu told me that both the FBI and Chinese intelligence had approached him. The FBI had questioned him at least twice, primarily about teachers sent by IUPUI's partner, Sun Yat-sen University in Guangzhou. "They are professors," he told the FBI. "I know them. I know their background."

In 2013, Xu was visiting China for a Confucius Institute study-abroad program when someone asked him to dinner, saying that a mutual friend would join them. The mutual friend turned out to be from Chinese intelligence—though he didn't have to say so. "I am Chinese. I know where he works. . . . I frankly tell my attitude. I am not interested to be a spy. I am not going to go further. The way I say it, they can tell. I am not a political person. They won't invite me for coffee, tea, or dinner again."

LIKE OTHER FBI field offices, Tampa's was keeping an eye on the Confucius Institute in its jurisdiction—the one sprouting at USF. "There's a lot of concern about Confucius Institutes," says Koerner, the former head of counterintelligence in Tampa. "Anytime there was the Chinese government with involvement in student populations, there's a reason for it. Chinese officials would come from the consulate in Houston ostensibly for receptions and other events, or to show a film on China, but actually to check on students. They want their tentacles in the student community. Who are the problems? The Falun Gong people? People bad-mouthing the regime? They need somebody to spot and assess who's a problem. The embassy needs to know which students it can rely on in technological fields to be helpful. Who it can recruit, what's their family background. Who's a dissident to stay away from."

Unaware of any FBI scrutiny, Peng embarked on an ambitious agenda. He ramped up the institute's course offerings and opened a cultural center. He persuaded leaders of Tampa's Chinese community to form a committee that donated more than ten thousand dollars to the institute, which reciprocated by training Chinese language teachers and sponsoring cultural events.

He also grew close to Xiaonong Zhang, a Nankai business professor who came to USF in 2007 as a postdoctoral fellow, reporting to Peng. She became a visiting faculty member at the Confucius Institute and then associate director for the spring 2009 semester. At the time, she and her husband, also a Nankai professor, were considering a divorce.

"Given my exceptional capacity, both academically and administratively, I had been admired by many women," Peng later wrote about his relationship with Zhang. "The fact that I was single unfortunately leaves more room for imagination by some."

During Peng's frequent travels, they exchanged affectionate emails, addressing each other as Little Sea Elephant and Big Sea Elephant. Her messages were longer and more passionate than his. "Yesterday I went through our correspondences and felt something special in my heart," she wrote to him in December 2007. "Maybe this is what's called 'passion developing with time.' I love the feeling I have when I communicate with you. I feel lonely when I am all alone at home. I miss you very much and I enjoy all the sweet memories we have together. I love you!"

When Peng went to Japan in March 2008, she wrote to "my dear brother Sea Elephant: You have left me again, for such a long time. Sadness arose in my heart the moment we waved good-bye to each other . . . maybe separation can help us truly be aware of our love and the existence and value of each other."

After he answered that he had arrived safely and missed her, too, she wrote, "I miss you very much, my dear brother. I always miss you whenever I am by myself. I miss your kindness, your smiles and your warm embrace. . . . Without you around, I feel the room is so cold and the night so quiet, and I don't quite know what to do."

"Dear SSE," Peng replied, presumably using an acronym for Small Sea Elephant. "So glad to get your lovely e-mail. I am missing you badly in Tokyo. I must bring you here some day in the near future. Tokyo has wonderful food. . . . Tomorrow we will buy a lot of Japanese food and bring them back to China and US. I am sure you will love them especially the Japanese soup!"

Zhang wrote back, "I had a good nap this afternoon, (I pretended you were the pillow next to me.) I am very happy that you can always think of me at happy moments. From the standpoint of romantic psychology, this shows that you love me a lot."

Peng: "Yes, I really wish that we were together. I wish we would be together again very soon."

Eventually, they had a bitter falling-out. Peng says she was angry because he rejected her advances. She says that she realized Peng has "a bad personality: dishonest, scheming, selfish and arrogant," and patched up her marriage.

In early March 2009, a year after the Confucius Institute opened, Zhang arranged to meet Maria Crummett, the dean of international affairs and Peng's boss, at a Starbucks in the USF library. She complained that Peng was micromanaging the faculty, requiring them to be in their offices at all times during the workweek and attend evening and weekend meetings, asking them to clean his office and car, and making inappropriate comments to female teachers. He had taken to asking one female professor, Baojing Sang, to stay in the office after everyone else had left, and was also calling Sang in the evenings, Zhang said.

Crummett consulted Provost Wilcox but took no action. Then, on March 27, Shuhua Liu Kriesel approached Eric Shepherd, a USF professor of Chinese language, to denounce Peng. Born in Shandong Province, on China's northeast coast, where her father was a teacher, Kriesel attended the University of Washington in Seattle. She moved in 2006 to Tampa, where she was assistant principal at a Chinese school and worked at the Confucius Institute as China projects coordinator. Peng had just fired her; her last day of work was March 24.

Over lunch with Shepherd, Kriesel accused Peng of "leaning against her or placing his arm around her while she was working at her computer," and of asking her to buy clothes, wash dishes, and fix meals for him. Like Zhang, she expressed concern about Peng's behavior toward Sang. She also raised the possibility of financial wrongdoing, saying Peng had requested that she falsify a Confucius Institute budget. On April 1, Zhang went to Shepherd's office and "recounted many of the same complaints and incidents" that Kriesel had.

Was it just coincidence that two women approached the same professor within five days with similar complaints against Peng? Shepherd says that each confided in him independently. "Either they were really, really good at concealing that they had planned everything together, or they didn't know the other was coming forward," Shepherd told me in August 2015 as we chatted in a USF conference room. They chose him, Shepherd added, because of his fluency in their native language. "The staff felt comfortable telling me. They were afraid it would come back on them. They wanted to express their concerns" in Chinese.

Zhang and Kriesel may also have sought out Shepherd because they expected him to be sympathetic. The friction between Peng and Shepherd was no secret. In the small world of China experts at USF, both were rising stars, and hence rivals. Shepherd had studied Chinese at Ohio State, where he earned his bachelor's, master's, and doctoral degrees, "because it was clear to me that the Chinese had a strategic advantage." They could take advantage of business and technology opportunities in the United States, but Americans lacked the linguistic ability to reciprocate in China. After teaching at Iowa State and Ohio State, he arrived at South Florida in 2008 and gained renown for his skill in teaching

Chinese by using the traditional storytelling art of *kuaishu*. Shepherd thought that Peng, as a specialist in international politics and business, was miscast running an institute of language and culture, and was mistakenly steering it toward academic research rather than teacher training and community outreach.

Like Peng's institute, Shepherd's study-abroad program for USF students in China received Hanban funding. From 2009 to 2012, Hanban "gave every student a scholarship," Shepherd said. "I know what their motive was. Our students came out of the program with a positive view of China." In 2010, Kriesel served as Shepherd's teaching assistant for one semester.

Peng contends that the FBI set him up using a time-honored tactic: enlisting people who had an animus against him. He suggests the following scenario: The FBI, which was scrutinizing Confucius Institutes nationwide, noticed that the director of South Florida's institute had been a bureau contact while at Princeton. The possibility of deploying Peng to penetrate the Confucius Institute network and reverse the direction of its espionage captivated the bureau. Because the FBI expected Peng to be reluctant, based on his evasiveness at Princeton and his refusal to stay in touch afterward, it needed leverage over him, such as a threat to his status at South Florida.

Peng speculates that the bureau first cultivated Kriesel. She was active as a volunteer in Tampa's Chinese-American community, helping to boost attendance at a Chinese church and Chinese-American Association of Tampa Bay events, so the FBI might well have found her useful. Perhaps she was initially unwilling to help the bureau with Peng but agreed once he began criticizing her work. At the bureau's instigation, he theorizes, she persuaded Zhang to complain to Crummett. But Crummett was slow to act, and the FBI may have worried that the USF administration was writing off Zhang as a vengeful ex-girlfriend. So, Peng speculates, the bureau persuaded Kriesel to come forward, too. Kriesel might then have told the FBI that the university had punished Peng.

Peng also suspects that the campaign against him was carefully timed. He was placed on leave less than a month before the university honored Madame Lin Xu, director general of Hanban and chief executive of the Confucius Institute headquarters in Beijing, with a "President's Global Leadership Award" at commencement exercises. If he were still director of the USF institute, Peng says, he would have coordinated Madame Xu's visit and cemented his relationship with her, making it harder for the FBI to imperil his position. Instead Peng, who had invited Madame Xu to South Florida, wasn't allowed to meet her.

University phone logs obtained through a public records request add to the intrigue. They show twelve calls from the mobile phone of Dianne Mercurio, the FBI special agent, to USF extensions in January and February 2009, shortly before the Zhang and Kriesel complaints. The university redacted the numbers she contacted, citing an exemption in Florida public records law for disclosing anything that could identify a confidential informant.

Zhang told me that she had never spoken to an FBI agent and never heard of Mercurio. I visited Kriesel's home in suburban Tampa twice, hoping to ask her the same questions. The first time, in 2014, her husband told me that she was resting and didn't want to be disturbed. When I returned in 2015, I encountered a man fishing in the pond out back. He told me that he had rented the house from the Kriesels, who had moved to Texas, and that Shuhua was spending a lot of time in China. He gave me their email address, which I wrote to, receiving no reply.

Professor Baojing Sang, whom Zhang and Kriesel had accused Peng of harassing, is another puzzle. She was back in China when I phoned her in 2014. She described Peng as a caring supervisor who had once arranged for a friend to pick up her mother and daughter at a Florida airport and take them to Walt Disney World.

"Maybe he is not a good manager, but he's a good scholar," she said. "I feel very sorry" about his troubles. "It was a shock."

She was unaware that Zhang and Kriesel named her in their complaints. "They should not be talking about me. Who gave them the power to talk about me?"

In June 2015, though, she emailed me, upset that I had cited her defense of Peng in my Bloomberg article. "I think you need to know what kind of person Peng is," she wrote, without elaborating.

AFTER SPEAKING WITH Kriesel and Zhang, Shepherd acted quickly. He notified Crummett and then accompanied Zhang to see a vice provost. On April 7, Crummett summoned Peng to her office and placed him on administrative leave with pay.

Stepping into the vacuum created by Peng's absence, Shepherd wielded more influence over USF's Confucius Institute. On a July 2009 visit to Beijing, he discussed the institute's mission with Hanban's director general, and passed along her views—which accorded with his own interest in teacher training—to Crummett and Provost Wilcox. Lin Xu, he told them, wanted USF to become the "focal center" for developing Confucius Classrooms in Florida elementary and secondary schools and could send "an unlimited number of teachers."

USF closed its inquiry into the sexual harassment allegations because Zhang and Kriesel didn't pursue them. "I was tired of telling the unpleasant facts again and again," Zhang told me.

Still, the university's probe uncovered an abundance of questionable activities, including a penchant for pornography. While searching Peng's university laptop, USF's audit and compliance office found "a large cache of sexually-related materials with disturbing thematic content."

According to a family friend, Peng's interest in pornography stemmed from a 1997–98 stint as a postdoctoral researcher at Tokyo's Waseda University. The material, which included images of women in bondage, related to his academic research, Peng told me. "SM and naked pictures are a very important part of the Japanese culture, and you do not fully understand Japanese culture without it."

Saying that "this discovery calls into question your judgment to serve in an administrative capacity," Provost Wilcox removed Peng as Confucius Institute director in August 2009, though he retained his professorship.

Storing porn on an employer's computer isn't against the law; otherwise, the prisons would be even more crowded than they are. But stealing is. Unfortunately for Peng, the auditors dug into his spending and accused him of bilking USF out of $15,950 in entertainment and travel expenses, mainly by pretending that he was doing research or attending conferences when he was on vacation or teaching at Chinese universities.

In 2004, for example, USF gave Peng $220 for what he described as a weekend research trip to libraries in the Miami area. Emails and photos told a different story. Peng, accompanied by his father and a friend, visited a museum and took a dip in the ocean.

Peng's response was an inimitable blend of admission and defiance: "Who said that you cannot swim in a research trip?"

In October 2006, USF reimbursed Peng $1,220 in expenses for a presentation he said he had given the previous January at the International Workshop on East Asian Political Economy, at Peking University. The auditors claimed that no such workshop took place, and that Peng had forged the letter of invitation on his laptop six months afterward. On the January dates given for the workshop, he was actually teaching at Nankai University, which both paid him and reimbursed him for airfare.

This and other disputed China workshops did take place, although there may have been discrepancies in dates and conference titles because he didn't bother to double-check them, Peng maintained. He also said that he drafted the invitations himself because workshop organizers weren't confident of their English. He acknowledged that he should have reported his outside income from Chinese universities to USF.

Peng also contended that he spent thousands of dollars of his own money to advance the Confucius Institute, entertaining influential guests from China and ensuring that USF officials visiting Beijing were properly received. "It might be a bit right that I do not know the university procedures well and do not distinguish university and private business very well," he wrote in response to the auditors. "However, I do it much to the favor of the university and my hard work has brought great benefits to the university."

Peng failed to separate university and private business in another way. The auditors found that he falsified official letters inviting friends and acquaintances from China to study at South Florida. Peng's letters to the Chinese students and scholars overstated stipends that USF would pay them, boosting their chances of visa approval. Although it is normally the department chairman's responsibility to issue such invitations, Peng instructed one recipient to ignore the chairman's letter and use his for the visa application instead.

Kate Head, who conducted the Confucius Institute audit as the university's associate director of audit and compliance, met on July 31, 2009, with a USF police detective and an agent for U.S. Immigration and Customs Enforcement, which then opened its own investigation. Peng, one immigration agent later reported, "somewhat appears to have traded favors as counterparts in Chinese academia helped him procure employment there and he tried to reciprocate the assistance. He helped a few individuals obtain positions at USF, as well as their corresponding visas, by overstating their qualifications for both."

Peng's favors for Chinese newcomers didn't end at the U.S. border. In a separate investigation, Peng's department at USF, Government and International Affairs, barred him from its graduate programs for three years because he gave answers from past master's degree exams to two Chinese students preparing to take the test. Peng said there was no rule against doing so, it was common in China, and the students needed a boost because of their poor English skills.

All the while, the FBI kept track of the auditors' investigation. Mercurio called the audit office three times on October 20, 2009, including one call to Kate Head's number. On November 12, two calls were placed from Head's phone to Mercurio.

Mercurio and Peng also had lunch several times. She asked him to reconnect with former schoolmates and colleagues at the Chinese security service so he could gather information about China's foreign policy strategies. But he sidestepped her overtures, and didn't contact the email address she gave him—snowbox35@yahoo.com. He was hoping that the auditors would clear him to return to the Confucius Institute.

No such luck. The 187-page University Audit & Compliance draft report was scathing. It laid out in exhaustive detail Peng's alleged "misuse" of USF funds and "providing of falsified letters of invitation," and, concluding that these activities appeared to meet the legal definitions of theft and fraud, referred them to police for criminal investigation.

University officials were appalled. President Genshaft, Provost Wilcox, and General Counsel Steven Prevaux "wanted to put you in jail for what is in the Head report," Steven Wenzel, Peng's civil lawyer and a former USF general counsel, told him later.

Peng's return to the Confucius helm seemed as unlikely as Taiwan conquering China. His professorship, and even his freedom, were in jeopardy. Despite his brave front, he realized he had little choice. Only the FBI could save him.

The bureau moved quickly to take advantage of his predicament. On November 17, a week after the draft report was sent to Peng, Mercurio and another agent took him to lunch. They discussed the audit and "particularly raised the issue of letters of invitation." When Peng said that he wasn't aware that sending inaccurate visa letters was a crime, Mercurio told him that "not knowing the law is not a defense. But how the violations are handled is more important. It all depends on whether the authority would pursue them or not." The unspoken message was that he needed powerful friends—like the FBI.

Peng understood. "I asked them whether they could help me," he later wrote. He promised to give her a list of his students in China. In return, "she also agreed that she would try to help with my matter, although she was not sure what they could do."

"Thank you for your willingness to help me at this difficult time of mine," Peng wrote the next day to the "snowbox" email address. "If the final report is very bad and I am severely punished, I will be in a very weak position to help you because I will surely lose my reputation in China and will no longer be invited. Then there will be little I can do for you. If you can help me and my status and reputation are kept, I promise I can do a lot for you. Please trust that most of the problems are caused by cultural differences and I am a truly high quality person."

Having reeled him in, and understandably reluctant to make a written promise to interfere with university discipline, Mercurio played it cool. "As I stated at lunch, I don't know if there's anything that I can do for you," she replied. "We can certainly keep in touch and deal with matters as they unfold. Since your troubles don't have anything to do with assistance to my office, there probably isn't much I can do. However, let me know your status, and if I can help you, I will."

THE CIA'S FAVORITE
UNIVERSITY PRESIDENT

On the crisp autumn afternoon of November 26, 2007, a black car picked up Pennsylvania State University president Graham Spanier at Washington's Dulles International Airport and whisked him to CIA headquarters in Langley, Virginia. Using his identification card embedded with a hologram and computer chip, he checked in at security and was greeted by the chief of staff of the National Resources Division, the CIA's clandestine domestic service. They proceeded to a conference room, where about two dozen chiefs of station and other senior CIA intelligence officers awaited them.

Spanier was expecting to brief them on the work of the National Security Higher Education Advisory Board, an organization he chaired and had helped create, which fostered dialogue between intelligence agencies and universities. First, though, the CIA surprised him. In a brief, confidential ceremony, it presented him with the Warren Medal that is, according to Spanier, the agency's highest honor for non-employees. Named after late chief justice Earl Warren, and enclosed in a handsome hand-carved wooden box, the medal was about four inches in diameter and resembled a large gold coin. The front depicted an eagle and was inscribed, "For Outstanding Service to the United States." The other side read, "To Dr. Graham B. Spanier. For your outstanding contributions to the national security of the United States of America. Thank you from a grateful nation."

The honor recognized Spanier's dedication to alerting college administrators to the threat of human and cyber-espionage, and to opening doors for the agency at campuses nationwide. A former family therapist and television talk-show host with an unruffled, empathetic manner and features—round face, white hair, blue eyes—reminiscent of Phil Donahue, Spanier soothed many an academic's anxieties about dealing with the CIA and FBI.

Since the intelligence agencies were going to meddle anyway, Spanier reasoned, they should do so with the knowledge and consent of university presidents. "My feeling was, If there's a spy on my campus, a potential terrorist, or a visiting faculty member you believe is up to no good, I know you'll be pursuing it," he told me in April 2016. "Here's the deal. Rather than break into his office, come to me, I have top-secret clearance, show me your FISA [Foreign Intelligence Surveillance Act] order, and I'll have someone unlock the door."

SPANIER'S CIA MEDAL—and a similar FBI award a year later—symbolized a reconciliation between the intelligence services and academia. The relationship has come full circle: from chumminess in the 1940s and 1950s, to the animosity during the Vietnam War and civil rights eras that I remember from my youth in Amherst, Massachusetts, and back to cooperation after the September 11, 2001, attacks. Their unequal partnership, though, tilts toward the government. U.S. intelligence seized on the renewed goodwill, and the red carpet rolled out by Spanier and other university administrators, to expand not only its public presence on campus but also covert operations and sponsoring of secret research. Except for the snubbing of *Game of Pawns*, the FBI movie about Glenn Shriver, federal encroachment on academic prerogatives met only token resistance.

The two cultures are antithetical: academia is open and international, while intelligence services are clandestine and nationalistic. Still, after Islamic fundamentalist terrorists toppled the World Trade Center, universities became part of the national security apparatus. The new recruiting booths at meetings of academic associations were one telling indicator. The CIA began exhibiting at the annual convention of the American Council on the Teaching of Foreign Languages in 2004, as did the FBI and NSA around the same time. Since 2011, the FBI, Office of the Director of National Intelligence, and NSA have participated on a panel at the Modern Language Association convention titled "Using Your Language Proficiency and Cultural Expertise in a Federal Government Career."

Today American universities routinely offer degrees in homeland security and courses in espionage and cyber-hacking, and vie for federal designation as Intelligence Community Centers for Academic Excellence and National Centers of Academic Excellence in Cyber Operations. They obtain research grants from obscure federal agencies such as Intelligence Advanced Research Projects Activity. Established in 2006, IARPA sponsors "high-risk/high pay-off research that has the potential to provide our nation with an overwhelming intelligence advantage," according to its website. To date, it has funded teams with researchers representing more than 175 academic institutions, mostly in the United States.

While almost all IARPA projects are unclassified, universities increasingly carry out secret but lucrative government research at well-guarded facilities. Two years after the 9/11 attacks, the University of Maryland established a center that conducts classified research on language for the Pentagon and intelligence agencies. Edward Snowden worked there in 2005 as a security guard, eight years before he joined government contractor Booz Allen Hamilton Inc. and leaked classified files on NSA surveillance.

The center is located off campus. Like many universities, Maryland forbids secret research on campus, but its transparency stops at the far side of its neatly trimmed lawns. "Classified research always occurs off campus . . . to ensure the integrity of sensitive work being done," Crystal Brown, Maryland's chief communications officer, told me. "Of course any research being done on campus upholds the spirit of academic freedom and an open environment."

Other universities have no such compunctions. "Classified research on campus, once highly controversial, is making a comeback," VICE News reported in 2015. The National Security Agency in 2013 awarded $60 million to North Carolina State University in Raleigh, the largest research grant in the school's history, to launch an on-campus laboratory for data analysis. "Due to the high degree of confidentiality required . . . specific funding, personnel numbers and facility details cannot be provided," a university news release stated. "Physical access to the lab itself will be restricted to individuals who have been issued a security clearance by the U.S. government."

Virginia Polytechnic Institute and State University, based in the southwest Virginia town of Blacksburg, established a private nonprofit corporation in December 2009 to "perform classified and highly classified work" in intelligence, cybersecurity, and national security. Two years later, the university planted its flag in prime intelligence community turf. It opened a research center across the Potomac River from Washington, D.C., in Ballston, an Arlington, Virginia, neighborhood brimming with CIA and Pentagon contractors. The center features facilities for "conducting sensitive research on behalf of the national security community."

Virginia Tech's quest for buried treasure sparked George Washington University in Washington, D.C., to rethink its ban on research—on or off campus—that is "not compatible with open communication of knowledge." Rather than be outdone in its own backyard by what one administrator belittled as a school from "out there in the middle of farm country," GWU adopted a plan in 2013 to "explore modifying its policies to allow some faculty and staff members to engage in classified research." It also envisions building a classified facility on the university's science and technology campus in Ashburn, Virginia.

"There is a lot of funding in this area, and we're not competitive for that funding," Leo Chalupa, GWU's vice president for research, told the *Baltimore Sun.*

Like many public universities across the country, the University of Wisconsin is searching for other income sources to offset a decline in state appropriations. After cutting its support per student by 20 percent from 2002–03 to 2012–13, Wisconsin allowed its university system to accept classified contracts, reversing restrictions dating back to campus protests against the Vietnam War. The university then joined with private companies to build a cybersecurity laboratory at a research park in Madison. Around the same time, its flagship Madison campus waived a cap on enrollment of out-of-state and international students, who pay higher tuition than in-state residents. Nobody seemed to notice that the combination of classified research and unlimited foreign enrollment amounted to an invitation for espionage.

U.S. INTELLIGENCE OFTEN meets informally with university higher-ups and gives presentations to faculty members about the espionage threat. Emails obtained through an open records request show such interactions at one public university, New Jersey Institute of Technology, in Newark, which has 11,325 graduate and undergraduate students. In February 2011, CIA director of science and technology Glenn Gaffney, an NJIT alumnus, visited administrators and board members there. "I am looking forward to continuing discussions on all of the topics we discussed including opportunities for students, faculty and researchers," an NJIT engineering dean wrote to the CIA afterward.

"Mr. Gaffney's visit to his alma mater was a great opportunity for him to revisit the campus, participate in a recruiting event with students, and thank the school for what the Engineering Sciences program did to prepare him for what became a successful career at CIA," a CIA spokesperson told me.

The following month, an FBI agent had lunch with NJIT's deans of engineering, computing sciences, and management at a private table at Don Pepe, a Portuguese restaurant near the bureau's Newark offices. The agent advised the deans to beware of foreign scholars, especially from China.

"There's a lot of visiting professors, and the FBI's concern is that a healthy percentage of them are intelligence agents," said Robert English, then interim dean of management, who organized the lunch at the agent's request. "They want to inform universities about potential agents coming over, and they want to warn faculty, if you're doing any research, make sure it's not on your hard drive when you go there."

Three years after the lunch at Don Pepe, the bureau hosted a career day at its Newark office for graduate students from the area's universities. Although the FBI hires only U.S. citizens, it pressed NJIT for thirty students from its computer science program, which is almost entirely made up of foreigners, primarily from India and China. The FBI "pushed me a lot," recalled James Geller, then the institute's chairman of computer science. He did his best to meet the quota, sending a contingent of eighteen students, all of whom were international. At the FBI's request, he provided their dates and places of birth and their passport numbers. "Attached please find all information on foreign nationals that has been supplied to me by NJIT CS [computer science] students who attended your event," Geller emailed the FBI in June 2014. The FBI may have wanted to refer them as potential employees to other intelligence agencies or contractors, monitor their activities, use them as informants, or all of the above.

"I was actually amazed they were willing to bring foreign students to their program," Geller told me.

If foreign students play ball, they may be rewarded. In 2014–15, FBI agents met twice with an Iranian graduate student in electrical engineering at the University of Nevada at Reno, asking him about Iran's infrastructure and nuclear program. Coincidentally or not, the student came up a winner soon afterward in the Diversity Immigrant Visa Program, known as the green-card lottery, granting him permanent U.S. residency. His odds of success were less than one in one hundred.

ACADEMIA WAS PRESENT at the CIA's creation. Its precursor, the Office of Strategic Services, founded in 1942, was "half cops-and-robbers and half faculty meeting," according to McGeorge Bundy, an intelligence officer during World War II and later national security adviser to presidents Kennedy and Johnson. The OSS was largely an Ivy League bastion. It attracted thirteen Yale professors in its first year, along with forty-two students from the university's class of 1943. A Yale assistant professor, under cover of acquiring manuscripts for the university library, became OSS chief in Istanbul.

When the CIA was established in 1947, the Ivy influence carried over. Skip Walz, Yale crew coach from 1946 to 1950, doubled as a CIA recruiter, drawing a salary of ten thousand dollars a year from each employer. Every three weeks he supplied names of Yale athletes with the right academic and social credentials to a CIA agent whom he met at the Lincoln Memorial Reflecting Pool in Washington. The "classic CIA resume of the 1950s" was "Groton, Yale, Harvard Law." In 1963, the Soviet Union expelled a Yale history professor, Frederick Barghoorn, whom it accused of spying for the CIA. Although the agency gradually expanded hiring from other universities, 26 percent of college graduates it employed during the Nixon administration had Ivy League degrees. It helped establish think tanks and research centers at several top universities, such as MIT's Center for International Studies in 1952. The CIA "was the primary funding source for the Center's first two years, and a sponsor of various research projects until 1966," according to the center's website.

Almost from its inception, the CIA cultivated foreign students, recognizing their value as informants and future government officials in their homelands. It learned about them not only through their professors but also through the CIA-funded National Student Association, the largest student group in the United States. With only 26,433 international students in the United States in 1950, about 3 percent of today's total, the CIA relied on the association to identify potential informants both at home and abroad.

The agency, which supported the student association as a noncommunist alternative to Soviet-backed student organizations, meddled in the association's election of officers and sent its activists, including future feminist icon Gloria Steinem, to disrupt international youth festivals. "In the CIA, I finally found a group of people who understood how important it was to represent the diversity of our government's ideas at Communist festivals," Steinem told *Newsweek* in 1967. "If I had the choice, I would do it again."

National Student Association staff members reported to the CIA on "thousands of foreign students' political tendencies, personality traits, and future aspirations." The CIA helped establish associations in the United States of students from Iran, Pakistan, and Afghanistan, as well as the Foreign Student Leadership Project, which enrolled students from Asia, Latin America, and the Middle East for a year at an American university. With an assist from the CIA, the number of foreign students in the United States almost doubled from 1950 to 1960.

Then it all unraveled. *Ramparts,* a monthly magazine that opposed the Vietnam War, reported in 1966 that a Michigan State University program to train South Vietnamese police had five CIA agents on its payroll. A year later, *Ramparts* revealed the CIA's involvement in the National Student Association, stirring a national outcry. The Johnson administration responded by banning covert federal funding of "any of the nation's educational or private voluntary organizations"—though not of their individual members or employees.

Privately, Johnson saw the hand of world communism—namely, the Soviet Union and/or China—in both the *Ramparts* exposé and the antiwar protests, and ordered the CIA and FBI to prove it. Both agencies dug into the personal lives of *Ramparts* staff, and "eleven CIA officers grew long hair, learned the jargon of the New Left, and went off to infiltrate peace groups in the United States and Europe." FBI penetration and surveillance—including illegal wiretaps and warrantless searches—expanded under Nixon but failed to turn up evidence of foreign funding.

The government's crackdown on its campus critics, along with CIA blunders such as the disastrous 1961 Bay of Pigs Invasion of Cuba, fractured the camaraderie between intelligence agencies and academe. In 1968 alone, there were seventy-seven instances of picketing, sit-ins, and other student protests against CIA recruiters. In 1977, a political science professor at Brooklyn College was denied tenure and promotion. The candidate had offended his colleagues by letting the CIA debrief him in a fifteen-minute telephone conversation after a research trip to Europe.

The disaffection was mutual. Just as Ivy League graduates began having doubts about joining the CIA, so older alumni who devoted their careers to intelligence agencies bridled at the antiestablishment campus mood. "It is not true that universities rejected the intelligence community; the community rejected universities at least as early," Yale historian Robin Winks wrote.

Hostility between the intelligence services and universities peaked with the 1976 report of the Senate Select Committee to Study Governmental Operations with Respect to Intelligence Activities, usually known as the Church Committee after its chairman, Senator Frank Church of Idaho. In the most comprehensive investigation ever of U.S. intelligence agencies, the committee documented an appalling litany of abuses, some undertaken by presidential order and others rogue. The CIA, it found, had tested LSD and other drugs on prisoners and students; opened 215,820 letters passing through a New York City postal facility over two decades; and tried to assassinate Cuban dictator Fidel Castro and other foreign leaders. The FBI, for its part, had harassed civil rights and anti–Vietnam War protesters by wiretapping them and smearing them in anonymous letters to parents, neighbors, and employers.

The committee also exposed clandestine connections between the CIA and higher education. The agency was using "several hundred

academics" at more than a hundred U.S. colleges for, among other purposes, "providing leads and, on occasion, making introductions for
intelligence purposes," typically without anyone else on campus being
"aware of the CIA link."

Bowing to the CIA's insistence on protecting its agents, the committee
didn't name the professors or the colleges where they taught. Typically,
they helped with recruiting foreign students. A professor would invite an
international student—often from a Soviet-bloc country, or perhaps Iran—
to his office to get acquainted. Flattered by the attention, the student would
have no clue he was being assessed as a potential CIA informant. The professor would then arrange for the student to meet a wealthy "friend" in
publishing or investing. The friend would buy the student dinner and pay
him generously for an essay about his country or his research specialty.

Unaware he was being compromised, the grateful student would
compose one well-compensated paper after another. By the time the professor's friend admitted that he was a CIA agent, and asked him to spy,
the student had little choice but to agree. He couldn't report the overture
to his own government, because his acceptance of CIA money would
jeopardize his reputation in his homeland, if not his freedom.

MORTON HALPERIN KNEW about this deception from conversations
with Church Committee staff and his own research. He found it "completely inappropriate" and intended to end it once and for all. The
committee's report showed him the way.

From a bookshelf in his office at the Open Society Foundations in
Washington, D.C., where he is a senior advisor, Halperin extracts the first
volume of the Church Committee report. He opens the faded, thumb-
worn paperback to a passage he had underlined forty years before: "The
Committee believes that it is the responsibility of private institutions and
particularly the American academic community to set the professional and
ethical standards of its members." That sentence sent him on a quest to
persuade colleges to stand up to U.S. intelligence agencies and curb
covert activity on their campuses. His mission would provoke an unprecedented confrontation between the CIA and the country's most famous
university. Its outcome would shape the relationship between U.S. intelligence and academia, and still has repercussions today.

Halperin had Ivy League credentials as impeccable as any CIA recruit's: a bachelor's degree from Columbia and a Yale doctorate, followed by six years on the Harvard faculty. A former White House wunderkind, who'd taken a top Pentagon post under President Lyndon Johnson before turning thirty and then joined the National Security Council staff under President Richard Nixon, Halperin had himself become a target of U.S. government covert operations, largely because of his misgivings about the Vietnam War. With the approval of his mentor, Henry Kissinger, then national security adviser, the Nixon administration tapped Halperin's home phone in 1969, suspecting him of leaking information about the secret bombing of Cambodia to reporters. It also placed him near the top of Nixon's notorious "enemies list."

Halperin had also clashed with the CIA over censorship. The agency contended that *The CIA and the Cult of Intelligence* (1974), on which Halperin had advised authors Victor Marchetti and John Marks, divulged classified information about technological methods for gathering intelligence. A federal judge ordered 168 deletions in the text, and at the CIA's request imposed a gag order on Halperin in 1974, prohibiting him from divulging the excised material.

As director of the Center for National Security Studies, a project of the American Civil Liberties Union, Halperin had lobbied Congress to create the Church Committee. He attended its hearings and testified before it, urging a ban on clandestine operations because they bypass congressional and public oversight and are incompatible with democratic values.

Armed with the Church Committee's recommendation, he approached Harvard and asked it to set rules for secret CIA activity on campus. He expected that any restrictions placed by the nation's oldest and most prominent university on CIA activity would spread throughout academe.

Harvard general counsel Daniel Steiner, whom Halperin contacted first, was sympathetic, and urged President Derek Bok to take up the issue. As it happened, Bok was already familiar with the Church Committee. Its chief counsel, Frederick A. O. ("Fritz") Schwarz Jr., was a family friend and Bok's former law student. Bok admired his political activism, especially on civil rights. As a third-year Harvard law student in 1960, Schwarz had organized a protest in Cambridge to support a sit-in by blacks at the lunch counter of a Woolworth's department store in Greensboro, North Carolina, that refused to serve them.

"I can still remember walking into Harvard Square on a rainy day," Bok said in a 2015 interview. "There in front of Woolworth's were Schwarz and another student picketing over Woolworth's refusal to serve Negroes in the South."

Bok had also met with Church Committee member Charles Mathias, a Republican senator from Maryland, and staff director William Miller, to discuss whether the committee should call for a federal law banning covert intelligence gathering on campus. Universities typically oppose any extension of federal power over academic decisions. Reflecting this view, Bok told Mathias and Miller at their meeting that colleges, not the government, should take the lead in curtailing covert operations. They agreed.

"The integrity of the institutions required it," Miller told me in 2015. "It could not be imposed from outside."

Bok appointed four Harvard sages to set standards as the Church Committee had advised. They included Steiner and Harvard law professor Archibald Cox, who had become famous in the 1973 "Saturday Night Massacre," when President Nixon fired him as special prosecutor for the Watergate scandal.

Steiner met with top CIA officials, including Cord Meyer Jr., who had overseen the agency's hidden role in the National Student Association. Based on their discussions, Steiner wrote to Meyer, "I would conclude that the CIA feels it is appropriate to use, on a compensated or uncompensated basis, faculty members and administrators for operational purposes, including the gathering of intelligence as requested by the CIA, and as covert recruiters on campus."

The Harvard wise men disagreed. Their 1977 guidelines prohibited students and faculty from undertaking "intelligence operations" for the CIA, although they could be debriefed about foreign travels after returning home. "The use of the academic profession and scholarly enterprises to provide a 'cover' for intelligence activities is likely to corrupt the academic process and lead to a loss of public respect for academic enterprises," they wrote.

Also forbidden was helping the CIA "in obtaining the unwitting services of another member of the Harvard community"—in other words, recruiting foreign students under false pretenses. To Bok and his advisers, this perverted the trust between professor and student on which higher education was built. Posing as a mentor, a professor might probe a foreign student's views on international affairs, or ask about his financial situation, not to guide him but to help the CIA evaluate and enlist him. And, once it snared the student, the agency might ask him to break the laws of his home country—a request that Harvard couldn't be a party to.

"Many of these students are highly vulnerable," Bok told the Senate in 1978. "They are frequently young and inexperienced, often short of funds and away from their homelands for the first time. Is it appropriate for faculty members, who supposedly are acting in the best interests of the students, to be part of a process of recruiting such students to engage in activities that may be hazardous and probably illegal under the laws of their home countries? I think not."

The Harvard committee acknowledged that its new rules made the CIA's job harder. "This loss is one that a free society should be willing to suffer," it said.

THE CIA SAW no reason to suffer. Admiral Stansfield Turner, CIA director from 1977 to 1981, believed that the agency should take advantage of the presence of foreign students on U.S. soil. Since recruiting foreigners in totalitarian countries is difficult, "it would be foolish not to attempt to identify sympathetic people when they are in our country," he wrote in his autobiography. "University personnel can sometimes help the CIA in this identification, though there clearly can be a conflict between a university official's doing that and fulfilling his responsibility to look after the student's best interests in and out of the classroom."

Turner rejected Harvard's guidelines—as well as another Church Committee recommendation that the agency tell university presidents about clandestine relationships on campus—and made clear that the agency had no intention of following them.

If professors want to help the CIA, Turner argued in correspondence with Bok, it's their right as American citizens, "a matter of choice or conscience." While the agency encourages scholars to notify their universities of their CIA ties, Turner went on, many are reluctant to do so for fear of hurting their careers. "These relationships are frequently kept confidential at the insistence of the individuals themselves, their concerns being that they might otherwise be exposed to harassment or other adverse consequences as a result of exercising their right to assist their Government."

In his narrative, the scholar-spies, rather than the foreigners they deceptively recruited, were at risk. Harvard's policy, he concluded, "deprives academics of all freedom of choice in relation to involvement in intelligence activities."

FOLLOWING THE MAXIM that the best defense is a good offense, the CIA promulgated its own "Regulation on Relationships with the U.S. Academic Community," which remains in effect today. Drafted by John Rizzo, a young lawyer who had recently joined the CIA from the Treasury Department, the one-page regulation ratified the status quo, permitting the agency to "enter into personal services contracts and other continuing relationships with individual full-time staff and faculty members."

The CIA would "suggest" that the staff or faculty member alert a senior university official, "unless security considerations preclude such a disclosure or the individual objects."

Since the Church Committee also raised concerns about CIA relationships with journalists and clergy, Rizzo drew up rules for dealing with them, too. It would have made sense for him to set the same standards for covert use of journalists and clergy as for academics, since there are obvious analogies between the three groups. All are expected to pursue their vision of truth, whether or not it conflicts with the national interest. All have captive flocks that trust them—students, readers and sources, and worshippers—making them potentially valuable as recruiters.

Yet Rizzo set a higher bar for journalists and clergy. To use them, unlike a professor, would require the personal approval of the CIA director. The reason for the double standard, Rizzo said in a 2015 interview, was purely pragmatic. Of the three groups, professors were by far the most important to the agency. By the Church Committee's reckoning, the CIA had relationships with fifty journalists and a handful of clergy, as measured against several hundred academics.

"Academics were active on lots of campuses," said Rizzo, who rose to become the agency's acting general counsel before leaving in 2009 for private practice. "The judgment was, the director can't approve every single one."

Harvard and the CIA bickered with one eye on the audience they wanted to impress: the rest of academia. One university, no matter how prestigious, couldn't stare down the CIA. But if other universities lined up behind Harvard, the agency would be hard-pressed to resist.

"I thought the Harvard policy would have a chilling effect," Rizzo said. "We all thought it was just the beginning, the canary in the coal mine."

So did Halperin, who set out like Johnny Appleseed to sow the Harvard guidelines across the country. To his shock, the soil was barren. Other universities were reluctant to follow Harvard's lead without documented evidence of covert CIA-faculty relationships, which the Church Committee had suppressed. University presidents wrote to the CIA, asking for particulars about cooperating faculty, which the agency declined to provide. Some professors complained that Harvard's rules would infringe on their academic freedom. Steiner, the Harvard lawyer, sought support from an association of general counsels at major universities, without success. After CIA director Turner lobbied University of Michigan faculty members, they voted down proposed guidelines.

Only ten schools adopted Harvard's policy even in diluted form. "Fortunately, very few other universities followed Harvard's example, and this did not become a continuing problem," Turner later wrote.

Rizzo was surprised that the Harvard policy "never got traction." It didn't even stop covert activities at Harvard, where professors risked being disciplined for hiding their CIA affiliations. "I don't remember hearing about any Harvard cooperators being scared off by the Bok guidelines," Rizzo said.

Forty years later, Halperin remains perplexed. "I thought once Harvard did it, everybody else would follow," he said. "Nobody did. It was a big disappointment. If we had been able to make it the norm on major campuses, it would have had impact. I was befuddled, bewildered, and frustrated. Finally, I just gave up."

THE FAILURE TO replicate the Harvard guidelines nationwide snuffed out the last chance to build a firewall between U.S. intelligence and academia. Critics of covert recruiting on campus lost momentum. Even as students from China began pouring into the United States, prompting the FBI and CIA to escalate campus recruiting, the pushback from academia diminished, especially after the Soviet invasion of Afghanistan in 1979. The alliance that had characterized the 1940s and 1950s began to reemerge.

In 1977, a year after the Church Committee report, a Boston-based CIA operative dropped by the office of an MIT physicist. It was the start of a long and delicate relationship in which the physicist would cooperate with the agency—and set limits on just how far his cooperation would extend.

He was heading a federally funded MIT initiative on nonproliferation and had acquired a security clearance at the request of the U.S. government. The agent explained that the CIA was eager to consult academic experts on nuclear issues. "There are several people in your department who are already helping us," the agent said. "You travel abroad and have interactions with foreign scientists."

After consulting with an MIT colleague, who confided that he was already advising the CIA, the physicist agreed to the agent's request, with the proviso that his assistance would be voluntary. "I was against the spread of nuclear weapons, but I didn't want to be considered an employee of the CIA," he said in 2015.

"I felt that proliferation was a serious problem and I might be able to make a contribution, but I also had some misgivings." He didn't tell other MIT faculty or administrators about his new role. "I didn't talk about it. You have the feeling most people at MIT don't want to know."

As he returned from trips to such countries as Austria, Germany, Japan, and Indonesia, the CIA would call and question him. Whom did you meet? Did you talk to so-and-so? What did you learn?

Though unpaid, having a CIA connection could be useful. For example, when the physicist wanted to learn more about Iraq's nuclear program, he would go to the CIA's covert office in a downtown Boston commercial building. There he would use the scrambler phone, a secure line on which he could discuss classified information, to call a scientist at the Oak Ridge National Laboratory, in Tennessee, who was an expert on the antiquated bomb-building method that Iraq favored.

From 1984 to 1986, while on leave from MIT as a visiting scholar with the U.S. Arms Control and Disarmament Agency, he was occasionally sent on sensitive missions. On one occasion, he consulted with the CIA station chief in Vienna, who had a diplomatic cover and a spacious office in the U.S. embassy, where the physicist showed up at the appointed time. Elegantly dressed in a three-piece suit, the chief greeted his guest, locked the door, returned to his large desk, and pushed a button. A wall of bookshelves swung around to reveal a room with a large hemispherical metal-meshed enclosure. Reminded of every spy film he had ever seen, the physicist laughed and said, "Can you do that again?"

The station chief led him into the cage, where they could talk about intercepted intelligence information without fear of surveillance. Half-apologetically, the chief explained that he came from a CIA family—his father had worked for the agency and so did his wife—but didn't have much scientific knowledge. The physicist said he understood, and explained the intercepts in laymen's terms for him.

Back with MIT, he traveled again, and his debriefings resumed. Of particular interest to the CIA were his interactions with the Iranian students who had been sent to study nuclear engineering at MIT in the 1970s before the downfall of the shah in 1979. Several had returned to Iran in the mid-1980s after the new regime there, which had suspended the nuclear program begun under the shah, decided to resume it. The CIA wanted the physicist's assessment of their capabilities.

Then, in the late 1990s, he was asked to work directly for the agency: to go to India and establish contact with various scientists in order to obtain information that the CIA wanted. For the physicist, that crossed a line. He was willing to tell the CIA about his trips and provide scientific savvy, but not to accept its assignments or use his academic status as a cover to gather information on its behalf. "I refused," he said. "I was not willing to act as an agent for the CIA. That was the last time I heard officially" from the agency.

However, he did hear once more—unofficially. In February 2005, he was a member of a small group of U.S. nuclear scientists who met at the Iranian mission in lower Manhattan with Mohammad Javad Zarif, then Iran's permanent representative to the United Nations and now its minister of foreign affairs. The scientists hadn't notified the U.S. government of the meeting, which aimed to seek common ground on Iran's nuclear program.

Shortly after the physicist returned home that evening, he received a phone call. "We understand you met with Zarif," a woman's voice said. "We'd like to discuss it." At a restaurant in Cambridge, he answered her questions about the discussion and his impressions of Zarif. He didn't ask how she learned about it.

THE CIA MOVED to mend the breach with academia. In 1982, it brought fourteen college presidents to its Langley headquarters to meet the director and other top officials. In 1977, it started a "scholars-in-residence" program in which professors on sabbatical from their universities were given contracts to advise CIA analysts and made "privy to information that would never be available to them on campus." In 1985, the agency added an "officers-in-residence" component, which placed intelligence officers nearing retirement at universities at CIA expense.

The effectiveness of the officers-in-residence program was "very mixed," said former CIA analyst Brian Latell, who ran it from 1994 to 1998. Before he took over, "we were sending Dagwood Bumsteads who should have been forced into retirement." Some were just hanging around campus with nothing to do. Latell set standards; the officers must have advanced degrees and be allowed to teach.

Some universities refused to participate. Latell sought to place a well-qualified officer with a doctorate and teaching experience at Yale. He enlisted support from senior faculty who fondly remembered the days when Yale professors and alumni forged the OSS. Nevertheless, Yale president Richard Levin rejected the proposal, Latell said. Asked about the incident, Levin said he had only a "vague recollection" of it.

At the University of California, Santa Barbara, the CIA officer in residence drew criticism by displaying a reticence more suited to his clandestine background than to the open academic culture. "Whether or not his 'no comments' and refusals to talk about subjects were excessive, he apparently felt that he had to minimize exposure and say very little," according to a CIA history of the program. Faculty initiated petitions against him, and a student protest "led to numerous arrests and the kind of flare-up that a host university and the Agency equally wish to avoid." He "inspired suspicion rather than confidence," and "quickly left."

At its peak, the program had officers in residence at more than a dozen universities, but the CIA has trimmed it back in recent years. The CIA and elite colleges both undervalued the program, Art Hulnick felt. The agency rarely invited the officers to talk about life on campus, while premier universities such as Harvard and MIT didn't consider them qualified to teach.

Boston University had no such qualms. After more than two decades at the CIA as an analyst, speechwriter for two directors, liaison to the German government, and academic affairs coordinator, Hulnick became an officer in residence at BU in 1989. The university assigned him a fourth-floor office—"In case they storm the building, they won't get you," his department chair joked—and he developed and taught courses on intelligence strategy. When his three-year stint in the program ended, he didn't return to the CIA. Instead he joined BU's international relations faculty and wrote two books and numerous articles before retiring in 2015.

After Hulnick's classes, he and his students routinely repaired to Cornwall's pub in Kenmore Square for refreshments. He sensed that some were foreign spies, who took his courses as a sort of in-service training. "I could tell," Hulnick said in a 2015 interview in his Brookline, Massachusetts, living room, which had framed maps on the walls and a keyboard that he occasionally plinked. "There's a certain level of jargon. They were trying to get the American take on how intelligence is supposed to work."

One Russian student, for instance, who had been to Thailand and spoke fluent Thai, had "all the hallmarks of a KGB officer." Hulnick had to buy lunch for another Russian as a prize for deciphering a coded message he wrote on the blackboard. "She had family connections to the Russian mafia, and a lot of them were ex-KGB. She came from that world."

Like universities, the CIA never forgets its alumni. One day its clandestine domestic arm, the National Resources Division, asked Hulnick if he knew any foreign students of interest.

"I said, 'I can point people out, but that's it,'" Hulnick recalled. He wouldn't arrange meetings. "They said, 'We'll take it from there.' I couldn't be involved beyond spotting a student."

One student whom Hulnick spotted for the agency in the 1990s came from Kuwait's ruling family. "He was in my class. We talked about it. I picked out the name. I asked him and he said, 'Yeah, I'm a prince.'"

THE CIA SUPPLIED not only teachers but also students, intervening in a cherished academic bailiwick: admissions. In some cases it arranged schooling for valuable foreign informants who were in danger and had to flee to the United States. "Foreign nationals who have worked in place for years, and have done a heroic service, at some point may need to be exfiltrated out of their home country," says Henry Crumpton, the former head of the CIA's National Resources Division. "During that resettlement process, the agency goes to great lengths to help them establish a new life with a new identity. A big part of that is finding jobs, which may require more education for the former agent who has defected and his family."

In other instances, the CIA compensated foreign agents by arranging their children's or grandchildren's admission to an American college and paying their tuition, typically through a front organization. "When you're recruiting a foreigner, you look at, 'What can I do for this guy?' Sometimes a guy will say, 'I want my daughter to go to a good American school,'" says Gene Coyle, who came to Indiana University as a CIA officer in residence. He retired from the agency in 2006 and is now a professor of practice at Indiana, teaching classes on national security and espionage history.

"The answer may be, 'We may be able to line her up with a scholarship from the Aardvark Society of Boston.' Instead of giving Daddy cold hard cash, when he has to explain where he gets it, his daughter gets the Aardvark Society second-born scholarship for people from Uzbekistan."

While the CIA can pull strings at top universities when it needs to, some informants ask for less selective colleges. A former CIA officer recalls that one source's request was easily granted: his son wanted to attend for-profit Strayer University, which accepts anyone with a high school diploma.

"We sent an awful lot of Arabs" to state universities in the Southwest, this ex-officer recalls. "They all wanted to study petroleum engineering. Those schools had a huge Arab population and they fit right in."

THE COMPOSITION OF the professoriate is undergoing a sea change. Tenured faculty who rose through the academic ranks are giving way to adjunct teachers and "professors of practice" with government or business backgrounds. As a result, more faculty members have national security experience. Some act as talent scouts, recommending students who would make good analysts or agents.

Dr. Jerrold Post was a pioneer among this growing breed. With a foot in both camps, he funneled a stream of prospects into U.S. intelligence.

As a Yale medical student, Post enjoyed reading Ian Fleming's James Bond novels in the library in his spare time. Then, as a resident in psychiatry at Harvard, he repeatedly made a Freudian slip on his typewriter, transposing the first two letters of the word *psychiatrist* to spell *spychiatrist*.

Despite this portent, Post seemed destined for a traditional academic career, until his path took an unexpected turn. After accepting an offer from Harvard's Department of Psychiatry, Post recalls, he received a call from someone he barely knew, who had been two years ahead of him at Yale medical school. His name was Herb.

"I understand you don't have a job for next year," Herb said.

"Actually, I do," Post said. But he agreed to have lunch with Herb at the Hickory Hearth in Washington's Georgetown neighborhood.

The luncheon conversation mystified Post. It was like a job interview in which the interviewer never says what the job is. Herb clearly knew a lot about Post, and elicited more.

Finally, Post asked, "Herb, are we here to talk about a job?"

With his teeth clamped together, presumably to prevent anyone from reading his lips, Herb hissed, "I'd rather not talk about it here."

Post grasped a wooden shutter. "Look, there are no electronic bugs here," he said.

Herb smiled. "You like that sort of thing, do you? Why don't you follow me in your car."

Herb crossed the Key Bridge to northern Virginia and parked at an overlook. Post followed him. So did a police car. Herb blushed. "This happened to me once before," he said. Post wondered if Herb, unaware that he was happily heterosexual, was about to make some sort of overture.

At the next overlook, they were alone. Herb reached into his pocket and removed a CIA secrecy agreement. "Before we talk, I want you to sign this," he said.

Post signed. Soon he agreed to start a pilot program to develop psychological assessments of world leaders for the president and secretaries of state and defense.

That was in 1965. For the next twenty-one years, Post ran the CIA's Center for the Analysis of Personality and Political Behavior, overseeing anthropologists, sociologists, political scientists, social and organizational psychologists, and other psychiatrists. His achievements included preparing profiles of Egyptian president Anwar Sadat and Israeli prime minister Menachem Begin before the landmark Camp David peace agreements in 1978. Post cautioned U.S. president Jimmy Carter to avoid arguing about biblical history with Begin, since both men fancied themselves experts on the subject.

Post enjoyed the intellectual adventure of crafting what he regarded as a new kind of intelligence, and presidents and cabinet members loved hearing about the personality quirks of their opposite numbers. Still, Post's work was controversial, and CIA directors weren't always receptive to it. "What he was doing wasn't in the mainstream," says Robert Jervis, a Columbia University professor of international politics and longtime CIA consultant. "A lot of people thought it was hocus-pocus."

In 1986, Post decamped to George Washington University, which was seeking closer ties with the federal government. As a professor of psychiatry, political psychology, and international affairs, he became a force unto himself. He founded a political psychology program, where he taught popular courses on leadership and the psychology of terrorism. Long frustrated by CIA secrecy, he relished the limelight bestowed by his frequent commentary on CNN, MSNBC, and other networks. After Iraq invaded Kuwait in 1990, he prepared a profile of Saddam Hussein at a newspaper's request, and testified before Congress about the Iraqi leader.

On the side, he consulted for intelligence agencies from his home office, where research assistants had to compete for space on the couch with his wire-haired dachshunds, Coco and Emily. His "hybrid world," as former student and research assistant Laurita Denny calls it, came in handy when protégés aspired to federal service. "I don't know another person who networks and maintains contacts as well as Jerry," says Denny, who now holds a national security post in the U.S. government. "He opened doors for students."

She added in a September 2015 email: "Jerry has been a part of restoring that historical closeness between the academic community and the intelligence community. Jerry's accessibility to students and his ability to network and retain connections with his prior colleagues definitely bridged an important gap."

Post told me that he only recommended students who knew about his CIA background and asked him for guidance. "I did not reach out to people as much as have people reach out to me," he said. "I was just trying to be helpful to students who wanted a government career."

A former student's memoir gives a different impression. John Kiriakou recalled that Post asked him to stay after class one day in 1988. Kiriakou, who was about to earn his master's degree, had just taken a job with the U.S. Office of Personnel Management. Post, who more than two decades earlier had withdrawn from another position to join the CIA, was about to persuade Kiriakou to do the same.

"I'd heard he had a big reputation as an expert in his field," Kiriakou wrote. "What I didn't know was that he was also a former employee of the CIA."

Post asked Kiriakou whether he had considered working for the CIA. Kiriakou said he hadn't. "It turned out that Dr. Post, because of his love for the agency, tried to identify potential CIA candidates among the undergraduate and especially graduate student body at GW. He told me he'd been impressed by my analytical and writing skills in his class, and it seemed clear, he added, that I had a great interest in foreign affairs and international power politics. He didn't know whether the CIA and I would be a fit, but . . . the work at the agency might appeal to me. At a minimum, it couldn't hurt to have some preliminary conversations with CIA people."

Kiriakou agreed, and Post called the CIA then and there. Within half an hour, Kiriakou "was ringing the buzzer to an unmarked office in an unmarked building in suburban Virginia" for an interview. After his hiring, he expressed his gratitude to Post by sending him a bottle of scotch.

Two years later, when Post gave a talk at the CIA, Kiriakou and several other young officers thronged the podium to thank him. "We all owed our budding careers to this wonderful man," Kiriakou wrote.

Kiriakou would spend most of his CIA career in the clandestine service, including heading the counterterrorism team in Pakistan that captured Abu Zubaydah, who was then believed—wrongly, as it turned out—to be one of Osama bin Laden's top lieutenants. Disillusioned by the CIA's use of waterboarding and other "enhanced interrogation techniques" on prisoners such as Zubaydah, Kiriakou resigned in 2004. He later served almost two years in federal prison for confirming the name of a covert CIA officer to a journalist.

Post continued placing students with intelligence agencies until he retired in 2015. When two young women received offers from the FBI in 2013, he congratulated them in front of the class.

"I just want you to remember that I wrote very strong letters for you," he told them. "At this point, I've had twenty-eight students who have gotten jobs with the intelligence community. I think I'm just about at critical mass. When I give the signal, it's time for the coup." As the honorees paled visibly, Post hastened to add, "Only kidding."

A generational shift also underlies the increasing ties between the intelligence community and academia. Baby boomer professors who grew up protesting the CIA-aided misadventures of the 1960s, from the Bay of Pigs to the Vietnam War, began to retire, replaced by those shaped by the Soviet invasion of Afghanistan, the first Gulf War, and 9/11. Younger faculty are more likely to regard the collecting and sifting of intelligence as a vital tool for a nation under threat and a patriotic duty compatible with—even desirable for—academic research.

Barbara Walter considers it a public service to educate the CIA. The University of California, San Diego, political scientist gives unpaid presentations on her specialty, civil wars, at think tanks fronting for the agency, sometimes for audiences whose name tags carry only their first names. When CIA recruiters have visited UCSD, she has helped them organize daylong simulations of foreign policy crises to measure graduate students' analytic abilities—and even role-played a CIA official. "I played one of the leads," she says proudly.

She's aware, though, that some older faculty colleagues frown on these activities. "One interesting thing for me is that my more senior colleagues would absolutely not be comfortable consulting with the CIA or intelligence agencies," she says. "Anybody who remembers or had exposure to the Vietnam War has this visceral reaction."

GRAHAM SPANIER WAS the exception to Walter's dictum. The Vietnam War didn't prejudice him against intelligence agencies.

As an undergraduate and graduate student at Iowa State University, Spanier told me, he had been an "establishment radical." Spanier, who didn't serve in the war because of student and medical deferments, led peaceful, law-abiding demonstrations against it but disapproved of more confrontational tactics, such as taking over administration buildings. Once, when a march threatened to turn unruly, he borrowed a police loudspeaker to urge calm.

"I had the greatest respect for law enforcement," he said. "I was always in the forefront of change, but I believed in working through the system. I wanted to be at the table, making change, rather than outside the building, yelling and having no effect."

As he advanced in his career, gaining a seat at the table of administrators who hammered out academic policy, he paid little heed to the Church Committee or to CIA and FBI activities. Then, in 1995, he was appointed president of Penn State. Because Penn State conducts classified research at its Applied Research Laboratory, Spanier needed a security clearance.

While he was being vetted, Spanier read newspaper accounts linking University of South Florida professor Sami Al-Arian and adjunct instructor Ramadan Shallah to Palestinian Islamic Jihad, an Iran-backed terrorist group. (Another foreign-born South Florida professor, Dajin Peng, then a newcomer to the faculty, would later be of interest to the FBI.) Spanier was struck by USF president Betty Castor's lament that she had no idea of Al-Arian's alleged fund-raising for terrorists and that the FBI had not given her "one iota" of information.

The soft-spoken Shallah had been named head of Islamic Jihad and vowed war against Israel. The director of the international studies center at USF was quoted as saying, "We couldn't be more surprised."

Spanier made his own vow: never to be surprised. As president, he thought, "I want to be the first to know, not the last."

He convened a meeting in his conference room of every government agency that might conduct an investigation at Penn State, from the FBI and CIA to the Naval Criminal Investigative Service (the university does Navy research) and state and local police departments. "What I said to them is, 'If there is a significant national security or law enforcement issue on my campus, you can trust me. I understand the importance and sensitivity of such matters. I would like you to feel comfortable coming to me to talk about it, rather than sneaking around behind my back.'"

They agreed to stay in touch. From then on, an FBI or CIA agent—or usually both—would drop by once a month to brief him or ask his advice, typically about counterintelligence or cybersecurity issues involving foreign students or visitors.

In 2002, David W. Szady became the FBI's assistant director for counterintelligence. A quarter century before, he had gone undercover at the University of Pittsburgh, posing as a chemist to befriend Soviet students. Now, like Spanier, he wanted to smooth relations between intelligence agencies and academia. Soon FBI and CIA officials asked Spanier to expand the Penn State experiment nationwide.

The result was the National Security Higher Education Advisory Board (NSHEAB), established in 2005 with Spanier as its chairman. It consisted, then as now, of twenty to twenty-five university presidents and higher education leaders, though some initially were nervous about their membership becoming public, fearing a campus backlash that never materialized. Spanier, conferring with the FBI and CIA, chose the members, primarily from prestigious research universities.

At the FBI, "nobody thought we could get it up and running," because academia was perceived as hostile turf, Szady says.

NSHEAB members receive security clearances and come to FBI and CIA offices periodically for classified briefings. The agenda for an October 2013 meeting at FBI headquarters, for example, included the investigation of Edward Snowden for leaking classified National Security Agency documents; the Boston Marathon bombing; Russian threats to laboratories and research; and Department of Defense–funded students abroad "being aggressively targeted" by Iranian intelligence. Afterward the FBI hosted a dinner for NSHEAB members at a gourmet Italian restaurant in downtown Washington.

"There's a real tension between what the FBI and CIA want to do and our valid and necessary international openness," says one NSHEAB member, Rice University president David Leebron. "But we don't want to wake up one morning and find out that there are people on campus stealing our trade secrets or putting our country in danger. We might be uneasy bedfellows, but we've got to find an accommodation."

THE FBI'S LEADERS impressed Spanier. "They are very familiar with the FBI's history and reputation going back to Hoover," he says. "What I observed was almost the opposite. They emphasized to the people out in the field and throughout headquarters to be very sensitive" to issues such as profiling students of a particular religion or nationality.

The FBI and Spanier reached an understanding that it would notify him or the board about investigations at U.S. universities. The bureau lived up to its word when it noticed Internet postings by a Penn State student urging Islamic jihadists to "write their legacy in blood" by attacking police stations, post offices, Jewish schools and day care centers, and other targets. "The FBI came to tell me that they had their eye on someone," Spanier says. "They were picking up chatter on the Internet. There were things that were pretty threatening." When agents tried to question the student in a parking lot in January 2011, he reached for a loaded handgun in his jacket, and was arrested. He was sentenced to 102 months in prison for soliciting terrorism and assaulting the FBI agents.

In return for being kept in the loop, Spanier opened doors for the FBI throughout academia. He gave FBI-sponsored seminars for administrators at MIT, Michigan State, Stanford, and other universities, as well as for national associations of higher education trustees and attorneys. Many of them arrived at his talks "with a healthy degree of skepticism," Spanier told me. Displaying his American Civil Liberties Union membership card to prove that he shared their devotion to academic freedom, Spanier would assure them that the FBI had changed since J. Edgar Hoover's henchmen snooped in student files. After reviewing "challenges" for FBI-university relations, such as their different cultures and views of authority, he would describe how the advisory board was providing a forum for communication and understanding. Then he would delve into the bureau's concerns about foreign students and foreign visitors, which were "initially a harder sell to an academic audience" worried about the FBI nosing around their classrooms.

He also acted as a go-between for the CIA with university leaders who weren't on the national security board. "What a CIA person can't do is call the president's office, and when the secretary answers, say, 'I'm from the CIA and I want an appointment.' It doesn't work, and it's not credible. Before anybody would do that, I would call the president. The presidents all knew me. They would take my call. . . . I would say, 'Someone from the CIA would like to come, there's no issue on your campus now'— occasionally there was an issue—most often it was a get-acquainted meeting. Sometimes I would just give the first name. 'Someone will call your assistant, it's Bob.' . . . That worked one hundred percent of the time."

Spanier facilitated CIA introductions to the presidents of both Carnegie Mellon and Ohio State universities. A Pittsburgh-based CIA officer began visiting Jared Cohon, CMU's president from 1997 to 2013, once or twice a year. "I know there was direct activity with selected faculty," Cohon says. "They were interested in what the faculty might have observed when they went to foreign conferences. My impression, what I heard from the CIA, was that it was more defensive than offensive. Trying to make sure those faculty weren't recruited by a foreign power.

"I was uneasy about it, and I am uneasy," he adds. "I'm a kid of the sixties, and I remember all the protests on campus. The idea of the CIA being on campus would have turned people crazy. Things have changed dramatically in that regard."

At Spanier's instigation, the FBI special agent in charge of southern and central Ohio brought a guest to see Ohio State's then president, E. Gordon Gee, in 2010. The stranger handed Gee a business card with only a first name and a phone number. "Tell me what you do," Gee said.

"I work for the CIA," the newcomer answered. "I'm a spy."

The spy had majored in theater and was "wonderfully jovial," Gee recalls. His purpose was to let Gee know that the CIA would be recruiting on campus, and not only Americans. "I think it was because of the significant foreign population at Ohio State," Gee says. "It was the first time in thirty years I ever had someone from the CIA visit."

Spanier frequently traveled abroad, visiting China, Cuba, Israel, Saudi Arabia, and other countries of interest to the CIA. On his return, the agency would debrief him. "I have been in the company of presidents, prime ministers, corporate chief executives, and eminent scientists," he told me. "That's a level of life experience and exposure you don't have as a case officer or even a State Department employee."

I asked if U.S. intelligence had ever instructed him to gather specific information; in other words, if he had ever acted as an intelligence agent. He smiled and said, "I can't talk about it."

His lofty contacts enabled Spanier to steer federal research funds to universities in general, and Penn State in particular. When Robert Gates, who as president of Texas A&M University had been Spanier's "close colleague" on the higher education advisory board, became U.S. secretary of defense in December 2006, they brainstormed about academia's role in national defense. The result was the Pentagon-funded Minerva Initiative, which supports social science research on regions of strategic importance to U.S. security.

At meetings with the CIA's chief scientist, or the head of the FBI's science and technology branch, Spanier invariably asked, "What's your greatest need?" He rarely heard the answer without thinking, We can do that at Penn State. Then he would approach the director of the appropriate Penn State laboratory, explain what the CIA or FBI wanted, and say, "Why don't you go and talk to them?"

Spanier resigned as Penn State president in November 2011 and as chairman of the National Security Higher Education Advisory Board soon afterward, during a firestorm over alleged child sex abuse by a former assistant football coach. University trustees hired Louis Freeh to investigate. He and Spanier had been friendly for years. Freeh had been FBI director when Spanier welcomed the bureau to Penn State. In 2005, Freeh had inscribed a copy of his memoir, *My FBI*, to Spanier with "warm wishes and appreciation for your leadership, vision and integrity."

Freeh's July 2012 report portrayed Spanier quite differently. It accused him of concealing the child sex abuse allegations from trustees and authorities and exhibiting "a striking lack of empathy" for victims. Spanier denied the allegations and sued Freeh and Penn State separately, contending that they scapegoated him. The university counter-sued. In March 2017, a jury in Harrisburg, Pennsylvania, convicted Spanier of one misdemeanor count of child endangerment for failing to report the abuse. Spanier's lawyer said he will appeal.

THANKS TO SPANIER, CIA and FBI agents could now stride onto campus through the main gate, with university presidents personally arranging their appointments with faculty and students. But, except possibly at Penn State, they still slipped in through the back door whenever it suited them, ignoring their pact with Spanier that they would inform university leaders of their campus investigations.

For example, the FBI didn't notify universities during the 2011 Arab Spring, when it questioned Libyan students nationwide, including

Mohamed Farhat, a graduate student at the State University of New York at Binghamton.

In Binghamton, a gritty industrial city nestled among hills near the Pennsylvania border, Farhat talked to me for two hours in November 2015 about himself and his encounters with the FBI. He spoke animatedly, holding nothing back, using expressive gestures to punctuate his fluent English. "I'm a talkative guy," he told me. "I am very truthful. I don't like hiding." Married with three children—the eldest, a daughter, born in Libya, and two sons born in the United States—he's battled numerous medical, emotional, and financial difficulties. His left eye was blinded in a teenage accident in a schoolyard, and he's suffered from diabetes and depression.

The son of an Islamic scholar and nephew of a Libyan general, Farhat grew up in Zliten, a town one hundred miles east of Tripoli. He studied electrical engineering at a technical college, but it bored him, and he discovered that he had an aptitude for English. Within a few years he was teaching English at every level from middle school to college.

When Saif al-Islam Gaddafi, son of dictator Muammar Gaddafi, decreed that the Libyan government would provide five thousand scholarships for study abroad, Farhat seized the opportunity. He arrived in the United States in December 2008 and, after a year of English language study in Pittsburgh, enrolled at SUNY Binghamton.

As democratic uprisings sprouted throughout the Arab world in 2011, Farhat canceled his classes for the semester and joined cyber-groups opposing the Gaddafi regime. There were about 1,100 Libyan students in the United States, and Farhat knew many of them. Soon friends began calling to let him know that the FBI had interviewed them and he should expect a visit, too.

A worried Farhat contacted Ellen Badger, then the director of SUNY Binghamton's international students office. She was accustomed to rebuffing FBI inquiries. When a university admits a foreign student or visiting scholar, it issues him or her a document required for a visa. It transmits the same information electronically to the departments of State and Homeland Security, but not the FBI, which, unlike the other two agencies, has no regulatory authority over this population. Unless the FBI had a subpoena, she could only provide it under the federal Family Educational Rights and Privacy Act with "directory information," which includes basic student data, such as dates of attendance, degrees and awards, and field of study.

"There was a clear understanding they [the FBI] were going to chat with me in the friendliest way, and would be happy with any information I could give," Badger says. "I would respond in the friendliest way and give them nothing. That's how the dance went."

She reassured Farhat: the FBI would probably come to her first, and she would take care of it. Instead, the FBI bypassed Badger. Because the CIA was "somewhat blind" regarding on-the-ground intelligence in Libya, the FBI had been assigned to question students about the situation there, one insider told me. Agents were instructed to interview Libyan students off campus, without alerting professors or administrators. To protect informants from exposure, the bureau wanted to be as discreet as possible. The FBI did glean some valuable nuggets; students in the Washington, D.C., area helped identify intelligence officers among Libya's diplomatic corps in the United States.

An agent knocked on the door of Farhat's apartment in a nondescript three-story brick building west of campus, showed identification, and said he wanted to schedule a time to talk to him. It never occurred to Farhat to refuse.

"I have no idea about rights," he says. "This is not part of our culture. To me, the FBI are the ultimate power."

Two agents showed up on the appointed morning. Removing their shoes as a sign of respect for Islamic culture, they sat at his kitchen table and unfolded a black-and-white map of Libya, asking where he was from.

It was the first of five visits from the FBI, each lasting more than an hour, over a period of two months. The same local agent came every time, accompanied by either of two agents with experience abroad; one spoke a little Arabic. At the initial interview, they explained that they wanted to make sure that he wasn't threatening, or threatened by, any pro-Gaddafi Libyans.

That mission reflected the bureau's concern that, since most Libyan students came on government scholarships, some might be loyal to Gaddafi—and planning acts of terror against the United States for supporting the revolution against him. That worry turned out to be misplaced. "The students hated Gaddafi," the insider recalled. "I don't want to say it was a waste of time, but we satisfied ourselves that there was no threat from the Libyans."

The agents proceeded to their other purpose: gathering intelligence. They asked Farhat about Libyan society and customs, and his life from secondary school on. Had he donated to Islamic groups or institutions? No. Transferred money to Libya? Once, to repay a debt. Joined the military? No. Did he learn at technical school how to build an electronic circuit? No, he joked, only how to change a lightbulb.

"They took lots and lots and lots of information from me," he says.

What disturbed Farhat most were the questions about his and his wife's friends and relatives, from other Libyan students to his uncles in the military. The agents wanted names, email addresses, phone numbers. Because they told him that they knew his email address and Facebook affiliations, he coughed up his most frequent contacts, figuring that the bureau could track them anyway.

"The idea that frustrated me was that they went into Facebook," he says. "They knew everything. I can't escape that. I don't like that."

By the fourth visit, Farhat says, "I was annoyed." The next time, he decided, would be the last. "I will tell them, 'No more,'" he promised himself. As it turned out, he never had to muster the courage to defy them, because on the fifth session they wrapped up, then never returned.

Farhat didn't tell Badger about the agents until afterward. "My reaction was regret," she says. "What you want to do in a situation like this is make sure students are informed of their rights. They don't have to answer any questions. They can decline a visit. They can set terms: 'I want the director of the international office there.' 'I want a faculty member there.' They have control.

"I never got to give that little speech."

8

. . . .

BUMPS AND CUTOUTS

The CIA agent tapped softly on the hotel room door. After the keynote speeches, panel discussions, and dinner, the conference attendees had retired for the night. Audio and visual surveillance of the room showed that the nuclear scientist's minders from the Islamic Revolutionary Guard Corps were sleeping but he was still awake. Sure enough, he opened the door, alone.

The agency had been preparing this encounter for months. Through a business front, it had funded and staged the conference at an unsuspecting foreign institution of scientific research, invited speakers and guests, and planted operatives among the kitchen workers and other staff, just so it could entice the nuclear expert out of Iran, separate him for a few minutes from his guards, and pitch him one-on-one. A last-minute snag had almost derailed the plans: the target switched hotels because the conference's preferred hotel cost seventy-five dollars more than his superiors in Iran were willing to spend.

To show his sincerity and goodwill, the agent put his hand over his heart. "*Salam habibi*," he said. "I'm from the CIA, and I want you to board a plane with me to the United States."

The agent could read the Iranian's reactions on his face: a mix of shock, fear, and curiosity. From prior experience with defectors, he knew the thousand questions flooding the scientist's mind: What about my family? How will you protect me? Where will I live? How will I support myself? How do I get a visa? Do I have time to pack? What happens if I say no?

The scientist started to ask one, but the agent interrupted him. "First, get the ice bucket," he said.

"Why?"

"If any of your guards wake up, you can tell them you're going to get some ice."

IN PERHAPS ITS most audacious and elaborate incursion into academia, the CIA secretly spent millions of dollars staging scientific conferences around the world. Its purpose was to lure Iranian nuclear scientists out of their homeland and into an accessible setting where its intelligence officers could approach them one-on-one and press them to defect. In other words, the agency sought to delay Iran's development of nuclear weapons by exploiting academia's internationalism, and pulling off a mass deception on the institutions that hosted the conferences and the professors who attended and spoke at them. Like the hero of the 1998 film *The Truman Show*, the conferees had no idea they were acting in a drama that simulated reality but was stage-managed from afar by a higher power. Whether the national security mission justified this manipulation of the professoriate can be debated, but there's little doubt that most of them would have balked at being dupes in a CIA scheme.

More than any other academic venue, conferences lend themselves to espionage. Popularized by globalization, these social and intellectual rituals have become ubiquitous. Like stops on the world golf or tennis circuit, they sprout up wherever the climate is favorable, and draw a jet-setting crowd. What they lack in prize money, they make up for in prestige. Although researchers chat electronically all the time, virtual meetings are no substitute for getting together with peers, networking for jobs, checking out the latest gadgets, and delivering papers that will later be published in volumes of conference proceedings. "The attraction of the conference circuit," English novelist David Lodge wrote in *Small World*, a 1984 send-up of academic life, is that "it's a way of converting work into play, combining professionalism with tourism, and all at someone else's expense. Write a paper and see the world!"

The importance of a conference may be measured not only by the number of Nobel Prize winners or Oxford dons it attracts, but by the number of spies. U.S. and foreign intelligence officers flock to conferences for the same reason that lawyers chase ambulances and Army recruiters concentrate on low-income neighborhoods: they make the best hunting grounds. As Willie Sutton famously said when asked why he robbed banks, "Because that's where the money is." While a university campus may have only one or two professors of interest to an intelligence service, the right conference—on drone technology, perhaps, or ISIS— may have dozens. If a spy has nothing to do, chances are he'll put some false business cards in his wallet and head to the nearest conference.

"Every intelligence service in the world works conferences, sponsors conferences, and looks for ways to get people to conferences," says a former CIA operative. Adds NYU professor Mark Galeotti: "Recruitment is a long process of seduction. The first stage is to arrange to be at the same workshop as a target. Even if you just exchange banalities, the next time you can say, 'Did I see you in Istanbul?'"

Conferences also provide valuable unclassified information on technology or government policy before it's published, with expert panelists available to clarify misconceptions or ambiguities. "Because the feedback in verbal exchanges is rapid, when there is something you don't understand, you can ask about it and clear it up, and when you find some new intelligence leads, you can pursue them," according to *Sources and Methods of Obtaining National Defense Science and Technology Intelligence* (1991), known as "China's Spy Guide."

The FBI warned American academics in 2011 to beware of conferences, citing this scenario: "A researcher receives an unsolicited invitation to submit a paper for an international conference. She submits a paper and it is accepted. At the conference, the hosts ask for a copy of her presentation. The hosts hook a thumb drive to her laptop, and unbeknownst to her, download every file and data source from her computer."

The FBI and CIA swarm conferences, too. At gatherings in the United States, says a former FBI agent, "foreign intelligence officers try to collect Americans; we try to collect *them.*" The CIA is involved with conferences in at least four ways: it sends officers to them, it sponsors them at its headquarters, and through Beltway fronts, so that the intelligence community can tap academic wisdom, and it mounts sham conferences to reach potential recruits and defectors from hostile countries.

The CIA monitors upcoming conferences worldwide and identifies those of interest, said David Albright, founder and president of the Institute for Science and International Security and an expert on nuclear proliferation. Suppose there is an international conference in Pakistan on centrifuge technology: the CIA would send its own agent undercover, or enlist a professor who might be going anyway to report back. If it learns that an Iranian nuclear scientist attended the conference, it might peg him for possible recruitment at the next year's meeting.

Intelligence from academic conferences can shape policy. It helped persuade the George W. Bush administration—mistakenly, as it turned out—that Saddam Hussein was still developing weapons of mass destruction in Iraq. "What our spies and informants were noticing, of course, was that Iraqi scientists specializing in chemistry, biology, and, to a lesser extent, nuclear power kept showing up at international symposia," former CIA counterterrorism officer John Kiriakou wrote in a 2009 memoir. "They presented papers, listened to the presentation of others, took copious notes, and returned to Jordan, where they could transmit overland back to Iraq."

Some of those spies may have drawn the wrong conclusions because they lacked advanced degrees in chemistry, biology, or nuclear power. Without expertise, agents may misunderstand the subject matter, or be exposed as frauds. At conferences hosted by the International Atomic Energy Agency in Vienna on topics such as isotope hydrology and fusion energy, "there's probably more intelligence officers roaming the hallways than actual scientists," says Gene Coyle, who worked for the CIA from 1976 to 2006. "There's one slight problem. If you're going to send a CIA guy to attend one of these conferences, he has to talk the talk. It's hard to send a history major. 'Yes, I have a PhD in plasma physics.' Also, that's a very small world. Everybody knows what institutes exist. If you say you're from the Fermi Institute in Chicago, they say, 'You must know Bob, Fred, Susie.'"

Instead, Coyle says, the agency may enlist a suitable professor through its National Resources Division, which has a "working relationship" with a number of scientists. "The National Resources people subscribe to all the computer sites that show what conferences are coming up in the next six months. If they see a conference in Vienna, they might say, 'Professor Smith, that would seem natural for you to attend.'

"Smith might say, 'I am attending it, I'll let you know who I chatted with. If I bump into an Iranian, I won't run in the opposite direction.' If he says, 'I'd love to attend, but the travel budget at the university is pretty tight,' I could see where the CIA or FBI guy would say, 'Well, you know, we might be able to take care of your ticket, in economy class.'"

A SPY'S COURTSHIP of a professor often begins with a seemingly random encounter—known in the trade as a "bump"—at an academic conference. One former CIA operative overseas explained to me how it works. Let's call him "R."

"I recruited a ton of people at conferences," R told me. "I was good at it, and it's not that hard."

Between assignments, he would peruse a list of upcoming conferences, pick one, and identify a scientist of interest who seemed likely to attend because he had spoken at least twice at the same event in previous years. R would assign trainees at the CIA and NSA to develop a profile of the target—where he had gone to college, who his instructors were, and so on. Then he would cable headquarters, asking for travel funding. The trick was to make the cable persuasive enough to score the expense money, but not so compelling that other agents who read it, and were based closer to the conference, would try to preempt him.

Next he developed his cover—typically, as a businessman. He invented a company name, used GoDaddy.com to build a website, and printed business cards. He created billing, phone, and credit card records for the nonexistent company. For his name, he chose one of his seven aliases.

R was no scientist. Unlike a physicist-agent of his acquaintance, he couldn't use a line like "You'd think they're trying to solve the Riemann hypothesis" as an icebreaker. Instead, figuring that most scientists are socially awkward introverts, he would sidle up to the target at the edge of the conference's get-together session and say, "Do you hate crowds as much as I do?" Then he would walk away.

"The bump is fleeting," R says. "You just register your face in their mind."

No one else should notice the bump. It's a rookie mistake to approach a target in front of other people. They might be minders assigned by the professor's own country to monitor him. They would report the conversation, compromising the target's security and making him unwilling or unable to entertain further overtures.

For the rest of the conference, R would "run around like crazy," bumping into the scientist at every opportunity. With each contact, called "time on target" in CIA jargon and counted in his job performance metrics, he insinuated himself into the professor's affections. For instance, having researched his publications, R would say he had read a wonderful article on such-and-such topic but couldn't remember the author's name. "That was me," the scientist would say, blushing.

After a couple of days, R would invite the scientist to lunch or dinner and make his pitch: his company was interested in research or consulting in the scientist's field, and would like to support his work. "Every academic I have ever met is constantly trying to figure how to get grants to continue his research. That's all they talk about." They would agree on a specific project, and the price, which varied by the scientist's country: "One thousand to five thousand dollars for a Pakistani. Korea is more." Once the CIA pays a foreign professor, even if he's unaware at first of the funding source, it controls him, because exposure of the relationship might imperil his career or even his life in his native country.

When the conference ended, and the professor was heading home, R would instruct him on security precautions: go to a cybercafé, use a thumb drive, protect your password. "The target is suspicious. 'Why do I have to drive thirty minutes to an Internet café?'" A possible answer: R's company was worried about competitors stealing its trade secrets.

"I'M SURPRISED THERE'S so much open intelligence presence at these conferences," Karsten Geier said. "There are so many people running around from so many acronyms."

Geier, head of cybersecurity policy for the German foreign office, and I were chatting at the Sixth Annual International Conference on Cyber Engagement, held in April 2016 at Georgetown University in Washington, D.C. The religious art, stained-glass windows, and classical quotations lining Gaston Hall enveloped the directors of the NSA and the

FBI like an elaborate disguise as they gave keynote addresses on combating one of the most daunting challenges of the twenty-first century: cyberattacks.

The NSA's former top codebreaker spoke, too, as did the ex-chairman of the National Intelligence Council, the deputy director of Italy's security department, and the director of a center that does classified research for Swedish intelligence. The name tags that almost all of the seven hundred attendees wore showed that they worked for the U.S. government, foreign embassies, intelligence contractors, or vendors of cyber-related products, or they taught at universities.

Perhaps not all of the intelligence presence was open. Officially, forty nations—from Brazil to Mauritius, Serbia to Sri Lanka—were represented at the conference, but not Russia. Yet, hovering in the rear of the balcony, a slender young man, carrying a briefcase, listened to the panels. No name tag adorned his lapel. I approached him, introduced myself, and asked his name.

"Alexander," he said, and, after a pause, "Belousov."

"How do you like the conference?"

"No," he said, trying to ward off further inquiries. "I am from Russian embassy. I don't have any opinions. I would like to know, that's all."

I proffered a business card, and requested his, in vain. "I am here only a month. My cards are still being produced."

I persisted, asking about his job at the embassy. (A subsequent check of a diplomatic directory showed him as a "second secretary.") He looked at his watch. "I am sorry. I must go."

The unclassified conference revealed no secrets. Instead, the speeches and panel discussions offered a bonanza of what is known in intelligence parlance as "open source": publicly available information that, especially when pieced together like a jigsaw puzzle with thousands of other tidbits, illuminates government policies or cutting-edge science. Such sources are of increasing interest to intelligence agencies.

"I built an open-source system for the CIA," Ray Van Houtte told me outside the auditorium. He's a system architect for CACI, a national security contractor in Arlington, Virginia. His system helps the CIA test hypotheses on topics such as cooperation between Iran and North Korea. The Chinese, he added, are "the experts" on gathering open-source material. "They have tens of thousands of people doing it every day."

The conference also provided an opportunity, and a pretext, for networking. Several years ago, a military attaché from a foreign embassy emailed conference organizer Catherine Lotrionte, a Georgetown professor and former assistant general counsel of the CIA, and asked to talk with her. He explained that he had gone to the first conference but missed the most recent one, and wanted to catch up.

The attaché visited her three times in the ensuing year. He brought her gifts—chocolates and gold coins stamped with his country's insignia—and asked her about cybersecurity events and experts in the United States. Lotrionte, who has a security clearance, was careful to share only unclassified information.

Then a U.S. intelligence agency let her know that it was investigating the attaché. He was neither a diplomat nor a cyber aficionado (which explained why his queries had seemed rather basic). He was a spy, assigned by his government's most senior military leaders to gather information about cybersecurity specifically from her.

The American agent mystified her by asking if the attaché was good-looking. "I said, 'You're targeting him, don't you know what he looks like?'"

She offered to end the acquaintance, but the agent said no. Instead, he gave her a list of questions for the attaché. Making a rough sketch on a napkin of possible chains of cyber-command in the attaché's country, he instructed her to ask how cybersecurity was organized there.

Lotrionte declined to help. "They wanted me to do their work for them," she said. She never learned the outcome of the investigation, but soon afterward the attaché stopped contacting her.

WHEN THE CIA wants John Booth's opinion, it phones him to make sure he's available to speak at a conference. But the agency's name is nowhere to be found on the conference's formal invitation and agenda, which invariably list a Beltway contractor as the sponsor.

By hiding its role, the CIA makes it easier for Booth and other scholars to share their insights at its conferences. They take credit for their presentations on their curriculum vitae without disclosing that they consulted for the CIA, which might alienate some academic colleagues as well as the countries where they conduct their research.

An emeritus professor of political science at the University of North Texas, Booth specializes in studying Latin America, a region where history has taught officials to be wary of the CIA. "If you were intending to return to Latin America, it was very important that your CV not reflect" these presentations, Booth told me in March 2016. "When you go to one of these conferences, if there are intelligence or defense agency principals there, it's invisible as a line on your vitae. It provides a fig leaf for participants.

"There's still some bias in academia against this. I don't go around in Latin American studies meetings saying I spent time at a conference run by CIA."

The CIA arranges conferences on foreign policy issues so that its analysts, who are often mired in classified details, can learn from scholars who understand the big picture and are familiar with publicly available sources. Participating professors are generally paid a thousand-dollar honorarium, plus expenses. With scholarly presentations followed by questions and answers, the sessions are like those at any academic meeting, except that many attendees—presumably, CIA analysts—wear name tags with only their first names.

Of ten intelligence agency conferences that Booth attended over the years, most recently a 2015 session about a wave of Central American refugee children pouring into the United States, the CIA and Office of the Director of National Intelligence directly ran only one or two. The rest were outsourced to Centra Technology Inc., the leader of a growing Beltway industry of intermediaries—"cutouts," in espionage parlance—that run conferences for the CIA.

"There always needs to be a cutout," Galeotti told me.

The CIA supplies Centra with funding and a list of invitees, who gather in Centra's Conference Center, near the Ballston Metro stop in Arlington, Virginia. It's "an ideal setting for our clients' conferences, meetings, games, and collaborative activities," according to Centra's website.

"If you know anything, when you see Centra, you know it's likely to be CIA or ODNI [Office of the Director of National Intelligence]," said Robert Jervis, the longtime CIA consultant. "They do feel that for some academics thin cover is useful."

Established in 1997, Centra has received more than $200 million in government contracts, including $40 million from the CIA for administrative support, such as compiling and redacting classified cables and documents for the five-year Senate Intelligence Committee study of the agency's torture program. Its executive ranks teem with former intelligence officials. Founder and chief executive Harold Rosenbaum was a science and technology adviser to the CIA. Senior vice president Rick Bogusky headed the Korea division at the Defense Intelligence Agency. Vice president for research James Harris managed analytic programs at the CIA for twenty-two years. Peggy Lyons, director of global access, was a longtime CIA manager and officer with several tours in East Asia. David Kanin, Centra analytic director, spent thirty-one years as a CIA analyst.

Like Booth, Indiana University political scientist Sumit Ganguly has spoken at several Centra conferences. "Anybody who works with Centra knows they're in effect working for the U.S. government," he said. "If it said CIA, there are others who would fret about it. I make no bones about it to my colleagues. If it fits in their craw, it's their tough luck. I am an American citizen. I feel I should proffer the best possible advice to my government."

Another political scientist, who has given four presentations for Centra, said he was told that it represented unnamed "clients." He didn't realize they were U.S. intelligence agencies until he noticed audience members with first-name-only name tags. He later ran into one or two of the same people at an academic conference. They weren't wearing name tags and weren't listed in the program, which only identified speakers, so few attendees knew they were intelligence analysts.

Centra strives to mask its CIA connections. It removed its executives' biographies from its website in 2015. The "featured customers" listed there include the Department of Homeland Security, the FBI, the Army, and sixteen other branches of the federal government—but not the CIA. When I phoned Rosenbaum and asked him about Centra holding conferences for the CIA, he said, "You're calling the wrong person. We have nothing to do with that." He then hung up.

I next dropped by Centra's offices on the fifth floor of a building in Burlington, Massachusetts, a northern suburb of Boston. The sign-in sheet asked visitors for their citizenship and "type of visit": classified or not.

The receptionist fetched human resources director Dianne Colpitts. She politely heard me out, checked with Rosenbaum, and told me that Centra wouldn't comment.

"To be frank, our customers prefer us not to talk to the media," she said.

THE GRAYBEARD OF CIA-concealment conferences is the RAND Corporation. Spun off from a military aircraft manufacturer in 1948, and best known for federally funded defense research, RAND has served as a CIA stand-in for decades. On July 14, 2015, for example, RAND hosted a CIA conference on the "dynamics of militia groups and the implications for Iraq and Syria."

Although the conference was unclassified, it was one of the best-kept secrets in Washington. It was closed to the media, and off RAND's website. The invitation to professors on the panel didn't mention the CIA. "The RAND Corporation, in collaboration with the U.S. government, is organizing a conference," it read. University of California, San Diego, political scientist Barbara Walter listed her presentation on her curriculum vitae under "Policy Briefings and Talks" simply as "RAND, Washington DC, 'Lessons for Iraq and Syria,' July 2015."

RAND hosts two such conferences a month, often under nondisclosure agreements with intelligence agencies. Even in RAND's internal budgets, the conferences are not designated as funded by the intelligence community but by a "generic, nondescriptive indication," a person familiar with the process told me. That way, if hackers penetrated RAND's system, they couldn't trace the money to the CIA.

Like RAND, another nonprofit, federally funded center for defense research fronts for the intelligence community. Established during World War II when the Navy brought in a group of MIT researchers to thwart German submarines, the Center for Naval Analyses, run by the nonprofit organization CNA, now works with a wide array of federal agencies.

Houchang Chehabi, a Boston University professor specializing in Iranian studies, told me that he participated in a CNA conference on Iran and religion in Arlington, Virginia, in 2012. There he encountered several of his former students who work for U.S. intelligence. The center never mentioned the CIA or any other intelligence agency as its client, he said.

If it had, he wouldn't have gone, for fear of hurting his reputation and being considered "not a genuine scholar, but a kind of expert who sells his knowledge to the highest bidder. . . . They know exactly what they're doing when they contract out these conferences." Like Centra, CNA declined comment.

THAT SAME YEAR, Chehabi attended a conference in Istanbul of the International Society for Iranian Studies. He was president of the society, which had decided to meet in Turkey because Iranian professors could obtain visas to travel there. The choice backfired when a media mouthpiece of Iranian hard-liners denounced the conference as a Zionist plot. While the conference did include Israeli participants, and was planning a panel on Iran-Israel relations, Iranian intelligence was likely also concerned that its scholars might be recruited by Western services, or defect. The attacks proved effective. Although sixty Iranians had submitted proposals, only five showed up, and only two delivered talks.

"I'm pretty sure, in various rooms at the hotel in Istanbul where the conference was held, there were people from Iranian intelligence," Chehabi said. "It maintains agents in Turkey, and it would be easy to sneak them into the hotel."

Iran's anxiety about its scholars' loyalty may have been justified. During the conference, an Iranian approached Chehabi in a corridor and told him that he had inside information and wanted to defect to the West. "My instinct was to believe him," Chehabi recalled. "He had his wife with him. They were both nervous. He seemed like somebody who wanted to risk everything."

Still, it could have been a setup, and Chehabi decided to err on the side of caution. "We're not in that business," he told the dissident. "This is an academic conference."

U.S. intelligence services, like Iran's, understand that conferences are a modern-day underground railroad for Iranian academics escaping to the West. The CIA has taken full advantage of this vulnerability. Beginning under President George W. Bush, the U.S. government had "endless money" for covert efforts to delay Iran's development of nuclear weapons, the Institute for Science and International Security's David Albright told me. One program was the CIA's Operation Brain Drain, which sought to spur top Iranian nuclear scientists to defect. The *Los Angeles Times* revealed the program in 2007 but didn't mention its use of academic conferences, which is described here for the first time.

Because it was hard to approach the scientists in Iran, the CIA enticed them to academic conferences in friendly or neutral countries, a former intelligence officer familiar with the operation told me. In consultation with Israel, the agency would choose a prospect. Then it would set up a conference at a prestigious scientific institute through a cutout, typically a businessman, who would underwrite the symposium with $500,000 to $2 million in agency funds. The businessman might own a technology company, or the agency might create a shell company for him, so that his support would seem legitimate to the institute, which was unaware of the CIA's hand. "The more clueless the academics are, the safer it is for everybody," the ex-officer told me. Each cutout knew he was helping the CIA, but he didn't know why, and the agency would use him only once.

The conference would focus on an aspect of nuclear physics that had civilian applications and also dovetailed with the Iranian target's research interests. The institute would invite many academics to give and attend presentations, with the CIA ensuring through its contacts that the scientist was on the list.

Typically, Iran's nuclear scientists also held university appointments. Like professors anywhere, they enjoyed a junket. Iran's government sometimes allowed them to go to conferences, though under guard, to keep up with the latest research and meet suppliers of cutting-edge technology—and for propaganda.

"From the Iranian point of view, they would clearly have an interest to send scientists to conferences about peaceful uses of nuclear power," Ronen Bergman told me. A prominent Israeli journalist, Bergman is the author of *The Secret War with Iran: The 30-Year Clandestine Struggle Against the World's Most Dangerous Terrorist Power*, and is working on a history of Israel's central intelligence service, the Mossad. "They say, yes, we send our scientists to conferences to use civilian technology for a civilian purpose."

The CIA officer assigned to the case might pose as a student, a technical consultant, or an exhibitor with a booth. His first job was to peel the guards away from the scientist. In one instance, kitchen staff recruited by the CIA poisoned the guards' meal, causing massive diarrhea and vomiting. The hope was that they would attribute their illness to airplane food or an unfamiliar cuisine.

With luck, the officer would catch the scientist alone for a few minutes, and pitch him. He had boned up on the Iranian by reading files and courting "access agents" close to him. That way, if the scientist expressed doubt that he was really dealing with the CIA, the officer could respond that he knew everything about him—and prove it. "I know you had testicular cancer and you lost your left nut," one officer told a potential defector.

Even after the scientist agreed to defect, he might reconsider and run away. "You're constantly re-recruiting the guy." Once he was safely in a car to the airport, the CIA coordinated the necessary visas and flight documents with allied intelligence agencies. It would also spare no effort to bring his wife and children to the United States—though not his mistress, as one scientist requested. The agency would resettle the scientist and his family and provide long-term benefits, including paying for the children's college and graduate school. Most of the defectors had doctorates and presumed that their children would someday, too.

ENOUGH SCIENTISTS DEFECTED to the United States, through academic conferences and other routes, to hinder Iran's nuclear weapons program, the ex-officer familiar with the operation told me. He said an engineer who assembled centrifuges for Iran's nuclear program agreed to defect on one condition: that he pursue a doctorate at MIT. Unfortunately, the CIA had spirited him out of Iran without credentials such as diplomas and transcripts. At first, MIT refused the CIA's request to consider him. But the agency persisted, and the renowned engineering school agreed to accommodate the CIA by waiving its usual screening procedures. It mustered a group of professors from related departments to grill the defector. He aced the oral exam, was admitted, and earned his doctorate.

MIT administrators denied any knowledge of the episode. "I'm completely ignorant of this," said Gang Chen, chairman of mechanical engineering. However, two academics corroborated key elements of the story. Muhammad Sahimi, a professor of petroleum engineering at the University of Southern California who studies Iranian nuclear and political development, told me that a defector from Iran's nuclear program received a doctorate from MIT in mechanical engineering.

Timothy Gutowski, an MIT professor of mechanical engineering, said, "I do know of a young man that was here in our lab. The thing about him, somehow I learned that he did work on centrifuges in Iran. I started thinking, What went on here?" Gutowski, who didn't recall the Iranian's name, described him as tall and handsome, with an engaging smile.

Another Iranian nuclear scientist, Shahram Amiri, disappeared on a religious pilgrimage to Saudi Arabia in 2009. He returned to Iran in 2010, claiming that the CIA had kidnapped him. U.S. officials said he defected by choice and was paid $5 million for information, but missed his family and decided to return home. Emails released in 2015, which were sent in 2010 to then–secretary of state Hillary Clinton from her aides, appear to support the U.S. version. After convicting Amiri of providing the United States with vital intelligence, Iran hanged him in August 2016.

Rather than abduct scientists, the CIA may have used other leverage. One impetus for defectors may have been fear of the consequences of saying no. According to the ex–intelligence officer, the CIA told them that if they stayed in Iran, they would be assassinated.

"You're a dead man walking," a CIA agent would warn a wavering scientist. "The U.S. and Israel have identified you as a key member of Iran's nuclear development program."

According to the same source, one scientist spurned the CIA because he didn't believe it would protect his children. "My children will have a better chance of living if they stay in Tehran," he told the CIA agent pitching him.

"We'll kill you," the agent replied.

"Only I will die," the Iranian said. "Otherwise, the IRGC [Islamic Revolutionary Guard Corps] will kill all of us."

The scientists had to take the CIA's threats seriously. Four Iranian nuclear scientists were assassinated between 2010 and 2012, and another wounded. The killings likely had two purposes: to deplete Iran's thin cadre of nuclear weapons experts, and to deter other Iranian scientists from joining the program. Iran accused the United States and Israel of complicity in the assassinations, which the United States denied. Iran convicted a man whom it described as a Mossad agent of one of the murders, and executed him in 2012.

The killings drew praise from a prominent right-wing politician. "On occasion scientists working on the nuclear program in Iran turn up dead," former Pennsylvania senator Rick Santorum said in 2011, while seeking the Republican presidential nomination. "I think that's a wonderful thing."

Under certain conditions, the U.S. government allows itself to assassinate foreigners. The U.S. ban on assassinations—imposed by executive order after the Church Committee disclosed that the CIA had tried to eliminate Fidel Castro and other foreign leaders—has been interpreted to exempt killings in self-defense against an imminent threat. Military force against "legitimate targets" in peacetime, "where such individuals or groups pose an immediate threat" to national security, "does not constitute assassination," a memorandum by lawyers for U.S. military and intelligence agencies concluded in 1989.

Still, it seems unlikely that the CIA itself assassinated the scientists. Since Congress authorized the use of force against those responsible for the September 11, 2001, attacks, the federal government has approved killing members of Al Qaeda and affiliated terrorist groups. But Iranian scientists were a different matter. Despite the covert U.S. campaign to sabotage Iran's nuclear program, including infecting its operations with the Stuxnet computer virus, the two countries were not at war, and the scientists were not terrorists. According to national security lawyers whom I consulted, the United States could lawfully have bombed Iranian nuclear facilities if the president determined that Iran was building a weapon for use against the United States or an ally, and killed researchers in the buildings or bunkers, but targeting a scientist directly would have stretched the rules.

Intelligence agencies sometimes make death threats as an intimidation tactic, without necessarily intending to follow through. According to David Albright, the CIA or an allied espionage service left two letters at the Switzerland home of German engineer Gotthard Lerch, a key lieutenant in the nuclear proliferation network of Pakistani physicist Abdul Qadeer Khan. The first warned Lerch of "grave consequences" if he sold centrifuge designs to Iran; the second bluntly stated that his body would be found in a river. Lerch continued to purvey nuclear technology, and was unharmed.

Bergman said it was likely that Israel assassinated the Iranian scientists, "with some sort of wink and nod from the Americans." He speculated that the United States "would inform Israel of its attempts to recruit this scientist or the other. While this is done, Israel wouldn't kill the guy. If it fails, Israel would have been notified and could make a call on whether to kill him."

U.S. intelligence did once lure a nuclear scientist to an academic meeting with the intention of killing him. However, the operation took place in wartime, when assassinating a civilian who contributes to the war effort may be justifiable as self-defense under international law. During World War II, the Office of Strategic Services, the precursor to the CIA, sent renowned spy and former major league catcher Moe Berg to a 1944 lecture that Werner Heisenberg, the head of Nazi Germany's atomic bomb program, had been persuaded to deliver in neutral Switzerland.

Switzerland was "the only place outside their own country where German scientists could attend scientific meetings, which they liked to do, not least because the schnapps, cheeses, and chocolates that were no longer available in Germany were still in ample supply in Zurich and Bern," Nicholas Dawidoff wrote in *The Catcher Was a Spy*, a 1994 biography of Berg.

The multilingual Berg, who posed as a Swiss physics student, carried a pistol. He had orders to shoot Heisenberg if the scientist gave any clue that Germany was close to making an atomic bomb. Heisenberg didn't, and "the pistol stayed in Berg's pocket."

At least two Iranian nuclear scientists traveled abroad to an academic conference less than a year before they were assassinated. Masoud Ali-Mohammadi, a professor of elementary particle physics at the University of Tehran, was killed outside his home in January 2010 by a remote-controlled bomb attached to a motorcycle parked next to his car. Ten months later, Majid Shahriari, a professor at Shahid Beheshti University, was being chauffeured down a Tehran boulevard when an assailant on a motorcycle pulled up next to his Peugeot, attached a bomb to the car, and blew him up.

Ali-Mohammadi "had participated in projects linked with Iran's nuclear program and had extensive information about it," Bergman said. Shahriari "played a key role in enabling Iran to increase its level [of] uranium enrichment," Sahimi told me in a December 2015 email.

Both professors had participated in a conference in December 2009 in Jordan of Project SESAME (Synchrotron-light for Experimental Science and Applications in the Middle East), a regional research center intended to foster scientific excellence and build bridges between countries. "Iranian intelligence is convinced that . . . the Mossad used this conference in order to either try to recruit them to become Israeli agents or bolster surveillance over the two scientists," according to Bergman.

Sahimi told me he finds it "plausible" that the CIA approached Ali-Mohammadi and Shahriari at the SESAME conference and asked them to defect. They would have refused, he said. "Both were Iranian patriots."

9
. . . .

HIDDEN IN THE IVY

In his application to Harvard University's John F. Kennedy School of Government, Kenneth Moskow wrote that his favorite hobby was climbing mountains with friends in foreign countries. And that's how he died, years later, collapsing of altitude sickness as he neared the volcanic rim of Mount Kilimanjaro, a two-hour hike from the summit, with a group of buddies, including former CIA colleagues. They took turns trying to resuscitate him, without success, and no medical support helicopter could fly up in the thin air.

More than one thousand mourners attended a memorial service at Harvard. Illinois U.S. senator Barack Obama, only six weeks away from being elected president, took time from campaigning to console Moskow's widow, writing to praise his "zest for life" and "adventurous and energetic spirit." As a tribute to his patriotism, his family was given the flag that flew over the U.S. Capitol on the day of his death.

The obituaries hailed Moskow as a CIA legend. He had grown up in a Boston suburb, with an itch for travel, studying abroad in Spain and hitchhiking Kerouac-style around the United States. After his undergraduate days at Harvard, where he'd won a bout in a Golden Gloves boxing tournament, he scrapped plans for law school—"there are enough lawyers," he said—and joined the agency. Dispatched to Spain, he disguised himself in a wig and tooled around Madrid in a red Mustang convertible.

He was always in a hurry. Following his next posting, in Cyprus, he enrolled in the Kennedy School's mid-career program, which offers a one-year master's degree in public administration, even though, at thirty years old, he was still early in his career and one of the youngest students. There he mingled with future government, business, and military leaders both from the United States and abroad. Fluent in Spanish, he fraternized with Latin American classmates, including ex–Guatemalan defense minister Héctor Gramajo and José María Figueres, who would soon be president of Costa Rica. "He had an awful lot of good connections from the school," his widow, Shelagh Lafferty Moskow, told me.

For many of his former Kennedy School classmates, his death in September 2008 at the age of forty-eight was a double jolt. Not only were they saddened by his premature passing—"he was a very popular guy, affable, clean-cut, smile on his face, good handshake," said one—but they were startled to learn that he had been a spy. He had told classmates and professors that he was a State Department diplomat, which was the same cover he used overseas. The photo roster for his Kennedy School class listed his experience as a political officer in the U.S. embassies in Madrid and Nicosia, Cyprus, and State Department foreign affairs officer, with "areas of interest" in "Government @ Business" and "International Affairs/Security."

"At least in my circle, I don't believe anyone knew that he worked for the CIA," said a Kennedy School classmate, Barbara Grob, who runs media campaigns for nonprofit groups in the San Francisco area. "Nobody said, 'By the way, did you hear Ken was in the CIA?' "

Caught in an awkward social situation, he did confide in one Kennedy School classmate. Clyde Howard, an actual State Department foreign-service officer, was eager to get to know someone he presumed was a colleague. "When I learned that Ken was supposedly an FSO, I introduced myself and asked him about his career at State, to see if we had friends in common," Howard recalled in an email. "He told me he was with the Agency, and asked me to keep that to myself. I had worked overseas with CIA guys who were under State cover, so I was used to that arrangement. . . . I didn't talk about him with my classmates."

As intelligence agencies invade universities, they've penetrated not just conferences and laboratories but the very core of the academic endeavor—the classroom. Moskow is one in a long line of CIA officers who have enrolled undercover at the Kennedy School, generally with Harvard's knowledge and approval, gaining access to up-and-comers worldwide. In a single year, 1991–92, at least three CIA clandestine officers attended the Kennedy School's mid-career program, all posing as State Department employees. For four decades the CIA and Harvard have concealed this practice, which raises larger questions about academic boundaries, the integrity of class discussions and student interactions, and whether an American university has a responsibility to accommodate U.S. intelligence.

Foreign services have placed undercover agents at the Kennedy School, too, but without its knowledge. At the most famous and prestigious public policy school in American academia, you never quite know whom you're sitting next to—or who they're working for.

Intelligence services flock to the Kennedy School because it's both the epitome of globalization and a conduit to the highest echelons of the U.S. government. Alumni have risen to become presidents or prime ministers in at least a dozen countries, from Ecuador to Liberia, Bolivia to Bhutan. No fewer than five graduates have served in Japan's cabinet since 2014. Closer to home, Obama's secretary of defense Ashton Carter was on leave from his regular job as a Kennedy School professor.

The notices on a hallway bulletin board one random morning in 2015 illustrated the school's vast and eclectic reach. They invited students to meet a Saudi prince; attend panels on leadership, organizing, and advocacy in Japan, Serbia, and Jordan; listen to television journalist Marvin Kalb on Vladimir Putin and Harvard professor/*New Yorker* writer Jill Lepore on the press and the polls; and learn about crisis communications inside the office of South Carolina governor Nikki Haley.

"The whole world comes to you," says one awed graduate.

That includes the CIA. Since the standoff between Derek Bok and Stansfield Turner in the 1970s, Harvard and the agency have kissed and made up. Papering over the differences between their cultures has required compromise on both sides, with the CIA becoming more transparent, and Harvard less so.

The newfound intimacy is most evident at the Kennedy School, where the relationship benefits both sides. As a professional school, its mission is to prepare students for government jobs, and the CIA is an important employer, as well as a source of expertise, funding, guest speakers, and a certain cachet. Long dominated by Ivy Leaguers, the CIA favors Harvard as a training ground for employees. It also wants to hire Kennedy School graduates, consult its professors, and cultivate its foreign students.

Once known as the refuge of out-of-office politicians, the Kennedy School now swarms with former intelligence brass. Speaking there in April 2015, CIA director John Brennan waved to "my former deputy" in the audience: Michael Morell. The former CIA deputy director is a non-resident senior fellow at the Kennedy School's Belfer Center for Science and International Affairs, along with ex–CIA director David Petraeus, who periodically holds court in a Belfer Center office, with fellows and students lining up to see him. Admiral Stansfield Turner, the former CIA director who feuded with then–Harvard president Derek Bok, sits on the editorial board of the Belfer Center's quarterly journal, *International Security*, as does General Brent Scowcroft, former chairman of the President's Foreign Intelligence Advisory Board. Legendary CIA intelligence officers Rolf Mowatt-Larssen and Charles Cogan are also affiliated with the center. Its director, Graham Allison, is on the CIA director's advisory board.

These connections are open, but others are less visible. The CIA has long had an understanding with the Kennedy School that its intelligence officers can attend programs undercover, as long as they don't violate the ban established by Bok on covert recruiting. Generally, clandestine officers inform the Kennedy School administration—but not their professors or classmates—that they work for the CIA. The school keeps it quiet.

In practical terms, this makes sense. Since the Kennedy School accepts open CIA employees such as analysts, it seems unfair to exclude case officers, who are not only the agency's eyes and ears in the field, but its heart and soul. Surrounded by international students, they couldn't acknowledge their real occupation without word getting back to Riyadh or Jakarta and imperiling their diplomatic status, so they have to stick to their foreign-service identities.

Yet the presence of students who are living a lie undercuts one of the Kennedy School's key educational goals. Its programs for future leaders are designed to overcome cultural differences and national prejudices through candid discussions with their counterparts from other countries about personal and work experiences. A student inhibited by the need to protect a false identity can't be completely frank. In that sense, the

CIA's clandestine officers displace other government employees who could contribute more to the learning experience, both in and out of the classroom.

"I'd be uneasy about anyone undercover," says Columbia professor Robert Jervis, a longtime CIA consultant and member of the *International Security* editorial board. "It's antithetical to the spirit of the university."

The issue of clandestine recruiting is particularly dicey. Without explicitly mentioning the enrollment of CIA officers in Harvard classes, the 1977 report by President Bok's top advisers on "Relationships Between the Harvard Community and U.S. Intelligence Agencies" deplored the use of "professors, administrators or possibly students" as recruiters: "[I]t is inappropriate for a member of an academic community to be acting secretly on behalf of the government. . . . The existence on the Harvard campus of unidentified individuals who may be probing the views of others and obtaining information for the possible use of the CIA is inconsistent with the idea of a free and independent university. Such practices inhibit free discourse and are a distortion of the relationship that should exist among members of an academic community."

Both the CIA and Harvard caution undercover intelligence officers against recruiting classmates. "It's a red line," one Harvard administrator told me. "Everybody understands it. We believe they honor it. I have had discussions, on behalf of the school, with senior CIA training people, to make sure they know the rules."

Still, even if a clandestine CIA officer doesn't formally enlist a foreign classmate—and no one monitors compliance—nothing prevents him or her from grooming a potential asset, perhaps over a beer at a Harvard Square bar or at one of the school's many social functions. After they graduate, the intelligence officer can then renew the acquaintance overseas, or at a Harvard reunion, and tap his old Kennedy School buddy for information, still without disclosing his CIA affiliation.

"Suppose a student is working for the CIA, and sitting next to a Russian, and says, 'Let's go have a beer,' and develops a friendship, then develops a paying relationship," says Professor Joseph Nye, a former dean of the school. "I don't see how you know it. I don't know how a dean would find out about it."

In its zeal to recruit the Kennedy School's foreign students, the CIA has occasionally overstepped. Since September 11, 2001, the agency twice approached one Kennedy School administrator. First, it asked him to identify students who were rising stars in Pakistan's government and police force, doubtless so it could develop them as assets. He declined. Second, it wanted to know which Palestinian National Authority officials taking executive education courses had impressed him. It offered to arrange, presumably through a front organization, for a Palestinian group to come to the school. He passed the idea to another administrator, and didn't hear of it again.

A foreign student once complained to Joseph McCarthy, a now-retired senior associate dean at the Kennedy School, that people unaffiliated with Harvard had taken him to lunch and tried to recruit him as a spy. "They made him feel uncomfortable," McCarthy says.

McCarthy dialed a phone number they had given the student. "Who are you?" he asked.

"We're an agency of the federal government. We can't tell you more than that."

When he called again, the number was disconnected.

Kevin Ryan, a retired U.S. Army brigadier general with intelligence experience, directs the Belfer Center's Defense and Intelligence Project, a hub for research and analysis in those fields. He told me that the CIA has met with him, asking to debrief him about his travel abroad and to be notified of foreign guest speakers. He refused.

"I don't want a relationship," he said. "I don't want anyone to think that what I do is connected to the U.S. government. My background is already one strike against me."

WHETHER BECAUSE OF Ryan's response or for other reasons, the CIA does not send representatives to the project's weekly seminars, even though other U.S. government and military officials often take part, along with Kennedy School students and fellows. But it can't resist the chance to cultivate decision makers enrolled in the Kennedy School's executive education programs. Considered cash cows for the school, such programs typically last two to four weeks and award certificates of attendance rather than degrees. In the Senior Executive Fellows program for federal managers and their foreign counterparts, participants who ostensibly work in foreign trade for the Commerce Department occasionally request two certificates—one in their official alias, and one in their real name.

"We accept people paid for and sponsored by the U.S. government even if we don't know their identity," a person familiar with that program told me.

To Tad Oelstrom, a former Air Force lieutenant general who oversees the Senior Executives in National and International Security program, having spies hidden in the student body can enhance the educational experience. About seventy students, half American and half foreign, take the two-week, $12,500 course, which is given twice a year and has trained many luminaries-to-be, including heads of the National Security Agency and Defense Intelligence Agency.

The student body probably includes foreign intelligence officers, Oelstrom told me. "We don't know who they are. You would suspect that some of them come here with other missions in mind."

As for U.S. agents, "Sometimes I know, sometimes I don't," though he may be aware that the CIA is paying their tuition. "We don't pry into their background." Generally, they tip off Oelstrom in advance, and he accommodates their cover. "We ask, 'What would you like reflected on the photo roster?'" If they want to be omitted from the roster, that's okay, too. He's not worried that they'll try to recruit classmates: "Agencies have been a part of the program for so long. I can't say it would never happen."

Foreign or domestic, Oelstrom says, spies are welcome. Discussions are unclassified, and classes help prepare students for the real, open, uncertain world, where intelligence leaks and espionage are a fact of life. For managers accustomed to secure environments, recognizing that they must be able to communicate without using classified information is part of learning to lead.

It's also fodder for jokes. When the students gather for the first time, they're given thirty seconds apiece to introduce themselves. "If someone says, 'I'm from the intelligence community, and my name is Jim Smith,' I go tongue-in-cheek, 'And his real name is . . .' It settles everyone down."

IN 1986, ROBERT M. Gates approached the Kennedy School with an unexpected proposal. Then the CIA's deputy director, Gates felt that the agency had become too cloistered and inward-looking. He was also fed up with finger-pointing between CIA analysts and White House policy makers over intelligence failures.

His concept, honed by discussions with the school, was that the CIA would pay it to run executive education courses for senior managers in U.S. intelligence. The classes would discuss case studies, developed by the school, on decision making that involved intelligence issues, from the Cuban Missile Crisis to the dissolution of the Soviet Union.

The Harvard Intelligence and Policy Program signified a rapprochement between the CIA and Harvard after the Bok-Turner confrontation. The program also became its own case study in the balancing of national security and academic freedom, and in the complexities of collaboration between an intelligence service built on secrecy and a university that bans classified research on campus.

"The CIA had as little experience of writing unclassified contracts as Harvard had of concluding contracts with an intelligence agency," Professor Philip Zelikow, who would become one of the main teachers in the program and oversee the case studies, later wrote.

Having recently endured a scandal over undisclosed CIA funding for a conference hosted by the director of its Center for Middle Eastern Studies, Harvard administrators were wary of Gates's overtures and fearful of another media bashing. "We thought we'd get clobbered," Albert Carnesale, then the Kennedy School's academic dean, told me.

To overcome Harvard's skepticism, the CIA broke with long tradition. It agreed that the program would be unclassified and, after months of wrangling, yielded its claim to prior review of material. It also facilitated case studies by declassifying documents and making people available for interviews. To Harvard's relief, media coverage at the program's launch in December 1987 was favorable: "CIA Waives Secrecy Rule for $1 Million Harvard Study," ran the *Boston Globe* headline.

The case studies and courses, which lasted one to three weeks, satisfied Harvard and the CIA enough that they renewed the contract throughout the 1990s. The negotiations, though, were always contentious. One year, the CIA still hadn't signed the contract on June 29, the day before Harvard's fiscal year ended. Nancy Huntington, the program administrator, called Harvard's general counsel to say that she and Professor Ernest May were fielding the program without funds and would go to jail tomorrow. The university got in touch with the CIA, which sent a courier with the contract.

George Tenet, who became CIA director in 1997, was less committed than his predecessors to the Harvard experiment. Then, in 1999, the Kennedy School developed a case study of the American response to the Soviet Union's invasion of Afghanistan. Titled *Politics of a Covert Action: The US, the Mujahideen, and the Stinger Missile,* it exposed the jousting behind President Reagan's decision in 1986, over the CIA's opposition, to send Stingers to the Afghan rebels.

Compelling and meticulously researched, the study identified three former CIA station chiefs in Pakistan. It also described the rapport between Muhammad Zia-ul-Haq, Pakistan's president from 1978 until his death in 1988, and William Casey, CIA director from 1981 to 1987. "Casey became Zia's closest contact in the Reagan administration," it reported.

The account of how it was outmaneuvered by an assistant under-secretary of defense and several members of Congress (including the Texas representative later lionized in the 2007 film *Charlie Wilson's War*) roiled the agency. "I was told they objected to naming Zia-ul-Haq so prominently; apparently they thought it was a secret he cooperated with the CIA," Kirsten Lundberg, its author, told me.

The CIA appeared to be "upset in general that the interviews were on the record; somehow it had been their impression that all the interviews were classified," Lundberg continued. "They wanted us to classify the entire case. Failing that, they wanted us to turn over all the interview transcripts and the tapes. We did not." Harvard attorneys backed the decision.

"The fight dragged on for months, and left bitterness," recalled Peter Zimmerman, a longtime Kennedy School administrator whose current title is senior associate dean for strategic program development. "It made it easy for the CIA to move on." Disillusioned with transparency, the CIA didn't renew the contract.

Although managers from the CIA's analytical branch made up most of the students, some came from the clandestine service and enrolled under aliases. The Kennedy School gave them end-of-course certificates with their names blanked out.

After one course ended, a CIA participant called Huntington in distress, asking her if the program was "private."

"What do you mean?" she asked.

"I ran into someone at the [Harvard] Institute of Politics and my cover was blown," he said.

Since the Harvard Intelligence and Policy Program classes were limited to American intelligence personnel, fictional identities posed no ethical obstacle. The use of cover in the mid-career program raises more serious issues. That one-year program typically has almost twice as many international students as Americans. Of the 214 participants in 2015–16, 79 were American, including 31 from the federal government and military. The 135 foreign students represented 75 countries; 36 came from Asia, and 24 from the Middle East. The estimated ten-month cost per student was $88,862, including $45,697 in Harvard tuition, an $8,040 mid-career surcharge, and $23,380 for room and board.

Americans and Russians, Arabs and Israelis, Turks and Armenians gather every Thursday for a student-led seminar. "Part of my job was to try to create an environment where all those people can get into a room and you don't have fistfights every day," recalls a former program staffer. "Some of the best conversations have a little tension in them. The trick is to create that environment, either in the classroom or out, without it boiling over. Sometimes it boils over."

The international roster reads like a CIA shopping list. "In my year, we had a Jordanian diplomat who became a senior adviser to the king," says a former CIA analyst. "A German diplomat. A Brazilian diplomat . . . There's no doubt that's a rich environment for conversations, dialogue, and introductions. It's always interesting to know what foreign officials are doing, and helpful to meet people who would serve as contacts overseas."

Mid-career participants also make valuable contacts outside the program. Because they can fulfill its eight-credit requirement by taking courses throughout the university, they get to know other Kennedy School and Harvard students. During school vacations, they go on student-organized treks worldwide, from Kenya to Korea. They're often greeted by influential alumni who arrange meetings with government and business honchos.

About twenty-five mid-career students traveled to Washington, D.C., on an October weekend in 2015. Their itinerary included the State Department, National Security Council, U.S. Institute of Peace, House

Armed Services Committee, and the Pentagon, where they met Rear Admiral Peter Fanta, a Kennedy School graduate. Accidentally separated from the group outside the White House, one student began chatting with the man next to her in line, who turned out to be an FBI special agent. When she told him that she was in the Kennedy School mid-career program, he asked if she had any interest in working for the FBI. "We're recruiting heavily," he said. "How about the CIA?"

Most mid-career graduates, including former CIA personnel, say that they learned a lot. Past and future government officials on the faculty "brought a wealth of their own experience to the table," said retired CIA officer Regis Matlak. They taught him to think about foreign affairs in a more sophisticated way by placing an issue in chronological context, tracing its historic roots, and avoiding simplistic analogies.

I can relate to the group dynamics. In 1998–99, I was a fellow in a Stanford University program for mid-career journalists. It was similar in many ways to the Kennedy School's mid-career program. Accompanied by spouses and children, experienced professionals from the United States and around the globe assembled in Palo Alto. We pondered the world's problems at weekly seminars, gravitated toward the same courses and professors, bonded on excursions to wine country and Monterey Bay, and enjoyed casual evenings of conversation and camaraderie in each other's homes. I voiced opinions freely—perhaps too freely!—and so did other fellows. Then we scattered again. Today, almost two decades later, I still feel a kinship with them. I keep in touch with several whom I consider friends for life, and eagerly await reunions.

My classmates were aware of my true occupation and employer, and accepted my attitudes and experiences at face value, as I did theirs. Had one of us been an undercover intelligence officer, though, he or she could have taken advantage of those trusting relationships to groom an informant or two.

AN ADMISSIONS COMMITTEE of more than twenty-five professors and administrators reviews mid-career candidates; each file is read multiple times. They're judged on three criteria: Can they handle the academic work? Are they outstanding at their jobs? Do they have potential to rise higher? CIA clandestine officers apply under their covers, typically as foreign-service officers. Furnished with strong recommendations—for example, "he'll make a great ambassador someday"—from embassy colleagues accustomed to safeguarding CIA covers, they're usually admitted. Once they arrive, they confess their secret to key Kennedy School administrators, who promise to honor it.

"We will protect your identity," said one administrator. "We serve the government. This is our government."

Their teachers are in the dark. "The weird thing is that the Kennedy School provides faculty with limited information about the students in their classes," says one professor. "We're just told that they're mid-career students. It would help me to teach them if I knew more about them."

Ironically, the State Department in recent years has preferred to send actual diplomats to the Kennedy School's main competitor in the mid-career field: a one-year master's program at Princeton's Woodrow Wilson School (where University of South Florida professor Dajin Peng earned his doctorate). It's a money-saving move: Princeton provides full scholarships to its fifteen to twenty students. The State Department's Foreign Service Institute does sponsor mid-career training for two economic officers a year, and they occasionally choose the Kennedy School.

Unlike the Kennedy School, the Wilson mid-career program does not accept CIA spies. "We never take operatives, we only take analysts," John Templeton, the school's director of graduate admission, told me. "We just basically feel that only the analysts should be part of our program. The operatives are not involved in setting policy." The school has made its policy clear to intelligence agencies, and they abide by it, he said. Since the analysts acknowledge their CIA employment, Princeton avoids having to condone false credentials. Another person close to the Wilson program said it strongly prefers students who can candidly share their professional experiences, because such dialogue is vital to the educational process.

I'm told that the Kennedy School's policy of enrolling mid-career CIA officers undercover continues to the present day. In 2013, for example, a Latin American publication outed a CIA agent who went through the mid-career program as a foreign-service officer several years before. However, naming those who attended clandestinely in recent years might endanger their safety or U.S. interests, especially if they still spy. Thus in this chapter the only CIA officers whom I identify as mid-career graduates participated in the program more than twenty years ago and no longer work in the clandestine service.

ROBERT SIMMONS WENT to Harvard twice—and concealed his CIA background both times.

Simmons and I met one morning in November 2015 in his Stonington, Connecticut, home, which overlooks a saltwater cove where Captain Kidd supposedly stashed some of his pirate treasure. The property has been in his family for more than a century. There's an American flag on a flagpole in the front yard, and a blue Chevrolet TrailBlazer in the driveway with the license plate GUNGHO. A delicately carved, wood-paneled 1840 door from a Buddhist temple in Taiwan adorns the front hall. We talked in a basement study lined with books, including the Church Committee report on an upper shelf.

A Haverford College graduate, Simmons earned two Bronze Stars in the U.S. Army in Vietnam. He joined the CIA in 1969 because it "knew more about what was going on in Vietnam than the military did." He ran a CIA interrogation center there, and then spent a year on leave as a special student in Asian studies at Harvard. He used a military cover, which didn't endear him to a Chinese-language instructor from mainland China. "I remember her saying that she didn't want to teach me Chinese because I might use it to kill Chinese."

His next CIA posting was Taiwan, where he gathered intelligence on its nuclear weapons program. After three years of quarreling with his station chief, he decided to pursue a master's degree at the Kennedy School. When the chief tried to bury his application, Simmons appealed to the U.S. ambassador to Taiwan, who sent it to Harvard through his own channels. The application portrayed him as a State Department economic officer.

The school not only accepted Simmons but gave him a scholarship, which made him uneasy. When he arrived at Harvard in 1978, he went to see then-dean Graham Allison; Zimmerman, who headed the mid-career program; and Albert Carnesale, his faculty adviser.

"I don't want to take your money if you don't know who I work for," Simmons recalls saying.

They told him they did know; the ambassador had hinted there was "something unusual" about the application. They pledged to keep his secret. (Zimmerman confirmed the incident, Carnesale said he didn't remember, and Allison declined to comment.) The program's photo roster listed Simmons's experience simply as "US Embassy, Republic of China, 1976–present."

I was startled to learn that the Kennedy School was already the CIA's wingman in 1978, which was the year I graduated from Harvard. My mind drifted back to my college days, when my friends and I would have been oblivious to any spies in our vicinity. We were too busy studying, listening to Bob Dylan or James Taylor records, and playing pinball and foosball in the Dunster House basement.

We wouldn't have crossed paths with Simmons anyway, because he rarely socialized with other students. He was married and lived off campus, and he also worried that a few beers might loosen his tongue. "If I disclosed my identity so quickly after leaving Taiwan, it could jeopardize my replacement."

Had Simmons revealed his CIA past to classmates, one interrogation technique he employed with wounded prisoners in Vietnam might have sparked the kind of lively discussion that is supposed to enhance the program's educational value.

"When prisoners were wounded, we had a 50 percent better chance of getting them to cooperate with us than if they were not . . . ," he told an interviewer for a 1997 book. "I knew some American doctors who helped me out from time to time. I'd bring in an American doctor with a big bag full of pills and devices and everything, and he'd put his gear on and listen to a heartbeat and go through a fairly elaborate routine, which seemed quite sophisticated to a peasant. Then the doctor would look at the wound and say, 'Oh, that looks very bad. It could get infected. You could lose that limb.'

"The prisoner would ask, 'What can you do?'

"I'd usually let the doctor go, and then tell the prisoner, 'We'd like to help, but it's hard to get the medicine. I can't do anything to help you without getting some sort of help in return.' That tended to work well."

The Geneva Conventions state that wounded or sick combatants "shall not wilfully be left without medical assistance and care." Prisoners of war may not be coerced or tortured physically or mentally to induce cooperation, or, if they refuse to answer, be "threatened, insulted, or exposed to any unpleasant or disadvantageous treatment of any kind."

Simmons told me he didn't violate those rules because "they weren't our prisoners." They were the responsibility of South Vietnam, which referred them to the CIA for questioning. If they cooperated, they could eat and sleep at the interrogation center, and American doctors would treat them; if not, they were returned to the South Vietnamese for medical care. Their information, he added, saved American lives.

After finishing the mid-career program, Simmons resigned from the CIA. It allowed him to list his agency employment on his resume as he sought work on Capitol Hill, where he quickly rose to be staff director of the Senate Intelligence Committee. Later, he taught a Yale University seminar on Congress and the intelligence community. His students included Samantha Power, Obama's U.S. ambassador to the United Nations. As a former CIA officer, he had to submit the syllabus to the agency for approval.

Simmons was narrowly elected to Congress in 2000 and served three terms as a Republican in a Democratic-leaning district. Especially after September 11, 2001, his credentials as a soldier and spy impressed both voters and his colleagues in the House, where he sat on the Armed Services, Veterans Affairs, and Homeland Security committees and was considered an expert on terrorism. After being defeated for reelection in 2008 and the Republican nomination for U.S. Senate in 2010, he made a modest political comeback in 2015 by being elected first selectman of Stonington.

Simmons may be the only undercover spy in the mid-career program to be honored on the Kennedy School's walls. Like other graduates who served in Congress, he rates a plaque in the school's Taubman wing.

THE CIA SENT Thomas Gordon to Amman, Baghdad, Beirut, Berlin, Bosnia, Egypt, Kuwait, London, Oman, Somalia, Washington, D.C.—and Harvard Square.

Agency recruiters first wooed Gordon when he was an undergraduate at Brigham Young University. After stints as a Houston policeman and a Navy officer, he joined the CIA in 1987. He had a knack for languages. Part Native American, he was already fluent in Navaho and Hualapai, and soon gained a working knowledge of German and Arabic. Among his responsibilities: tracking a fledgling terrorist organization called Al Qaeda.

He was between assignments when CIA higher-ups summoned him. They told him that a year of training would help him move up the ladder, and presented an array of options including the National War College, Princeton, and the Kennedy School. When he couldn't decide, they chose for him. "They called me back the next day and said, 'We're going to send you to Harvard for a year.' . . . I think it's one or two or three a year that they'll try to send there."

He was admitted to the mid-career program as a State Department foreign-service officer but sensed that the school was aware of his real job. "I think they had some kind of a wink and a nod. A couple people there at the Kennedy School talked to me like I wasn't a foreign-service officer. I got the impression they were amenable to my coming there."

The CIA, which paid his way, cautioned him not to recruit anyone at Harvard. "We got the brief before I left—we were not to be doing our normal job when we get there. I said, 'Sure.'

"But of course, in that line of work, you keep your line open for future consideration. It's like going into the NFL Draft. You meet people you might end up knowing later in your career. My associations that I made there came in handy later. . . . As corny as it is, there's a camaraderie. I can pick up the phone and call anyone on the alumni list—I was there in 1992, can I get your thoughts on this?"

Upon arrival, he checked in with the CIA office in Boston as a courtesy, and then devoted himself to academic life. Aside from the usual run of courses on foreign policy, he studied federal Indian law at Harvard Law School, and picked the brain of Kennedy School professor Joseph Kalt, an expert on Native American economic development.

Maintaining his cover was no harder than it had been overseas, though at least one classmate was skeptical. "What he was saying about his background didn't add up," says Bryan Welch, then editor of the Taos, New Mexico, News. "I recall the vague feeling that there must be something else going on there."

Gordon also occasionally ran into CIA colleagues such as Ken Moskow, who had attended the mid-career program the year before. "I knew him in passing, and then back at the office. Sitting down with him a few times when he came back to Cambridge. And then overseas a couple times."

After Harvard, Gordon resumed pursuing Al Qaeda. He left the CIA's employ in 1996 but continued working for U.S. intelligence as an independent contractor. "I've spent an inordinate amount of time in Iraq and Afghanistan over the last decade."

In 1998, he was elected an Arizona state representative as the ultimate long shot, a Republican write-in candidate in a Democratic district. "I was out here, noticed nobody filed, threw my name in." The next year he was embroiled in a bizarre scandal that led to media exposure of his CIA background.

At the time, the province of Kosovo was fighting for independence from Serbia. A naval reservist, Gordon persuaded an Arizona congressman to give him a special permit to travel to the Balkans, on the grounds that he'd been ordered to deploy there. That explanation was bogus, as the congressman learned when an irate general contacted him, complaining that Gordon was causing trouble. Gordon issued a statement that he couldn't discuss the details because he'd spent most of his career in "intelligence or special operations," prompting the *Arizona Republic* to reveal that he had worked for the CIA. It also reported that the agency had fired him, which Gordon denies. He pleaded guilty in 2001 to entering a military installation for an illegal purpose, and paid a ten-dollar fine.

Gordon told me that his commanding officer in the reserves had unofficially blessed his trip. He went to the Balkans to avenge an old friend from CIA training who had been killed in Al Qaeda's 1998 bombings of U.S. embassies in Kenya and Tanzania. Osama bin Laden was backing the Muslim rebels, so Gordon was on Serbia's side. "I was there with special ops—we helped some Iranians and Al Qaeda guys to leave the country." Unfortunately, the Serbs didn't realize it, and imprisoned him. "They just knew I was an American wandering around."

In 2010, Gordon flirted with a run for governor of Arizona, but withdrew. Today, as the head of a community development group on a Native American reservation, he puts the lessons of his Harvard education on Indian law and economic development to good use. "My time at Harvard has enabled me to do good things for tribes here. I went there fully thinking, I'll be chief of station somewhere and retire in obscurity. I end up being more reservation related."

Kiowa Gordon, one of his eight children, is an actor best known for playing a Native American werewolf in the Twilight Saga. On his Twitter page, Kiowa describes his parentage this way: "Born in Berlin, Germany, to a spy and a Hualapai."

TWO OF TOM Gordon's mid-career classmates in 1991–92 wore their cover so well that they fooled even him into believing they were U.S. diplomats. Actually, Eric and Gayle von Eckartsberg were spies like him.

Their entries in the photo roster portrayed both husband and wife as State Department officers in the U.S. embassy in Tokyo. Eric specialized in international environmental policy and nuclear nonproliferation, and "researched and wrote on U.S.-Japan bilateral science issues and Japanese technology policy." Gayle, in the embassy's political section, had a background in "international political assessment and analysis" and "experience in research and reporting on Japanese political scene."

Eric told me in a January 2016 email that "my employment cover was later rolled back and I am able to publicly acknowledge that I worked for CIA from 1983–1994." At Harvard, he said, he was "exclusively engaged as a full-time student under a professional development program." He and Gordon "probably shared a beer or two at some point" but "never discussed work since neither of us were working while at school."

Gayle "was at the K school purely as a student as well, and can't comment on anything related to her previous government service," Eric said. However, one of her Harvard professors told me that he later learned she worked for the CIA.

Gordon found out about the von Eckartsbergs when he returned to the agency from Harvard. "Somebody dropped their name," he said.

The von Eckartsbergs impressed their classmates. "They were very cordial and extremely interesting people," Bryan Welch said. "They shared interesting insights from—I thought—the foreign service."

Upon earning their master's degrees, they moved to New York, where Gayle was assigned to the United Nations. Returning to Japan for a visit, they lunched with former Kennedy School classmates there, including

Eiichi Funada, who later became commander of Japan's Self-Defense Force fleet.

Eric's memory of the lunch is hazy, but it would have been a "purely personal" event, not a recruiting trip, he told me. "I've visited Japan many, many times since the K-school and none of it was for that kind of work."

Both von Eckartsbergs soon left the clandestine service. Gayle, who had taken Professor Joseph Nye's course at the Kennedy School, served as his special assistant when he became National Intelligence Council chairman in 1993 and assistant secretary of defense the following year. Later, she worked as an executive for In-Q-Tel, the CIA's investment arm, identifying commercial technologies that could help with intelligence collection and analysis. She's currently director of plans, policy, and operations for the Pacific Division of the U.S. Marine Corps.

Eric is a senior vice president for an information technology company; his LinkedIn page touts him as an "experienced sales, business development, and strategy executive with record of delivering solid revenue growth to early and mid-stage start-ups" and "deep knowledge of Federal national security and defense markets."

In a tenth-reunion report to classmates, Gayle sustained her former cover, describing the United Nations as her "last bona-fide tour as a U.S. Foreign Service Officer." The Kennedy School, she told them, "changed my life. You know what I mean—insight, context, contacts, retooling, focus, new opportunity, you name it. The promise of the Kennedy School experience was and is very real to me. Thanks to my classmates and teachers for this experience, and here's to continuing the tradition."

DONALD HEATHFIELD HAD impeccable credentials. He had earned a bachelor's degree in economics at York University in Toronto and a master's in business administration at a Parisian school, where he stayed on as international director of development.

As a mid-career applicant, "I went through a detailed screening procedure that included tests, motivation letters and recommendations," he later told a Russian magazine. "By that time, I already had an MBA diploma and a specialist in world economy diploma as well as experience in creating and managing businesses. So I didn't differ from other candidates in terms of training level."

Heathfield did differ from most of them in another respect: both his name and nationality were false. In 2010, a decade after graduating from the program, he was unmasked as one of the ten Russian spies who had slinked into American society as "illegals," gathering intelligence on their own without the diplomatic immunity enjoyed by embassy personnel. (Others included Lydia Guryeva, who under the alias Cynthia Murphy scouted Columbia Business School classmates and professors.) His real name was Andrey Bezrukov: "Heathfield" was borrowed from a dead Canadian. A backstory as a Canadian diplomat's son who went to an international school in the Czech Republic was concocted to explain his Eastern European accent.

It isn't just the CIA that sends spies to the Kennedy School; foreign intelligence services, whether allied or hostile, also covet access to future leaders. Russia, in particular, "has intensified its activity in the U.S. under Putin," says Kennedy School administrator Sergei Konoplyov. "It might send people for short executive education courses. It's cheap, there's no suspicion. The person comes from Alfa Bank in Moscow, makes friends, hands out lots of business cards, and continues the relationship afterwards. 'Maybe you come to Moscow?' "

The Kennedy School is typically informed of the U.S. agents who enroll undercover, but not of their foreign equivalents. Rumors, though, run rampant: a favorite pastime might be called "Guess the Spy." One year, a student from the British government attracted speculation. A mid-career tradition is that students introduce themselves to classmates in fifteen wacky seconds, taking an awkward stab at cheerleading or opera singing. The presentations used to be videotaped, a practice since discontinued. Displaying the renowned British reserve, the official refused to participate.

"He was super-convincing," recalls a former school administrator. "I thought he was going to have a breakdown. I wasn't surprised when, months later, somebody came by and said, 'I'm pretty sure he's in MI6.' "

By contrast, "Heathfield" fit in well with his class, which included future Mexican president Felipe Calderón. An energetic networker, he led Canadian students on a Scotch-tasting excursion, which they christened "the Royal Canadian Scotch Stagger," and organized a spring tour of wine caves in France. He struck classmates as "a flavorful conversationalist," "very friendly, but also somewhat mysterious," and "always very vague about his career ambitions."

After graduation, he attended Kennedy School reunions and visited classmates around the world, ostensibly to keep up friendships. More likely, he was nurturing informants. "In Singapore, in Jakarta—he knew what everyone was doing," one said. "If you wanted to know where anybody was at, Don would know."

He also hobnobbed with professors and pundits at World Future Society meetings, and started a software design firm to help governments predict trends. Assigned by Moscow to gather information on "Western estimation" of Russian foreign policy, and on U.S. policy on topics from Central Asia to terrorists' use of the Internet, Heathfield chatted up a George Washington University professor who had served as a national security aide to then–vice president Al Gore. A federal planner for nuclear weapons development told Heathfield about bunker-busting warheads that Congress had recently authorized.

His wife, Elena Vavilova, posed as a Canadian named Tracey Lee Ann Foley, and worked for a real estate firm in Somerville, adjacent to Cambridge. Russian intelligence had trained them both in espionage techniques such as invisible writing and steganography, or embedding messages in digital photographs. For two years until their arrest, their older son, Timothy, attended the Elliott School of International Affairs at George Washington University. Located across from State Department headquarters, the school prepares students for foreign-service and intelligence careers. The *Wall Street Journal* reported that, before his parents were caught, Timothy had agreed to spy for Russia and go there for espionage training. Timothy and his parents have denied it.

The family spoke no Russian in its apartment near Harvard Square. "In order to win, we need to understand," Bezrukov later explained. "In order to understand, we need to love. So you must love the country in which you work." He added, "I like many of the features of the American people, such as optimism, resourcefulness, willingness to make necessary changes, the ability to fairly and quickly recognize and correct their mistakes."

Arrested while celebrating Timothy's twentieth birthday, Heathfield and Foley pleaded guilty to conspiracy to act as unregistered agents of a foreign government. The Kennedy School rescinded his degree. The precautions that Russia had taken to conceal Heathfield's identity amused his former Kennedy School dean, Joseph Nye. After all, Bezrukov didn't need to falsify his name and homeland to penetrate the mid-career program; a foreign-service cover would have sufficed, as it does for CIA agents.

"He could have signed up as a Russian student and found out the same information," Nye told me. "I make friendships with a lot of foreign students all the time. Are some of them FSB [Russian counterintelligence]? Possibly. I must have shaken his hand."

Although Timothy and his younger brother, Alexander, were born in Toronto, the Canadian government stripped them of their citizenship. Alexander challenged the ruling but a federal court upheld it in August 2015 on the grounds that his parents came to Canada as Russian spies, fraudulently obtaining citizenship and passports to "establish their legend," or backstory.

Returning to Moscow in a spy swap, Bezrukov was hailed as a hero. He became an adviser to ex–intelligence officer Igor Sechin, who is President Vladimir Putin's right-hand man and the chief executive of Rosneft, the state-controlled oil giant. Bezrukov's wife, Vavilova, is an adviser at Norilsk Nickel, a Russian mining company, according to her LinkedIn page.

On his LinkedIn page, "Donald Heathfield aka Andrey Bezrukov" highlights his Kennedy School degree, without mentioning that it was revoked. He also lists a 1983 diploma in history from Tomsk State University in Russia that was nowhere to be seen on his mid-career program bio. It would have given him away.

SHORTLY AFTER BECOMING CIA director in September 2011, General David Petraeus visited the Manhattan office of billionaire precious metals investor Thomas S. Kaplan. They had lunch in a conference room adorned with backlit digital replicas of paintings out on loan from Kaplan's private collection of Rembrandts, one of the largest in the world. Petraeus was impressed by the vibrant, colorful copies, barely distinguishable from the originals.

They talked first about the Middle East. Petraeus was the architect of the counterinsurgency strategy that helped stabilize a disintegrating Iraq, and Kaplan had a keen interest in the region. Then the general got down to business. He needed Kaplan's help with a promising idea: sending spies to graduate school.

Petraeus, who has a master's degree and doctorate from Princeton's Woodrow Wilson School, favored closer ties between the CIA and universities. He invited university professors to Langley to brief analysts on China and other topics, and then enjoy dinner with him afterward in the director's dining room.

Clandestine officers, Petraeus thought, had fewer advanced degrees, and fewer opportunities for graduate education, than analysts. Between assignments, they could benefit from an academic year fine-tuned to their individual instructional needs, from languages to economics. Since there was always internal resistance to freeing up officers for training— "We're famous for pulling people out of language school halfway through because of a new mission somewhere"—he would call them "Director's Fellows," to show he was pushing the program. They would go to the best schools: Harvard, Yale, Princeton, Stanford, and Johns Hopkins's School of Advanced International Studies.

"The thinking was to provide them an opportunity to go off for a year and really to build intellectual capital for their future assignment," Petraeus told me. "And then to enable them to have an out-of-your-intellectual-comfort-zone-experience. Such experiences have always been very important for me. When people have asked me, what enabled you to think out of the box the way you did the first year in Iraq as a division commander when we had the responsibilities of an occupying force and basically began to rebuild a nation after toppling its leadership, I often said that the biggest experience was graduate school. . . . For me, and for a lot of others I know, graduate school was tremendously formative. Among the takeaways for me was a very salutary experience with individuals who were exceedingly bright but saw the world through a very different lens."

He also wanted the fellows to mix with other U.S. and international students. "We didn't want them squirreled away by themselves," he said. He didn't expect any inappropriate recruiting. "They know the boundaries. You can have wonderful intellectual exchanges without trying to recruit somebody or exposing something sensitive."

Trouble was, Petraeus didn't have funding for the fellowships. Then he remembered Kaplan once telling him, "Let me know if you ever need anything." Now he reminded the billionaire of his promise. Kaplan readily agreed to pay for the program, and reached out to their mutual friend, Graham Allison, director of the Kennedy School's Belfer Center.

Allison, who has expanded the center into an empire of more than 150 faculty members, researchers, practitioners, and fellows, was glad to help the CIA. The trepidations expressed by Kennedy School administrators a quarter century earlier about collaborating with the CIA on the Intelligence and Policy Program had largely disappeared. While the ethical issues associated with enrolling spies, such as the use of false identities and the potential for covert recruiting, are valid concerns, they didn't come up in early discussions about the fellowships, Petraeus told me.

In the program's first year, two clandestine CIA officers had fellowships at Belfer. One was exactly the kind of candidate Petraeus had in mind; he had just left as chief of an important Middle Eastern station and was preparing for another key position in the region. Asked if the fellow used a cover, Petraeus said, "I know that some people at Harvard knew who he was. He probably was not declared, but I don't recall."

Engulfed in a scandal over allegedly providing classified information to a biographer with whom he was having an extramarital affair, Petraeus resigned as CIA director in November 2012. Although he talked to his successor, John Brennan, about the program during the transition, the agency's interest in it quickly waned—much as its support for the Harvard Intelligence and Policy Program faded after Robert Gates left.

"It's so difficult to break someone free for a year," Petraeus told me. "It takes senior leadership that's really committed to it. Your desires collide with reality, and the urgency of the moment, which is very real, crowds out such opportunities. We likely had new requirements in places like Syria and Iraq and others that one can imagine."

Now called the Recanati-Kaplan Foundation Fellowships, the revamped program "educates the next generation of thought leaders in national and international intelligence," according to the Belfer Center website. It caters primarily to analysts rather than spies: typically, two from U.S. intelligence agencies other than the CIA, and one each from France and Israel. They spend a year at the Belfer Center on research related to national security. In 2015–16, for instance, a Pentagon intelligence analyst studied "Transnational organized criminal networks that impact the economic stability and security of the U.S. and its allies," while an Israeli military intelligence officer examined "Middle East regional dynamics and counterterrorism."

Virtually no one at Harvard outside the Belfer Center appears to have heard of the Recanati-Kaplan program. Largely unstructured, it has no required courses or grades, and only recently began issuing certificates. Graham Allison himself is the "principal investigator," or faculty adviser for the fellows' research.

"No one's undercover or lies about who they are," Kevin Ryan told me. As the center's director of defense and intelligence projects, he oversees the program. But "we don't hang a sign on the wall saying they're from the intelligence community."

While the Kennedy School insisted on full editorial control over the Intelligence and Policy Program case studies, it has been willing to cede authority over the Recanati-Kaplan fellows' research. In some cases, Ryan said, fellows have submitted their papers to their agencies for prepublication review. In other instances, they have asked him to omit their authorship. Since the center doesn't publish anonymous work, "we keep it in-house."

Petraeus meets with the fellows at least once a year. "It's always great fun to compare notes with them," he said. So does Kaplan. At one such session, the billionaire rambled on about his charity, Panthera, which protects imperiled big cats such as tigers, lions, jaguars, and leopards and their habitats, and boasted that he had foreseen Saddam Hussein's 1990 invasion of Kuwait, according to an attendee.

The partnership with France and Israel likely reflects Kaplan's affinity for both countries—and their governments. Although born and raised in the United States, with a doctorate in history from Oxford, he is something of a Francophile. He learned French as a student in Switzerland, and two of his children were born in Paris.

At a March 2014 ceremony at Manhattan's 92nd Street Y, France's then-ambassador to the United States bestowed his country's premier award on Kaplan, inducting him into the prestigious Legion of Honor, established by Napoleon in 1802. Before Petraeus, former U.S. ambassador to the United Nations Mark Wallace, and other luminaries, François

Delattre pinned the insignia on Kaplan, who was natty as always in a three-piece suit and matching pocket square.

In a speech, Delattre hailed Kaplan's services to France: dissuading the French government from selling the historic Fifth Avenue mansion that houses the embassy's cultural services, by paying to install a bookstore there; loaning his Rembrandt collection to the Louvre; and creating the Kennedy School fellowships.

"The program has brought France together with the United States and Israel, which I much appreciate, the three countries together, in order to improve intelligence analysis and cooperation," Delattre said.

Like Israeli prime minister Benjamin Netanyahu, Kaplan strongly opposed the Obama administration's deal with Iran. The son-in-law of Israeli investor Leon Recanati, Kaplan has been a key backer of United Against Nuclear Iran (UANI), an advocacy group that includes former intelligence chiefs of Israel, Germany, and the United Kingdom on its advisory board.

UANI sought to pressure companies to stop doing business with Iran by exposing their violations of the sanctions then in place. "As much as United Against Nuclear Iran may not have had Tomahawk missiles and aircraft carriers at its disposal, we've done more to bring Iran to heel than any other private sector initiative and most public ones," Kaplan said in 2014.

Proceedings in a lawsuit against UANI hinted at a covert relationship with U.S. intelligence. When a shipping magnate targeted by UANI sued for defamation, the Obama administration intervened, saying that disclosure of the group's files could hurt national security. In March 2015, after reviewing classified declarations submitted by the U.S. government, a federal judge dismissed the lawsuit, ruling that "allowing the litigation to proceed would inevitably risk the disclosure of state secrets."

GIFTS AND AWARDS from the military and espionage services of former Soviet-bloc countries adorn the third-floor office of Sergei Konoplyov, director of the Kennedy School's Black Sea Security Program. They include medals from Ukrainian and Armenian intelligence, a plaque from the president of Romania, and an unopened bottle of champagne with Konoplyov's photograph on the label. The inscription reads, "This sparkling wine was produced and bottled in the secret cellars of the Ministry of Defense of the Republic of Moldova in the honor of Mr. Sergei Konoplyov."

A former Soviet military officer, Konoplyov was never a spy himself, he assured me—but so coyly that he seemed to enjoy being disbelieved. His alma mater, the Military Institute of Foreign Languages in Moscow, was a "nest of spies," and he was eager to be recruited so he could shop at stores closed to ordinary Russians, but somehow Soviet intelligence overlooked him.

He wants to write a book titled "From the KGB to the KSG," he jokes. "If I were working for the Russian government, I would be a perfect asset. I know everyone, including the Defense Secretary, Ashton Carter. There are a lot of sources here at the Kennedy School."

After the Soviet Union collapsed, he worked in Ukraine and at the Eurasia Foundation, which fostered private enterprise and democracy in the newly independent states. He was a mid-career student in 1996–97 and has stayed at the Kennedy School ever since, running executive education programs for military and intelligence officials of former Soviet-bloc countries. Some take place in Cambridge, others in Eastern Europe. In 2015, for instance, Harvard cosponsored a five-day program in Bucharest with the Romanian Intelligence Service on "Security in the Black Sea Region: Shared Challenges, Sustainable Future." Konoplyov spoke at the opening ceremony, and Tad Oelstrom participated in a panel discussion on "Framing border(less) perspectives in the Black Sea region: Human vs. national vs. transnational security." About half of the seventy attendees were Romanian intelligence officers.

Konoplyov's programs provide a neutral back channel for resolving emergencies and disputes in the region. In 2005, a desperate phone call from a Russian admiral to an American counterpart whom he had met the year before at the Kennedy School prompted the United States and Britain to rescue a Russian submarine tangled in fishing nets in the depths of the Pacific Ocean.

In 2009, Romania exposed a Ukrainian spy ring and expelled its military attaché, testing the friendship that the heads of the two countries' intelligence services had formed at—where else?—the Kennedy School.

"Why didn't you tell me first?" the Ukrainian asked the Romanian, according to Konoplyov. "The president called and I feel bad."

They quarreled and the Romanian said to Konoplyov, "I won't talk to Ukrainians. They aren't reliable."

So Konoplyov invited the same Ukrainian and a different Romanian to an executive education program and told them to communicate. At first, the Ukrainian refused. But by the end, Konoplyov says, "I saw them sitting in Dunkin' Donuts and talking."

ONE KENNEDY SCHOOL classmate saw through Ken Moskow's cover. An Arizona real estate developer and lawyer who served in naval aviation during the Vietnam War, Richard Shaw also had worked in foreign counterintelligence. When they first met, Moskow told Shaw that he was a foreign-service officer. "I said, because I have some background myself, 'Let's put that crap aside. We both know who you really work for,'" Shaw recalls. "He kind of looked shocked. We proceeded on, and were good friends and business partners."

Moskow used his year at the Kennedy School to rethink his career plans. After earning his master's, he quit the CIA and went into real estate with Shaw in Mexico. He kept in touch with other classmates, and attended José Figueres's 1994 presidential inauguration. When Figueres's term ended in 1998, he and Moskow became partners in Costa Rican real estate.

It's unclear whether, or when, Moskow's Latin American classmates learned of his CIA background. Shelagh Moskow, his widow, said he wouldn't have told them about it during the mid-career program. She didn't know Moskow at Harvard—they would elope to Paris in 2000—but based her conclusions on subsequent conversations. Ken knew Latin Americans would be leery of the CIA, and he would have needed the agency's permission anyway, she said. "He was very serious about what those rules were, abiding by those rules. There's a strong culture in the agency of not talking."

However, one Latin American classmate said that Moskow's CIA connection was no secret. "Everybody knew Mr. Moscow [*sic*] was part of the CIA as so many of the students at Kennedy school," said a spokeswoman for Roque Sevilla, an Ecuadorian businessman and conservationist. According to Shaw, Figueres (who didn't respond to requests for comment) and the now-deceased Guatemalan defense minister Héctor Gramajo were clued in, too.

While Moskow's "cards were always held close to the vest," his agency past was "common knowledge" among his Harvard buddies, Shaw said. "It is certainly true that he would not have broadcast that information beyond that little tight circle." For example, "he wouldn't travel around with businesspeople in Mexico or Costa Rica and say, 'By the way, I'm from the government.'"

Moskow still dropped by the Kennedy School, and he and Konoplyov became close friends. They surfed on Martha's Vineyard and traveled to Ukraine, homeland of Moskow's ancestors. When I asked Konoplyov whether the CIA stayed in touch with Moskow during the 1990s, he reminded me of Vladimir Putin's dictum that "there is no such thing as a former KGB man."

"It's easy for the CIA to go to Ken and say, 'There's a conference, can you go there and talk to these people?'" Konoplyov continued. "Ken would say, 'Of course.' If you're the CIA, FBI, Stasi, you don't need someone on the payroll if you have friendly connections."

Soon Moskow was a current CIA man again. After the September 11, 2001, attacks, he reupped. As a Paris station chief, he dashed across Europe and former Soviet republics to keep weapons of mass destruction out of the hands of terrorists, before retiring from the agency again in 2006 to spend more time with his family.

In his twenty-fifth-anniversary report to his Harvard undergraduate classmates in 2008, he acknowledged to them for the first time that he had been "recruited into the CIA" soon after graduation and "served as an undercover operations officer." Seemingly sensing that his time was running short, he added, "With the recent passing of parents of college friends and watching both our own and friends' children grow, it makes one further recognize the importance of taking advantage of each day and opportunities as they arise."

Though startled to learn posthumously of the CIA officer in their midst, his Kennedy School classmates told me that they understand the reasons for the deception. Had they found out at the time, they might have been less forgiving, but the climate has changed.

"I have a different feeling about intelligence agencies and the work they do given 9/11," said Barbara Grob, the West Coast media relations specialist. "Prior to 9/11, I would have been quicker to be judgmental. As a dyed-in-the-wool liberal, I've shifted on it. I don't feel strongly that we have to know that about people."

10

. . . .

"I AM KEEPING YOU OUT OF JAIL"

This isn't J. Edgar Hoover's FBI. The *Untouchables* stereotype of ex-policemen pursuing mobsters and crooked politicians no longer fits. After Hoover's death in 1972, the bureau began hiring women as agents for the first time since he'd become director almost half a century before; by 2012, they made up almost 20 percent of the force. Agents come from all walks of life, including former computer scientists, human resources specialists, airline pilots, even journalists.

Today's FBI is a hybrid, an intelligence service grafted onto traditional law enforcement. It reports to the director of national intelligence as well as the attorney general. Increasingly, it operates worldwide, with seventy-eight offices and suboffices in U.S. embassies from Kuala Lumpur to Caracas, coordinating with the CIA and security agencies in the host countries.

After the 9/11 attacks, the bureau's priorities shifted from catching mobsters, drug traffickers, and white-collar criminals to preventing terrorism, foreign espionage, and cyberattacks. This transition steered the FBI's gaze to academia. The bureau's target "is not just the more traditional spies passing U.S. secrets to foreign governments. . . . It is also students and scientists and plenty of others stealing the valuable trade secrets of American universities and businesses."

Dianne Mercurio epitomizes this transformation. Her path was both typical of the modern FBI and startling in its swift ascent. Like Dajin Peng, the professor whom she recruited, she had known little but success in her career, and was confident, perhaps overly so, in her ability to handle any situation.

Also like Peng, she became a Floridian in adulthood; her roots lay elsewhere. The second child of Dale and Marilyn Farrington, Dianne Leigh Farrington was born in 1968 in Burlington, Vermont, where her father worked as a draftsman for General Electric's Armament Division. The division manufactured automatic weapons for U.S. troops during the Vietnam War, and Dale Farrington shared patents for two devices that improved the machine guns' performance—a lubricating device and a "muzzle brake torque assist."

When Dianne was four, her father transferred to a GE division in Greenville, South Carolina. The Farringtons bought a home on Candlewood Court in nearby Mauldin, which was evolving from a farming village into a middle-class bedroom suburb. Its population rose to 23,808 in 2012, up 52.1 percent from 2000. Predominantly white, Republican, and Protestant, one of the few South Carolina cities with a higher household income and lower poverty rate than the national average, Mauldin is known for fiscal conservatism and police speed traps. "It used to be a big red dot on the AAA travel maps," says John Gardner, Mauldin's former planning and economic development director.

Mauldin High School was built in 1973, the same year that the Farringtons moved to the city, and renovated in 2002, the year that Dale Farrington retired from General Electric. With a 91.9 percent graduation rate, and average SAT scores of 503 in critical reading and 506 in math, it is considered one of South Carolina's best public high schools. Future NBA Hall of Famer Kevin Garnett may be its most notable former student, though his arrest following a racial melee in the hallway prompted his transfer to Farragut Career Academy in Chicago for his senior season.

At Mauldin High, Dianne Farrington was a solid student and a standout athlete. A member of the girls' basketball, powderpuff football, track, and cross-country teams, she set school records in the 400 and 800 meters, and was a state champion in the 800.

"She was a lot of fun in the workout settings and socially as well," recalled track and cross-country teammate Dana Purser House, now cross-country coach at Bluffton High in South Carolina. "She and I would go back and forth competing, pushing each other." House, who transferred to Mauldin High as a sophomore, said some teammates treated her as an interloper, but not Dianne. "She was always very nice with regards to that. We had a mutual respect."

Delmer Howell, her high school coach, wasn't surprised that she became an FBI agent. "She was a leader on the team," he said. "She has the kind of intelligence and perseverance they're looking for."

Her college choice demonstrated her independence and self-assurance. While Mauldin High graduates typically stayed in-state at Clemson or the University of South Carolina, Dianne headed to the University of North Carolina at Chapel Hill. "We had very few kids who got into UNC, it was tough for out-of-staters," said Martha Oakhill, her guidance counselor. Surprisingly, Dianne didn't run track in college, though she played ice hockey as a club sport. She majored in psychology.

After graduating in 1990, she moved to Tampa and then returned to North Carolina. In 1994, she became a social worker for Orange County, which includes Chapel Hill. Based in the county seat, Hillsborough, she helped run a subsidized day care program for foster and low-income children that enabled their parents to work or go to school. She impressed supervisors and colleagues alike as efficient and unflappable.

If another social worker was anxious at the last minute about whether a family would qualify for the program, Dianne "was one to say, 'Don't worry, I'll get it done, day care will pay,'" recalls one social worker, Patty Clarke. "She was a great team player. If she didn't get her stuff done, money wouldn't get paid to day care, and kids would get kicked out. It never happened."

Robert Brizendine, who shared an office with Dianne, realized that she was destined for greater things. "She was a very intelligent young woman who took the job because she needed something to do. There wasn't a great deal of future in social work, particularly the position she was in," he says. "She had the capability of doing something more meaningful, and more lucrative as well. . . . She was definitely overqualified."

She confided in Brizendine and others that she had a more challenging career in mind—one that few social workers aspired to. She was applying to the FBI, and they might be contacted for background checks. She kept in top physical shape, running and working out, preparing herself for the bureau's grueling training regimen.

"I knew from the beginning that she was interested in the FBI," says Deanna Shoffner, her social work supervisor. "She talked about it. She wanted a different career. Going to the FBI was quite unusual. I didn't know anybody else who had done it in all my years in social services."

Applicants to become FBI agents must be U.S. citizens between the ages of twenty-three and thirty-six-and-a-half, with a bachelor's degree and three years of work experience. They're disqualified for having a felony conviction, a student loan default, or failure to file tax returns or pay court-ordered child support. Hiring is highly selective; in fiscal year 2011, the FBI had 22,692 applicants for 543 vacancies.

Dianne met the criteria, and beat the odds. Hired in 1997, she completed mandatory training at the FBI Academy in Quantico, Virginia, and was assigned to the Tampa office. She paid her dues by probing a variety of crimes, and joined the FBI's Innocent Images International Task Force against child pornography. She helped investigate a Florida pastor, Lawrence Kilbourn, whose daughter had found a videotape showing him molesting girls aged six to twelve. Kilbourn "made statements to" Mercurio "as to his alleged videotaping of sexual acts with young girls," according to a court document. Kilbourn pleaded guilty to state and federal charges and was sentenced to seventeen years in prison.

On a trip back to Chapel Hill, Dianne got together with old friends and told Brizendine that she found FBI work fulfilling and enjoyable. Her personal life was blossoming as well. She married Matthew Mercurio, a State University of New York graduate who works as a medical device distributor. They have two daughters, who attend a private school in Tampa and, like their mother, are athletic. Dianne herself ran the Nike Women's Marathon in San Francisco in 2008, shortly after turning forty.

Like many Floridians during the boom, the Mercurios speculated in real estate. From 2004 to 2006, they bought and sold at a substantial profit three lots in The Cliffs at Glassy, a development about forty-five minutes' drive from her parents' home in Mauldin featuring a golf course designed by Tiger Woods and breathtaking views of the Blue Ridge Mountains. A fourth lot, which they acquired in 2007 and held on to, dropped in value as The Cliffs sank into Chapter 11 bankruptcy in 2012.

SOON AFTER THE Kilbourn case, Mercurio expressed interest in a transfer to the counterintelligence squad. Its head, J. A. Koerner, chose her for the coveted slot over several other applicants. "She was good at working people," he says. "She could talk to them, and get them to talk to her. On a scale of one to ten, she was an eight or nine." She was also "a good shot," and instructed other agents in firearms.

The terrorist attacks of September 2001 stunned the FBI, especially the Tampa office. Three hijackers had attended flight school in Venice, Florida, within Tampa's jurisdiction. The bureau shifted every available agent into Koerner's domains, counterterrorism and counterintelligence. "On September 10, 2001, I had seventeen people working for me. On September 12, I had a hundred and seventeen."

The biggest target was Sami Al-Arian, the USF computer professor accused of bankrolling Palestinian terrorists. (His case, as we've seen, led Pennsylvania State University president Graham Spanier to reach out to the FBI and CIA.) Although Mercurio interviewed one of Al-Arian's alleged co-conspirators on the day of their arrest in 2003, she caused some waves within the bureau by avoiding any deeper entanglement in what was a quagmire of Dickensian, Jarndyce versus Jarndyce proportions.

"A lot of people didn't want to work it because there were ten years of tapes, interviews, translations, documents, plus a lot of press attention. It was under a microscope," says one insider. Mercurio "was assigned to it. She said no. If I was a supervisor, you don't get to say no."

Koerner says he didn't want to put Mercurio, a counterintelligence agent, on a counterterrorism investigation. He had another beat in mind for her: Chinese espionage. Chinese efforts to penetrate Tampa's research facilities had worried Koerner for years. In the 1990s, China's consulate in Houston had offered a Chinese student at the University of South Florida an incentive to spy: if he would provide information about his friends working for defense contractors in Tampa, his ailing parents in China would be allowed to move closer to a medical clinic. The student briefly cooperated with Chinese intelligence before contacting the FBI and asking how to extricate himself. Its advice, which he followed successfully, was to tell the Chinese official that "the FBI saw me talking to you."

Before retiring from the FBI in 2004, Koerner began to give China-related cases to Mercurio, and she took courses on China. Her beat occasionally brought her to South Florida's campus. In March 2011, for instance, she and another FBI agent questioned Hao Zheng, an associate professor of computer science, about a Chinese graduate student in his classes, Zheng said in a telephone interview.

"I was a little bit nervous," Zheng said.

While it's not clear how Mercurio first came across Dajin Peng's name, she was likely aware of the concern at FBI headquarters about Confucius Institutes and began keeping tabs on the one sprouting at USF and its director. Presumably she also developed sources in Tampa's Chinese community, in which Peng was active on behalf of the Confucius Institute.

Mercurio must have discovered Peng's FBI file, because she phoned Nick Abaid, the agent who had cultivated him at Princeton. She struck him as "a fairly new agent who was feeling her way in the Chinese field."

In December 2009, a month after the draft audit accused him of expense account and visa transgressions, Peng flew to China to teach there over the holiday break, as was his custom. On his return, the Department of Homeland Security examined his computers and discovered a document titled "FBI and I," in which Peng briefly recounted his relationships with Abaid and Mercurio.

Mercurio "knows very well about my case and has detailed information about the USF Confucius Institute," Peng wrote. "She even suspected that the CI has spying missions. I had to explain to her that the CI is a purely academic and cultural institution and it has no spying mission at all. Then she asked me to help to get some information," such as the names of students in the graduate business courses Peng taught in China for mid-career executives. "I also found that the FBI knows all the information the investigators know as the investigation proceeded."

Peng had written it at the request of the criminal lawyer he had just hired, Stephen Romine, a former prosecutor. Romine recognized that the

FBI might play a role in the case, and he was also concerned that Mercurio might exploit her access to Peng to elicit information damaging to him. But a homeland security officer thought he'd caught a spy reporting to the Chinese government. The officer alerted Mercurio, who "got really nervous" until Romine cleared up the confusion, Peng said.

Mercurio continued to monitor the university's audit. USF police called her office twice on December 17, 2009; one conversation lasted more than fourteen minutes. When the final audit and compliance report came out on January 28, 2010, it was virtually identical to the earlier draft. That day, Mercurio spoke on her mobile phone for twelve minutes with university police. "It is my understanding that she is asking USF police to not do anything with their case until she can assess your situation," Romine emailed Peng on February 17, after conferring with Mercurio.

"Until she can assess your situation" was a tactful way of saying, "Until you decide to spy."

"She made no promises regarding your cooperation and stopping any charges against you," Romine continued. "They will evaluate everything only at this point. She has agreed to not question you about the allegations involving USF."

On the afternoon of March 9, Mercurio met with Peng and Romine in the lawyer's office. They agreed that Peng would cooperate with the FBI, and Mercurio would advocate for him with the university. It was in the FBI's interest for the university to let Peng off easy, not only because he would be in her debt, but also because he would be less useful as an informant if he were to lose the professorship that gained him entrée to Chinese intellectuals, government officials, and business executives.

When Mercurio left the office, Peng asked the lawyer how long he would have to help the FBI. After some years of "good service," he could ask to quit, Romine replied.

The answer dismayed Peng. While he feigned enthusiasm, he inwardly had no desire to spy for the FBI. His childhood had taught him to avoid intelligence agencies, and he also worried about his safety. "I would rather rot in a U.S. jail than a Chinese jail," he once told Professor Harvey Nelsen, his mentor. Still, he preferred to avoid incarceration in either country, and just now an American prison was the more imminent threat. He had to play along.

And thus they tangoed. Sometimes accompanied by another agent, Mercurio would pick up Peng in a brown sedan at his drab suburban apartment, and they would head to an Olive Garden off Bruce B. Downs Boulevard for lunch. The Olive Garden was far enough from the USF campus that he was unlikely to be recognized, and FBI agents liked its pseudo-Italian fare.

When they pulled in at the restaurant, they would often sit talking in the parking lot first. Peng would hand Mercurio the bills from his most recent China trip for reimbursement. Either she didn't know that USF and the Chinese universities where he taught were also paying his travel expenses, or she didn't care.

In their regular corner booth, Mercurio would order a chicken Caesar salad, while Peng chose the more expensive surf 'n' turf. Then, behind a veneer of friendship and conviviality, the sparring would begin. As in a labor negotiation or diplomatic summit, each side sought to achieve as much of its own agenda as possible. Peng wanted Mercurio to keep him out of prison and restore him to his former glory as Confucius Institute director. She wanted him to spy on China, the Confucius Institutes, and Tampa's Chinese community.

At first, she would toss softball questions. How did ordinary Chinese feel about their government? What was his analysis of Chinese policy on Taiwan or Tibet? Peng would pontificate at length, as if lecturing to his USF students. She listened with every sign of interest and gratitude. Stroking his ego, she assured him that his insights would go straight to the president.

Next she got down to specifics. What government officials would he meet on his next China trip? How could the FBI persuade a certain Chinese-American professor, businessman, or bureaucrat to cooperate—would he be most susceptible to money, a promotion, a green card? What were the names and occupations of Peng's Chinese friends working in Hong Kong and Macau? Which of his colleagues and students at South Florida were acting suspiciously? Egging him on, she would complain that other China-born professors at USF weren't doing their part for the FBI.

Peng would supply a few driblets, but soon his gaze would become wary, his tone evasive. Once, she suggested that he consider a venture outside academia, running a front company that the bureau would establish and fund. It wouldn't work, Peng said, because he needed affiliation with USF and the Confucius Institute as cover or else he couldn't do what the FBI wanted—get closer to Chinese government officials.

He would love to cooperate, he told her, but first the university needed to end its smear campaign against him. After all, without credibility, he was useless to the FBI. It was up to her to save him—for both their sakes.

HIS LAWYERS CAME to the same conclusion. After hammering out the deal with Mercurio, Romine and Peng's civil lawyer, Steven Wenzel, developed an unusual defense strategy: leave it to the FBI. The attorneys would use a "soft approach" to "buy some time" so that "developments on the other aspect of this . . . might greatly assist you in the present controversy with USF," Wenzel emailed Peng on March 19.

Counting on an outside agency to sway academic discipline, normally the prerogative of university administrators and faculty, might seem like a forlorn hope, but it was shrewd politics. The evidence against Peng was compelling, and his lawyers would be hard-pressed to change university president Judy Genshaft's mind. The FBI might have more clout. Whether or not the bureau had tipped USF off about Al-Arian's indictment, Genshaft was likely grateful for its handling of the case and haunted by the public outcry against the university after O'Reilly's broadcast.

Bucking the FBI wasn't the way for Genshaft to repair USF's image and appease its military constituents. It also wasn't her inclination. Genshaft's relations with liberal faculty members had been somewhat strained since the American Association of University Professors had condemned USF for violating Al-Arian's due process rights by dismissing him before his trial without giving him an opportunity to respond to the charges against him. She was also insecure, rarely sending emails for fear that they would become public. Gordon Gee, former president of Ohio State, where Genshaft had worked for sixteen years, calls her a "nervous Nellie." Trained in counseling and school psychology (she and Mercurio shared a background in social work), she was less apt to make a fuss about academic independence than, say, a former law school dean like Derek Bok. Nor was Robert Wilcox, a native of Great Britain who became USF's provost in 2008, likely to stand up to FBI meddling; his expertise was in physical education and sports.

Wenzel soon began sending Peng sunny bulletins. "Things seem to be going well for you and I am glad," he emailed Peng on April 30. "I've not heard anything from the University which is consistent with what we had all thought might happen as a result of your cooperation." A week later, he proclaimed, "I am most happy to see that the mess got reversed. No one has acknowledged that to me directly but I was assured that was going to happen."

"There is no real issue at USF now," Peng replied. "[M]y case has actually been stopped. In fact, they are working hard trying to reinstate me as the director for the Confucius Institute."

The declaration of victory was premature, as the university convened a five-member faculty committee to review Peng's case and recommend discipline. "We both think the matter is over but today Diana [*sic*: Peng's misspelling of Dianne] told me that the University has to let the panel run its course," Peng emailed Wenzel on May 12.

With a lawyer's caution, Wenzel usually avoided naming the FBI and Mercurio in his emails. They were "our friends," and the faculty review was "this thing." As he wrote to Peng on May 25, "our friends and I are working to get this thing stopped but that is taking longer than I had hoped." He added on May 28, "Our friends are working with me and I am optimistic that they will be successful also."

Again, Wenzel's optimism was short-lived. On July 1, an email from Wenzel warned Peng that if the faculty committee recommended firing him or revoking his tenure, the media would report it, which was the last thing that the FBI wanted. "My conversations with our friends makes it clear to me that you are owed no value to them if there is negative publicity about you," Wenzel wrote. "I leave to you and Mr. Romine the exploration of what losing these friends means to you."

The alternative, Wenzel wrote, was settling with the university, but the terms would be harsh. "Our friends tell me the University will not settle your issues unless you give up tenure," he wrote. Peng would have to forfeit his job security, and risk being fired at any time.

Six days later, after talking to USF officials, Wenzel reiterated that the university insisted Peng relinquish his tenure. "They told our friends that and have never told our friends anything differ [*sic*]." At best, USF "might be willing to consider some adjunct teaching."

Peng was aghast. During the faculty review, he learned for the first time that sexual harassment complaints by Xiaonong Zhang and Shuhua Liu Kriesel had triggered the audit. That revelation, combined with Wenzel's news that the FBI was nudging him to give up his professorship, sent his anxious mind into a whirl. He became convinced that the bureau was conspiring with his accusers and USF.

The federal immigration investigation was another irritant. When Peng returned to O'Hare International Airport in Chicago that same summer from China, Homeland Security agents copied the images on his three laptop computers and external hard drive, seeking evidence to support a criminal prosecution for visa fraud. They found "no materials which could be used to defraud the admissions process." They would close their investigation in November, concluding that while Peng's "disregard for laws, regulations and ethical standards in academia were well documented by the USF audit," his "questionable statements with respect to visa procurements were not proven to be false . . . and no conspiratorial acts were found."

PENG VENTED HIS frustration on his lawyer. "Please do not growl at me," Wenzel responded on July 18. "It was not until you began cooperating with our friends that we could even consider giving USF a response. You may remember that before that there was a great deal of concern about your liberty and that that was more important than your job. You and me and Mr. Romine all said that to each other repeatedly.

"What I don't think you understand is that the administration of USF at the highest level has made up its mind. There is nothing you're going to say to change what the president thinks or what her lawyer thinks or what the Provost thinks. . . . You may remember that we were offered the opportunity [to] take a year's salary and to submit resignation. That was a certain sign from the president about her intentions. . . . As for what our friends [sic] advice is, you need to understand they will tell you what ever they want you to hear so that you will continue to be helpful [to] them."

"I get the point," Peng replied. "I have no choice but to fight."

Peng badgered Mercurio as well, asking the FBI to pay Wenzel's fees. "Any compensation my office offers will be as a direct result of your cooperation," she answered on July 31. "Remember I am keeping you out of jail as well, and it's difficult to put a price on freedom."

He, Mercurio, and another agent talked during this period in a parked car outside Peng's apartment. Unhappy with the tone of their questions, Peng blurted out, "I know you suspect I'm a Chinese spy."

They didn't deny it, and just looked at each other. "Oh, a spy," one of them said. Peng felt that he'd broken a taboo, like the boy who dared to say that the emperor was naked.

Unable to sleep at 3:27 a.m. on August 11, he lashed out at Mercurio in an email. "I am willing to serve my country utilizing my special capacity and resources," he wrote. "But I have to be treated in an honorable and fair way. . . . Even if you and USF can twist my arms and force me into a more unfair deal, it is going to hurt our common course in the long run. Please let USF not to mistreat me further. . . . I have made huge contribution to USF and am running huge risks to contribute to the USA." He added a plea: "As an effective social workers [*sic*], you can play a critical role here, since you r [*sic*] the only one all three sides trust now."

Mercurio was fed up. "You are making false allegations about my office which I do not appreciate," she replied. "My office has not caused your legal troubles to extend, but rather have protected you in the best ways possible. . . . Your assistance to my office is not considered substantial, only minimal at this point. Therefore, understand that I have stuck my neck out for you thus far, knowing that substantial assistance may never happen. A thank you, instead of a list of demands, would be nice for a change."

A thank-you was deserved, because Mercurio was making headway. "We've come a long way from the University's demand that you be fired before the next academic year," Wenzel told Peng on August 17. "You have received in exchange for your concessions lifelong employment with all tenure rights."

By the next day, Mercurio was brokering the final terms between USF and Peng. "It took more than two hours for the FBI to convince me to accept the conditions I e-mailed you Monday," Peng told Wenzel. "However, USF is still demanding much more. . . . I do not want a fight between USF and me, especially because it will involve Dianne, who I think has helped me a lot so far . . . Dianne just called. . . . I am glad that she told me that USF position IS NOT FINAL and is willing to go back to the table. She called a few USF people and left a message in your voice mail. I told her . . . that I will absolutely stick to the terms I agreed to FBI on Monday."

"She is the only one to get USF to budge (make a movement)," Wenzel replied. "We are dependent on her."

On August 19, Wenzel told Peng that Mercurio "called me after speaking with you and speaking with the president at length." From August 18 to August 26, she and USF general counsel Steven Prevaux called each other seven times, twice for more than fifteen minutes. He also phoned her extension at the FBI office six times between July and December 2010, once for a forty-five-minute conversation.

On August 24, 2010, sixteen months after he was placed on leave, Peng and the university reached a settlement that had Mercurio's fingerprints all over it. USF fined him ten thousand dollars and suspended him without pay from December 2010 to December 2011. While the agreement permanently barred Peng from having "administrative responsibility" for the Confucius Institute, it promised that, after his suspension, he would develop a "Confucius Institute linkage" at USF's branch campus in nearby St. Petersburg, "with appropriate and new Partner(s) in China."

Mercurio had preserved Peng's freedom, his tenured professorship, and the bureau's potential access to Chinese policy makers and Confucius Institute insiders. USF police never brought charges against him, despite the auditors' findings. The FBI was so deeply involved in the settlement that "it was acting as though it was the provost," said Professor Nelsen. Asked if the FBI's influence, along with his own legal acumen, was responsible for saving Peng's job, Wenzel said, "That's about right."

The leniency of the punishment astounded faculty members familiar with the allegations against Peng—but not with the FBI's intervention. "How in the world could he not be fired was the feeling I heard from everyone," Eric Shepherd said.

The university contends that the FBI's advocacy had no effect. The discipline "was consistent with its past practice and appropriate for the serious misconduct," and Genshaft "was extremely unhappy with the FBI's continued attempts to insert itself," according to USF spokeswoman

Lara Wade-Martinez. Genshaft and Wilcox declined to answer written questions that I sent them.

EMBOLDENED BY HER triumph, Mercurio stepped up her advocacy for Peng. With a CIA officer in tow, she showed up at the office of South Florida senior vice president Karen Holbrook, who had been assigned on the day of the settlement to supervise Peng's development of the Confucius Institute affiliate in St. Petersburg.

The visitors told Holbrook that Peng had been an FBI informant at Princeton and vouched for his ability and patriotism. In essence, they conveyed the message to his new boss that he was under their protection. "They were coming to tell me what they knew about him," Holbrook told me during a 2014 conversation in the waterfront mansion that she and her husband, Jim, an oceanographer, own on Sarasota Bay. "It was favorable."

The CIA officer likely accompanied Mercurio because the agency, which takes the lead on overseas espionage, was hoping to run Peng as an asset in China. The combined presence of the two powerful intelligence services would have intimidated many a university administrator. Not Holbrook. A newcomer to USF and thus unscarred by the Al-Arian uproar, Holbrook had a more formidable academic resume than either Genshaft or Wilcox. A cell biologist, she had been provost of the University of Georgia from 1998 to 2002, and president of Ohio State University from 2002 to 2007. She also recognized the tensions between national security and academic freedom. As graduate dean at the University of Florida in the 1990s, she had rejected an FBI request to see student files, but had been overruled. She wasn't about to roll over for the bureau now.

Like the intelligence agents, Peng may have underestimated Holbrook. Reluctant to be exiled to St. Petersburg, he conceived a grander position for himself. He would run, on USF's main campus, one of four research centers that Hanban leaders told him they planned to establish and fund in the United States. He pitched the idea to Holbrook in her office on October 12, 2010.

At first, Holbrook was charmed. "I really quite enjoyed talking to him at the beginning," she said. The USF administrators who dumped Peng in her lap hadn't told her about the allegations against him. Then Maria Crummett, Peng's ex-boss, enlightened her. Holbrook read the audit report. "I decided, that was something I didn't want to get into. That's when I stopped interacting with him." Moreover, Hanban funding for the research center, his pet project, didn't materialize.

Holbrook didn't hear from the CIA officer again, but Mercurio phoned her eight times from October 15 to December 1, 2010, and probably went to see her a second time. Mercurio also called General Counsel Prevaux twice.

On November 17, with Peng five weeks away from starting his suspension, Mercurio emailed Holbrook, urging her to include him in festivities planned for an upcoming visit to USF by a Chinese dignitary. She was likely referring to the leader of a delegation from USF's Confucius Institute partner, Nankai University, which would arrive in Tampa later that month. "As we discussed in our last meeting," Peng's "credibility is critically at stake," Mercurio wrote. He "has been functioning for over a year on promises of a show of resolve to his overseas contacts" and "will be rendered completely ineffective if no show of support is given by USF in the very near future."

Unless Peng is on hand to welcome the guest, she warned, he "will appear extremely rude and disrespectful." His absence could "generate a high level of suspicion" and cause him to "lose face." If Holbrook found it awkward for Peng to attend the public events, at least she could arrange a "brief, private meeting."

It didn't seem to occur to Mercurio that Holbrook might not care as much as she did about whether Peng was an effective spy—as against whether he was an effective teacher or scholar. His "credibility does not just affect his dealings with USF, but has national security implications on a large scale," the FBI agent wrote.

Holbrook didn't respond. Instead, she forwarded the email to Provost Wilcox. "I find it all extremely troubling on a number of levels," he replied. USF forbade Peng to meet with the VIP.

That month, Peng told Mercurio that he had a wonderful idea. USF should establish a branch campus in China as a base for spying. After all, many American universities were opening branches overseas and several, including Johns Hopkins, had planted the flag in China. Why not USF?

Actually, Peng's suggestion was a delaying tactic, his best yet, the product of hours of racking his brain for ways to escape the FBI's grip. A branch campus, he knew, would require numerous approvals and be snarled in Chinese red tape. He could put off spying for years.

Mercurio took the bait. On December 1, she emailed Holbrook again. After acknowledging the "radio silence" with which Holbrook had greeted her previous request, she brought up Peng's proposal. Peng "recently mentioned the possibility of exploring a USF branch campus in China, a difficult task for U.S. universities," she wrote. "Of course, it would all hinge on current support from USF, which was promised in several venues this summer."

USF administrators were outraged. In their eyes, they had tried to cooperate with the FBI, but establishing a branch campus as a springboard for American spies would be a gross violation of academic values. If discovered, it would destroy the school's reputation and get other American universities kicked out of China.

On December 5, Holbrook brushed off Mercurio: "I need to be very clear about the institutional position before I speak with Peng again, and perhaps before you and I confer as well." After Christmas, she passed the message to Wilcox. "This is the email I received from Dianne Mercurio that upset Judy (and me as well)," she wrote to the provost. "This seems to me to be a very unfortunate situation and I do not think we want to be involved any longer."

Wilcox: "And a USF Branch Campus in China, no less! I agree, that personal and institutional integrity suggests that we should not participate. Let's talk!"

Holbrook: "Yes, very problematic, What do you think were the promises re: the branch campus??? This should be a priority for discussion."

With a push from Peng, Mercurio had gone too far. The FBI's clout at South Florida was waning—and so was its infatuation with Peng. At a meeting in an airport hotel, FBI agents asked him to take a lie detector test. It was clear that they still suspected he was spying for China. Peng replied that he would be glad to take a polygraph to prove he wasn't. But when they told him that the questioning would be more comprehensive, he balked, saying it was an invasion of privacy.

Upset by the request, Peng accused the FBI in the June 4, 2011, *St. Petersburg Times* article of orchestrating the university investigations of him. Six days later, whether by retribution or coincidence, federal immigration officials resumed their scrutiny of Peng. Although his status was "previous subject, closed case," a new entry in his file ordered an "extensive search for documentation of contacts in China, expenditures, and financial transactions. Search computers, phones, and electronic media if possible."

Much as Chinese intelligence wasted time and money on Glenn Shriver, the FBI had misjudged Peng. Perhaps, despite the bureau's evolving mission, it still understood mobsters better than it did college professors. Mercurio gave him an ultimatum: if he was still interested in working with the FBI, he had to come to its Tampa office for a tape-recorded conversation. Peng never showed up.

THAT SHOULD HAVE marked the end of Peng's travails at South Florida. He could have served his suspension and quietly returned to teaching. Except that he couldn't resist retaliating against the "Little Sea Elephant" who had denounced him. And Mercurio was no longer rushing to his rescue.

What set him off was a decision by Nankai University, USF's Confucius Institute partner, to suspend him from teaching in its mid-career business program. Nankai cited the St. Petersburg Times coverage that questioned why USF didn't fire him. Peng inferred that his ex-flame, Xiaonong Zhang, and her husband had supplied the articles to Chinese authorities.

In October and November 2011, Nankai leaders found themselves bombarded by angry letters, ostensibly from an ever-growing number—20, 36, 40, and finally 46—of "overseas Chinese." Depicting Peng as a victim of persecution by South Florida, the FBI, and Nankai, the anonymous authors urged Nankai to reinstate him and suspend Xiaonong Zhang for bringing false complaints against him in revenge for being spurned romantically. Otherwise, they threatened to circulate the missives to "the top leadership of all relevant organs of the Chinese government," presidents of China's top twenty universities, all of Nankai's deans, teachers, and students, and domestic and overseas media.

"The professor who has made great sacrifices for the motherland and major contributions to Nankai is framed by bad people at Nankai, persecuted by U.S. authorities, and suspended from teaching without reason, while the actual culprit is allowed to continue teaching," wrote "Thirty-six overseas Chinese of the Greater Tampa Bay area in the United States, who have made major contributions to the Confucius Institute of Nankai University."

Nankai officials had little doubt as to the epistles' true author: Peng. "Although he did not use his own email address, judging from the language, he wrote the letter himself," Naijia Guan, Nankai's vice president for international affairs, emailed Kun Shi, who had taken over as director of the USF Confucius Institute. Peng concedes that the prose style is similar to his own but says his supporters wrote the letters. Their pressure led Nankai to lift his suspension after a few months, he says.

Guan reacted to the epistolary onslaught by canceling Nankai's partnership in the institute. Peng "extremely affected the friendship of our two universities, and we cannot tolerate such abominable behavior," she wrote on November 8, 2011, to Holbrook, who remonstrated with her to no avail.

South Florida administrators were furious at Peng. Once again, they wanted him gone. "Some decisions will be made by USF very soon that will adversely effect [sic] your continued employment there," Robert McKee, who had represented Al-Arian and was now Peng's lawyer, cautioned him on November 23.

The university offered Peng a buyout plus the opportunity to resign rather than be fired. He rejected it. It was "disappointing and somewhat surprising to learn" that Peng had turned down "a very generous settlement proposal," USF general counsel Prevaux wrote to McKee on November 28. "Consequently the university must now pursue its own course of direct action."

USF considered firing Peng for cause, but "it became clear that the case for termination would require the testimony of witnesses in China who could prove difficult to locate, interpreters and multiple document translations," according to university spokeswoman Wade-Martinez. Instead, after administrative and faculty reviews, Peng received "the most severe progressive discipline administered to any tenured USF faculty member in the last decade."

The university suspended him without pay from June 2013 through August 2015 for damaging its relationship with Nankai and Hanban.

It also accused him of trying to broker agreements with Hanban, violating a clause in his 2010 settlement that prohibited him from representing himself as a USF employee or negotiating contracts on the university's behalf while on suspension. Peng's defense was that he had apprised USF administrators of these discussions and told Hanban he was suspended.

The grounds for Peng's second suspension involved no crimes, unlike the alleged expense account and visa scams behind his first, and it could be argued that he was exercising legitimate free speech rights. Nevertheless, without the FBI in his corner, Peng's penalty was twice as harsh.

In June 2013, Peng filed a grievance through the faculty union, contending that the university was retaliating against him for refusing to spy on China. It was "by far the most exotic case we've ever had," said Robert Welker, a business law professor and the union's negotiator.

That November, the university offered to shorten Peng's suspension to one year. Under the proposed settlement Peng would have "no responsibilities for the Confucius Institute or any international exchange program of any kind." He would also agree that neither he nor USF "had interactions with external agencies that were inappropriate, unlawful, or unethical." That clause, which Welker said was inserted by the university, would have prevented Peng from criticizing USF's relationship with the FBI.

Peng spurned the deal. He preferred to serve out his suspension rather than conceal the FBI's role and give up hope of participating in international programs. After the university rejected his grievance and an appeal, the statewide faculty union decided against pursuing the case further.

At an orientation session for new faculty in 2013, USF senior vice provost Dwayne Smith dropped by the union's table and began discussing Peng's grievance with Welker and Paul Terry, an education professor and the union president. Smith, who represented the university in grievance discussions, told them that Peng should be careful because the government had enough evidence to put him in prison for twenty years.

Although his union was fighting the suspension, Terry agreed that Peng had gotten off lightly. Terry was surprised that the university hadn't fired Peng. Perhaps, he surmised, USF feared that its history of caving in to Mercurio and the FBI would become public if Peng were dismissed. "I kept saying, 'He might have something on the university.'"

IN AUGUST 2015, Peng's second suspension ended. He was living alone; his father had been killed in December 2014, at the age of eighty-nine, when a car hit him near the USF campus. In a eulogy, Peng said that his father had instilled in him a passion for world affairs—and the ability to withstand pressure.

I flew to Tampa for Peng's return to teaching. Carrying backpacks, laptops, and even the occasional skateboard, about forty students poured into the first meeting of his course on "China Today." Peng, though, was nowhere to be found. Compensating for his unpaid suspension, he'd booked teaching gigs in China up to the last minute. When thunderstorms delayed his flight from Beijing, he missed his connection in Chicago.

Instead of Peng, an elderly bald man wearing a flower-print shirt was writing discussion topics on a whiteboard, such as "Oldest Continuous Civilization." It was Peng's mentor, Emeritus Professor Harvey Nelsen. He explained to the students that he was filling in for Peng, "who had an event preventing him from getting here." He added that Peng was "completely sound of mind and body," as if they doubted it.

"You're going to enjoy Professor Peng," Nelsen continued. "He's a real kick. All the student evaluations on him were right through the roof, the highest in the department. He's got this great Chinese accent that takes some getting used to." Nelsen then launched into an anecdote about a student who told him that Peng was "extraordinary, the only professor I know who got his PhD in prison."

"Not prison," Nelsen had replied. "Princeton." The student wasn't far off the mark, I thought, remembering Mercurio's "I am keeping you out of jail" email.

Peng made it to Tampa for the first session of "Introduction to Japan," which he was also teaching that semester. He even had time beforehand to bask in his USF office, from which his suspension had barred him. The narrow, windowless third-floor office overflowed with books in both Chinese and English. Dominating one wall, a Chinese world map depicted

China in the center, relegating the United States to the upper right. It reminded me of the famous *New Yorker* magazine cover "View of the World from 9th Avenue." Because the earth is round, Peng explained to me, every country can put itself in the middle of its map.

Even with the travel fiasco, he seemed calmer and more relaxed than I'd ever seen him. We headed to the classroom, where forty-eight students assembled. Precisely at 5 p.m., he asked them, mock seriously, "Are you ready? Should I teach in English, Japanese, or Chinese?"

He wanted to know how many of them had been to Japan, and a dozen hands went up. He turned to a black student in a baseball cap, who hadn't raised his hand. "Have you been?"

"No."

"Next time I go, I will bring you," Peng said, deadpan.

A female student mentioned that she had just visited China. Peng feigned disbelief. "I was there, I didn't see you."

Peng may have been an incompetent or even unethical administrator, and miscast as a spy, but he proved to be a delightful teacher. Sauntering around the oppressively warm room in his white shirt with rolled-up sleeves, he held the undergraduates' attention for three hours. He leavened his theme that Japan and the United States are cultural opposites—Japan is homogeneous and collaborative, the U.S. heterogeneous and individualistic—with riffs of humor and repartee, the spoonfuls of sugar that made the educational medicine go down. He made jokes at the students' expense and his own, played the fool, shared personal experiences, offered exotic rewards for right answers, and in general acted like a cross between a talk-show host and a Borscht Belt comedian.

Japan, he told them, has a population of 127 million people, primarily on four islands. Which is bigger in landmass, he asked one student, California or Japan?

"California," correctly answered the student, whose name was Michael.

"Should I give him prize?" Peng wondered aloud. "Do you like money?" he asked Michael. With a flourish, he pulled a bill with Mao Zedong's picture on it out of his pocket. Unfortunately, Michael forfeited the Chinese currency because he couldn't identify Mao: Peng relayed it to another student who recognized the Chinese leader.

Instead of Asian money, students who couldn't answer Peng's questions had to be content with his standard reassurance: "That's okay. If you know everything, I lose my job."

As Peng described Japan's vulnerability to natural disasters, including tsunamis, earthquakes, and typhoons, he noticed a student smiling. "Why are you so happy about typhoons?" he asked her. Later, Peng pointed to her as he bantered with another student: "Do you know who is the most happy person in this room? She is."

Occasionally, he flashed his accustomed braggadocio. "Have any of you been to Waseda University?" was his segue into boasting that Waseda, where he had studied as a Social Science Research Council fellow, "is one of the two best private universities in Japan," producing more prime ministers, billionaires, and literature prize-winners than any other. He was "the only one selected" for the fellowship, which was "the most prestigious social science" award, "a big honor for me."

Like any experienced comic, Peng knew the value of a running gag. "Have you been to Hong Kong?" he asked a student.

"No, but I'd like to visit," she said.

"Next time I go, I bring you," Peng said, for the umpteenth time. Then he delivered the punch line, with impeccable timing. "I have a good suitcase." As his audience tittered, I realized that, unlike most people who deal with the FBI, Peng enjoyed the last laugh.

NO-SPY ZONE

After the FBI ended its courtship of Dajin Peng, it sought to erase any trace of the entire affair. Understandably, the bureau didn't want the public to know about its bungled recruiting of a university professor to spy on China.

That meant suppressing agent Dianne Mercurio's 2010 emails to Karen Holbrook, then University of South Florida senior vice president. Citing "national security implications on a large scale," Mercurio had urged the university to make a "show of support" for Peng before a visiting Chinese delegation and to explore opening a branch in China—presumably as a base for U.S. intelligence.

Emails to state institutions, such as USF, are normally considered public documents under Florida law. However, in an April 2012 letter to the university's lawyer, the FBI claimed to own the emails and demanded that USF surrender them.

"These communications were explicitly marked as being 'confidential,' 'sensitive,' and 'for official use only,'" Steven Ibison, then special agent in charge of the bureau's Tampa office, wrote in a letter cosigned by an FBI lawyer. "All copies of these communications must be returned to the FBI as soon as practicable. This law enforcement sensitive information is the property of the United States government and was loaned to your client on the condition that it remain confidential." Underscoring its tough tone

and implied threat of litigation, the FBI enclosed copies of two legal prece-
dents that it interpreted to support its demand.

The university withstood the pressure. Abiding by Florida law, it
retained custody of the emails—and later supplied them to me, over the
FBI's objections, in response to my public records request.

I had first asked Ibison about Peng before learning about the demand
letter. I didn't get very far. "I honestly can't remember any details of that
case," he told me in 2014. He had left the FBI and was in charge of security
for Noble Energy Inc. in Houston. "I've been out of the business so long.
I'm not trying to avoid your questions." He did remember Mercurio—
"Dianne's a good agent"—and acknowledged that he had approved FBI
operations at universities.

When USF provided me with his letter soon afterward, I phoned Ibison back and pointed out that he had written to the university only two
years before. He continued to claim selective amnesia. "You've got to
understand, there's five hundred people in the Tampa division," including about two hundred agents, Ibison said. "I'm not trying to blow smoke.
I just honestly don't recall the letter or the case."

During our first conversation, Ibison discussed the relationship between
intelligence agencies and academia in general terms. "There is a tension," he
told me. "The bureau always walks that fine line, trying to handle educators
a little differently. Obviously, we have a large number of foreign educators,
foreign students, coming into our country with a certain amount of information, intelligence, that can be gleaned from them. It wouldn't be unusual
that there are those folks here to gather intelligence on us.

"The bureau understands it's kind of sacred ground when you go into
a university. There are higher levels of authority before an agent walks
onto a campus, different levels of approval that have to be gained. . . .
Education is kind of one of those areas where people including myself
put it on a higher pedestal."

U.S. INTELLIGENCE OFFICIALS like Ibison pay tribute to the special status of universities, but their actions belie their words. Far from being a
"sacred ground" off-limits to espionage, academia is like a well-trampled
city park, once pristine but now littered with candy wrappers, broken
glass, and dog droppings.

What a former government official told me in the early stages of my project—"Both sides are exploiting universities"—proved to be true. Foreign and U.S. spy services alike prey on students and professors through deception and intimidation. China entrapped Glenn Duffie Shriver by paying him to write essays, the same trick that U.S. agents play on scientists at academic conferences. American intelligence pressured Peng and Carlos Alvarez to spy and Iranian nuclear scientists to defect, much as China warned a Chinese student at South Florida that his parents' medical care depended on his cooperation. All services take advantage of students' ideological fervor, as Cuba did with Marta Rita Velázquez and Ana Belén Montes.

Forty years ago, after the Church Committee revealed the CIA's ties to universities, the agency defeated the Harvard-led campaign to ban intelligence gathering by academics and deceptive recruiting of foreign students. Since then, the stigma on campus against working for U.S. intelligence—which was the main reason the CIA gave for hiding its relationships with professors—has faded. After 9/11, Graham Spanier and other university administrators welcomed U.S. intelligence, yet it still goes behind their backs, as in the FBI questioning of Libyan students like Mohamed Farhat. Invited or not, openly or not, U.S. intelligence today touches virtually every facet of academic life. Its influence likely equals or surpasses its previous peak in the 1950s, when it focused on a narrow swath of elite universities, and the population of foreign students in the United States was far smaller than it is today.

To weigh the impact of this shift on national security and academic culture, it's best to distinguish between overt and covert intelligence operations on campus. Most of the aboveboard activities, from sponsoring research to recruiting U.S. citizens for staff positions, appear on balance to be beneficial. Their openness fits academic values, and they may make America safer. For example, academic research funded by Intelligence Advanced Research Projects Activity, such as analyzing how groups gain followers on social media, or detecting key phrases in conversations in noisy cafés or obscure languages, might erode privacy, but it could predict a terrorist attack.

Public appearances by intelligence bigwigs foster student awareness and discussion of public policy. CIA director John Brennan often speaks on campuses, though protesters shouting "drones kill kids" and "U.S. out of the Middle East" thwarted his talk at the University of Pennsylvania in April 2016.

Recruitment events, which used to spur similar demonstrations, replenish the CIA's ranks. They take place on campuses nationwide, and are advertised in student and university media. At twenty-five to thirty-five universities each year, the agency tests the analytic skills of potential applicants by simulating a foreign affairs crisis. In April 2015, during a three-hour simulation at Harvard, thirty students—chosen by lottery from 130 who had signed up—advised five CIA analysts on responses to an imaginary oil and gas explosion in an Arctic region where Russia and the United States both had territorial claims.

The CIA wanted to limit participation to twenty-five students, "but we had so much interest that we went to thirty," organizer Eliza J. DeCubellis, a Harvard sophomore, told me. "As soon as you mention the CIA, anything to do with covert operations, students are very intrigued. After years of mistrust, people now are really interested in what the CIA actually does."

In September 2015, I attended a more traditional recruiting session. About fifty students and recent alumni from Harvard University's adult education extension school crowded into the reading room of its career services office to listen to pitches from three CIA employees: two women, and a man in a bow tie.

The trio emphasized that the CIA is education-friendly, offering student internships, tuition reimbursement for in-service courses, bonuses for mastery of "mission-critical" languages, and a chance to do academic-style research but with real-world impact. "I didn't want to work for a think tank," said one woman, a CIA analyst. "Here I know immediately, the president's reading it."

The other woman said she majored in aerospace engineering at MIT, and had been looking for industry jobs when the CIA invited her for an interview. "I thought it was a hoax; it turned out one of my professors had called them."

They showed a slide presentation of the CIA's organizational chart, starting with the clandestine Directorate of Operations: "the sexy side of the agency, the one movies are made about," as the analyst described it. Its job "is to recruit people to commit espionage against their own governments." Left unmentioned was that some of those people are foreign students and professors.

In the question-and-answer session, audience members expressed concern about the impact of a CIA career on social and family life. "You have to be comfortable not talking about your successes or your failures," said the analyst. "I go to a party with people who aren't CIA officers, I don't talk about work. I find I'm more interesting that way." Employees can tell their spouses that they're in the CIA, but not their children, because "children talk." Her husband is an FBI agent, and most of their friends work for the FBI or CIA. "They understand."

The other woman said she had planned to work at the CIA for a few years and then enter the corporate sector. Instead, "I got hooked," she said.

"Like heroin," the analyst replied.

Even rejects from such recruiting events may prove valuable to U.S. intelligence. While unsuitable for staff positions, they often have skills— such as fluency in foreign languages—conducive to spying overseas. "Eighty-five percent of those interested parties would never qualify for a position," a former federal law enforcement official told me. The CIA and FBI "then have this mailing list of names of people who sometimes are really, really talented and really, really crazy. They couldn't pass the screening but they could be very helpful. They could never be an employee but they could be an asset."

IN A SENSE, this overt presence may pave the way for, or legitimize, the covert U.S. operations in academia with which this book has been principally concerned. Because they're hidden, their effect is harder to judge, but they seem of little advantage to national security, and corrosive to academic culture.

There may be professorial James Bonds, or real-life Indiana Joneses, but I didn't find them. As far as I could tell, using professors as spies tends to backfire. Accustomed to their low-risk tenured positions, where about the worst thing that can happen is being snubbed at a cocktail party, they don't adjust well to the high-stakes world of espionage. Often they're reluctant, like Peng. Or they're modestly effective, like the professor whom the FBI fielded as a double agent against Russia. If they're caught spying by a foreign government or terrorist group, not only would they be in danger; so would their friends, collaborators, and sources. Other researchers might be denied visas, depriving the U.S. public and policy makers of possibly vital information and knowledge.

Generally, professors are more comfortable briefing U.S. intelligence when they return from their travels, or speaking at conferences run by CIA fronts. Such half-hidden complicity—the conference talks are usually listed on resumes, without reference to the CIA—is less perilous and more compatible with academic ethics than spying, but could still hamper academic research and credibility abroad.

Recognizing the ethical tangles, Theodore Postol drew a careful line, balancing his loyalties to his country, to science, and to his students. Postol, who retired in 2014 from the MIT faculty, aided U.S. intelligence but stopped short of spying.

I've been friendly with Ted for a quarter century, ever since I profiled him for the *Boston Globe Magazine* in 1992. Always good copy, the expert on missile defense had been especially newsworthy in the wake of the first Gulf War. After millions of American television viewers thrilled to watch U.S.-made Patriot missiles destroy Iraqi Scud missiles launched at Israel, Postol spoiled the celebration. He contended that virtually all of the Patriots had missed the Scuds; the appearance otherwise had been an optical illusion caused by the insufficient speed of television cameras. The Pentagon and Raytheon, the defense contractor that produces the Patriots, disputed his findings, but he was proven correct.

I knew Ted to be skeptical and scrappy, a classic whistle-blower. He fought with his neighbors, his university, and the national security establishment. For example, following the Patriot dispute, federal agents visited his office to complain that an article he had written for an academic journal about the missiles' failure contained classified information, even though he had based his analysis on public sources. Fed up with being hassled, he eventually chose not to renew his security clearance.

That is why I was somewhat surprised to learn, when we chatted for this book, that U.S. intelligence had been tapping his expertise behind the scenes for years. After 9/11, his brilliance mattered more to the intelligence community than his pugnacity, and an agent in the FBI's Boston office contacted him. As the FBI shifted priorities to meet the terrorist threat, the agent had switched from organized crime to counterterrorism, and universities were his beat. Postol met with him three or four times

a year for more than a decade. Sometimes the agent would call beforehand and ask to bring a friend, which meant that a CIA officer would
join them.

Postol educated them about weapons of mass destruction, and passed
along research that he and his students had conducted exposing flaws in
Russian satellite systems and U.S. missile defenses. When he returned
from Russia or China, he supplied his "general impressions." He hit it off
with the FBI agent, who became a regular guest speaker in Postol's MIT
course on the technology and politics of weapons of mass destruction.
The class included both international students and future U.S. military
officers in the Reserve Officers' Training Corps (ROTC). "His presentations were excellent, and very carefully designed to provide general information about the FBI's techniques for monitoring and reacting to potential
attacks on the public," Postol told me.

Still, Postol avoided sharing names and specifics, especially those of
his students, with the FBI and CIA. "I'm trying to be helpful to these
people, at the same time I'm not an agent for them," he says. "They've
occasionally asked me questions that got close to the boundary. I said, 'It's
not a good idea to talk about it.'" To make sure everything was aboveboard, he told the Russians and Chinese that he was talking generally to
the CIA, without revealing their "direct discussions."

SINCE NONCITIZENS AREN'T allowed to work for the CIA and FBI as staff
employees, public recruiting sessions generally exclude international
students and researchers. Secretly, though, U.S. intelligence pursues
them. Because they can blend into their native societies and have contacts there, they're potentially more helpful than even linguistically gifted
Americans. The downside is that they also wash out at a significant rate.

"There are a lot of people in schools in the U.S. who are potentially of
interest when they go home," a former CIA officer told me. "They get targeted whether they're nuclear scientists or come from a country where
we have problems with Islamic extremism. Getting them to agree in theory" to go home and help the CIA "isn't a great trick. You start paying
them; all college students need money. And even if I say it's all voluntary, somewhere in his mind he never thinks of any conversation with a
security service as voluntary. All of that works in your favor. 'Sure, I'll

talk to you, this is painless, I'm not risking anything, I feel I have a contact in the government.'

"Maybe he agrees, and then he never goes home. He falls in love and lands a job and never leaves the U.S. Or the day comes" when the CIA wants him "to go back on foreign soil. It's no longer fun and games. It's real. You have the issue: if he goes abroad, will he do anything?"

Cultivating foreign scientists at academic conferences may be more productive than on campus, though so many intelligence services circulate at such events that they may cancel each other out. It's possible that enrolling undercover CIA officers next to foreign businesspeople and officials in mid-career and executive education programs, as at Harvard's Kennedy School, reaps dividends in the form of useful intelligence sources abroad, but it also undermines the candor and trust vital to education.

Ishmael Jones, the pseudonymous former intelligence officer who wrote a scathing memoir about the CIA, suggested to me that the agency devotes too much time and manpower to U.S. universities. "I believe our national security agencies need to be focusing on foreign targets located in foreign countries," Jones emailed me in October 2014. "Instead, working with US colleges lets agencies do soft, low-risk, nonthreatening kinds of things that let everyone look busy but don't accomplish much. A case officer can take a leisurely drive over to the nearest college and chat with a professor or student and give Headquarters the sense that operations are being generated. It's much nicer than traveling through a sweaty foreign country to a meeting with an agent in a nasty hotel room at which a hostile security service can come bursting in at any moment."

The strongest justification for pervasive U.S. espionage in academia is that hostile countries are doing it, too. With the influx of Chinese and Iranian students, the proliferation of Confucius Institutes, and Russia's enthusiasm for academic espionage under an ex-KGB president, foreign spying on campus appears to be surging, in some cases jeopardizing U.S. national and economic security. Duke graduate student Ruopeng Liu funneled Pentagon-funded research to China; Cuba recruited its most effective agent, Ana Belén Montes, through a Johns Hopkins classmate; and Russia insinuated Andrey Bezrukov, Lydia Guryeva, and other "illegals" into prominent universities, though possibly to less advantage than it hoped. Glenn Duffie Shriver went from Michigan to Shanghai for a college study-abroad program and ended up taking seventy thousand dollars from Chinese intelligence to try to penetrate the U.S. government. We know about Montes, Bezrukov, and Shriver—and about cyberhacks by foreign intelligence into academic networks—only because U.S. investigators exposed them. It's likely that some foreign spies remain hidden in U.S. student bodies or faculties today.

Even foreign agents who don't imperil America's security may undermine the credibility of its universities. Fairly or not, the revelation that Carlos Alvarez was working for Cuban intelligence placed the Harvard workshop and other programs that he led under a cloud.

As American and foreign agents converge on campus, university administrators avert their gazes, making no complaints and taking no precautions. They don't want to appear unpatriotic, or alienate research funders, by pushing back against U.S. intelligence. Nary a peep is heard from university authorities when the FBI or CIA, without notifying them ahead of time, hassles international students and professors. South Florida softened Peng's punishment to accommodate the FBI's plans to make him a spy. Owing much of its cachet to its intimate relationship with the federal government, which hires its graduates and supplies it with A-list speakers and visiting fellows, Harvard's Kennedy School enrolled undercover CIA agents in a mid-career program, without informing either faculty members or other students about them.

If universities act as accomplices for U.S. intelligence, they're passive bystanders to foreign espionage. The values of diversity and internationalism, which invigorate U.S. higher education and attract so many foreign students, also make it vulnerable. Devoted to collaboration, Duke professor David Smith was late to recognize that a graduate student in his lab, Ruopeng Liu, was taking advantage of him and passing Pentagon-funded research to China. Even after Smith began to suspect him, Duke gave Liu a doctorate. UMass Boston paid no attention to the visiting scholars, affiliated with China's spy university, who snooped on one academic conference after another.

Universities don't bother to protect their research by requiring science graduate students to learn about intellectual property law, or by signing agreements with foreign collaborators that safeguard each side's ideas. They plunge ahead with study-abroad programs in China and Russia, and vie for Boren fellowships that have aroused suspicion in Russia and elsewhere by requiring recipients to spend a year after-ward in a national security position. Yet they rarely warn students at orientation sessions to watch out for foreign intelligence services. Few schools screened *Game of Pawns*, the FBI's overwrought wake-up call.

Their motives for ignoring foreign espionage aren't entirely altruistic. They'd rather not offend countries on which they've become depen-dent for tuition revenue, researchers, and branch campuses. They welcome Confucius Institutes—which are funded and staffed by a Chinese gov-ernment affiliate, sanitize China's history and policy, and may at times be tapped to collect intelligence—as a low-cost option for teaching Chi-nese language and culture. Eager for full-paying international students, Marietta College went even further, initiating a partnership with a uni-versity run by China's security ministry.

Like their institutions, individual professors may put global prestige ahead of intellectual property. John Reece Roth, an emeritus professor of electrical engineering at the University of Tennessee, was convicted in 2008 of using graduate students from China and Iran on U.S. Air Force research that was off-limits to foreigners, and taking a laptop with restricted files to China. Roth wasn't a Chinese spy. He was simply proud of his renown there. He found it hard to believe that a country where two uni-versities had named him an honorary professor, where his lectures drew large audiences, and where both volumes of his book *Industrial Plasma Engineering* were available in translation, could have any duplicitous intent. When I visited him in 2012 in federal prison in Ashland, Kentucky, he was devising a makeshift Mobius strip to catch red ants swarming across the floor of his cell and feasting on candy bar scraps. "I still have some inventing ability," he told me.

Academics ignore espionage at their peril. As long as American uni-versities conduct vital research, place alumni and faculty in the upper ech-elons of government and business, and—perhaps most important—remain a bastion of access and international culture in a fearful, locked-down world, they will attract attention from intelligence services. Ultimately, unless they become more vigilant, spy scandals could undermine their values, tarnish their reputations, and spur greater scrutiny of their gover-nance, admissions, and hiring.

Alternatively, universities could recognize these dangers and sum-mon the will to curb foreign and domestic espionage. They could adopt the 1977 Harvard prohibition on students and faculty spying or covertly recruiting for the CIA, extend it to intelligence services worldwide, and punish violators with dismissal, expulsion, or degree revocation. They could raise campus awareness of deceptive recruiting and research theft, and make it a priority to investigate complaints. They could declare themselves no-spy zones, where students and professors of all nationalities would devote themselves to learning without being shadowed by deceptive pitches and purloined research. Such a ban might be hard to enforce, but even if universities couldn't become completely spy-free sanctuaries, they could at least make intelligence services think twice before infiltrating them.

EACH YEAR SEES a swelling in the ranks of international students in the United States, and of American students going to college abroad. U.S. universities have eighty-two foreign campuses, more than twice as many as any other country. However, terrorism fears, tensions with China and Russia, and nativist sentiment could inhibit further growth. Over the objections of leading universities, the Obama administration proposed in 2016 to bar foreign students from corporate-funded defense research in fields such as munitions, nuclear engineering, and satellite technology. The wave of nativist fervor that propelled Donald Trump to the presidency could lead to more sweeping restrictions.

That would be a shame, because higher education is one of the few industries in which the United States still leads the world. International students not only fill academia's coffers but also provide cheap labor for its research. U.S. graduate programs couldn't survive without them. After earning doctorates in science and engineering, about two-thirds stay in the United States for at least five years, bringing new energy and ideas to American companies rather than competitors overseas. When China began sending students to the United States in 1978, Deng Xiaoping expected that 90 percent would come home. Instead, after the Tiananmen Square crackdown, most Chinese recipients of U.S. doctorates stayed put. From that perspective, China and other countries have little choice but to spy on American universities; they need to compensate for losing so much talent.

I observed the brain drain firsthand one morning in April 2016. Benefiting like a spy from academic openness, I slipped through an unlocked door into the lobby of a Duke science building, where candidates for master's degrees in electrical and computer engineering were displaying their final projects to examiners.

Almost all of the budding engineers were Chinese. Two floors above, in Professor David Smith's lab, Ruopeng Liu had appropriated his colleagues' ideas. But Liu had returned to China six years before, and these graduate students seemed guileless and effervescent, especially Wankun Zhu. The daughter of economics professors, she had created a website that recommends movies for people based on their opinions of films they had seen. "Users do not need to search for new movies themselves; we can provide recommendation of movies that is highly likely to cater to their taste," she said. She told me cheerfully that she used a mix of real and fake data, since her site wasn't yet getting feedback.

Zhu was looking forward to starting a job with Google in June. She chose to stay in the United States, she told me, because starting salaries in Silicon Valley are higher than in China, making housing more affordable. "Also the air quality and working environment in the U.S. is better."

Another exhibitor from China, Wen Bo, created a site to predict winners in World Cup matches, using variables such as FIFA world ranking, shots on target, possession rate, and having a superstar or not.

Zhu grew up in Yunnan Province, home of the Stone Forest, where Glenn Shriver wandered off the path. Bo planned to work for Cisco Systems Inc., curriculum provider to Thorildsplans Gymnasium in Stockholm, where Marta Rita Velázquez teaches. In the global village of academia, six degrees of separation is more than enough to find a spy.

NOTES

INTRODUCTION: THE FBI GOES TO COLLEGE

xi The reconstruction of the first meeting between Dajin Peng and Dianne Mercurio is primarily based on interviews with Peng and his neighbor, as well as "FBI and I," an account that Peng wrote for his lawyer in December 2009. While Mercurio declined to be interviewed for this book, her emails to Peng and to University of South Florida administrators provide valuable information about her role.

xii "pending investigation into allegations": Maria Crummett letter to Peng, April 7, 2009.

xiv Amy Carter: The description of the Amy Carter case is based on press accounts such as Matthew L. Wald, "Amy Carter Is Acquitted Over Protest," *New York Times,* April 16, 1987.

xv Rochester Institute of Technology: Daniel Golden, "In From the Cold: After Sept. 11, The CIA Becomes a Growing Force on Campus," *Wall Street Journal,* October 4, 2002.

xv the growing threat of foreign espionage: Daniel Golden, "American Universities Infected by Foreign Spies Detected by FBI," Bloomberg News, April 9, 2012.

xvi "voluminous": Email from Clara Williams, custodian of records, New Jersey Institute of Technology, April 28, 2015.

xvi eight FBI personnel: Letter from Attorney Gary Potters, representing New Jersey Institute of Technology, to U.S. District Court Judge Leda Dunne Wettre, December 17, 2015: "Over two separate days, approximately eight FBI personnel reviewed NJIT's contemplated production of documents."

xvii "not overly concerned": Gregory M. Milonovich, email message to UC Davis associate chancellor and chief of staff Karl Engelbach and Lori Hubbard, assistant to the associate chancellor, May 20, 2015.

xvii   increasingly means: The full Joint Chiefs of Staff definition of intelligence is "[i]nformation and knowledge about an adversary obtained through observation, investigation, analysis, or understanding." Other definitions are cited at: http://www.au.af.mil/au/awc/awcgate/cia/define_intel.htm.

xviii   "strengthen ties w. classmates": Complaint, FBI Agent Maria L. Ricci, *USA v. Richard Murphy, Cynthia Murphy, et al.*, U.S. District Court in Manhattan, June 25, 2010, p. 36.

xix   heading overseas: Data on Americans studying abroad and foreign students in the United States come from the Institute of International Education's "Open Doors" reports.

xix   more than 160: Data on American-style campuses abroad were provided by Kyle Long, a Columbia University doctoral student who is writing his dissertation on the subject.

xx   rose by 44 percent: Data on foreign-born and Chinese-born scientists and engineers working at U.S. colleges: National Science Foundation, National Center for Science and Engineering Statistics, Scientists and Engineers Statistical Data System, 2003 and 2013, special tabulations (2015), Lan and Hale.

xx   "ideal place": FBI White Paper, "Higher Education and National Security: The Targeting of Sensitive, Proprietary, and Classified Information on Campuses of Higher Education," April 2011.

xx   In a 2012 poll: The poll of staff who work with international students was taken during a NAFSA: Association of International Educators webinar, "When Federal Agents Come Calling: Educating Campus Stakeholders," March 22, 2012.

xx   "3 primary areas": Milonovich email message to members of the National Security Higher Education Advisory Board, May 19, 2014.

xx   a friend of his: The source for this anecdote is Muhammad Sahimi, a professor of petroleum engineering at the University of Southern California and an expert on Iranian nuclear and political development.

xxi   "a plethora of commercial aliases": Ishmael Jones (pseudonym of a former CIA officer), *The Human Factor: Inside the CIA's Dysfunctional Intelligence Culture* (New York: Encounter Books, 2008), pp. 51–52.

xxi   "posing as a pointy-headed college professor": Ishmael Jones, email message to author, October 11, 2014.

xxiii   "most energetic and incompetent": Jones, *The Human Factor*, p. 278.

xxiii   "nascent nuclear program": Ibid., p. 272.

xxiii   "a scientific conference specifically designed . . . nuclear program": Ibid., pp. 286–87.

xxiii   The professor who pretended to help Russian intelligence requested anonymity.

1: CLOAK OF INVISIBILITY

3   I am grateful to Michael Standaert, a freelance journalist based in Shenzhen, and his researcher, Su Dongxia, for their assistance with this chapter. Michael interviewed Ruopeng Liu, visited Kuang-Chi's facilities in Shenzhen, and gathered information on the anniversary party and on Shenzhen's Peacock Program, among other contributions.

3   Brandishing a light saber: A video of the anniversary party can be seen at
     http://mp.weixin.qq.com/s?__biz=MzA4MjIxMTExNQ==&mid=417787100
     &idx=1&sn=0733b433d9f6e289a419e52b24e13f31&scene=4#wechat_redirect
     and at http://mp.weixin.qq.com/s?__biz=MzA4MjIxMTExNQ==&mid=41793
     6634&idx=1&sn=43b2255cf6ed0253c1dc44dbc87469fa&scene=4#wechat
     _redirect.

4   "No matter how thrilling": Translation by Kean Zhang.

4   "Elon Musk of China": Wu Nan, "'Elon Musk of China' Aims to Give the World
     a Commercial Jetpack—But Is It Just Flight of Fancy?," *South China Morning
     Post*, April 7, 2015.

4   an astounding total: The patent data were displayed in a video presentation at
     Kuang-Chi's exhibit hall.

5   according to an agenda: NSHEAB Agenda, October 23–24, 2012, FBI head-
     quarters, attached to an August 31, 2012, email message from Brenda M. Fleet
     to NSHEAB members. Arizona State University provided the email and attach-
     ment to the author in response to a public records request.

5   shown to an invitation-only audience: The FBI video was shown at the National
     Intellectual Property Protection Summit; see https://summit.fbi.gov/agenda.html.

6   whom he surveyed: John Villasenor, "Intellectual Property Awareness at
     Universities: Why Ignorance Is Not Bliss," *Forbes*, November 27, 2012.

6   "the use of students": Defense Security Service, "2015 Targeting U.S. Tech-
     nologies: A Trend Analysis of Cleared Industry Reporting," p. 21, Figure 9.

6   forming the backbone: Data on doctorates earned by foreign students come
     from a 2015 Pew Research Center study: http://www.pewresearch.org/fact
     -tank/2015/06/18/growth-from-asia-drives-surge-in-u-s-foreign-students/.

6   "Foreign intelligence services": David Szady, "The Lipman Report," July 15, 2014.

7   American taxpayers fund: National Science Foundation, National Center for
     Science and Engineering Statistics, 2016. Federal Funds for Research and
     Development: Fiscal years 2014–2016. Detailed Statistical Tables. Arlington,
     VA. Available at https://ncsesdata.nsf.gov/fedfunds/2014/.

9   "a group that played blackjack": David Smith email message to the author,
     May 19, 2006.

9   After five years of litigation: The case was *Kelly v. First Astri Corporation*. For
     the California appellate decision, see http://caselaw.findlaw.com/ca-court-of
     -appeal/1224276.html.

9   "I was lucky enough": David Smith email message to the author, April 15, 2016.

9   "I said, 'By the way'": Pendry's recollection of the San Antonio meeting is in a
     2015 video, "Celebrating 15 Years of Metamaterials," available on YouTube.

9   "I and my group": David Smith email message to the author, April 14, 2016.

10   employed a stage magician and a filmmaker: Philip Ball, *Invisible: The Danger-
     ous Allure of the Unseen* (Chicago: University of Chicago Press, 2015), pp. 2–6
     and 247–53.

10   coauthored an article: J. B. Pendry, D. Schurig, and D. R. Smith, "Controlling
     Electromagnetic Fields," *Science*, June 23, 2006, pp. 1780–82.

10   unveiled the first successful cloak: D. Schurig, J. J. Mock, B. J. Justice, S. A.
     Cummer, J. B. Pendry, A. F. Starr, and D. R. Smith, "Metamaterial Electromag-
     netic Cloak at Microwave Frequencies," *Science Express*, October 19, 2006.

10 "can make light curve": David R. Smith and Nathan Landy, "Hiding in Plain Sight," *New York Times*, November 17, 2012.

10 "I would never have imagined": David Smith email message to the author, April 15, 2016.

11 "very difficult to evaluate": Ibid.

11 Liu began taking a train: http://blog.sciencenet.cn/blog-49489-278391.html.

11 "He conducted his research": Tie Jun Cui email message to the author, June 20, 2016.

12 "He was really more": David Smith email message to the author, April 14, 2016.

13 "had been extremely paranoid": David Smith email message to the author, April 25, 2016.

13 "The majority of collaborations": David Smith email message to the author, May 19, 2016.

14 "By the way, I have seen": Tie Jun Cui email message to the author, June 21, 2016.

14 "properly scientific": Tie Jun Cui email message to the author, June 20, 2016.

14 "supposed to find": Email message from the postdoctoral fellow to the author, April 25, 2016.

14 "With me believing": David Smith email message to the author, April 25, 2016.

14 "Being new to all": David Smith email message to the author, May 19, 2016.

15 "I'm not positive": David Smith email message to the author, February 11, 2017.

15 "He began trying to add constraints": David Smith email message to the author, April 14, 2016.

15 a program called Project 111: "China to Undergo Brain Gain Through Plan 111," http://www.china.org.cn/english/China/181075.htm.

16 Xi Xiaoxing: Matt Apuzzo, "U.S. Drops Charges That Professor Shared Technology with China," *New York Times*, September 11, 2015.

16 A study by Thomas Nolan: Nolan's study, "Trends in Trade Secret Prosecutions," was first presented at a meeting of the Chinese Biopharmaceutical Association in Qingdao, China, on July 3, 2012, and then at a meeting in New York of the National Association of Criminal Defense Lawyers, October 22, 2015. Updated data, including conviction rates, may be found at http://jeremy-wu.info/fed-cases/latest-statistics-on-fedcases/.

16 China accounts for: IP Commission Report, http://www.ipcommission.org/report/IP_Commission_Report_052213.pdf, pp. 2–3.

17 FBI report: Counterintelligence Strategic Partnership Intelligence Note, "Chinese Talent Programs." It describes the Zhao and Liu cases.

17 "soon welcomed": http://english.cas.cn/about_us/introduction/201501/t20150114_135284.shtml.

18 he hoped that 90 percent would return: Denis Fred Simon and Cong Cao, *China's Emerging Technological Edge: Assessing the Role of High-End Talent* (New York: Cambridge University Press, 2009), p. 219.

18 the U.S. government allowed them to stay: Ibid., p. 218.

18 Thousand Talents: The description of the Thousand Talents program and its perks is based on David Zweig and Huiyao Wang, "Can China Bring Back the Best? The Communist Party Organizes China's Search for Talent," working paper, Center on China's Transnational Relations, March 2012, pp. 18–20.

18 "the most assertive government": Ibid., p. 4.

18   In the 296: Yu Wei and Zhaojun Sen, "China: Building an Innovation Talent Program System and Facing Global Competition in a Knowledge Economy," *Brain Circulation*, 2012.

18   Of Chinese students who received: Table 3-29, Science and Engineering Indicators 2014, www.nsf.gov/statistics/seind14/index.cfm/char.

18   Hong Ding: Wang Zhuoqiong, "China Fishing in Pool of Global Talent," *China Daily*, April 16, 2009.

19   rejected a full-time offer: Yitang Zhang, telephone interview, November 2, 2015. Zhang said his arrangement was unique and not part of a talent program.

19   "migratory birds": Simon and Cao, *China's Emerging Technological Edge*, p. 245.

20   "I really had wanted him": David Smith email message to the author, May 22, 2016.

20   "This is the point": David Smith email message to the author, April 14, 2016.

21   "As time progressed": Ibid.

21   "A bunch of smart people": David Smith email message to the author, May 19, 2016.

22   Smith heralded the advance: Richard Merritt, "Next Generation Cloaking Device Demonstrated," *Duke Engineering News*, February 2009, http://den .pratt.duke.edu/february-2009/cloaking-device.

22   "It all just fell apart": Smith email message to the author, April 15, 2016.

23   "did make a positive scientific": John Pendry email message to the author, January 12, 2016.

23   "limited interactions": Ibid.

24   publishing its proceedings: Tie Jun Cui, David Smith, and Ruopeng Liu, *Metamaterials: Theory, Design, and Applications* (New York and London: Springer, 2010).

24   "There was no mention": David Smith email message to the author, April 14, 2016.

25   "representing someone else's work as your own": https://gradschool.duke.edu /academics/academic-policies-and-forms/standards-conduct/prohibited -behaviors.

25   "It would have been very difficult": David Smith email message to the author, April 18, 2016.

25   "going to get the best students": Lindsey Rupp, "Duke's Board Will Consider Groundbreaking Expansion into China," *Chronicle*, December 4, 2009.

29   Shenzhen's Peacock Program: Wu Guangqiang, "The Peacock Program's Great Success," *Shenzhen Daily*, May 16, 2016, http://www.szdaily.com/content/2016 -05/16/content_13358994.htm.

29   municipal records show: The Shenzhen Municipal Science and Technology Bureau provided the $13.7 million figure in response to a request under China's public records law.

29   interview on Phoenix Television: http://v.ifeng.com/news/society/201603 /010d8df7-eae2-414d-bacb-32b663f5ea1f.shtml.

29   In 2012, Liu was chosen: "President Liu Was Appointed Subject-Matter Expert of '863' Program," http://www.kuang-chi.com/en/index.php?ac=article&at =read&did=989.

29   Xi Jinping: www.kuang-chi.com/htmlen/details/139.html.

29   bought a controlling share: Sally Rose, "Hong Kong Investor to Lift Jetpack,"
     http://www.stuff.co.nz/business/65173346/hong-kong-investor-to-lift-jetpack.

30   Liu and two other Kuang-Chi scientists: The other applicants were Lin Luan
     and Chaofeng Kou. On April 14, 2015, examiner Patrick Holecek issued the
     "final rejection," available at http://portal.uspto.gov/pair/view/BrowsePdfServ
     let?objectId=I8HDVH8HPXXIFW4&lang=DINO. U.S. patent 9219314 was issued
     on December 22, 2015.

31   "has not demonstrated": David Smith email message to the author, April 14, 2016.

31   "The prospect of true invisibility": Ibid.

31   "Ruopeng was not really capable": Michael Schoenfeld email message to the
     author, forwarding responses from David Smith, February 5, 2016.

32   "certainly Ruopeng would": Ibid.

32   which raised $62 million: Michael J. de la Merced, "Kymeta Raises $62 Million
     in Investment Led by Bill Gates," *New York Times*, January 11, 2016.

32   "At all points": Michael Schoenfeld email message to the author, forwarding
     responses from David Smith, February 5, 2016.

32   "I now look for signs": David Smith email message to the author, April 14, 2016.

2: THE CHINESE ARE COMING

34   The phone rang at 3 a.m.: Former president Carter recounted the story of Frank
     Press's phone call in a 2013 speech at the U.S.-China Relations Forum in
     Atlanta: https://www.cartercenter.org/news/editorials_speeches/jc-what-us
     -china-can-do-together.html.

35   "I had no idea": The source for Atkinson's account is Richard C. Atkinson,
     "Recollections of Events Leading to the First Exchange of Students, Scholars
     and Scientists Between the United States and the People's Republic of China,"
     2006, http://rca.ucsd.edu/speeches/Recollections_China_student_exchange
     .pdf.

36   "Chinese intelligence flooded": Michael Sulick, *American Spies: Espionage
     Against the United States from the Cold War to the Present* (Washington, DC:
     Georgetown University Press, 2013), p. 159.

36   Accustomed to hosting visiting scholars: Daniel Golden, "American Universi-
     ties Infected by Foreign Spies Detected by FBI," Bloomberg News, April 8, 2012.

37   Wentong Cai: The account of Wentong Cai is taken from documents in his
     criminal case in U.S. District Court in New Mexico. The Bo Cai quotation
     comes from his plea agreement, filed July 23, 2014. The plea agreement also
     quotes Wentong's "we finally obtained support" email. The description of angu-
     lar rate sensors is based on Applied Technology Associates' website, www.aptec
     .com/ars-14_mhd_angular_rate_sensor.html.

37   "Me and my cousin Bo": This and Wentong's statement "I feel so unfortunate"
     are both in an April 23, 2015, letter to the court. He received his Iowa State
     "research excellence" award on August 10, 2013, and was married on August 20,
     2013.

38   A study conducted for this book: Data on Chinese defendants in espionage-
     related crimes who attended U.S. universities come from a study by Lili Sun,

with help from David Glovin. For her research, Sun relied on cases archived at cicentre.com, the online site of the Centre for Counterintelligence and Security Studies, as well as Bloomberg Law, FBI.gov, Justice.gov, and news reports. In some cases, defense attorneys provided their clients' educational backgrounds.

38   Ahmad Jabbari: The CIA's approach to Jabbari was reported by Frances FitzGerald in "The CIA Campus Tapes," *New Times*, January 23, 1976.

39   Of 400 Soviet exchange students: "Final Report of the Select Committee to Study Governmental Operations with Respect to Intelligence Activities," known as the Church Committee, 1976, p. 164.

39   "young radical high-fliers": Christopher Andrew and Vasili Mitrokhin, *The Sword and the Shield: The Mitrokhin Archive and the Secret History of the KGB* (New York: Basic Books, 1999), p. 57.

39   "By the early years": Ibid., p. 58.

40   "youngest major spy": Ibid., p. 129.

40   "It was important that there should be no monopoly": Widely quoted, for example, in http://spymuseum.com/major-events/spy-rings/the-atomic-spy-ring/.

40   "talent-spotters": Andrew and Mitrokhin, *The Sword and the Shield*, p. 217.

40   "The scientific contacts": Ibid., p. 107.

41   sought sensitive information: Data on spying by Soviet scientists come from "Soviet Acquisition of Militarily Significant Western Technology: An Update," September 1985, released by the CIA Historical Review Program in 1999.

41   "spotting and assessing": Ibid., p. 22.

41   KGB had placed Boris Yuzhin: Yale Richmond, *Cultural Exchange and the Cold War: Raising the Iron Curtain* (University Park: Pennsylvania State University Press, 2003), p. 36.

41   "largely taught a new generation": Christopher Lynch, *The CI Desk: FBI and CIA Counterintelligence as Seen from My Cubicle* (Indianapolis: Dog Ear, 2009), p. 41.

42   "How can one ride": I. C. Smith, email message to the author, July 20, 2015.

42   "They were invaluable": Ibid.

43   Wu-Tai Chin: Sources regarding Wu-Tai Chin include Smith, news coverage of his trial, and Sulick, *American Spies*, pp. 159–64. The "eclipse" quotation is from p. 164. For a fictionalized version of the Chin story, see Ha Jin, *A Map of Betrayal* (New York: Vintage International, 2015).

44   "I took the position then and now": I. C. Smith, email message to the author, February 23, 2015.

44   "I sat with the two": I. C. Smith, email message to the author, August 8, 2015.

44   "It was those golden youth": I. C. Smith, email message to the author, February 23, 2015.

45   "He knew that they had been lied to": Ibid.

45   "We would not ask": I. C. Smith, email message to the author, February 24, 2015.

45   "Some agents even brought in their families": I. C. Smith, email message to the author, August 8, 2015.

45   "It was well down the whole effort": Ibid.

46   "Taiwan, feeling betrayed": I. C. Smith, email message to the author, August 7, 2015.

46   "An immense tension existed": Jones, *The Human Factor*, pp. 53–54.

48   "My proposals": Smith, email message to the author, February 24, 2015.

48   "Academic Security Awareness Program": The proposal for the program was included among FBI communications that Texas A&M University provided in response to my public records request.

49   ranks third in national security funding: William M. Arkin and Alexa O'Brien, "The Most Militarized Universities in America," *VICE News*, November 5, 2015; Federal Science and Engineering Support to Universities, Colleges and Nonprofit Institutions, FY 2013.

3: SPY WITHOUT A COUNTRY

52   I am indebted to Paul O'Mahony, senior editor at *The Local* in Stockholm, for his reporting for this chapter, including visits to Thorildsplans Gymnasium and the Spånga neighborhood, and a phone interview with Morgan Malm.

52   It periodically sends students: See, for example, http://thorildsplansgymnasium .stockholm.se/te13d-och-te13e-aker-till-san-francisco.

53   an indictment was unsealed: "Unsealed Indictment Charges Former U.S. Federal Employee with Conspiracy to Commit Espionage for Cuba," U.S. Department of Justice press release, April 25, 2013.

53   "one of the most damaging spies": "Cuba's Global Network of Terrorism, Intelligence and Warfare," hearing before the House Committee on Foreign Affairs Subcommittee on the Western Hemisphere, statement submitted by Michelle Van Cleave, May 17, 2012.

54   "known to actively target": FBI Private Sector Advisory, "Cuban Intelligence Targeting of Academia," September 2, 2014.

55   Harvard, Yale, Columbia, New York University: All of the universities except Johns Hopkins are cited in Jose Cohen, "El Servicio de Inteligencia Castrista Y La Comunidad Academica Norteamericana," 2002, http://www6.miami.edu /iccas/Cohen.pdf. I added Johns Hopkins because of its proximity to Washington and because it was the nexus for Myers, Velázquez, and Montes. Orlando Brito Pestana—like Cohen, a defector from Cuban intelligence—identifies its leading academic targets as Princeton, Harvard, Yale, Columbia, Stanford, Duke, Georgetown, and George Mason. Pestana, "La Penetracion Del Servicio De Inteligencia De Cuba En El Sector Academico De Estados Unidos," *Cuba in Transition*, Vol. 25, *Papers and Proceedings of the Twenty-Fifth Annual Meeting*, 2015.

55   "and even invitations to visit Cuba": FBI advisory, "Cuban Intelligence Targeting of Academia."

56   Almost every lawyer: The description of Don Miguel's life and family comes from interviews with faculty colleagues and family friends as well as his obituary: Daniel Rivera Vargas, "Fallece ex juez Miguel Velazquez Rivera," *El Nuevo Dia*, December 14, 2006.

57   "to read, learn, work hard": http://www.chkd.org/Our-Doctors/Our-Pediatricians /PDC-Pediatrics/Nivea-Velazquez,-MD/.

57   a distinct minority: https://en.wikipedia.org/wiki/Puerto_Rico_political_status
      _plebiscites.

58   an independent confederation: Phone interview with Arturo Lopez-Levy,
      June 29, 2016.

58   "two wings of the same bird": The poem is by Lola Rodriguez de Tio (1843–
      1924).

58   "Cuba was working very hard": Luis Dominguez forwarded my list of questions
      to Pestana and sent me the responses in a March 3, 2016, email message.
      Dominguez then translated the responses into English over the phone.

59   "Princeton, divest": Phone interview with Nilsa Santiago.

59   "commit itself completely": Daily Princetonian, April 14, 1978, p. 3.

59   She organized a Latino Festival: "Latino Festival Schedule of Events," Daily
      Princetonian, March 29, 1977, p. 6.

59   a Third World Cultural Festival: Daily Princetonian, December 13, 1976,
      p. 3.

59   "the descendant of an African woman": Marta Rita Velázquez, "Race Rela-
      tions in Cuba: Past and New Developments," senior thesis, May 2, 1979, p. 80.
      Made available courtesy of Seeley G. Mudd Manuscript Library, Princeton
      University.

60   "continued this oppression": Ibid., p. 70.

60   "the defender of a powerful racist class": Ibid., p. 74.

60   "The government has instituted": Ibid., pp. 78–79.

60   "a brief period of field research": Ibid., p. 4.

61   an impressive roster: https://en.wikipedia.org/wiki/Paul_H._Nitze_School_of
      _Advanced_International_Studies#Notable_alumni.

61   "voiced that opinion freely": Scott W. Carmichael, True Believer: Inside the
      Investigation and Capture of Ana Montes, Cuba's Master Spy (Annapolis, MD:
      Naval Institute Press, 2007), p. 51.

62   edited a journal on immigration law: Curriculum vitae, Marta Rita Velázquez,
      provided by Stockholm school district. Translated by Paul O'Mahony.

62   a legal intern: Grand jury indictment, Marta Rita Velázquez, U.S. District
      Court for the District of Columbia, February 5, 2004, p. 2.

62   taught a course at SAIS on Cuban history: SAIS communications director
      Lindsey Waldrop, email message to the author, February 10, 2016.

62   "gained her first real insight": Office of the Inspector General of the Depart-
      ment of Defense, "Review of the Actions Taken to Deter, Detect and Investigate
      the Espionage Activities of Ana Belen Montes," June 16, 2005, p. 17, http://www
      .dodig.mil/pubs/documents/05-INTEL-18.pdf.

63   "U.S. Relations with Latin America": Waldrop email to the author, February 10,
      2016.

63   Kendall Myers taught: My account of Kendall and Gwendolyn Myers is based
      on documents in their U.S. District Court case, including their June 4, 2009,
      indictment and an affidavit by FBI Special Agent Brett Kramarsic. It is also
      taken from media accounts, including Toby Harnden, "Spying for Fidel: The
      Inside Story of Kendall and Gwen Myers," Washingtonian, October 5, 2009,
      and Carol Rosenberg and Lesley Clark, "The Curious Case of Alleged Cuban Spy
      Kendall Myers," Miami Herald, June 14, 2009.

63   "Everything one hears about Fidel": Kramarsic affidavit, p. 9.

64   "looking for someone to translate": Inspector general's report, "Review of the Actions Taken," p. 9.

64   "expressed wish": Velázquez indictment, p. 10.

64   "It has been a great satisfaction": Ibid.

65   "unhesitatingly agreed": Inspector general's report, p. 9.

65   the technique required tensing: Jim Popkin, "Ana Montes Did Much Harm Spying for Cuba. Chances Are, You Haven't Heard of Her," *Washington Post Magazine*, April 18, 2013.

65   Montes applied to the Office of Naval Intelligence: Carmichael, *True Believer*, p. 55.

65   withheld her master's degree . . . until 1989: Dennis O'Shea, Johns Hopkins executive director for media relations, email message to the author, giving the date as 1989, February 2, 2016. "American Spies," by Sulick, gives the date as 1988, p. 269.

66   "By day, she was a buttoned-down GS-14": Popkin, "Ana Montes Did Much Harm Spying for Cuba."

66   "She successfully opposed": Phone interview with Chris Simmons, December 5, 2015.

67   controversial Defense Department assessment: "The Cuban Threat to National Security," Defense Intelligence Agency, November 18, 1997, https://fas.org/irp /dia/product/980507-dia-cubarpt.htm. On Montes's role, and criticism of the assessment: interview with Daniel Fisk.

67   exceptional intelligence analyst: Carmichael, *True Believer*, p. 56.

68   Pinned to the wall: Ibid., p. 145.

68   As she ate lunch alone: Popkin, "Ana Montes Did Much Harm Spying for Cuba."

68   "Montes compromised all": Van Cleave testimony before the House Committee on Foreign Affairs Subcommittee on the Western Hemisphere, May 17, 2012.

68   "What makes Ana Montes so extraordinary": Carmichael, *True Believer*, pp. 138–40.

69   Born in Cuba, Alvarez: This summary of Alvarez's background and career is based on filings in his case in U.S. District Court in Miami, 05-20943, including his curriculum vitae and his "Memorandum in Aid of Sentencing and Request for Downward Departure."

69   about seventeen thousand Cuban-American students: Jorge Duany email message to the author, December 16, 2015.

69   a Cuban psychologist: "Memorandum in Aid of Sentencing," p. 6, and FBI interrogation of Alvarez, which identifies her as Mercedes Arce: http://www .latinamericanstudies.org/espionage/Alvarez-spy-1.pdf.

70   In an ironic twist: Juan O. Tamayo, "Aide to Cuba's Ricardo Alarcon Sentenced to 30 Years for Spying," *Cuba Confidential*, February 8, 2014, https:// cubaconfidential.wordpress.com/2014/02/09/aide-to-cubas-ricardo-alarcon -sentenced-to-30-years-for-spying/.

70   "personal meetings, messages": "United States' Sentencing Memorandum and Response to Carlos Alvarez's Request for Downward Departure," February 26, 2007, p. 2.

70   "sensitive information": Ibid., p. 3.

70   "heavy dosage of idealism": Letter from Carlos Alvarez to American Psycho-
      logical Association ethics committee, provided by Herbert Kelman.

70   "mid-eighties": Ibid.

71   "Since you helped": "Appendix B: Representations Made to Carlos Alvarez
      During His Interrogations," court filing, February 21, 2007.

71   lobbied Cuban authorities in Havana: Letter from Herbert Kelman to Judge K.
      Michael Moore, February 6, 2007.

72   took no disciplinary action: Letter from Patricia Dixon, APA Office of Ethics,
      to Alvarez, July 8, 2010.

73   She briefed Chamorro: Interview with Daniel Fisk.

73   more than $700 million: Velázquez curriculum vitae.

74   "forces of freedom": "Prime Minister Palme's Visit to Cuba," State Department
      cable, July 5, 1975, https://wikileaks.org/plusd/cables/1975STOCKH03203_b.html.

74   married in March 1996: Nancy Vega Ramos, Puerto Rico director of vital sta-
      tistics, email message to the author, August 3, 2016.

75   "It has always been a characteristic": Nigel West, email message to the author,
      February 19, 2015.

76   had studied at Harbin Institute: See Semenko's LinkedIn page, https://www
      .linkedin.com/in/mikhailsemenko.

76   earned a bachelor's degree: Lydia Guryeva's degrees: Nicole Bode, "Suspected
      Russian Spy Earned Degrees at Columbia, NYU," https://www.dnainfo.com
      /new-york/20100630/manhattan/suspected-russian-spy-earned-degrees-at
      -columbia-nyu.

76   "strengthen . . . ties": Ricci, Complaint, p. 36.

76   "clean": Ibid., p. 36.

76   "v. usefull": Ibid., p. 34.

76   She also cultivated: Jason Horowitz, "Clinton Confidant Believes He Might
      Have Been Spies' Target," Washington Post, June 29, 2010.

76   "You were sent to USA": FBI Agent Maria L. Ricci, Complaint, USA v. Richard
      Murphy, Cynthia Murphy et al., June 25, 2010, p. 5.

77   He criticized U.S. foreign policy so vehemently: James Barron, "Curiosities
      Emerge About Suspected Russian Agents," New York Times, June 29, 2010.

77   pretended it was a wrong number: Stepan Kravchenko, a Moscow-based
      reporter for Bloomberg News, contacted Guryeva for me.

77   "a positive response . . . will come of it": FBI Agent Gregory Monaghan, Com-
      plaint, USA v. Buryakov, Sporyshev, and Pobodnyy, U.S. District Court in New
      York, January 23, 2015. The complaint doesn't name the university, but Time
      magazine identified it as NYU: Massimo Calabresi, "Sloppy Russian 'Spymasters'
      Burn a Deep Cover Operative in New York," Time, January 26, 2015, http://time
      .com/3683373/russian-spy-arrest-new-york/.

77   Montes expected to spend: Carmichael, True Believer, pp. 68–82.

77   also implicated Montes: "Review of the Actions Taken," p. 63.

78   "raised the evidence threshold": Chris Simmons email message to the author,
      May 30, 2016.

78   an unrepentant statement: http://www.latinamericanstudies.org/espionage
      /montes-statement.htm.

78 only met their Cuban handlers: Harnden, "Spying for Fidel."

79 "I have great admiration": Kramarsic affidavit, p. 20.

79 "deserve every honor in this world": Harnden, "Spying for Fidel."

79 "Our overriding objective": Sulick, *American Spies*, p. 280.

79 Sweden bans extradition: http://www.government.se/government-of-sweden/ministry-of-justice/international-judicial-co-operation/extradition-for-criminal-offences/.

80 Velázquez became a Swedish citizen: Government's Motion to Modify Sealing Order, October 5, 2011, p. 2.

80 "undoubtedly aware": Ibid.

80 where he attended: https://www.iaea.org/About/Policy/GC/GC48/GC48Inf Documents/English/gc48inf-16-rev1_en.pdf.

80 and Lisbon: http://www.docsrush.net/2820487/north-south-centre-of-the-council-of-europe.html.

80 the extradition treaties that Austria and Portugal have: http://www.mcnabbas sociates.com/Austria%20International%20Extradition%20Treaty%20 with%20the%20United%20States.pdf; http://www.mcnabbassociates.com/Portugal%20International%20Extradi tion%20Treaty%20with%20the%20United%20States.pdf.

80 She taught English: Velázquez's teaching positions in Vienna and Portugal are listed in her curriculum vitae.

81 Jorge Velázquez: https://www.linkedin.com/in/jorge-velazquez-83434946.

81 the Obama administration was considering trading Montes: J. P. Carroll, "Tupac's Cop-Killer Aunt Chilling in Cuba May Finally Face Justice In U.S.," *Daily Caller*, June 6, 2016, http://dailycaller.com/2016/06/06/tupacs-cop-killer -aunt-chilling-in-cuba-may-finally-face-justice-in-u-s/.

81 California congressman . . . denounced: Devin Nunes, "This Traitor Belongs in Jail, Not Free in Cuba," *Wall Street Journal*, July 14, 2016.

82 A 2013 study by a consultant: Carmelo Mesa-Lago, "The Potential Role of FIU in a Future Cuba," July 17, 2013.

82 administered the Test of English: Lindsay Gellman, "For First Time, International University Admissions Tests Coming to Cuba," *Wall Street Journal*, June 17, 2015.

82 where 17 percent: http://www.scb.se/en_/finding-statistics/statistics-by-subject -area/population/population-composition/population-statistics/aktuell-pong /25795/yearly-statistics—the-whole-country/26040/.

83 They bought it in 2013: *Mitt I Västerort* (newspaper), September 10, 2013, http:// arkiv.mitti.se:4711/2013/37/vasterort/MIVT-20130910-A-029-A.pdf.

84 earning about four thousand dollars a month: Robert Waardahl, email message to the author, June 15, 2016.

84 who graduated from another Stockholm high school: Ingmar Kviele graduated from Kungsholmen Gymnasium. Perhaps aspiring to follow his father into diplomacy, he attended the international section, where classes were taught in English.

84 has signed petitions: http://onedayseyoum.com/en.jointhefight.php. http://namninsamling.se/index.php?nid=9102&fnvisa=namn.

84 that has assailed the Castro regime: https://www.amnesty.org/en/countries /americas/cuba/.

4: FOREIGN EXCHANGE

85   gathered to dedicate: The tree dedication ceremony and the session on "The Future of U.S.-Russia-China Relations" were both part of the McDonough Leadership Conference, which I attended at Marietta on April 1–2, 2016.

86   "elite institute for preparing": Political Minister-Counselor Jonathan Aloisi, communication from U.S. Embassy in Beijing to Secretary of State, Washington, D.C., November 2002.

87   they can fulfill its general education requirements: Marietta spokesman Tom Perry email message to the author, May 9, 2016.

87   hosts twenty to twenty-five: Interview with Mark Schaefer.

88   pay board but no tuition: Interview with Yolanda Feng, UIR exchange student.

88   stay for free: Tom Perry email message to the author, July 11, 2016.

88   sponsored joint conferences: For instance, the Marietta-UIR Summer Palace Forum in Beijing in June 2013 and June 2015. http://news2.marietta.edu/node /10109.

88   a 2013 book: Luding Tong and Helen Xu, *Emotional Appeals and Advertising Strategies in Modern China* (Beijing: University of International Relations Publishing House, 2013).

88   Marietta's choir performed: Tom Perry email message to the author, May 6, 2016.

89   replete with greenery: I am indebted to Michael Standaert for the visual description of UIR.

89   specializes in teaching: The description of UIR's specialties and research institutes is based on its website, en.uir.cn.

89   "key national universities": http://en.uir.cn/uniqueness.html.

89   On a subcampus: www.prcstudy.com/uni_university_of_international_relations .shtml.

90   placed under the security ministry in 1965: Gerald Chan, *International Studies in China: An Annotated Bibliography* (Commack, NY: Nova Science, 1998), p. 17.

91   "Training for most MSS intelligence officers begins": Stratfor, May 24, 2010, https://www.stratfor.com/analysis/special-series-espionage-chinese -characteristics.

91   "qualified students with a lack of foreign contacts": Ibid.

92   Fei-ling Wang: "China Releases Detained U.S. Professor," Associated Press, August 10, 2004, http://www.nbcnews.com/id/5665726/ns/world_news/t/china -releases-detained-us-professor/.

92   "pays most": David Shambaugh, "China's International Relations Think Tanks: Evolving Structure and Process," *China Quarterly*, no. 171 (September 2002).

93   A 2011 CIA report: Open Source Center, "Profile of MSS-Affiliated PRC Foreign Policy Think Tank CICIR," August 25, 2011.

93   joint doctoral program: en.uir.cn/international_politics.html.

93   Of 636 bachelor's degree recipients: http://www.uir.cn/data/upload/ufq8 yrnYz7XRp9S6MjAxNMTqsc8=_R3DtKb.pdf. Translated from Chinese by Kean Zhang.

93   A LinkedIn site for UIR alumni: https://www.linkedin.com/edu/alumni ?companyCount=3&id=11401&functionCount=3&unadopted=false&trk =edu-cp-com-CC-titl.

94   Xie Tingting: Her LinkedIn site lists her master's at UIR, and her positions at Emory and the Charhar Institute: https://www.linkedin.com/in/tingting-xie -2a37a640.

94   "focuses specifically": David Shambaugh, "China's Soft-Power Push: The Search for Respect," *Foreign Affairs*, July/August 2015.

94   is a senior fellow: http://charhar.china.org.cn/2015-09/28/content_36700161 .htm.

94   At his urging: Phone interview with Yawei Liu, October 27, 2016.

94   to observe the January 2011 referendum: Tingting is listed in "Observing the 2011 Referendum on the Self-Determination of Southern Sudan," Carter Center Final Report, p. 55.

95   diplomatic conundrum: For China's relationship to Sudan, see Larry Hanauer and Lyle J. Morris, "Chinese Engagement in Africa: Drivers, Reactions, and Implications for U.S. Policy," 2014 RAND Report.

95   "a sensitive nature": Phone interview with David Carroll, April 4, 2016.

96   "core values": http://w3.marietta.edu/About/mission.html.

96   endowment: For Marietta's and Denison's endowments, see National Association of College and University Business Officers 2015 endowment study, http:// www.nacubo.org/Documents/EndowmentFiles/2015_NCSE_Endowment _Market_Values.pdf.

96   Middle Eastern contingent: "Fall Enrollments for Full-Time Undergraduate International Students," table provided by Perry, email message, February 19, 2016.

96   fifty thousand dollars up front: Interviews with Jeremy Wang, Robert Pastoor, and Ron Patterson.

96   Marietta first gained a toehold in 1985: Sherry Beck Paprocki, "The Changing Face of Marietta College," *Marietta*, Autumn 2006.

97   a tenure-track position: Phone interview with Michael Taylor.

97   an early member: The description of Yi Lirong's career and imprisonment is based on Chinese-language articles posted on Xiaoxiong Yi's website, such as https://xiaoxiongyi.wordpress.com/category/my-father/. I am indebted to Kean Zhang for translating them.

97   moved to a housing complex: The account of Xiaoxiong Yi's childhood, exile, and education is based on a State Department cable, "Portrait of Vice President Xi Jinping: 'Ambitious Survivor' of the Cultural Revolution," November 16, 2009, which was made public by WikiLeaks in 2011. Internal evidence identifies Xiaoxiong Yi as the unnamed professor cited in the cable. The "groomed to become" and "descended into the pursuit" quotations both come from the cable.

99   He He Li, who attended Marietta: Perry email message to the author, May 2, 2016.

99   four-page cable: Aloisi, communication from U.S. embassy to State Department, November 2002.

100   Yi overruled her: Rees-Miller email message to the author, May 4, 2016.

103   "It was a lot of talking": Paprocki, "The Changing Face of Marietta College."

103   UIR opened its own summer program: The description of the summer program is based on two UIR documents obtained from the University of Massa-

chusetts Boston under a public records request: "2014 UIR Summer School Visiting Professor Agreement" and "Explanations on UIR 2014 Summer School Courses."

104   Deborah McNutt: http://xiajixueqi.uir.cn/view.php?cid=24&tid=106. She declined to comment.

104   had his heart set: Phone interview with Xing Li, April 7, 2016. His honorary professorship at UIR is listed on his curriculum vitae: http://pds.aau.dk/pds /file/2892185.

105   the UIR-Aalborg initiative: http://www.en.aau.dk/education/master/develop ment-international-relations/specialisations/china-international-relations. The academic journal is called the *Journal of China and International Relations.*

105   one of its biggest export markets: http://www.worldsrichestcountries.com/top _denmark_exports.html.

105   "As long as the joint program": Li Xing email message to the author, April 8, 2016.

106   two visiting scholars: UMass Boston supplied me with the resumes of Rihan Huang and Wang Hui. Shorter bios are available at http://archive.constant-contact.com/fs154/1102184412683/archive/1115578661485.html.

107   agreed to promote: UMass Boston also provided a copy of its memo of under-standing with UIR.

107   "China should seize": Xie Tingting, Huang Rihan, "The European Refugee Crisis from the Perspective of International Migration Governance," https:// journals.aau.dk/index.php/jcir/article/view/1310/1065.

108   Marietta's Beijing office: I am indebted to Jessica Meyers, an American journal-ist in Beijing, who visited the Marietta office there for this book.

108   no aberration: The decline in Chinese enrollment at Marietta comes from the "Fall Enrollments" table, and in overall enrollment from a Perry email message to the author, February 18, 2016. The overall numbers are based on full-time-equivalent day students.

109   "Portrait of Vice President Xi Jinping": Available at https://wikileaks.org/plusd /cables/09BEIJING3128_a.html.

109   a posting on Chinese social media: http://junqing.club.sohu.com/shilin/thread /vpcl68bqpc. Translated for the author by Kean Zhang.

109   extended their partnership: "Marietta Signs Cooperative Agreement with International University," *Olio,* http://news2.marietta.edu/node/1417.

5: SHANGHAIED

112   donated two hundred dollars: Posting on www.gvsu.edu/gvnow/2001/giving -spirit-2904.00000.htm#sthash.xsp0Da2x.dput, December 20, 2001.

112   He trash-talked Chinese opponents: Phone interview with Michael Weits.

112   laughed at him: Phone interview with Geling Shang.

112   He clambered all over the rocks: Phone interview with Peimin Ni.

113   "dynamic global network": See, for example, http://steinhardt.nyu.edu/faculty _positions/art/visual_arts_AP_tenure_track.

113   study-abroad centers: http://www.nyu.edu/global/global-academic-centers .html.

113   By requiring its Shanghai students: http://shanghai.nyu.edu/academics/study
       -away/out.

113   branches in Qatar: https://www.washingtonpost.com/local/education/in-qatars
       -education-city-us-colleges-are-building-an-academic-oasis/2015/12/06
       /6b538702-8e01-11e5-ae1f-af46b7df8483_story.html.

113   Carnegie Mellon also offers degrees: http://www.cmu.edu/global/presence/.
       A complete list of branch campuses abroad, including the Booth School's and
       Duke's, is located at http://www.globalhighered.org/?page_id=34.

114   "convening space": http://centerbeijing.yale.edu/event/2014/10/opening-ceremony
       -yale-center-beijing.

114   more than tripled: "IIE Releases Open Doors 2015 Data," http://www.iie.org
       /Who-We-Are/News-and-Events/Press-Center/Press-Releases/2015/2015-11
       -16-Open-Doors-Data.

114   Goucher College: http://www.goucher.edu/study-abroad.

114   fifth most popular destination: http://www.iie.org/Research-and-Publications
       /Open-Doors/Data/US-Study-Abroad/Leading-Destination.

114   five-year goal: http://uschinastrong.org/initiatives/100k-strong/.

114   study-abroad office: www.alliance-exchange.org/policy-monitor/04/07/2015
       /state-department-announces-launch-study-abroad-branch.

114   an Institute of International Education initiative: www.iie.org/Who-We-Are
       /News-and-Events/Press-Center/Press-Releases/2015/2015-10-01-IIE
       -Announces-Impact-Of-Generation-Study-Abroad#.V4Yv1PkrLIU.

114   In both Abu Dhabi and Qatar: Vivian Salama, "Abu Dhabi Bankrolls Students
       as NYU Joins Sorbonne," Bloomberg News, September 15, 2010, http://www
       .bloomberg.com/news/articles/2010-09-14/abu-dhabi-bankrolls-students-as
       -nyu-joins-sorbonne-in-uber-swanky-gulf.

115   Michigan State University president: Daniel Golden, "American Universities
       Infected by Foreign Spies Detected by FBI," Bloomberg News, April 8, 2012,
       http://www.bloomberg.com/news/articles/2012-04-08/american-universities
       -infected-by-foreign-spies-detected-by-fbi.

116   Oriental Daily News: The publication's name was translated from the Chinese
       by Leon Slawecki. The article was published on November 19, 1984.

117   "When service desks were moved": Leon Slawecki, "Starting Up: The Johns
       Hopkins Center in Nanjing, China," paper presented at ASPAC '89, Honolulu,
       Hawaii, June 30, 1989, p. 12.

117   Larry Engelmann: Larry Engelmann and Meihong Xu told their story in
       Daughter of China: A True Story of Love and Betrayal (New York: Wiley, 1999).
       The book contains some errors—for example, it identifies Slawecki as "Sloane"—
       but Gaulton confirmed the key events.

118   Six foot two: Much of the account of Glenn Shriver's parents is based on records
       provided by Kent County, Michigan, circuit court. That includes Jon Michael
       Shriver's physical description, his employers, and the details of his separation
       and divorce from Karen Sue Shriver and his nonpayment of child support. I
       found his first marriage and divorce on ancestry.com.

119   ten years in prison for dealing heroin: Lisa E. Kinney, director of communica-
       tions, Virginia Department of Communications, email message to the author,
       February 3, 2016.

119   became lifelong friends with his teacher: In a letter to the judge in Glenn Duffie Shriver's case, Michael Neal wrote, "Glenn's father Jon and I have remained friends since he was a student in my college English courses in the late 1970's." Jon was in prison at the time.

119   Glenn visited his father and half brother during summers: David Wise, "Mole-in-Training: How China Tried to Infiltrate the CIA," *Washingtonian*, June 7, 2012.

119   He traveled to Barcelona: Ibid.

119   "I knew early on": Sentencing hearing, U.S. District Court, Alexandria, Virginia, January 21, 2011.

120   His mother married Luis Chavez: Marriage license, Kent County, Michigan, March 11, 1997; Judgment of Divorce, Ottawa County, Michigan, September 22, 2003.

120   Grand Valley had 18,579 students in 2000: https://www.gvsu.edu/ia/history-of -enrollment-degrees-awarded-7.htm.

120   Amway cofounder: Shandra Martinez, "Billionaire Rich DeVos Is GVSU's Largest Donor at $36M," http://www.mlive.com/business/west-michigan/index.ssf /2016/01/how_billionaire_rich_devos_acc.html, January 4, 2016.

120   2.5 grade point average: Phone interview with Rebecca Hambleton, Grand Valley director of study abroad; https://www.gvsu.edu/studyabroad/partnershipnon -gvsu-academic-policies-667.htm.

121   Boren Awards: David Boren described the origins of the awards in a speech, "Global Education in the 21st Century: A National Imperative," October 12, 2010. A video of his address is at http://www.borenawards.org /multimedia.

121   the program provides: http://www.iie.org/programs/Boren-Awards-for-Inter national-Study.

121   with priority given: Jessica S. Wolfanger, Sara M. Russell, and Zachary T. Miller, "Boren Scholarship and Fellowship Survey," October 2014, https://www .cna.org/CNA_files/PDF/DRM-2014-U-007929-Final.pdf.

122   "The most important thing": "David Boren: Breaking the Language Barrier," video at http://www.borenawards.org/multimedia.

122   "linking university-based research": Letter to Senator Boren in February 1992, quoted in David J. Comp, "The National Security Education Program and Its Service Requirement: An Exploratory Study of What Areas of Government and for What Duration National Security Education Program Recipients Have Worked" (PhD diss., Loyola University, 2013).

122   University of California, Berkeley, deferred participation: Ibid.

123   increasingly prestigious and selective: For scholarships, https://www.borenawards .org/document/download/boren_scholarship_summary_stats_41.pdf; for fellowships, https://www.borenawards.org/document/download/boren_fellowship _summary_stats_42.pdf.

123   American University in Washington, D.C., led the nation: http://www.american .edu/careercenter/news/CC_2014_Awards_Roundup.cfm.

123   7.5 percent work for the CIA: Wolfanger, Russell, and Miller, "Boren Scholarship and Fellowship Survey," p. 35.

123   "life-changing experience": Ibid., p. 85.

124   "a recent incident": Letter from Dean Chappell of the FBI's Strategic Partner-
      ship Unit to NSHEAB members.

124   under the Boren rules: "Boren Fellowship Handbook," 2015, p. 17, https://www
      .borenawards.org/document/download/current_year_fellowship_handbook
      _182.pdf.

125   he answered an ad: My account of Glenn Shriver's recruitment by Chinese
      intelligence primarily draws on the following sources: the "statement of
      facts" in *U.S.A. v. Glenn Duffie Shriver* in federal court in Alexandria, Virginia;
      Wise, "Mole-in-Training"; a November 21, 2016, email from retired CIA
      counterintelligence officer Philip Boycan; interviews with other people famil-
      iar with the events, who requested anonymity; and *Game of Pawns: The Glenn
      Duffie Shriver Story*, the FBI movie about his case, available at https://www
      .youtube.com/watch?v=R8xlUNK4JHQ.

125   "Shriver was able to present": Email message from Philip Boycan to the author,
      November 21, 2016. All subsequent quotations from Boycan are from the same
      email.

126   "we can be close friends": Statement of facts.

126   "some secrets or classified information": Ibid.

126   tattoo supply: Wise, "Mole-in-Training."

126   Du Fei: Ibid.

130   "compelling true story": Email invitation January 10, 2013, from Brenda M.
      Fleet to "counterintelligence strategic partner" for the January 30, 2013, *Game
      of Pawns* premiere at U.S. Navy Memorial and Naval Heritage Center. Also,
      http://wfocitizensacademy.org/film-screening-game-of-pawns/.

131   "Are we doing anything": The April 28, 2014, email correspondence between
      Sullins and Maurer was provided by the University of South Florida in response
      to a public records request.

132   Alexander van Schaick: Jean-Friedman-Rudovsky and Brian Ross, "Exclu-
      sive: Peace Corps, Fulbright Scholar Asked to 'Spy' on Cubans, Venezue-
      lans," ABC News, February 8, 2008, http://abcnews.go.com/Blotter/story
      ?id=4262036.

134   "Glenn and I are doing really well": Email message from Karen Chavez to Allen
      Dale, September 15, 2015.

134   "How much does it pay?": Email message from Karen Chavez to Allen Dale,
      September 17, 2015.

6: AN IMPERFECT SPY

137   *St. Petersburg Times:* Kim Wilmath, "USF Professor Is Impugned, but Employed,"
      St. Petersburg Times, June 4, 2011; "Tenure Shouldn't Shield Unethical Acts at
      USF," editorial, *St. Petersburg Times*, June 9, 2011. The newspaper is now known
      as the *Tampa Bay Times*.

138   "I am not allowed to use my office": Dajin Peng, email message to the author,
      July 22, 2014. He probably meant "tapped" instead of "taped."

139   Wuhan: The description of Wuhan comes from "Wow! Wuhan's back," *China
      Daily*, September 7, 2012, http://usa.chinadaily.com.cn/weekly/2012-09/07
      /content_15741178.htm.

145 regularly ranks among the top fifteen universities: "Points of Pride," USF Office of Decision Support, Planning and Analysis, http://www.usf.edu/about-usf/points-of-pride.aspx.

145 Nine of the top ten: For defense contractors in the Tampa area, see "Defense & Security," Tampa Hillsborough Economic Development Corporation, http://tampaedc.com/defense-security/.

146 *The O'Reilly Factor*: Partial transcript, http://www.foxnews.com/story/2003/02/20/transcript-oreilly-interviews-al-arian-in-september-2001.html. This doesn't include O'Reilly's "hotbed of militants" statement, which is cited here: http://web.usf.edu/uff/AlArian/Fall.html.

147 Neil Genshaft: Campaign contributions from the Federal Election Commission, fec.gov.

147 Richard Beard: The *St. Petersburg Times* reported on Beard's objections to the settlement, and on the radio interview with Al-Arian, in Meg Laughlin, "USF Considered $1M payoff to Al-Arian," February 8, 2007.

148 a retired three-star general: For General Steele, military partnerships, and the memorandum of understanding, see http://www.usf.edu/world/centers/military-partnerships.aspx; http://www.usf.edu/world/documents/world-index/centcomagreement.pdf; and http://www.research.usf.edu/absolute-news/templates/usfri-template.aspx?articleid=561&zoneid=1.

148 On a website for grading their professors: www.ratemyprofessors.com.

149 the 2005 divorce terms: Peng's divorce is in Hillsborough County court, family law division.

150 Peng rapidly secured: The establishment of the USF Confucius Institute, its funding, and the Wilcox and Crummett correspondence are described in Peng, "My Open Response to the Second Investigation of Me by the USF Provost's Office."

150 at least $1 billion: Confucius Institute statistics are at http://english.hanban.org/node_7586.htm. China's 2013 spending is in Confucius Institute Annual Development Report 2013, http://www.hanban.edu.cn/report/pdf/2013.pdf.

151 attached a caveat: Daniel Golden, "China Says No Talking Tibet as Confucius Funds U.S. Universities," Bloomberg News, November 2, 2011.

151 American Association of University Professors: "On Partnerships with Foreign Governments: The Case of Confucius Institutes," https://www.aaup.org/report/confucius-institutes.

151 "a cover-up for a gigantic system": Fabrice de Pierrebourg and Michel Juneau-Katsuya, *Nest of Spies: The Startling Truth About Foreign Agents at Work Within Canada's Borders* (Toronto: HarperCollins, 2009), p. 160.

152 Kent State partnered with Shanghai Normal University: http://einside.kent.edu/Management%20Update%20Archive/news/announcements/success/DollarsSense.html.

153 donated more than ten thousand dollars: Peng, "My Open Response."

153 considering a divorce: Xiaonong Zhang letter to the author, September 28, 2014.

153 "admired by many women": Peng, "My Open Response."

153 Sea Elephant: "Some Love Letters from Xiaonong Zhang to Professor Dajin Peng," an exhibit in a March 22, 2012, memorandum from USF senior vice

provost Dwayne Smith to Provost Ralph Wilcox, "Review of Dr. Dajin Peng's Actions While on Suspension."

154   "a bad personality": Xiaonong Zhang email message to the author, September 28, 2014.

154   "dishonest, scheming": Ibid.

154   Zhang arranged to meet: The complaints by Zhang and Kriesel against Peng are contained in two USF incident report forms. They were filed by Maria Crummett and Eric Shepherd in April 2009.

155   Born in Shandong Province: http://www.tampabaychineseschool.com/admin /teacher/TeacherClassDescList.aspx.

155   Shepherd had studied Chinese at Ohio State: http://languages.usf.edu/faculty /data/eshepherd2013_cv.pdf.

156   traditional storytelling art: "USF's Chinese Storyteller," http://news.usf.edu /article/templates/?a=2818.

156   Kriesel served as Shepherd's teaching assistant: Interview with Shepherd; Lara Wade-Martinez email to the author, January 5, 2015, confirming Kriesel was hired as a teaching assistant on March 16, 2010.

156   She was active: For her participation in the Chinese-American Association of Tampa Bay, see http://lists.cas.usf.edu/pipermail/taiwan/2010-September.txt and https://www.corporationwiki.com/Florida/Lutz/chinese-american -association-of-tampa-bay-incorporated-5866431.aspx.

156   helping to boost attendance: Shuhua Kriesel, resume, provided by Peng.

156   the university honored Madame Lin Xu: http://dspace.nelson.usf.edu/xmlui /bitstream/handle/10806/14079/USFSP_CommencementAwardees.pdf ?sequence=1.

157   University phone logs: USF provided records of calls between the university and Mercurio's cell phone on September 11, 2014, and between the university and her office phone on December 9, 2014.

157   accompanied Zhang to see a vice provost: Shepherd's incident report form.

158   passed along her views: Shepherd email message to Wilcox and Crummett, June 7, 2009.

158   "large cache": Provost Office Response by Dwayne Smith, Senior Vice Provost, to Peng's complaint to the USF Office of Diversity and Equal Opportunity.

158   Provost Wilcox removed Peng: Wilcox letter to Peng, August 25, 2009.

158   the auditors dug into his spending: The audit's findings are contained in University Audit and Compliance 09-968, Confucius Institute Misuse of Funds.

158   "Who said that you cannot swim": Peng, "My Open Response."

159   "It might be a bit right": Peng, "Response to Ms. Head's Investigation Report."

159   Kate Head: The Department of Homeland Security redacted names from email correspondence setting up the July 31, 2009, meeting between USF officials and immigration agents. However, internal evidence from the emails, including Kate Head's fax number and a reference to the "nice facility" at University Audit and Compliance as a potential meeting place, indicates that she participated.

159   "somewhat appears to have traded favors": Department of Homeland Security investigation report, November 15, 2010.

160   barred him from its graduate programs: Mohsen Milani letter to Dwayne Smith, December 13, 2009.

160   "wanted to put you in jail": Wenzel email message to Peng, July 18, 2010.

160   "particularly raised the issue . . . not sure what they could do": Peng, "FBI and I."

161   "Thank you for your willingness": Peng email message to Mercurio, November 18, 2009.

161   "We can certainly keep in touch": Mercurio email message to Peng, November 19, 2009.

7: THE CIA'S FAVORITE UNIVERSITY PRESIDENT

162   Warren Medal: The account of Spanier receiving the medal is based on an interview with Spanier, and on photos he provided of the medal.

164   convention of the American Council on the Teaching of Foreign Languages: Marty Abbott, ACTFL executive director, email messages to the author, September 2 and 8, 2015.

164   Modern Language Association: Rosemary Feal, MLA executive director, email message to the author, September 16, 2015.

164   "high-risk/high pay-off research": www.iarpa.gov.

164   more than 175 academic institutions: Interview with IARPA director Jason Matheny.

164   research on language for the Pentagon: https://www.casl.umd.edu/who-we-serve /governmentprofessional/.

164   "Classified research always occurs": Crystal Brown, email message to the author, August 16, 2016. She also confirmed Snowden's employment.

164   "Classified research on campus": William M. Arkin and Alexa O'Brien, "The Most Militarized Universities in America: A VICE News Investigation," *VICE News*, November 6, 2015, https://news.vice.com/article/the-most-militarized -universities-in-america-a-vice-news-investigation.

165   "Due to the high degree": Mick Kulikowski, "NC State Partners With National Security Agency on Big-Data Lab," *NC State News*, August 15, 2013.

165   "perform classified and highly classified": Committee on Research, Committee Minutes, August 28, 2011, http://www.bov.vt.edu/minutes/11-08-29minutes /attach_p_08-28-11.pdf.

165   "conducting sensitive research": http://www.hume.vt.edu/about/facilities.

165   "out there in the middle": Alyssa Bruns and Cory Weinberg, "GW Looks to Capitalize on Covert Research," *GW Hatchet*, October 29, 2012. Leo Chalupa, vice president for research, made the statement.

165   "explore modifying": "Vision 2021: A Strategic Plan for the Third Century of George Washington University," https://provost.gwu.edu/files/downloads /Strategic%20Plan.pdf.

165   "There is a lot of funding": Tricia Bishop, "Universities Balance Secrecy and Academic Freedom in Classified Work," *Baltimore Sun*, September 13, 2013.

165   Wisconsin allowed its university system to accept classified contracts: Warren Cornwall, "Shh! Wisconsin Seeking to Get In on Secret Cybersecurity Research," January 8, 2015, www.sciencemag.org.

165   waived a cap on enrollment: "Regents Approve Lifting Cap on Out-of-State Students at UW-Madison," www.wisconsin.edu/news/archive/regents, October 9, 2015.

166   "Mr. Gaffney's visit to his alma mater": Email to the author from a CIA spokes-
       person, November 30, 2016.

166   a private table at Don Pepe: They asked for a private table after an FBI agent
       expressed concern in a February 21, 2011, email message that "we would not
       be able to discuss matters as in depth in a public place . . . as much as I love Don
       Pepe's food."

167   "Attached please find all": James Geller email message to FBI agent, June 12, 2014.

167   agents met twice with an Iranian graduate student: Phone interview with Susie
       Askew, director of the international student office at the University of Nevada,
       Reno.

167   "half cops-and-robbers": Robin Winks, Cloak and Gown: Scholars in America's
       Secret War (London: Collins Harvill, 1987), p. 115. The numbers of Yale profes-
       sors and students joining OSS, and the anecdotes about the Yale assistant pro-
       fessor in Istanbul and crew coach Skip Walz, also come from Cloak and Gown.

167   "classic CIA resume": Tim Weiner, Legacy of Ashes: The History of the CIA
       (New York: Anchor Books, 2008), p. 107.

167   26 percent of college graduates . . . had Ivy League degrees: Winks, Cloak and
       Gown, p. 446.

168   "primary funding source": http://web.mit.edu/cis/pdf/Panel_ORIGINS.pdf.

168   National Student Association: The account of the CIA's penetration of the asso-
       ciation is based on Karen M. Paget, Patriotic Betrayal: The Inside Story of the
       CIA's Secret Campaign to Enroll American Students in the Crusade Against
       Communism (New Haven, CT: Yale University Press, 2015).

168   Gloria Steinem: Ibid., pp. 214–27. The February 27, 1967, quotation from News-
       week is cited on p. 380.

168   "thousands of foreign students' political tendencies": Ibid., pp. 399–400.

168   a Michigan State University program: Warren Hinckle, Sol Stern, and Robert
       Scheer, "The University on the Make," Ramparts, April 1966.

168   The Johnson administration responded: Loch K. Johnson, America's Secret
       Power: The CIA in a Democratic Society (New York: Oxford University Press,
       1989), p. 158.

169   "eleven CIA officers": Weiner, Legacy of Ashes, pp. 329–30.

169   seventy-seven instances: Ralph E. Cook, "The CIA and Academe," Studies in
       Intelligence, Winter 1983, p. 35; approved for release July 29, 2014.

169   Brooklyn College: Johnson, America's Secret Power, p. 167.

169   "It is not true": Winks, Cloak and Gown, p. 441.

169   "several hundred academics . . . providing leads": Book 1, "Final Report of the
       Select Committee to Study Governmental Operations with Respect to Intelli-
       gence Activities," p. 452.

170   "The Committee believes": Ibid., p. 191.

171   A federal judge ordered 168 deletions: Jane Mayer, "CIA Gag Order on Halperin
       Modified," Washington Star, October 4, 1980.

172   "I would conclude that the CIA feels": Correspondence from Daniel Steiner to
       Cord Meyer Jr., October 11, 1977.

172   Their 1977 guidelines prohibited: The Harvard guidelines promulgated by the
       Committee on Relationships Between the Harvard Community and U.S. Intel-
       ligence Agencies may be found in "National Intelligence Reorganization and

Reform Act of 1978, Hearings Before the Select Committee on Intelligence of the United States Senate," pp. 643–48. The "willing to suffer" quotation is on p. 648. Bok's "highly vulnerable" quotation is on p. 640.

173   "it would be foolish": Stansfield Turner, *Secrecy and Democracy: The CIA in Transition* (Boston: Houghton Mifflin,1985), p. 108.

173   "a matter of choice": Turner correspondence to Bok, May 15, 1978; Hearings Before the Select Committee on Intelligence, p. 659.

174   the CIA promulgated: The text of the CIA regulation is on p. 660 of the Intelligence Committee hearings.

175   After CIA director Turner lobbied: Ernest Volkman, "Spies on Campus," *Penthouse*, October 1979.

178   The CIA moved to mend: On CIA initiatives to bring college presidents and scholars-in-residence to Langley, see Cook, "The CIA and Academe," p. 39.

178   "Whether or not his 'no comments'": John Hollister Hedley, "Twenty Years of Officers in Residence," https://www.cia.gov/library/center-for-the-study-of-intelligence/csi-publications/csi-studies/studies/vol49no4/Officers_in_Residence_3.htm.

183   A former student's memoir: John Kiriakou with Michael Ruby, *The Reluctant Spy: My Secret Life in the CIA's War on Terror* (New York: Skyhorse, 2009), pp. 14–15, 24.

185   Betty Castor's lament: Anita Kumar, "Al-Arian Issue Looms for Castor," *St. Petersburg Times*, July 11, 2004, http://www.sptimes.com/2004/07/11/State/Al_Arian_issue_looms_.shtml.

185   "We couldn't be more surprised": Gustav Niebuhr, "Professor Talked of Understanding But Now Reveals Ties to Terrorists," *New York Times*, November 13, 1995. The surprised administrator was Mark T. Orr, director of the university's international studies center.

186   The agenda for an October 2013 meeting at FBI headquarters: Dean W. Chappell III, FBI's Strategic Partnership Unit, email message (with attached agenda) to NSHEAB members, September 29, 2013, provided by the University of Texas at Austin in response to my public records request.

186   the FBI hosted a dinner: Chappell email message to NSHEAB members, October 21, 2013.

187   it noticed Internet postings: https://archives.fbi.gov/archives/pittsburgh/press-releases/2013/pennsylvania-man-sentenced-for-terrorism-solicitation-and-firearms-offense.

187   He gave FBI-sponsored seminars: "Partial List of Talks Given on Behalf of the FBI," provided by Graham Spanier to the author.

189   Minerva Initiative: http://minerva.dtic.mil/overview.html.

189   Louis Freeh: See report at https://www.documentcloud.org/documents/396512-report-final-071212.html.

189   Spanier . . . sued Freeh and Penn State separately: See http://www.pennlive.com/news/2016/02/spanier_files_breach_of_contra.html.

8: BUMPS AND CUTOUTS

193 The CIA agent tapped: The opening scene is based on an interview with a former intelligence officer with firsthand knowledge of the incident.

195 "Because the feedback": Taken from William C. Hannas, James Mulvenon, and Anna B. Puglisi, *Chinese Industrial Espionage: Technology Acquisition and Military Modernization* (New York: Routledge, 2013), p. 26.

195 The FBI warned American academics: FBI white paper, "Higher Education and National Security: The Targeting of Sensitive, Proprietary, and Classified Information on Campuses of Higher Education," April 2011.

196 "What our spies and informants were noticing": Kiriakou, *The Reluctant Spy*, p. 154.

198 Sixth Annual International Conference: https://msfs.georgetown.edu/Cyber Conference2016.

202 Centra has received more than $200 million in government contracts: Jason Leopold, "The CIA Paid This Contractor $40 Million to Review Torture Documents," *VICE News*, July 27, 2015.

203 Barbara Walter listed: http://gps.ucsd.edu/_files/faculty/walter/walter_cv.pdf. The RAND conference is on p. 10.

204 a media mouthpiece of Iranian hard-liners denounced: http://www.iranhrdc .org/english/news/press-statements/1000000165-restrictions-on-academic -freedom-underscore-events-at-conference-for-iranian-studies.html.

205 The *Los Angeles Times* revealed the program: Greg Miller, "CIA Has Recruited Iranians to Defect," *Los Angeles Times*, December 9, 2007.

207 Emails released in 2015: Courtney Fennell, "Cryptic Clinton Emails May Refer to Iranian Scientist," CNN, September 2, 2015, http://www.cnn.com/2015/09 /02/politics/clinton-email-shahram-amiri/.

207 Four Iranian nuclear scientists were assassinated: The killings were widely reported. See, for example, Tom Burgis, "Timeline: Assassinated Iranian Scientists," http://blogs.ft.com/the-world/2012/01/timeline-assassinated-iranian -scientists/.

207 Iran convicted a man: "Iran Hangs 'Mossad Agent' for Scientist Killing," Reuters, May 15, 2012.

208 "On occasion scientists": Michael Ono, "Santorum Says He Would Bomb Iran's Nuclear Plants," ABC News, January 1, 2012, http://abcnews.go.com /blogs/politics/2012/01/santorum-says-he-would-bomb-irans-nuclear -plants/.

208 concluded in 1989: The 1989 legal opinion on assassinations was prepared by W. Hays Parks, chief of the international law branch of the international affairs division of the Office of the Judge Advocate General of the Army. Lawyers for the Departments of Defense and State, the CIA, and the National Security Council concurred in it.

208 "grave consequences": David Albright, *Peddling Peril: How the Secret Nuclear Trade Arms America's Enemies* (New York: Free Press, 2010), p. 209.

209 "the only place outside their own country": Nicholas Dawidoff, *The Catcher Was a Spy* (New York: Vintage Books, 1995), p. 164.

209 "the pistol stayed": Ibid., p. 205.

9: HIDDEN IN THE IVY

211 his favorite hobby: Phone interview with Shelagh Lafferty Moskow, January 15, 2016.

211 They took turns trying to resuscitate him: Kevin Ryan email message to the author, February 9, 2016.

211 More than one thousand mourners: SYA website, http://alumni.sya.org/s/833 /global.aspx?sid=833&gid=1&pgid=473.

211 Barack Obama: Ibid.

211 given the flag: Ibid.

211 won a bout: "Scoreboard," *Harvard Crimson*, January 13, 1983.

211 "there are enough lawyers": Joe Holley, "Ex-CIA Agent Ken Moskow; Died Atop Mount Kilimanjaro," *Washington Post*, October 6, 2008.

212 disguised himself in a wig: Shelagh Lafferty Moskow.

213 one in a long line: I pored over the mid-career program's annual photo rosters in the Kennedy School library, looking for students who might have been undercover CIA officers: for example, those who described themselves as political officers in a U.S. embassy with a working knowledge of Farsi or Arabic. I then cross-checked those names on the Internet, and in interviews with other sources and/or the graduates themselves, to determine if in fact they had worked for the CIA.

213 risen to become presidents: //en.wikipedia.org/wiki/John_F._Kennedy_School _of_Government#Notable_alumni.

213 No fewer than five: The five graduates who have served in Japan's cabinet are Yasuhisa Shiozaki, Yoko Kamikawa, Yoshimasa Hayashi, Yoichi Miyazawa, and Toshimitsu Motegi.

214 former intelligence brass: The list of experts and fellows at the Belfer Center may be found on its website: http://belfercenter.ksg.harvard.edu/experts/index .html?filter=T&groupby=1&type=.

214 on the CIA director's advisory board: http://belfercenter.ksg.harvard.edu /experts/199/graham_allison.html.

215 "[I]t is inappropriate": Hearings Before the Select Committee on Intelligence of the United States Senate on the National Intelligence Reorganization and Reform Act of 1978, p. 645, http://www.intelligence.senate.gov/sites/default/ files/hearings/952525.pdf.

216 occasionally request two certificates: Background interview with Kennedy School administrator.

217 two-week, $12,500 course: https://exed.hks.harvard.edu/Programs/nis/ overview.aspx.

217 including heads of the National Security Agency: Interview with Tad Oelstrom.

218 "The CIA had as little experience": Ernest R. May and Philip D. Zelikow, eds., *Dealing with Dictators: Dilemmas of U.S. Diplomacy and Intelligence Analysis, 1945–1990* (Cambridge, MA: MIT Press. 2006), p. xi.

218 a scandal over undisclosed funding: See Michelle M. Hu and Radhika Jain, "Controversy Erupts Over Professors' Ties to the CIA," *Harvard Crimson*, May 25, 2011, http://www.thecrimson.com/article/2011/5/25/research-cia -harvard-betts/.

219   with their names blanked out: May and Zelikow, *Dealing with Dictators*, p. ix.

222   Princeton provides full scholarships: http://wws.princeton.edu/admissions
       /mpp/financial-aid.

224   "When prisoners were wounded": Mark Moyar, *Phoenix and the Birds of Prey:
       Counterinsurgency and Counterterrorism in Vietnam* (Lincoln: University of
       Nebraska Press, 2007), pp. 104–5.

224   Geneva Conventions: See https://www.icrc.org/customary-ihl/eng/docs/v2_rul
       _rule110 and http://www.un.org/en/preventgenocide/rwanda/text-images
       /Geneva_POW.pdf.

225   his credentials as a soldier and spy: David Lightman, "Simmons' Resume Sud-
       denly an Asset," *Hartford Courant*, November 12, 2001.

225   Thomas Gordon: Gordon's resume is available at http://thisainthell.us/blog/?p
       =57518. The Houston Police Department confirmed his employment there.

227   prompting the *Arizona Republic* to reveal: Chris Moeser, "Gordon in CIA,
       Fired, Sources Say," *Arizona Republic*, July 24, 1999, p. 1.

227   He pleaded guilty: U.S. District Court for Arizona, Case CR 01-00164-
       001-PHX-VAM.

228   On his Twitter page: Kiowa Gordon's Twitter page, https://twitter.com
       /circakigordon.

229   "I went through a detailed screening procedure": *Russian Reporter* (weekly
       magazine), 2012. Translated from the Russian by Stepan Kravchenko.

230   A backstory as a Canadian diplomat's son: Abby Goodnough, "Suspect in Spy
       Case Cultivated Friends Made at Harvard," *New York Times*, June 30, 2010.

230   Scotch-tasting excursion: Ibid. Goodnough's article is also the source of the
       "flavorful," "very vague," and "In Singapore" quotations.

231   wine caves: Jonathan Saltzman, Shelley Murphy, and John Ellement, "Alleged
       Spies Always Strived for Connections," *Boston Globe*, June 30, 2010.

231   "very friendly": Ibid.

231   attended Kennedy School reunions: FBI report, "Higher Education and National
       Security," 2011.

231   started a software design firm: Evan Perez, "Alleged Russian Agent Claimed
       Official Was His Firm's Adviser," *Wall Street Journal*, July 2, 2010.

231   "Western estimation": *Complaint v. Heathfield, Foley, et al.*, FBI agent Maria
       Ricci, U.S. District Court for the Southern District of New York, http://cryptome
       .org/svr/usa-v-svr.htm 6/25/10.

231   agreed to spy for Russia: Devlin Barrett, "Russian Spy Ring Aimed to Make
       Children Agents," *Wall Street Journal*, July 31, 2012.

231   "In order to win": *Russian Reporter*.

232   rescinded his degree: Naveen N. Srivatsa, "Harvard Kennedy School Revokes
       Degree Awarded to Russian Spy," *Harvard Crimson*, July 16, 2010.

232   "establish their legend": *Vavilov v. the Minister of Citizenship and Immigration*,
       http://caselaw.canada.globe24h.com/0/0/federal/federal-court-of-canada
       /2015/08/2015fc960.shtml.

232   largest in the world: Speech by French ambassador Francois Delattre, March 5,
       2014, http://www.ambafrance-us.org/spip.php?article5421.

234   Engulfed in a scandal: Michael D. Shear, "Petraeus Quits; Evidence of Affair
       Was Found by FBI," *New York Times*, November 9, 2012.

234 Recanati-Kaplan: My account of the genesis of the fellowships is based on an interview with Petraeus. Kaplan and Allison declined to comment.

234 "educates the next generation of thought leaders": http://belfercenter.ksg .harvard.edu/fellowships/recanatikaplan.html.

235 a Pentagon intelligence analyst studied: The American studying criminal networks was Kim Benderoth; the Israeli studying counterterrorism was Gilad Raik. Their research topics are no longer listed on the Belfer Center website.

235 Panthera: https://www.panthera.org/.

235 He learned French as a student in Switzerland: Delattre speech.

236 "The program has brought France together": Video of Delattre speech, http:// frenchculture.org/archive/speeches/france-honors-tom-kaplan-legion-honor.

236 a key backer of United Against Nuclear Iran: Eli Clifton, "Document Reveals Billionaire Backers Behind United Against Nuclear Iran," https:/lobelog.com.

236 "As much as United Against Nuclear Iran": Video of speech by Tom Kaplan as he received French Legion of Honor medal, http://frenchculture.org/archive/speeches /france-honors-tom-kaplan-legion-honor. The words aren't in the published text.

236 Obama administration intervened: Matt Apuzzo, "Justice Department Moves to Shield Anti-Iran Group's Files," *New York Times*, July 27, 2014.

236 "allowing the litigation to proceed": Opinion and Order, U.S. District Court Judge Edgardo Ramos, *Victor Restis and Enterprises Shipping and Trading S.A. v. United Against Nuclear Iran et al.*, 13 Civ. 5032, March 23, 2015.

237 "Security in the Black Sea Region": The agenda is available at www.harvard -bssp.org/files/agenda%202015.doc.

237 a desperate phone call: Alvin Powell, "Russian, U.S. Admirals Talk to Save Sub," *Harvard University Gazette*, October 20, 2005.

238 "Everybody knew Mr. Moscow": Adriana Rivas email message to the author, January 25, 2016.

239 now-deceased Guatemalan defense minister: Gramajo's participation in the mid-career program was controversial because he had allegedly overseen murders and torture of political dissidents in Guatemala. At the Kennedy School graduation ceremony in 1991, he was served with papers in a lawsuit brought by eight Guatemalans in a U.S. court, accusing him of human rights abuses. Four years later, he was found civilly liable, and was prohibited from entering the United States. A swarm of bees stung him to death at his ranch in 2004.

10: "I AM KEEPING YOU OUT OF JAIL"

241 the bureau began hiring women as agents: Suzanne Stratford, "FBI Celebrates 40th Anniversary of First Female Agent," fox8.com/2012/08/13/fbi-celebrates -40th-anniversary-of-first-female-agent/.

241 they made up almost 20 percent: There were 13,907 agents, of whom 2,707, or 19.5 percent, were women, according to "Today's FBI: Facts & Figures," 2013– 14, p. 51.

241 Agents come from all walks of life: Ibid., p. 47.

241 It reports to the director: Ibid., p. 5.

241 seventy-eight offices and suboffices: Ibid., p. 8.

241   the burean's priorities shifted: FBI director Robert S. Mueller III, prepared
       statement before the Senate Judiciary Committee, June 2002, https://global
       .nytimes.com/2002/06/06/politics/06APMTEX.html?pagewanted
       =all&position=top.

241   "is not just the more traditional spies": https://www.fbi.gov/investigate/counter-
       intelligence.

242   born in 1968 in Burlington, Vermont: I traced her family history through birth,
       marriage, and death certificates available on Ancestry.com.

242   shared patents for two devices: "Frequency Responsive Lubrication System,"
       July 9, 1968, United States Patent 3,391,602; "Muzzle Brake Torque Assist for
       Multi-Barrel Weapons," November 21, 1972, United States Patent 3,703,122.

242   her father transferred: Phone interview with George Dewey Brooks.

242   Its population rose: "Population Trends for the 25 Largest SC Cities, 2000 to
       2012," provided by John Gardner.

242   lower poverty rate: "Economic Status Indicators: Greenville County and
       Municipalities," provided by John Gardner, based on American Community
       Survey 2008–2012 and 2010 U.S. Census.

242   Dale Farrington retired: Email from GE spokeswoman, January 9, 2016.

242   With a 91.9 percent graduation rate: South Carolina State Report Card 2015,
       Mauldin High School, https://ed.sc.gov/assets/reportCards/2015/high/c/
       h2301014.pdf.

242   his arrest following a racial melee: "After Getting Arrested in a Race Riot,
       Kevin Garnett Drove Himself to Escape Rural S.C. and Become Highest-Paid
       Player in NBA History," http://atlantablackstar.com/2015/02/24/kevin-garnetts
       -took-inspiring-road-rural-s-c-highest-paid-player-nba-history/, February 24,
       2015.

242   standout athlete: Mauldin High yearbook; interview with Coach Delmer How-
       ell; *1984–85 Palmetto's Finest Record Book*, p. 104.

243   She majored in psychology: University of North Carolina alumni records.

243   she became a social worker for Orange County: Donna Davenport, human
       resources analyst, Orange County, email message to the author, October 20, 2015.

244   must be U.S. citizens between the ages: "Today's FBI: Facts & Figures," p. 48.

244   22,692 applicants: Ibid., p. 47.

244   according to a court document: W. Bryan Park II, "Affidavit Seeking Oral Tes-
       timony and Production of Documents From Task Force Agent Robert Sheehan
       and F.B.I. Special Agent Dianne Farrington," *Florida v. Lawrence Kilbourn*,
       Case Number 99-3807, March 10, 2000.

244   medical device distributor: www.linkedin.com/in/matt-mercurio-4048875.

244   Nike Women's Marathon: http://www.marathonguide.com/results/browse.cfm
       ?MIDD=2224081019&Gen=B&Begin=1939&End=2038&Max=4881.

244   Cliffs at Glassy: I looked up the Mercurios' purchases and sales of lots at: viewer
       .greenvillecounty.org/countyweb/disclaimer.do.

245   dropped in value: County records show that the Mercurios bought the lot for
       $232,000 in 2007. It was valued at $138,080 in 2015.

245   sank into Chapter 11 bankruptcy: Case No. 12-01220, U.S. Bankruptcy Court
       for South Carolina, http://www.scb.uscourts.gov/pdf/court_postings/Cliffs
       _order.pdf.

245 Mercurio interviewed one of Al-Arian's alleged co-conspirators: Interview with Kerry Myers, who headed the Al-Arian criminal investigation. The government listed her as a possible witness, but she didn't testify.

245 if he would provide information: Interview with Koerner.

246 "a little bit nervous": Zheng email message to author, September 14, 2014.

247 On the afternoon of March 9: The date is confirmed by a March 5, 2010, email message from Romine to Peng: "We can do it Tuesday afternoon then. I will meet with you for about half an hour before she arrives."

248 In their regular corner booth: This scene is reconstructed from interviews with Peng and is consistent with their email correspondence.

249 American Association of University Professors had condemned: "Academic Freedom and Tenure: University of South Florida," 2003, https://www.aaup .org/report/academic-freedom-and-tenure-university-south-florida.

249 his expertise was in physical education: http://www.usf.edu/provost/documents /leadership-cv/wilcox-2012withoutrefcv.pdf.

251 agents copied the images: "Report of Investigation," Department of Homeland Security, Immigration and Customs Enforcement, November 15, 2010, provided in response to a public records request.

251 "no materials which could be used to defraud . . . no conspiratorial acts were found": Ibid.

253 Peng and the university reached a settlement: "Settlement and General Release Agreement Between Dr. Dajin Peng and the University of South Florida Board of Trustees," August 24, 2010.

254 assigned on the day of the settlement: Fax from General Counsel Steven Prevaux to Wenzel, August 24, 2010.

254 He pitched the idea to Holbrook: The meeting time and place were confirmed in an email message from Holbrook's executive administrative assistant, Beth Beall, to Peng, October 8, 2010.

255 probably went to see her: Holbrook thought so, but wasn't sure.

255 which would arrive in Tampa later that month: "Nankai University Delegation Visits USF," *USF World News*, November 28, 2010, http://global.usf.edu /wordpress/?p=672.

257 Otherwise, they threatened to circulate: Letter from "Thirty-Six Overseas Chinese of the Greater Tampa Bay Area," Exhibit 19, Memo to Dr. Ralph Wilcox from Dr. Dwayne Smith re: Review of Dr. Dajin Peng's actions while on suspension, March 22, 2012.

258 "Although he didn't use his own email address": Email message from Naijia Guan to Shi Kun, November 11, 2011, Exhibit 8, Memo to Dr. Ralph Wilcox.

258 "extremely affected": Letter from Guan to Karen Holbrook, November 8, 2011, Exhibit 3, Memo to Dr. Ralph Wilcox.

258 "it became clear that": Lara Wade-Martinez, "USF Response to Dan Golden," October 17, 2014.

258 The university suspended him: "Notice of Suspension," letter from the provost's office to Peng, May 23, 2013.

259 the university offered to shorten: "Settlement and General Release Agreement Between the University of South Florida Board of Trustees and Dr. Dajin Peng," proposed agreement that expired November 8, 2013.

11: NO-SPY ZONE

263 a letter cosigned by an FBI lawyer: Ibison and James P. Greene, chief division counsel, sent the letter on April 4, 2012, to Greg W. Kehoe, USF's lawyer.

264 over the FBI's objections: Lara Wade-Martinez, email message to the author, February 2, 2015.

265 detecting key phrases in conversations: See, for example, the IARPA-funded Babel project, https://www.iarpa.gov/index.php/research-programs/babel.

265 "drones kill kids": Ally Johnson, "Protests Shut Down CIA Director's Talk at Penn," *Daily Pennsylvanian*, April 1, 2016.

266 At twenty-five to thirty-five universities each year: Lara C. Tang, "CIA Hosts Recruitment Event on Campus," *Harvard Crimson*, April 2, 2015.

268 Postol spoiled the celebration: Daniel Golden, "Missile-Blower," *Boston Globe Magazine*, July 19, 1992.

270 wrote a scathing memoir: Jones, *The Human Factor*.

272 When I visited him in 2012: Daniel Golden, "Why the Professor Went to Prison," *Bloomberg Businessweek*, November 1, 2012.

273 more than twice as many: http://www.globalhighered.org/. The United Kingdom is second with thirty-eight.

273 to bar foreign students: Julia Edwards, "U.S. Targets Spying Threat on Campus with Proposed Research Clampdown," Reuters, May 20, 2016, http://www.reuters.com/article/us-usa-security-students-idUSKCN0YB1QT.

273 about two-thirds stay: "Five-Year Stay Rates for U.S. S&E Doctorate Recipients with Temporary Visas at Graduation, by Selected Country/Region/Economy," Table 3-29, Science and Engineering Indicators 2014, http://www.nsf.gov/statistics/seind14/index.cfm/chapter-3/c3s6.htm#s3.

274 "Users do not need to search": Wankun Zhu email message to the author, June 20, 2016.

SELECTED BIBLIOGRAPHY

Abrahams, Harlan, and Arturo Lopez-Levy. *Raúl Castro and the New Cuba*. Jefferson, NC: McFarland, 2011.

Albright, David. *Peddling Peril: How the Secret Nuclear Trade Arms America's Enemies*. New York: Free Press, 2010.

Andrew, Christopher, and Vasili Mitrokhin. *The Sword and the Shield: The Mitrokhin Archive and the Secret History of the KGB*. New York: Basic Books, 1999.

Ball, Philip. *Invisible: The Dangerous Allure of the Unseen*. Chicago: University of Chicago Press, 2015.

Bergman, Ronen. *The Secret War with Iran: The 30-Year Clandestine Struggle Against the World's Most Dangerous Terrorist Power*. New York: Free Press, 2008.

Blum, William. *The CIA: A Forgotten History*. London and Atlantic Highlands, NJ: Zed Books, 1986.

Carmichael, Scott W. *True Believer: Inside the Investigation and Capture of Ana Montes, Cuba's Master Spy*. Annapolis, MD: Naval Institute Press, 2007.

Chan, Gerald. *International Studies in China: An Annotated Bibliography*. Commack, NY: Nova Science, 1998.

Crumpton, Henry A. *The Art of Intelligence: Lessons from a Life in the CIA's Clandestine Service*. New York: Penguin Group, 2012.

Dawidoff, Nicholas. *The Catcher Was a Spy*. New York: Vintage Books, 1995.

De Pierrebourg, Fabrice, and Michel Juneau-Katsuya. *Nest of Spies: The Startling Truth About Foreign Agents at Work Within Canada's Borders*. Toronto: HarperCollins, 2009.

Eftimiades, Nicholas. *Chinese Intelligence Operations*. Reed Business Information, 1994.

Faddis, Charles S. *Beyond Repair: The Decline and Fall of the CIA*. Guilford, CT: Lyons Press, 2010.

Fialka, John J. *War by Other Means: Economic Espionage in America*. New York: Norton, 1997.

Hannas, William C., James Mulvenon, and Anna B. Puglisi. *Chinese Industrial Espionage: Technology Acquisition and Military Modernization*. New York: Routledge, 2013.

Johnson, Loch K. *America's Secret Power: The CIA in a Democratic Society*. New York: Oxford University Press, 1989.

Jones, Ishmael. *The Human Factor: Inside the CIA's Dysfunctional Intelligence Culture*. New York: Encounter Books, 2008.

Kiriakou, John, with Michael Ruby. *The Reluctant Spy: My Secret Life in the CIA's War on Terror*. New York: Skyhorse, 2009.

Latell, Brian. *Castro's Secrets: Cuban Intelligence, the CIA, and the Assassination of John F. Kennedy*. New York: Palgrave Macmillan, 2012.

May, Ernest R., and Philip D. Zelikow, eds. *Dealing with Dictators: Dilemmas of U.S. Diplomacy and Intelligence Analysis, 1945–1990*. Cambridge, MA: MIT Press, 2006.

Mills, Ami Chen. *C.I.A. Off Campus: Building the Movement Against Agency Recruitment and Research*. Boston: South End Press, 1991.

Moyar, Mark. *Phoenix and the Birds of Prey: Counterinsurgency and Counterterrorism in Vietnam*. Lincoln: University of Nebraska Press, 2007.

Paget, Karen M. *Patriotic Betrayal: The Inside Story of the CIA's Secret Campaign to Enroll American Students in the Crusade Against Communism*. New Haven, CT: Yale University Press, 2015.

Richmond, Yale. *Cultural Exchange and the Cold War: Raising the Iron Curtain*. University Park: Pennsylvania State University Press, 2003.

Rizzo, John. *Company Man: Thirty Years of Controversy and Crisis in the CIA*. New York: Scribner, 2014.

Roche, Edward M. *Snake Fish: The Chi Mak Spy Ring*. New York: Barraclough, 2008.

Shorrock, Tim. *Spies for Hire: The Secret World of Intelligence Outsourcing*. New York: Simon & Schuster, 2008.

Simon, Denis Fred, and Cong Cao. *China's Emerging Technological Edge: Assessing the Role of High-End Talent*. New York: Cambridge University Press, 2009.

Sulick, Michael. *American Spies: Espionage Against the United States from the Cold War to the Present*. Washington, DC: Georgetown University Press, 2013.

Turner, Stansfield. *Secrecy and Democracy: The CIA in Transition*. Boston: Houghton Mifflin, 1985.

Weiner, Tim. *Legacy of Ashes: The History of the CIA*. New York: Anchor Books, 2008.

Winks, Robin. *Cloak and Gown: Scholars in America's Secret War*. London: Collins Harvill, 1987.

Xu, Meihong, and Larry Engelmann. *Daughter of China: A True Story of Love and Betrayal*. New York: Wiley, 1999.

ACKNOWLEDGMENTS

While I have long covered higher education, reporting and writing *Spy Schools* required me also to understand espionage and intelligence agencies, a world I'd encountered mainly in novels and movies. Aware of my limitations and unsure of my judgment, I have depended more than ever on the kindness of family, friends, colleagues, and, yes, strangers.

First, I would like to thank my smart, tireless agent, Lynn Johnston, who not only marketed and advocated for this book but also skillfully edited my proposal. Serena Jones, my editor at Holt, guided and shaped *Spy Schools*, kept me on track, and was a constant source of insight and good advice. Her editorial assistant, Madeline Jones, was also a pleasure to work with.

I am indebted to my sister, Olivia Golden, my lifelong friend Katie Hafner, and my friend and former colleague David Glovin for reading the manuscript at various stages and improving it with their wise counsel. My friends Charles Stein, Mina Kimes, and Kirsten Lundberg made helpful suggestions on various chapters.

Because *Spy Schools* is international in scope, I enlisted the help of journalists based abroad. Michael Standaert, Su Dongxia, and Jessica Meyers contributed outstanding reporting in China, and Paul O'Mahony and Stepan Kravchenko did the same in Sweden and Russia, respectively. Kean Zhang translated documents from the Chinese and researched Chinese-language websites. Ronen Bergman shared his expertise on U.S.-Israeli intelligence activities regarding Iran's nuclear weapons program.

I am grateful to Nigel West, I. C. Smith, Mark Galeotti, and others for taking the time to enlighten me about the basics of intelligence work. David Major generously gave me access to the CI Centre database. Lili Sun compiled an authoritative list of Chinese defendants in espionage cases who attended U.S. universities. Also helpful with research advice and contacts were James Bandler, Renee Dudley, Michael Smith, Shai Oster, Prashant Gopal, Priscilla Lee, John Hechinger, Peter Toren, and Jeffrey Richelson. Nirmala Kannankutty at the National Science Foundation and Sharon Witherell at the Institute of International Education were invaluable sources of data on foreign researchers and students in the United States. Sara Logue, an archivist at Seeley G. Mudd Manuscript Library at Princeton, provided Marta Rita Velázquez's senior thesis and other documents.

My lawyers at the Reporters Committee for Freedom of the Press, especially Katie Townsend and Adam Marshall, as well as local counsel Bruce S. Rosen, brilliantly pursued my open records case involving New Jersey Institute of Technology and the FBI. Due to a quirk of state law, we included a New Jersey resident as a co-plaintiff, and Holt's Tracy Locke fulfilled that role admirably.

My thanks also go to the public relations professionals at universities and government agencies who cheerfully responded to my requests and endured my badgering, especially Lara Wade-Martinez at the University of South Florida, Dennis O'Shea at Johns Hopkins, Lindsey Waldrop at the School of Advanced International Studies, Mark Johnson at Arizona State, and Susan McKee at the FBI.

Without University of South Florida professor Dajin Peng, this book would not exist. He contacted me about his predicament, supplied me with key emails and documents, and answered my questions for hours on end. Laurie Hays, Jonathan Kaufman, John Brecher, and Tom Moroney encouraged my Bloomberg articles about Peng, which Gary Putka and Peter Jeffrey edited with care. Katherine Kriegman Graham, Bloomberg's newsroom counsel, advised me on open records requests for the Peng articles, and also connected me with the Reporters Committee for Freedom of the Press. John Ring at Bloomberg's Boston bureau came to my rescue during many a computer-related office mishap. Reto Gregori, deputy editor in chief at Bloomberg News, granted me the leave of absence during which much of this book was reported and written.

My family was supportive far beyond my fondest hopes. My sister, Olivia, helped me conceptualize key themes and sections, especially the conclusion. My son, Steven, set up my home office, assembled my personal computer, stored my files, transferred open records documents from discs, and enthusiastically solved my every digital need. My beloved wife and best friend, Kathy, offered countless sagacious suggestions, accompanied me on reporting trips, and did her best to keep me from obsessing.

There are many other people who deserve credit, but for various good reasons they shared their information and insights anonymously. I hope they enjoy this book, and take pride in their vital contributions.

INDEX

Daniel Golden is a senior editor at ProPublica, a nonprofit newsroom specializing in investigative journalism. He won a Pulitzer Prize in 2004 for his *Wall Street Journal* articles on admissions preferences at elite colleges, which became the basis for his bestselling book, *The Price of Admission*. A series that he edited about how U.S. companies dodge taxes by moving their headquarters overseas won *Bloomberg News*'s first and only Pulitzer in 2015. In 2011, his *Bloomberg News* series about for-profit colleges exploiting veterans, low-income students, and the homeless was named a finalist for the Pulitzer Prize for public service. He has also won three George Polk awards.